Interpersonal Conflict

Eighth Edition

Interpersonal Conflict

Eighth Edition

William W. Wilmot

Joyce L. Hocker

Connect
Learn
Succeed™

The McGraw-Hill Companies

Mc Graw Hill

Connect
Learn
Succeed™

Published by McGraw-Hill, an imprint of The McGraw-Hill Companies, Inc., 1221 Avenue of the Americas, New York, NY 10020. Copyright © 2011, 2007, 2001, 1998, 1995, 1991, 1985, 1978. All rights reserved. No part of this publication may be reproduced or distributed in any form or by any means, or stored in a database or retrieval system, without the prior written consent of The McGraw-Hill Companies, Inc., including, but not limited to, in any network or other electronic storage or transmission, or broadcast for distance learning.

This book is printed on acid-free paper.

1 2 3 4 5 6 7 8 9 0 WFR / WFR 0

ISBN: 978-0-07-338513-6
MHID: 0-07-338513-1

Vice President, Editorial: *Michael Ryan*
Sponsoring Editor: *Katie Stevens*
Managing Editor: *Meghan Campbell*
Developmental Editor: *Craig Leonard*
Marketing Manager: *Pamela Cooper*
Project Manager: *Michelle Gardner, Laserwords Private Limited*
Manuscript Editor: *Tally Morgan*
Design Manager: *Margarite Reynolds*
Cover Designer: *Mona Grigaliunas, Asylum Studios*
Production Supervisor: *Louis Swaim*
Media Project Manager: *Jennifer Barrick*
Composition: *10/12 Goudy by Laserwords Private Limited*
Printing: *Worldcolor*

Library of Congress Cataloging-in-Publication Data

Wilmot, William W.
     Interpersonal conflict / William W. Wilmot, Joyce L. Hocker.—8th ed.
          p. cm.
     Includes bibliographical references and index.
     ISBN-13: 978-0-07-338513-6
     ISBN-10: 0-07-338513-1
     1. Interpersonal conflict. 2. Conflict (Psychology) I. Hocker, Joyce L. II. Title.
HM1121.W56 2011
303.6'9—dc22

                                        2009036073

The Internet addresses listed in the text were accurate at the time of publication. The inclusion of a Web site does not indicate an endorsement by the authors or McGraw-Hill, and McGraw-Hill does not guarantee the accuracy of the information presented at these sites.

www.mhhe.com

This book is dedicated to the memory of:

Wally and Viola Wilmot

and

Janice Hocker Rushing 1948-2004

Brief Contents

Contents

Preface

The study and application of conflict resolution principles have come a long way since our first edition in 1978. Back then, conflict management was a new addition to the field of communication. Now we know that conflict skills can be learned. We are glad so many of our colleagues champion and teach courses related to conflict resolution. The world needs these skills. In this eighth edition, we have kept the core of our thinking and philosophy while incorporating new best practices.

Noticeable changes in this edition are (1) a new chapter on emotion in conflict. Reviewers and long-time users asked for a chapter dealing in a focused way with emotion. Thanks for your prodding. We hope the chapter will add helpful new ideas to your teaching. (2) Key ideas about conflict prevention are now integrated into the book rather than separated into a chapter. (3) We shifted chapter 7 toward a focus on "Mapping Your Conflicts," since the previous assessment focus seemed to our reviewers to be more detailed than most teachers wanted to teach. We keep the popular systems focus and add "Macro" and "Micro"–level conflict maps to help gain perspective on conflict. (4) We have added many more in-depth cases, providing a lens on different perspectives from different conflict parties. We hope the more complex and expanded cases will provide a way for students to see that given enough information, different points of view all make sense. We have made a major effort to improve the writing, organize the chapters more tightly when needed, and enliven the style of the book.

Long-time adopters will notice many changes. Let us know what you think. For those wanting to trace the origins of ideas, we have carefully rechecked all the references so you won't be led astray. You will also notice that while we kept the best application activities, new ones have been added throughout.

Chapter 1, "The Nature of Conflict," keeps the resilient definition of conflict that has withstood decades of use. That definition orients you to the rest of the book, and you will see it reflected throughout. We added an extended example showing several "tries" at conflict resolution, and expanded suggestions on how to create a supportive, constructive environment rather than a defensive climate. The escalatory and avoidance spirals have been retained but simplified. The chapter ends with opportunities you have for learning and growing by studying conflict.

Chapter 2, "Perspectives on Conflict," looks at personal experiences and how they shape one's view of conflict. All of our experiences, from early family to current workplace and personal relationships, repeatedly shape and reshape us. We kept, but shortened, the section on conflict metaphors, and kept the section on gender and culture filters.

Chapter 3, "Interests and Goals," has become a cornerstone chapter for understanding why conflicts happen. The TRIP acronym helps people understand what the drivers of conflict are, and allows us to predict when we will get into conflict, and over what. This chapter will assist you in seeing why conflicts are repeated and seem to have no end. Clarity of goals brings hope for resolution.

Chapter 4, "Power: The Structure of Conflict," retains the relational view of power crafted in earlier editions, while updating examples and applications. We add a definition of interpersonal power. A case study is extended as the parties "try again" to deal with their conflict more productively. The chapter shows you how to assess your power and to increase power for all parties. The sections on power imbalances and how to balance power successfully in conflicts are retained and clarified.

Chapter 5, "Styles and Tactics," retains the five-style treatment that has benefited from continued research. The thrust of this chapter remains an examination of when each style is useful and when it has limitations. Bullying, verbal aggressiveness, and violence are clearly designated as destructive choices, not styles, and the research is updated. An extended case with opportunities for "What would you do now?" has been added as an application.

We have added an entirely new chapter on "Emotions in Conflict," Chapter 6. We define emotion, discuss how emotions function in conflict, present misconceptions about emotions, and explain the developmental theory of adaptive emotions. A comprehensive list of feeling words is included, with several applications, so students can practice working with feelings. Positive emotions stimulate conflict resolution; they are given weight along with emotions experienced as negative. We present an extended case dealing with emotions, inviting students to respond to the various iterations of the conflict. We end with practical options for reducing strong emotions in conflicts.

Chapter 7, "Mapping Your Conflicts," has been rewritten to address the perspective of people in conflict rather than outsiders assessing conflict. We retain and rewrite the "systems" nature of all conflicts, giving a readable trip through systems theory. We have shortened the treatment of system patterns, triangles, and coalitions. We include the two popular conflict assessment guides, which have proved useful for the major paper in the course in many universities.

Chapter 8, "Interpersonal Negotiation," has been tightened and reorganized to reflect everyday negotiation. A new section on principled negotiation reflects the latest work at the Project on Negotiation at Harvard University. The section on the language of collaboration has been expanded.

Chapter 9, "Third-Party Intervention," benefited from a major reorganization; we think you will find it clearer. We discuss helping, intervention when the parties decide and resolve their conflicts, and outside intervention when an outsider decides. We have added a section on communication coaching as one mode where the parties are empowered by a facilitator.

Chapter 10, "Forgiveness and Reconciliation" (by Gary W. Hawk), presents forgiveness and reconciliation from the interpersonal perspective. This reflects recent research in the field of communication. Misconceptions about forgiveness are discussed. Two perspectives are presented in detail: forgiveness as a decision and forgiveness as a process. Suggestions are presented for when people are stuck. An expanded section on apology has been added. A new section on receiving forgiveness and forgiving oneself has been included. Reconciliation is presented as a "late stage in the journey." An extended multicultural example (from Hawaii) concludes the chapter.

We hope you will learn from this edition. Let us know any responses you have—we receive each comment gratefully as we think of ways to make this project continue to be helpful. Best wishes as you begin this journey of discovery!

Bill Wilmot and Joyce Hocker

Acknowledgments

To the Reader from Bill Wilmot

The journey we all take in dealing with conflict in our lives is ongoing. In my own case, I have numerous people who have supported, inspired—and yes—challenged me.

Melanie Trost, my wife, deserves special kudos for helping me stay connected and centered. Her own career in hospice keeps the blessings of this life in focus. Melanie always leads with a kind heart and sparkling intellect, never wavering from kindness toward others. We pursue our interconnected Montana dreams in our log home in the mountains, relying on the miracles of satellite Internet to stay connected to the wider world. As a friend of mine said, "Bill, I can't believe you found a woman to live up there with you!" Then there is that dog, Rosie, who communicates her needs with unwavering clarity. When she wants something, she simply comes up and stares at me, making it quite clear that I should know exactly what she needs. I try to respond properly, because I certainly would not want a conflict with her, given those teeth. And Angus, a one-year-old Aussie, has just joined our pack. Keep that delightful energy going Gus.

My son Jason and daughter Carina have enlivened our family gatherings by bringing four children into the mix. When they along with Kate convene at the family cabin, TeePee, in Wyoming, the energy in the room is considerable! It will be fun to see how Sydney and Evan resolve their dispute over whether to call me "papa Bill" or "Grandpa Bill," with Karson and Luke watching from the wings. It is fascinating to have discussions with Jason and Carina about many of the topics of this book, since the little ones give them a chance almost every hour to practice their conflict management skills.

I have a diverse group of friends who continue to be central. Elaine Yarbrough and Mike Burr and I have had a 30-year friendship that continues to deepen. I also have the opportunity to work around the world with Elaine, who is simply the best workshop presenter ever. Thanks for your ongoing support and assistance through all the changes in our lives. Roy Andes stays connected as a special friend, who has seen me through some significant life challenges, and is almost as good a telemark skier as I am! I love coming to "the tabin," recalling our good times in our ghost town "shabin" (not quite a shack, not quite a cabin). The "shabin" set the forces into motion for me to live full time at Georgetown Lake, Montana, a truly special place.

Curt Carlson, CEO of SRI International, deserves special thanks for a supportive and exciting work life. As the Discipline of Innovation work continues to improve with the help of incredible teams of people from SRI, we will undoubtedly keep experiencing even more continuous improvement. If our dream of creating innovation centers around the world comes true, there will be even more important work ahead of us. Curt, thanks for showing people how to never give up, keep teamwork front and center, and focus on important problems. Our book *Innovation: The 5 Disciplines for Creating What Customers Want* is now out in English, Chinese, and Korean with other languages to come. My heartfelt thanks for your unwavering faith in me, Curt. I tell everyone I work with our mantra—"iterate, iterate, iterate."

Paul Wilson, who owns Tamarack Construction, literally kept our house (built by someone else) from falling in. Paul has an eye for detail coupled with terrific treatment of his customers and friends that is legendary. In addition, as our outdoor activities continue to expand, I can't wait to take his two boys, Luke and Connor Wilson, to that secret lake with no name I told them about. I hope our business ventures continue to be successful. The one that failed was still cheaper than getting an MBA degree.

Bob Inkster, at St. Cloud State University, has been a true joy to stay in touch with. After all, it was "more than two years" ago that we were undergraduate students at the University of Wyoming. Bob continues to be a driving force in the mediation program at SCSU along with great folks like Jeff Ringer. They have put together one of the strongest mediation programs in the country.

In my work intervening with conflicted work teams, the strength of the analysis shared in this book continues to be validated. You will see some of their actual disputes reflected anonymously in selected case studies. In my workshops on conflict and when I train mediators, the participants continue to teach me about things I don't know or misunderstood. Thanks to all of you who put up with my jokes. It has been fascinating to do this work across many cultures, from South Africa to Singapore, and each time I learn something important. In every workshop I tell stories about Wes Shellen. For eight years, we had repetitive conflicts, made a decision to work on our relationship, and ended up being very close friends. Wes died of cancer at an early age, but his influence is there every time I tell a story or have a conflict with someone else. He taught me about relational needs in a way I will never forget. The turning point for us was the day when he said, "Bill, it would be better if you worried less about my karma and more about your own."

My family had more influence then they could have known. Grandfather Chalmer Wilmot, who only went to the third grade in school, was a Wyoming homesteader and one of the few who was tough and resourceful enough to not fail. His encouragement to "travel somewhere" I have managed to take to the maximum. My mother and father made it clear that college was the route to opening up life opportunities, and without that focus I would have been running an automobile service station early in my life. My two older sisters, other than holding me down and tickling me until I cried "uncle," were very supportive in my early life. Jeri taught me how to dance, and Joyce came back much later as a source of support during some of my life changes.

Joyce Hocker, coauthor, continues to lead the way with improving both our writing skills. As you read this edition, you will feel the impact of her dedication to making our thoughts crisper and words more parsimonious. My spiritual teachers still are beacons of light during dark times. My prime connection is now with Ven. Thubten Chodron of Sravasti Abbey who continues to impact thousands of people around the world. What a pleasure to get to know true exemplars of how to work with all the internal emotions and thoughts that bubble up and cause conflict.

To the Reader from Joyce Hocker

I marvel that the project I began in 1971, my dissertation on conflict resolution, still evolves as this book evolves. My life is defined and enriched by my continued passion for conflict resolution and peacemaking. I remain convinced that we can trust the principles about which we write and which remain a challenge in everyday life.

I dedicate this eighth edition, again, to Janice Hocker Rushing, my beloved younger sister who was Professor of Communication at the University of Arkansas when she died quickly and unexpectedly in 2004. Janice's brilliant intellect informed all the early editions of this book; she was its most involved and perceptive reviewer from the first through the sixth editions. She taught from the book, gave us creative feedback, and used the most complete set of teaching files for the course I have ever seen. Janice's spirit of loving kindness and appreciative inquiry continue to inform everything I write. I often think, "How would Janice say this?" Janice encouraged me to write from my mind and heart, and she continues to influence me in powerful and creative ways.

My husband Gary Hawk contributed to this book in multilayered ways. He revised his chapter on forgiveness and reconciliation, drawing from years of teaching this and other courses for the Davidson Honors College at the University of Montana. Gary's excellent writing set a high standard for me as I revised. I am deeply appreciative of Gary's ongoing research and thinking in forgiveness and reconciliation. Gary patiently put up with having a wife who was either at work or at home writing. Expert woodworker that he is, he built us a gorgeous cherry dining table which I promptly took over with stacks of materials for months. Toward the end, he commented that he would be glad to see the top of the table again. Gary understood and supported my desire to dive into this project, knowing how important the ideas are. He has generously supported me through five editions of this book. He talks with me about the deeper challenges of couples communication (as we work with couple clients), reconciliation, truth-telling, and dialogue. I am blessed to have Gary as my partner in life and glad he is a part of this book. Janice always said that Gary is "as deep as a well." He is; our conversations on topics in the book have informed my thinking for years. Our tuxedo cat, Lonestar, helped by doing what cats do—sitting on piles of paper, walking across the computer, and insisting on sitting on my lap late at night. He kept me company in the late hours.

I continue to feel gratitude and admiration for the contributions of my coauthor, Bill Wilmot. Bill draws from his innovative consulting work in ways that expand the ideas and applications in this book. Bill and I bring complementary gifts to this long project. He keeps an eye out for the latest organizational research, is unfailingly enthusiastic about the project, and has a welcome "can do" attitude. He managed to meet deadlines and work on this edition while traveling the world as a consultant. I appreciate his work in reorganizing several chapters that were in need of clearer thinking; he provided that perspective beautifully. Right at the end, Bill took on the task, with our research assistant Kathi Butler, of checking every single reference in the book.

I am gifted with superb colleagues. Chris Fiore of the Department of Psychology at the University of Montana, is my partner in a long-term communication skills training project and ongoing staff development for the Division of Diabetes Treatment and Prevention of the Indian Health Service. Chris and I practiced many of the concepts in the book in our work; we wrote and revised late at night in Albuquerque hotels, then revised again after we role-played and filmed our conflict resolution demonstrations. Thank you, Chris! Kelly Acton, MD, and Lorraine Valdez, Director and Deputy of the Diabetes Program of the Indian Health Service, have given me the chance for over a decade to work with their excellent staff in different ways. I especially appreciate Kelly's encouragement to make these ideas "user friendly" for people who are not in the field of communication. On one of these consulting trips Chris Fiore declared, "you need a research assistant," then sent Kathi Butler to me for help with the project, especially the new chapter on emotion in conflict. Kathi's research skills as a Clinical Psychology doctoral student proved essential. She brought articles to my home in the cold, dark, snowy days of winter, annotated and thoughtfully organized in a way that I could readily use. Kathi talked through ideas with me, found resources, encouraged me to add topics that I would not have thought of, and kept excellent track of my references, checking them all with Bill as we finished. Thank you, Kathi, for your intellectual gifts as a thinker, your skills as a researcher, and your human gifts of encouragement and compassion. Anne de Vore, Jungian analyst and longtime friend, is responsible for pointing me toward the research in the developmental theory of emotion. She discussed her ideas about emotion with me in a way that helped shape a massive field. I am grateful to Anne for her ongoing support of me for 33 years. Anne embodies the highest principles of conflict resolution from the inside out. Diane Haddon, friend and therapist in my building, patiently listened to me talk about this project for months and encouraged me and cheered me on. I am deeply grateful for all those lunches, workouts, and our ongoing friendship.

Every writer needs a writing group, I now see. Thank you to Leslie Burgess and Candace Crosby, who read drafts of parts of this project and helped me clarify new ideas, cases, and approaches. They are perceptive and kind-hearted critics and I trust them to find just the right perspective on a topic. I am glad we are supporting each others' writing projects in such a productive way. Yes, let's go to Mexico next year and write there! Sally Brown, my assistant, kept the business going while I was writing, provided all kinds of work-related support, and compiled the excellent index for this edition. I couldn't do what I do without Sally.

A few of my psychotherapy clients have graciously granted me permission to use parts of their stories, with all the identifying details changed, of course. In every case they gave me permission to write from their lives. I appreciate them for their stories and even more for the rich work I am privileged to do with them as a psychologist. I am also privileged to be involved again in my home association, the National Communication Association, especially with the Ethnography Division, which hosts writing about real people, from the heart and mind. Art Bochner, Carolyn Ellis, Tom Frentz, and others inspire and encourage me. Tom, my brother-in-law, encourages, or rather pushes, me to write and keep writing. Thank you, Tom, for your unfailing interest in my writing and how this project was coming along. You remind me of Janice when she was little: "Are you finished yet?" (So we can write something together, in this case.) Gale Young of California State–East Bay is not only my dear friend but kept reminding me she was going to have to teach from this book so I should make it good. I hope we have. Colleagues in NCA keep me inspired to update and work with these important ideas. I think of recent PhDs teaching with this text and try to make it teachable and inspiring.

My family of origin gave me the nascent ideas and the lived experience for everything in this book. My brother Ed is a clear-thinking man of peace and integrity who shares our unusually positive family experience with me, in memory. We keep the Hocker family values and experience alive in our Colorado cabin that our parents built, that now Tom Frentz, Ed and Gary and I maintain. I still hear our father Lamar's words as he gave sermons in a calm, reasoned, and deeply felt cadence. He and my mother personally involved all of us in social justice issues that gave rise to our shared passion for conflict resolution. We remember our mother Jean for her pragmatic, optimistic, factual, encouraging character. She was our first writing teacher. Grandmother Freddie

Lightfoot told me, as a child, "you can do anything you want to." Janice's voice lives always in me as an ongoing loving, inner dialogue. My family gave me a start in everything that remains important in my life, including this book.

From Both of the Authors

We hope this book informs and inspires you. We are very grateful to Craig Leonard, our development editor, who provided the most helpful summary of reviews ever. Thank you to our excellent reviewers Janice Barrett, Lasell College; Michael Monsour, University of Colorado-Denver; Linda Nickerson, University of Idaho; Gilda Parrella, Loyola University-Chicago; Amanda Retberg, Wisconsin Lutheran College; and Roseanna Ross, Saint Cloud State University. We welcome any suggestions or questions. Please let us know of any errors you spot. We'd love to know what you think of this edition; you can contact us by e-mail at:

Bill Wilmot
Professor Emeritus
University of Montana
wwwilmot@aol.com

Joyce L. Hocker
Faculty Affiliate
University of Montana
joyhocker@aol.com

Supplements

For Instructors: A password-protected instructor's manual is available online at www.mhhe.com/wilmot8e. Please ask your McGraw-Hill representative for access information.

For Students: True/false quizzes, multiple choice quizzes, and Application boxes are available on the Online Learning Center (www.mhhe.com/wilmot8e).

The eighth edition of *Interpersonal Conflict* is available as an eTextbook at www.CourseSmart.com. CourseSmart is a new way to find and buy eTextbooks. At CourseSmart you can save up to 50% off the cost of a print textbook, reduce your impact on the environment, and gain access to powerful Web tools for learning. CourseSmart has the largest selection of eTextbooks available anywhere, offering thousands of the most commonly adopted textbooks from a wide variety of higher education publishers. CourseSmart eTextbooks are available in one standard online reader with full text search, notes and highlighting, and email tools for sharing notes between classmates. For further details, contact your sales representative or go to www.coursesmart.com.

Part One

Conflict Components

Chapter 1

The Nature of Conflict

In conflict, be fair and generous.

Why Study Conflict?

Conflict is a fact of human life. It occurs naturally in all kinds of settings. Nations still struggle, families fracture in destructive conflicts, marriages face challenges and often fail, and the workplace is plagued with stress.

The study of conflict should be viewed as a basic human requirement and the practice of constructive conflict as an essential set of interpersonal skills (Sillars, 2009). We have confidence that your lives will be enriched by what you will learn in this course, and what you will continue to learn for the rest of your lives. Welcome to the process!

Mental health improves with a constructive conflict process. The National Institute of Mental Health funded a decade of studies of depression as one of the major public health problems of our time. Depression affects one's personal relationships and results in millions of dollars lost in the workplace due to missed days; then there are the medical and counseling costs. Effective conflict management is one aspect of interpersonal therapy, a well-researched counseling technique for dealing with depression. When people experience conflicts, much of their energy goes into emotions related to those conflicts. They may be fearful, angry, resentful, hopeless, or stressed. Adding to one's repertoire for resolving conflicts reduces a common stressor. Ineffective resolution of interpersonal disputes adds to depression and hopelessness. Eating disorders, physical and psychological abuse of partners (O'Leary et al. 1989), and problem drinking (Murphy and O'Farrell 1994) also are associated with destructive conflict environments.

Family Relationships

Our **family of origin** socializes us into constructive or destructive ways of handling conflict that carry over directly into how romantic relationships are later handled (Koerner and Fitzpatrick 2002). For example, step families' conflicts are destructive 95 percent of the time (Baxter, Braithwaite, and Nicholson 1999).

Severe parental conflict predicts both internal and external conflicts for adolescents (Turner and Barrett 1998). Many parents try to protect their children from exposure to their marital conflicts, but when children are present, often the conflicts are even worse and more destructive than when the parents fight alone (Papp, Cummings, and Goeke-Morey 2002).

Family research is quite clear about the systemwide effects of **destructive marital conflict.** First, negative conflict between the parents reduces the family's network of friends and creates more loneliness (Jones 1992). Conflict between the parents tends to both change the mood of household interactions and shift the parents' attention to the negative behaviors of their children (Jouriles and Farris 1992). Parental conflict has a direct negative impact on the children. Communication patterns between fathers and their young adult children seem to have a circular relationship—the young adults treat their fathers the way they were treated (Dumlao and Botta 2000). Conflict between parents predicts well-being of the children, with more conflict associated with maladaptive behavior on the part of the children (Dunn and Tucker 1993; Garber 1991; Grych and Fincham 1990; Jouriles, Bourg, and Farris 1991). Finally, the effects of destructive conflict patterns suggest that "ongoing conflict at home has a greater impact on adolescent distress and symptoms than does parental divorce" (Jaycox and Repetti 1993, 344). Parents who either avoid conflict or engage in negative cycles of mutual damage directly influence the children's subsequent lives. A modest relationship exists between mothers who avoid conflict and their daughters' marital satisfaction (VanLear 1992). On the other end of the continuum, children who are exposed to harsh discipline practices at home (which coincide with a negative and hostile relationship between the parents) are more at risk for aggression, hyperactivity, and internalizing by withdrawing, having somatic complaints, and experiencing depressive symptoms (Jaycox and Repetti 1993). The family effects also reach beyond the immediate environment. One study demonstrated that children from high-conflict homes had much stronger negative reactions while watching a video of angry adults than did children from low-conflict homes (El-Sheikh 1994).

The number of conflicts experienced does not seem to predict poor health and well-being as much as whether the individuals perceive the conflict to be resolvable (Malis and Roloff, 2006). Through studying the practices presented in this book, you may predict that your conflicts can be resolved. This belief and resulting experience will actually improve your physical health and well-being.

Simply stated, the level of conflict and how destructive it is affect all areas of family well-being. If you, as a present or future parent, change your own conflict resolution skills, you will affect everyone in your families, present and future. As you look back on your own family history, you probably know the truth of this statement.

Children and adults who were physically and sexually abused as children face significant difficulties in their later conflicts. It is not possible to generalize completely, because many people exhibit remarkable resilience and effectiveness in their lives despite terrible abuse. Yet common responses to abuse, including the verbal abuse of yelling and the silent treatment, are hypervigilance; difficulty relaxing; withdrawal at the first sign of tension or conflict; floating away, or dissociating; and not knowing or expressing what one really wants. Children's own attitudes toward marriage are directly affected by the conflict between their parents. If their parents have frequent conflict, children have a much less favorable attitude toward marriage (Jennings, Salts, and Smith 1991). A child's general feeling of self-worth are directly affected by interparental conflict (Garber 1991). This means that it isn't primarily a question of whether parents divorce or not that affects the children; rather, it is the level of conflict present in either the intact family or the restructured family that impacts the children.

The study of conflict can pay big dividends in your personal relationships. If you are an adolescent or a parent of an adolescent, it will come as no surprise to you that it takes about 10 years after an adolescent leaves home for parents and children to negotiate roles that bring them closer to equality than they were in their earlier parent–child relationship (Comstock 1994). At the heart of this negotiation is the conflict process. The study of conflict can assist in this process of redrawing family boundaries, letting you see which styles backfire, and which ones work best.

Love Relationships

We all know that love relationships provide a rigorous test of our ability to manage conflict. Siegert and Stamp (1994) studied the effects of the "First Big Fight" in dating relationships, noting that some couples survive and prosper, whereas others break up. These communication researchers tell us quite clearly that "the big difference between the nonsurvivors and survivors was the way they perceived and handled conflict" (357). "What determines the course of a relationship . . . is in a large measure determined by how successfully the participants move through conflict episodes" (Wilmot 1995, 95).

While married individuals are generally healthier than unmarried persons, if you are married and in conflict, your health is likely to be poorer than that of single people (Burman and Margolin 1992). Hostile behavior during conflictual interactions seems to relate to changes in one's immune system, resulting in poorer overall physical health (Kiecolt-Glaser et al. 1996). Wives appear to suffer more from hostile conflictual situations than do husbands (Kiecolt-Glaser et al. 1996).

One key skill in all long-term committed relationships is conflict management—certainly, the data on marriages suggest this is true (Gottman 1994). The presence or absence of conflict does not determine the quality of a marriage; rather, how the couple handles conflictual situations determines the quality of the relationship (Comstock and Strzyzewski 1990). Even beliefs about conflict are more important to marital happiness than whether or not the two partners actually agree with one another (Crohan 1992).

How you handle conflict spreads to other members of your family. For example, it has been noted that adult children who are taking care of their parents usually have high levels of conflict with siblings (Merrill 1996). Learning effective skills for dealing with your younger brother or sister is far better than engaging in a family dispute that will affect your children and subsequent generations as well.

The Workplace

So far, we have presented the reasons for studying conflict in personal relationships. In addition, **conflicts at work** present important challenges that affect your career development. "Conflict is a stubborn fact of organizational life" (Kolb and Putnam 1992, 311). We carry our interpersonal relationships into our workplaces; work life and private life intertwine. One study surveyed workers and found that almost 85 percent reported conflicts at work (Bergmann and Volkema, 1994). With an increasing awareness of cultural diversity and gender equity issues, it is imperative that we become familiar with issues surrounding promotions and harassment. In fact, one can see communication training in organizations as a form of preventive conflict management (Hathaway 1995). Managers need to learn conflict skills to intervene in disputes in their organization (Yarbrough and Wilmot 1995).

Ongoing, unresolved workplace conflict also has negative effects that reach far beyond the principal parties. If the executive director of a nonprofit agency and her board cannot get along, employees tend to take sides, fear for their jobs, and, like those above them, wage a campaign discrediting the other group. Health care environments present the probability of damaging conflicts. For instance, when doctors and nurses engage in destructive conflict, the patient suffers. When nurses, who often are the person who knows the patient's situation most intimately, withdraw, patient illness and death rises (Forte 1997). Serious interprofessional conflict results in an alarmingly higher number of medical errors than when teamwork is not in conflict (Baldwin, Jr. & Daugherty, 2008).

Ignoring workplace conflict sets destructive forces in motion that decrease productivity, spread the conflict to others, and lead to lower morale. In one organization, the CEO was on the verge of reorganizing the structure, affecting 600 people, so that two *wow!* vice presidents would not have to talk to one another!

Some of the advantages to studying organizational conflicts include:

- As an employee, you can learn how to get along with

    Fellow employees

    Your manager

    The public

- You will be perceived as more skilled

- You will be able to help prevent workplace conflicts

- As a supervisor, you can begin to

    See conflicts coming

    Learn productive responses

    Get more cooperation from employees

    Help employees resolve their disputes with one another

    Keep interpersonal conflicts from spreading to other parts of the organization

    Teach teams how to handle their own conflicts

As you will see in chapter 9, "Third-Party Intervention," you might study conflict so you can be of help to others experiencing interpersonal conflict. To be of most help you will need specific intervention skills, but understanding conflict dynamics is an absolute prerequisite for being an effective helper to others—children, friends, family, and work associates.

The Importance of Skill Development

The skills of conflict management are not intuitively obvious. For example, it isn't just the people who call one another names who have relationship difficulties deriving from conflict. It has been clearly demonstrated that "couples who never engage in conflict are at long-term risk" (McGonagle, Kessler, and Gotlib 1993, 398). In conflict, we must learn to "do what comes unnaturally." If we do what we have always done, we will keep getting the results we have always gotten—results that may keep us mired in the same old patterns. Who would imagine, for instance, that moving toward bad news, instead of away from bad news, is often the better strategy? How many of us intuitively know to tell more and more of the truth when a conflict is becoming destructive rather than keeping quiet or yelling?

Unresolved conflict has a tremendous negative impact. It directly affects the parties themselves. In personal relationships, unresolved conflict leads to drifting away from one another and sometimes jettisoning the relationship entirely. In the workplace, it leads to low productivity and being fired. Therefore, we need to activate effective skills in relationships for the following reasons:

- Your mental health will be improved as you learn to deal with conflict constructively.
- The long-term satisfaction in your family, in your love, relationships and at work hinges on how well you manage conflict.
- People around you will benefit from your improved skills.
- The overall health and mental health of everyone around you depends partly on successful conflict resolution.

Conflict management draws upon the skills of **emotional intelligence.** This popular concept is defined as "the capacity for recognizing our own feelings and those of others, for motivating ourselves, and for managing emotions well in ourselves and in our relationships" (Goleman 1998, 317). Later in the book we will discuss management of emotions in detail. As you can see at this point, recognizing feelings, self-motivation, and dealing with feelings are skills that pervade all of conflict management. Workplaces now ask employees to be excellent with "people skills"—the precise skills useful in conflict management.

Why is emotional intelligence so important for conflict management? Let's look at the twenty competencies organized into four clusters that describe emotional intelligence (p. 7).

Notice that the first three clusters must be mastered before you can effectively operate within the Social Skills area. We will lead you through concepts and exercises that will help you develop skills in all these areas. We see this as a lifelong process, needed in intimate relationships, family communication, workplace communication, and community and worldwide leadership. For example, you may have a long-standing conflictual relationship with one of your siblings. When you begin to see each other much less frequently, the daily irritations may well subside, giving you an opportunity to approach each other differently. Yet, hurts and fights from the past may make it difficult to create a new relationship. The ideas in this book will give you some starting places for finding new ground with your families.

Why study conflict? Because if we don't, we are more likely to repeat the damaging patterns we see on the job and in our homes. Examining the dynamics of conflict will allow us to unpack those dynamics, see what brings on destructive moves, and build more

EMOTIONAL INTELLIGENCE — 20 competencies

SELF-AWARENESS

1. Emotional self-awareness
2. Accurate self-assessment
3. Self-confidence

Key to master these

SELF-MANAGEMENT

4. Self-control
5. Trustworthiness
6. Conscientiousness
7. Adaptability
8. Achievement orientation
9. Initiative

SOCIAL AWARENESS

10. Empathy
11. Organizational awareness
12. Service orientation

SOCIAL SKILLS

13. Developing others
14. Leadership
15. Influence
16. Communication
17. Change-catalyst
18. Conflict management
19. Building bonds
20. Teamwork and collaboration

(Goleman 1995)

Application 1.1

Discuss with a small group what you believe are your three key strengths from the list above. What are three areas that you believe, or have been told, need development? Name and describe some people you know who model certain areas of emotional intelligence. What do you notice that they do?

productive options for ourselves both at work and at home. Since the first edition of this book was published in 1978, writers have agreed that conflict is not different from "regular" communication but is a part of the ongoing flow of the communication between human beings. We might define ourselves as being "in conflict," of varying intensities, many times a day or week. Even people who vastly prefer peace, harmony, and calm interaction find themselves involved in situations that are tense, escalating, and uncomfortable. Truly, we do not have the option of staying out of conflict unless we stay out of relationships, families, work, and community. Conflict happens—so we had best be prepared for it.

Son and Mother

The following dialogue may be familiar to you in tone, if not in content:

Son (Thinking through how to talk with his mother and make a request for more financial help): *My graduation expenses cost a lot more than I thought they would. I had to pay for the senior trip, the dinner, and all kinds of things I didn't know would come up. I don't know how I'm going to pay for my car insurance this summer. I promised Mom that I would pay for my graduation expenses and personal expenses in June out of my summer job. But I haven't been able to find one yet. I'm kind of scared. I know she hasn't planned on spending more money on my personal expenses. I guess I overestimated what I could earn, and how quickly. I'm kind of embarrassed to have to ask for help. But I don't know what else to do.*

Son: Mom, I have not been able to save as much money as I hoped to for my graduation expenses and personal expenses in June. And while I'm looking for work, as you know, I haven't found anything yet except for split-shift fast food work, which we both agreed would be my last resort. No benefits, either. So, while I hate to ask, I am wondering if you could help me financially until I get a full-time job. Then we can work out a pay-back schedule and a budget for me.

Mother (*Thinking about how to respond to her son*): *I do realize that graduation cost more than we thought it would. And I've been surprised at how few jobs there are. But it's also true that I didn't budget any extra money, and my hours at the hospital have been cut back some. I don't know what to do. He's my son and I know he needs help, but on the other hand, I think he needs to take whatever job he can find right away, even if he changes later. I would have to borrow the money to pay for all those extra expenses. But I guess I should. He needs the help.*

Mother: I do know that everything cost more than both of us thought it would. I want to help you out, of course. You may not know that my hours have been cut and we are on a very tight budget here at home. Would you be willing to take whatever job you can find for now, and then switch when you find something better? I think we can work this out.

The mother and son are engaged in interpersonal conflict. Their conflict results from their particular communication choices. The son asks for extra help; the mother makes a decision first rather than asking questions. The next few interactions may well escalate toward damage of their ongoing relationship. The son may be uncertain how he will look for work if he can't drive. He may want to save money he was given for graduation for other purposes. Yet he also wants his mother's recognition of him as an adult, and he wants to be seen as responsible. The mother wants, presumably, to help her son find work, to teach him to manage money, and to preserve a give-and-take relationship between them. She doesn't want to alienate her son, but she doesn't want to feel taken advantage of or to go against an agreement. Their individual and relational goals can only be met through creative conflict interactions. When conflict is viewed as a problem to be solved instead of a battle to be won or interaction to be avoided, creative solutions can be found.

In the Chinese language the character for conflict is made up of two different symbols: one indicates danger whereas the other indicates opportunity. As you think about these two approaches, decide whether you respond first to conflict as a dangerous, obstructive dilemma or whether you experience conflict as a welcome opportunity for change. The *I Ching* teaches that the wise person in conflict remains clearheaded, inwardly strong, and ready to meet his or her opponent halfway (Wilhelm 1977). At the beginning of your study of conflict, we ask you to consider the possibilities inherent in conflict. By the end of the course, we hope you come to experience the activity as an important means of growth rather than a failure or a negative event to be avoided at all costs.

Chinese symbol Danger and Opportunity

Application 1.2 — My Basic Approach to Conflict

Where are you on the following ratings describing your approach to conflict?

I love peace and harmony and will go to great lengths to avoid conflict.

I sometimes will willingly engage in conflict, but only if I can see no other good choice.

I like the give-and-take of a good verbal conflict and am not particularly wary of getting involved.

I enjoy constructive conflict. My adrenaline gets going and I like to see what can come of it. I even seek out conflict at times.

I count on conflict to help clear the air, solve problems, and get us to a "different place."

People can change their conflict behavior by studying this book and participating in class exercises, you will be able to understand your present conflict behavior, make choices to engage in new behavior during conflicts, and thus act as a change agent in times of crisis and turbulence. Your approach to conflict is not an inborn set of responses but rather a developed repertoire of communication skills that are learned, refined, and practiced. You don't have to remain the way you have been in the past.

⚬Preventing Destructive Conflict

At this point in the book and your conflict class, our fervent hope is that you have developed curiosity about conflict. **Prevention** of conflict presents a paradoxical task. On the one hand, we now know that conflict is one of the normal states of human communication; on the other hand, we would like to do what we can to prevent destructive, time-wasting, relationship-harming conflict. We'd like to enhance the possibility of creative change and decrease the probability of destructive conflict. To prevent means *"to anticipate, to forestall, to come before, to be in readiness for an occasion, to deprive something of power, to hold or keep back, and to deal with beforehand."* Prevention implies taking advance measures against something, to forestall something from its course. Prevention implies taking effective measures to ward off something destructive. We've all used the saying, "An ounce of prevention is worth a pound of cure." How might we prevent destructive conflict?

The Rescue Crew: A Fable

Once upon a time, in a beautiful meadow close to town, a group of friends was having a picnic on a sunny spring day. They'd brought along a kayak and a canoe for playing in the river, some softball equipment, great food, and some music. They had several backpack tents and sleeping bags in case they decided to stay overnight. It was spring break and all the friends were elated to be out of classes and just hanging out. Jack and Stacey jumped in their canoe and began to explore the other side of the river. Suddenly Stacey saw what looked like a person floating downstream. Sure enough, it was a woman who had been battered by the river rocks and was almost dead. The group sprang into action: someone knew CPR and revived her, someone else made temporary bandages for her wounds, and they called the EMTs on their cell phones. Just as they were loading her into the ambulance, the whole scene was repeated, with two more people needing rescue. The whole sequence continued. The friends called for help, and people responded generously. Soon an emergency tent city was set up, people brought in food and water, medical personnel volunteered their time, and organizers raised money, for the bodies kept coming, and the sturdy group of volunteers was over-whelmed by the urgent needs of the wounded and drowning people. Not everyone could be saved.

After a few weeks, a construction crew had set up a more permanent shelter with emergency medical equipment and some basic housing for the volunteers. Media crews visited to document the extraordinary tragedy and generous helping response. Some conflicts began to develop among the leadership; the people who had been on the original picnic claimed that they knew the most about the situation and should be elected as leaders of the new rescue organization. Names were suggested for the group. One evening a young man from a different town arrived to help. He immediately began running at full speed up the river. The rescue crew yelled at him to get back and help with the food preparation for the volunteers and victims. "Where the heck do you think you're going?" one of the leaders yelled. "I'm going upstream to see who's pushing all these people in the river. Come help me see what's happening and get this stopped now!" the runner replied.

As the fable illustrates, there's no reason to spend all our energy taking care of disasters. We need to find out what's causing them, then put energy into preventing further disasters.

Romances break up, families extend estrangements over years, and intractable conflicts damage peoples' enjoyment of work. Violence at home, at school, and in the wider society can be reduced by teaching people conflict resolution (Johnson and Johnson 1996). We mention "passion," which means *to suffer with*. Passionate conflict prevention involves staying with a situation long enough to make a difference rather than avoiding. Even with a wide repertoire of conflict resolution skills, most of us would rather prevent or avoid conflict than have to process it. On the international scene, conflict prevention could keep thousands or even millions of people from death or destruction. Our well-being as a globe depends on learning to prevent devastating conflict (Wenger and Mockli 2003).

Read

When you have experienced many conflicts that actually turn out better than you might have feared, you will become more hopeful and encouraged. We know that conflict resolution is a set of skills that can be learned, you can improve your skills and be a force for change in others.

Conflict Defined

All interpersonal conflicts, whether they occur between family members, romantic partners, students and teachers, employees and supervisors, work teams, or groups, have certain elements in common. One of the popular **definitions of conflict,** offered by Coser (1967), asserts that conflict is "a struggle over values and claims to scarce status, power, and resources in which the aims of the opponents are to neutralize, injure, or eliminate the rivals" (8). Note that this definition grew out of the cold war, in which conflict between the United States and the former U.S.S.R. dominated Western approaches to conflict. Conflict was definitely viewed as a win-lose situation. In 1973 Deutsch maintained that "conflict exists whenever incompatible activities occur . . . an action which prevents, obstructs, interferes with, injures, or in some way makes (resolution) less likely or less effective" (156). Mack and Snyder (1973) suggested that two parties must be present, along with "position scarcity" or "resource scarcity," in addition to behaviors that "destroy, injure, thwart, or otherwise control another party or parties, . . . the parties can gain (relatively) only at each other's expense" (36). All of these early social science definitions help us distinguish conflict from simple "strain," "disagreement," or "controversy" (Simons 1972; Schmidt and Kochan 1972). Conflict varies in intensity. It may be seen as a (1) mild difference, (2) disagreement, (3) dispute, (4) campaign, (5) litigation, or (6) fight or war (Keltner 1987). Another approach shows conflict ranging from avoidance to violence (Moore, 1996).

For purposes of this book, **conflict** is defined as follows:

> *Conflict is an expressed struggle between at least two interdependent parties who perceive incompatible goals, scarce resources, and interference from others in achieving their goals.*

Perception is at the core of all conflict analysis. In interpersonal conflicts, people react as though there are genuinely different goals, there is not enough of some resource, and the other person actually is getting in the way of something prized by the perceiver. Sometimes these conditions are believed to be true, but sorting out what is perceived and what is interpersonally accurate forms the basis of conflict analysis.

Careful attention to the elements that make up conflict will help you understand an apparently unresolvable conflict. When conflicts remain muddled and unclear, they cannot be *re-solved*, or solved a different way.

An Expressed Struggle

An *interpersonal* approach to conflict management focuses on the communicative exchanges that make up the conflict episode. **Intrapersonal conflict**—internal strain that creates a state of ambivalence, conflicting internal dialogue, or lack of resolution in one's thinking and feeling—accompanies **interpersonal conflict.** One may endure intrapersonal conflict for a while before such a struggle is expressed communicatively. If you are upset with your father yet you do not write him, or you phone him less often and avoid expressing your concern, do you have a conflict?

[handwritten margin note: Intrapersonal Conflict]

Application 1.3	My Intrapersonal Conflicts

Think of an intrapersonal strain you may be feeling right now, or felt for a while in the past. What is the struggle you feel? Think of a picture or metaphor to describe what you are feeling. What words describe the internal strain? Have you ever lived through an intrapersonal conflict that did not ever become expressed? If you answered yes to this question, ask yourself if you might have expressed the conflict ever so slightly in some way. How might you have expressed the internal conflict nonverbally, or by actions you did not take?

People involved in conflicts have perceptions about their own thoughts and feelings and perceptions about the other's thoughts and feelings. Conflict is present when there are *joint communicative representations* of it. The verbal or nonverbal communication may be subtle—a slight shift in body placement by Jill and a hurried greeting by Susan—but it must be present for the activity to be interpersonal conflict. Therefore, although other conditions must also exist before an interaction is labeled "conflict," Jandt (1973) asserts, "Conflict exists when the parties involved agree in some way that the behaviors associated with their relationship are labeled as 'conflict' behavior" (2). Often, the communicative behavior is easily identified with conflict, such as when one party openly disagrees with the other. Other times, however, an interpersonal conflict may be operating at a more tacit level. Two friends, for instance, may both be consciously avoiding the other because both think, "I don't want to see him for a few days because of what he did." The interpersonal struggle is expressed by the avoidance. **Intrapersonal perceptions** are the bedrock upon which conflicts are built; but only when there are communicative manifestations of these perceptions will an "interpersonal conflict" emerge.

Communication is the central element in all interpersonal conflict. Communication and conflict are related in the following ways:

- Communication behavior *often* creates *conflict*.
- Communication behavior reflects *conflict*.
- Communication is the vehicle *for the productive or destructive management of conflict*.

Thus, communication and conflict are inextricably tied. How one communicates in a conflict situation has profound implications for the residual impact of that conflict. If two work associates are vying for the same position, they can handle the competition in a variety of ways. They may engage in repetitive, damaging rounds with one another, or they may successfully manage the conflict. Communication can be used to exacerbate the conflict or to lead to its productive management.

The following example explains how to move a conflict from an internally experienced strain to an interpersonal communication:

Leslie: (To new husband, Greg, referring to Greg's 15-year-old son.) I've noticed Brennan is using my towels and other stuff from my bathroom instead of the things from his bathroom. Do you think he's annoyed because he can't share our bathroom any more? Or he is just being thoughtless? I don't want to share our bathroom and I can't stand it when he leaves damp towels all over the place!

Greg: I don't know. He hasn't said anything. Do you want me to check it out, or do you want to?

Leslie: (Sigh.) Well, I'm uncomfortable, but it's my job to check it out. I won't make assumptions. I'll just ask him.

This situation could have escalated into a "war of the towels," or been handled unproductively by the stepmom leaving curt notes, the stepson avoiding contact, and both building up negative assumptions about the other. As it happened, the boy did admit to his new stepmother that he was irritated. He and his father had lived together for years without bothering much about which towel was whose, and he resented being told which bathroom and towels to use. Leslie had a chance to say what privacy and neatness meant to her. The three of them talked it through, defusing what could have been a big conflict that would have been over the wrong things (towels instead of the new relationships).

Most **expressed struggles** become activated by a *triggering event*. A staff member of a counseling agency is fired, setting off a series of meetings culminating in the staff's demand to the board that the director be fired. Or, in a roommate situation, Carl comes home one night and the locks are changed on the door. The triggering event brings the conflict to everyone's attention—it is the lightning rod of recognition.

Interdependence

Conflict parties engage in an expressed struggle and interfere with one another because they are **interdependent**. "A person who is not dependent upon another—that is, who has no special interest in what the other does—has no conflict with that other person"

(Braiker and Kelley 1979, 137). Each person's choices affect the other because conflict is a mutual activity. People are seldom totally opposed to each other. Even two people who are having an "intellectual conflict" over politics are to some extent cooperating with each other. They have, in effect, said, "Look, we are going to have this verbal argument, and we aren't going to hit each other, and both of us will get certain rewards for participating in this flexing of our intellectual muscles. We'll play by the rules, which we both understand." Schelling (1960) calls **strategic conflict** (conflict in which parties have choices as opposed to conflict in which the power is so disparate that there are virtually no choices) a "theory of precarious partnership" or "incomplete antagonism." In other words, even these informal debaters concerned with politics cannot formulate their verbal tactics until they know the "moves" made by the other party.

[margin note: Interesting]

Parties in strategic conflict, therefore, are never totally antagonistic and must have **mutual interests,** even if the interest is only in keeping the conflict going. Without openly saying so, they often are thinking, "How can we have this conflict in a way that increases the benefit to me?" These decisions are complex, with parties reacting not in a linear, cause–effect manner but with a series of interdependent decisions. Bateson (1972) presents an "ecological" view of patterns in relationships. As in the natural environment, in which a decision to eliminate coyotes because they are a menace to sheep affects the overall balance of animals and plants, no one party in a conflict can make a decision that is totally separate—each decision affects the other conflict participants. In all conflicts, therefore, interdependence carries elements of cooperation and elements of competition. In true conflicts, the parties are "stuck with each other."

[margin note: Elements of both cooperation and competition]

Even though conflict parties are always interdependent to some extent, how they perceive their mutuality affects their later choices. Parties decide, although they may not be aware of this decision, whether they will act as relatively interdependent agents or relatively independent agents. Both or all may agree that "we are in this together," or they may believe that "just doing my own thing" is possible and desirable. A couple had been divorced for three years and came to a mediator to decide what to do about changing visitation agreements as their three children grew older. In the first session, the former husband seemed to want a higher degree of interdependence than did the former wife. He wanted to communicate frequently by phone, adopting flexible arrangements based on the children's wishes and his travel schedule. She wanted a monthly schedule set up in advance, communicated in writing. After talking through their common interest in their children, their own complicated work and travel lives, the children's school and sports commitments, and their new spouses' discomfort with frequent, flexible contact between the former partners, they worked out a solution that suited them both. Realizing that they were unavoidably interdependent, they agreed to lessen their verbal and in-person communication about arrangements while agreeing to maintain e-mail communication about upcoming scheduling. They worked out an acceptable level of interdependence.

An example of negotiating interdependence occurred with Katie, a junior in college, and her mother, Sharon. Katie wanted to set up a 30th anniversary party for her parents, who live just two hours from her college. Her mother, Sharon, kept saying on the phone, "Don't bother. Don't go to any trouble. It's not worth it." Katie persisted that she and her younger sister really wanted to do this (she insisted that they were interdependent). Mom stopped answering the phone and returning e-mails. Katie drove home the next weekend and asked Mom to talk the whole thing through with her. Katie learned that Mom was so angry with Dad for ignoring the upcoming event that she wanted to withdraw. She couldn't imagine enjoying a party that came only from her kids while she was simmering with resentment at her husband. So Katie talked to Dad about helping plan the party. Mom told her husband that she had been feeling hurt and slighted. They all got involved and had a good time. Now, notice that it was *not* Katie's role to play therapist with her parents—but she helped by asking them to talk to her and to each other. In a healthy family, everyone can talk to every other member. This builds healthy interdependence.

Sometimes parties are locked into a position of **mutual interdependence** whether they want to be or not. In some cases, interdependent units do not choose to be interdependent but are so for other compelling reasons. Some colleagues in an office, for instance, got into a conflict over when they were to be in their offices to receive calls and speak with customers. One group took the position that "what we do doesn't affect you—it's none of your business." The other group convinced the first group that they could not define themselves as unconnected, because the rest of the group had to be available to fill in for them when they were not available. They were inescapably locked into interdependence. If a working decision was not made, the parties would have almost guaranteed an unproductive conflict, with each party making choices as if they were only tenuously connected.

When you are stuck in unproductive interdependence, these conflicts turn into **gridlocked conflicts,** according to Gottman (1999)

You Know You're in Gridlock When . . .

- The conflict makes you feel rejected by your partner
- You keep talking but make no headway
- You become entrenched and are unwilling to budge
- You feel more frustrated and hurt after you talk than before
- Your talk is devoid of humor, amusement, or affection
- You become more entrenched over time so you become insulting during your talks
- More vilification makes you more polarized, extreme, and less willing to compromise
- Eventually you disengage emotionally or physically or both

(Gottman 1999, 132–133)

Think about how you feel when you are gridlocked in traffic. You may feel full of road rage, derisive of the stupid other drivers, furious at the system, defeated and hopeless, or numb and tuned out. The same emotions happen in a gridlocked interpersonal conflict. Trying harder often doesn't work. That's when you need to try smarter instead of harder. When nothing is working, try something different. Destructive conflicts rely on the same old (unproductive) stratgegies.

Most relationships move back and forth between degrees of independence and interdependence. At times there will be an emphasis on "me"—what I want—and on

Most relationships — Move between independence and interdependence

separateness, whereas at other times "we"—our nature as a unit—becomes the focus. These are natural rhythmic swings in relationships (Frentz and Rushing 1980; Galvin and Brommel 1982; Baxter 1982; Stewart 1978). Just as we all need both stability and change, conflict parties have to balance their independence and dependence needs.

Relationship and interdependence issues precede other issues in the conflict. Actually, these negotiations over interdependence permeate most conflicts throughout the course of the relationship, never becoming completely settled. A helpful practice is to address the interdependence issue openly in ongoing, highly important relationships. In more transient and less salient relationships, the interdependence may be primarily tacit, or understood.

Perceived Incompatible Goals

What do people fight about? (We use the word *fight* to mean verbal conflict, not physical violence.) People usually engage in conflict over goals that are important to them. One company had an extreme morale problem and asked for our help. The head cashier said, "All our problems would be solved if we could just get some carpet, because everyone's feet get tired—we're the ones who have to stand up all day. But management won't spend a penny for us." Her statement of incompatible goals was clear—carpet versus no carpet. But as the interviews progressed, another need emerged. She began to talk about how no one noticed when her staff had done good work and how the "higher-ups" only noticed when lines were long and mistakes were made. There was a silence, then she blurted out, "How about some compliments once in a while? No one ever says anything nice. They don't even know we're here." Her stated needs then changed to include not only carpet but self-esteem and increased attention from management—a significant deepening of the goal statement. Both goals were real, carpets and self-esteem, but the first goal may have been incompatible with management's desires, whereas the second might not; the need for recognition may have been important to both the cashiers and management.

We do not support the overly simple notion that if people just worked together, they would see that their goals are the same. Opposing goals are a fact of life. Many times, people are absolutely convinced they have opposing goals and cannot agree on anything to pursue together. However, if goals are reframed or put in a different context, the parties can agree. Recently a student teacher's supervisor outlined her goals for the student. Included in the list was the demand that the student turn in a list of the three most and least positive experiences in the classroom each week. The student asked to be transferred to another teaching supervisor. The chair asked why, saying, "Ms. Barker is one of our best supervisors." The student said, "That's what I've heard, but I can't be open about my failures with someone who's going to give me my ending evaluation. That will go in my permanent files." In a joint discussion with the supervisor and the student, the chair found that both were able to affirm that they valued feedback about positive and negative experiences. Their goals were more similar than they had thought; the means for achieving them were different. The supervisor agreed to use the list as a starting point for discussion but not to keep copies; the student agreed to list experiences so the supervisor would not feel that the student was hiding her negative experiences. Trust was built through a discussion of goals. Perceptions of the incompatibility of the goals changed through clear communication. *Are you noticing that it's difficult to resolve conflict without talking with each other?*

Goals are perceived as incompatible because parties want (1) the same thing or (2) different things. First, the conflict parties may want the same thing—for example, the promotion in the company, the one available scholarship, or the attention of the parents. They struggle and jockey for position in order to attain the desired goal. They perceive the situation as one where there "isn't enough to go around." Thus, they see their goal as incompatible with the other person's because they both want the same thing.

Second, sometimes the goals are different. Mark and Tom, for example, decide to eat out. Mark wants to go to Bananas and Tom wants to go to Pearl's. They struggle over the incompatible choices. Sometimes the goals are not as opposed as they seem. Two roommates would like to move out of the dorm and into an apartment. After looking around, Janet tells Allison that she thinks she'd "better just stay put." Allison was, naturally, hurt. As they talked about the situation, Janet told Allison she was afraid Allison wanted to spend more than Janet was able to. They found an acceptable budget and agreed to stick with it, thus resetting their goals more clearly. Of course, many times the content goals seem to be different (like which restaurant to go to), but beneath them is a relational struggle over who gets to decide. Regardless of whether the participants see the goals as similar or different, **perceived incompatible goals** are central to all conflicts.

Sometimes the surface goals differ but underneath is an ongoing relational struggle

Perceived Scarce Resources

A resource can be defined as "any positively perceived physical, economic or social consequence" (Miller and Steinberg 1975, 65). The resources may be objectively real or perceived as real by the person. Likewise, the scarcity, or limitation, may be apparent or actual. For example, close friends often think that if their best friend begins to like someone else too, then the supply of affection available to the original friend will diminish—a **perceived scarce resource.** This may or may not be so, but a perception that affection is scarce may well create genuine conflict between the friends. Sometimes, then, the most appropriate behavior is attempting to change the other person's perception of the resource instead of trying to reallocate the resource. Ultimately, one person can never force another to change his or her valuing of a resource or perception of how much of the resource is available, but persuasion coupled with supportive responses for the person fearful of losing the reward can help.

Money, natural resources such as oil or land, and jobs may indeed be scarce or limited resources. Intangible commodities such as love, esteem, attention, and caring also may be perceived as scarce. A poignant example concerns dropouts in the school system. By watching videotapes of classroom interactions, researchers could predict by the fourth grade which students would later drop out of school. The future dropouts were those students who received very limited eye contact from the teacher, either by their own doing or the teacher's. They became nonpersons, at least nonverbally. The glances, looks, smiles, and eye contact with the important person in the room became a scarce resource upon which the students were highly dependent. Often children fight with one another over this perceived scarcity—teacher attention. Or they fight with the teacher, resulting in a gain of that resource. A child would rather get negative attention than none. When rewards are perceived as scarce, an expressed struggle may be initiated.

*And sometimes resources really **are** scarce.*

In interpersonal struggles, two resources often perceived as scarce are **power and self-esteem.** Whether the parties are in conflict over a desired romantic partner or a change in work hours, perceived scarcities of power and self-esteem are involved. People engaged in conflict often say things that may be easily interpreted as reflecting power and self-esteem struggles, such as in the following scenarios:

> "She always gets her own way." (She has more power than I do, and I feel at a constant disadvantage. I'm always one down.)

> "He is so sarcastic! Who does he think he is? I don't have to put up with his mouth!" (I don't have ways to protect myself from biting sarcasm. It feels like an attack. I feel humiliated. The only power I have is to leave.)

> "I refuse to pay one more penny in child support." (I feel unimportant. I don't get to see the children very often. I've lost my involvement with them. Money is the only way I have to let that be known. I don't want to feel like a loser and a fool.)

> "I won't cover for her if she asks me again. She can find someone else to work the night shift when her kids get sick." (I feel taken advantage of. She only pays attention to me when she needs a favor.)

Regardless of the particular subjects involved, people in conflict usually perceive that they have too little power and self-esteem and that the other party has too much. Of course, with each person thinking and feeling this way, something needs to be adjusted. Often, giving the other person some respect, courtesy, and ways to save face removes the need to use power excessively. *Remember, people usually think the other person has more power and self-esteem. We don't perceive other people the way they perceive themselves.*

Interference

People who are interdependent, perceive incompatible goals, and want the same scarce resource still may not meet the conditions for conflict. *Interference,* or the perception of interference, is necessary to complete the conditions for conflict. If the presence of another person interferes with desired actions, conflict intensifies. Conflict is associated with blocking, and the person doing the blocking is perceived as the problem. For instance, a college sophomore worked in a sandwich shop the summer before her junior year abroad. She worked two jobs, scarcely having time to eat and sleep. She was invited to a party at a cabin in the wilderness, and she really wanted to go. She worked overtime on one day then asked for a day off from the sandwich shop, but the employer was reluctant to say yes, because the student was the only one the employer trusted to open the shop and keep the till. For an angry moment, the employer, who was interfering with what the student wanted to do, seemed like the main problem. Goals appeared incompatible, no one else was available to open (scarce resource), and the two parties were interdependent because the student needed the job and the owner needed her shop opened and the cash monitored. She was about to say, "No. I'm sorry, but I can't cover you." The student volunteered to train someone else, on her own time, to cover for her. The problem was solved, at least for this round, and the conflict was avoided. But if the student had quit in disgust or the employer had said no, both would have sacrificed important goals.

Another example of **perceived interference** involves Kelly, who prizes time alone in a lookout tower each summer. She plans for the weeks and looks forward to that solitude each year. When her two college-age daughters asked to join her, Kelly hesitated, saying she didn't think there was enough room. The daughters were disappointed and hurt, because they had been away at college and thought this would be a wonderful way to all be together. Mom could have told them she loved solitude and asked whether they could figure out some way so they could be together, but her quiet time could be maintained. For instance, the daughters love to hike and might have been glad to plan several days of hiking. Instead, the situation stayed unresolved and hurt feelings simmered.

Being blocked and interfered with is such a disturbing experience that our first "take" is usually anger and blame. We will discuss later the difference in *intent* and *impact*. For now, we suggest you adopt this radical idea:

> *You do not know what other people are thinking unless you enter into honest dialogue. You don't know their intention without dialogue. You can't read minds. Conversation is the best approach.*

From Destructive to Constructive Conflict

Conflicts move from episode to episode in a continually unfolding pattern of interaction between the prime parties. The moves and interpretations of each party influence those of the others. Nowhere can we more clearly see the interlocking effects of moves and countermoves than in **destructive conflicts.**

Conflict interaction can be productive or destructive depending on many factors, including the context in which it occurs (Camara and Resnick 1989) and the kinds of communication used. Conflict is potentially costly to all parties; these costs can exceed the gains if the conflict is drawn out before some kind of settlement is reached (Boulding 1989). If all participants are dissatisfied with the outcomes of a conflict and think they have lost as a result (Deutsch 1973), then the conflict is classified as destructive.

In one office two large men got into a loud, shouting and shoving match. After their boss called them into his office and talked through the conflict with them, the two men said "it's over. It's nobody else's business." However, other office workers were upset. An outside facilitator was called in to talk through the situation, including pointing out to the "fighters" that they had spread a feeling of threat and fear throughout the office. Others were avoiding them, and as a result, not getting their work done.

Several characteristics of spiraling destructive conflict can be identified. Participants can sometimes rescue a destructive interaction, making the overall effect more positive, but if the interaction continues to be characterized by the following descriptions, the overall result will be a destructive, win-lose experience for all parties. Gottman (1999) refers to the following four communication practices as the "**four horsemen of the apocalypse,**" meaning that when these four behaviors "ride in" to a relationship, the end is near (see figure 1.1).

Figure 1.1   The Four Horsemen of the Apocalypse

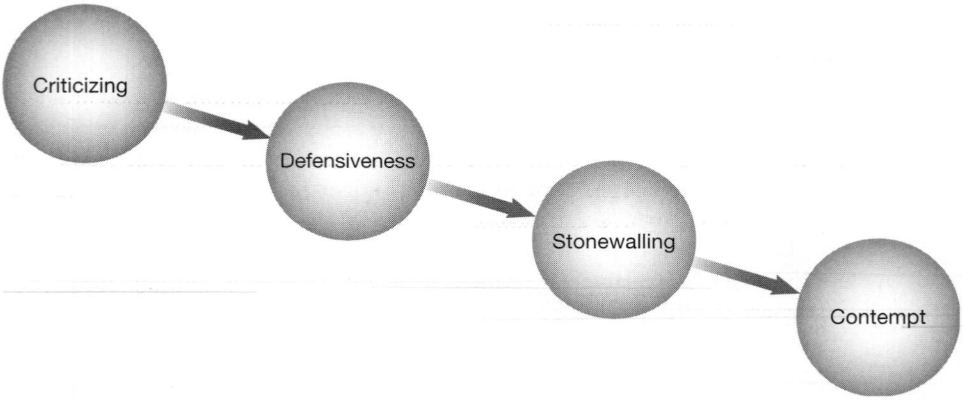

Criticizing

Defensiveness

Stonewalling

Contempt

The Four Horsemen

Critical Start-Up Sets the Tone for Any Conflict

The first moments of a conflict interaction—the **critical start-up**—can set the scene for a constructive or a destructive conflict. In fact, in Gottman's research (1999) the first minute of conflict with married couples predicts for 96 percent of the couples studied whether they will stay together or divorce. This amazing finding results primarily from the way the conflict is entered, or engaged. Criticism makes a harsh start-up. When wives escalate from neutral feeling to negative feeling quickly, right at the beginning, the outlook for the marriage remains bleak. Women criticize more than men do in marital conflicts. (We'll get to what men do that is equally destructive!) When a conflict begins with a critical statement, the conflict is likely to escalate quickly. Any conflict that begins with "you always" or "you never" is likely to have a destructive effect. For instance, the following example shows a harsh start-up:

> Pamela: You are the most selfish man I know! My mother is sick, maybe terminally, and you can't stir yourself to drive 30 miles for her birthday. Great. Now I get to tell my Mom that I'm married to a narcissistic jerk! Could you think of someone else for a change?

Application 1.4	From Criticism to Constructive Complaints

In your small group, practice changing criticisms to complaints. Think of destructive criticism, maybe that you have used, or that others have used against you, and practice brainstorming about how to change these critical comments to legitimate complaints. Don't be afraid to make the complaints strong and assertive—they need not be soft and wishy-washy. Remember to avoid blame, use I statements, describe instead of judging, and leave the door open for change. Practice transforming criticism into descriptive complaints, while remaining honest.

Another critical or harsh start-up might sound like this:

Pamela: I knew you wouldn't remember to call your friend and tell him you have to visit my mother. I have to do all the social work around here.

Many times, one person will criticize to get the other person's attention, to indicate how awful she or he is feeling, to try to make the conflict important enough to resolve, or to vent frustration or despair. However, none of these reasons, though understandable, is a good enough reason to begin interaction with criticism. Instead, you can turn a harsh start-up into a constructive complaint.

A Constructive Complaint

- Use an "I" statement.
- Describe the undesirable behavior.
- Use neutral, not judgmental, language.
- Ask for a specific, behavioral change.

A constructive complaint can be helpful. A destructive complaint includes blame and the attribution that there is something wrong with the other person, not just the behavior. The following is an example of a constructive complaint:

Pamela: I am upset that we are not going to see my Mom together. I have asked you three times to clear your weekend so we could both go see her. Next weekend is her birthday. She is sick and I want to see her, and I want you to come with me. I am frustrated and impatient with the excuses you've given me. I hope you will come. I don't want to have the kind of marriage where I have to see my folks by myself. This makes me feel sad and as though I don't have a partner. It would mean a lot to me if you would come, and let me know very soon so I can tell Mom.

Defensiveness Characterizes Destructive Conflict

When people use defensive communication, they are communicating a desire to protect themselves against pain, fear, personal responsibility, or new information. In an emotionally charged issue, if a person can listen to learn about oneself and the other, defensiveness drops away (Paul and Paul 1987). When defensiveness predominates, many destructive outcomes occur, such as power struggles, boredom, lack of fun and joy, chronic fighting, emotional pain and distance, and a desire to retaliate (Paul and Paul 1983, 1987). Defensiveness implies that one is warding off an attack. Notice that the metaphor for conflict that underlies the need to defend is a negative metaphor, war or attack. When you are defensive, you might whine, deflect, attack, and further defend. The interaction can get to look and sound like Ping-Pong.

Barbara: Every time I try to talk to you about my day, you launch into complaints and whining about how bad life is for you. You never listen to me. (Notice that Barbara is in fact attacking, criticizing, and blaming.)

Mark: If I didn't get my two cents' worth in, you'd talk all evening. All you ever do is complain. I decided weeks ago that every time you come home with some "poor me" tale, I'll match you. Besides, I have a right to be heard too. You aren't the only important one in this family.

Barbara: If things are so rotten for you in this relationship, why are you sticking around? All I'm asking for is a little empathy, but I guess that's beyond you.

You can easily see that neither Barbara nor Mark is the least bit interested in learning, only in attacking and defending. This interaction will undoubtedly escalate or lead to hostile withdrawal.

Defensiveness comes from a misguided sense of righteous indignation, expressed poorly. Another word for defensiveness might be contrariness. Some people seemingly can't help adopting a devil's advocate or contrary point of view. For them, conversation is a battle of wits. They enjoy the game of "batting ideas around" and are often very good at the performance. The pursuit of mutual understanding may seem boring and unchallenging (Yankelovich 1999, 141). Contrariness and defensiveness impede constructive conflict.

interesting

In this destructive complaint, Barbara and Mark might sound more like this. Sure, this approach takes more time and care . . . but it's the only approach that works (Gottman 1999).

Barbara and Mark Try it Again

Barbara: I've been noticing something that troubles me and is making me upset. When I come home and tell you about my day, which I look forward to, it seems that you immediately start to tell me about your day, making it sound horrible. I don't feel heard. And I'm not listening to you, either. Something isn't working.

Mark: I think you're right. I often feel that you get all the air time. I'm afraid that if I don't speak up, you'll talk all evening about your bad day. I'm not proud of this, but I really don't want to hear so much about your awful work situation.

Barbara: Thanks for being honest. It makes me feel less crazy. I do want to hear about you, good and bad things. I'd like for you to let me know you hear and understand me. I can easily imagine doing the same thing for you. I do care about you.

Mark: I haven't liked myself very much, that's for sure. I've been trying to teach you not to complain—but I've been doing the same thing to you. Let's start over.

In the previous example, Barbara and Mark began to create a more supportive climate instead of a defensive climate. People in a defensive climate are touchy, irritable, quick-tempered, and harsh.

Creating a Supportive Climate Rather Than a Defensive Climate

One of the best descriptions of defensive communication was written by Jack Gibb in 1961. It is so useful we suggest you memorize the categories. This schema will help you moderate your own defensiveness very effectively—if you pay attention to your own language. First, learn to recognize your own and others' defensiveness for what it is. Then, practice the "support side" of the following suggestions. **Defensive climates**—rather than **supportive climates**—are created when people use the following kinds of language:

- *Evaluation rather than description.* Judgmental and evaluating language leads to a defensive response in the other person. No one enjoys being "graded," especially as inadequate. Instead, use neutral and nonblaming language. Rather than saying, "You are closed-minded on this . . ." say "You really like the idea of going camping instead of kayaking. Are you open to some other options?"

- *Control rather than problem solving.* When you try to control the other person, you might insist on details, shut down communication, or simply say, "No way I'm going to do that." (Instead, say, "We can solve this problem. I'll listen to you; I ask you to listen to me." "Let's generate several possibilities.")

- *Strategy rather than spontaneity.* In strategic communication, the other person feels manipulated and managed. When you are communicating spontaneously, you are free of deception and are communicating honestly, in a straightforward way. Rather than saying "I'll get back to you on that," say, "I'm not comfortable with that idea. Let's keep talking."

- *Neutrality rather than empathy.* No one likes to feel like a "case" or a "type." When a doctor says to a patient with cancer, "That's the protocol we use in this kind of cancer," the patient will feel dismissed or made into an object. Instead, the doctor could say, "This is my best advice based on my experience and the research. What do you think? Will this work for you?"

- *Superiority rather than equality.* No one likes to be talked down to. If you indicate that you are more powerful, smarter, or more experienced than the other person, you will create defensiveness. Rather than "You'll see that I'm right when you have more experience," say, "I feel strongly about this. What is your experience?" Rather than "you have no idea how to negotiate with your boss," say "I have some ideas about how you might negotiate with your boss. Let me know if you want to hear them."

- *Certainty rather than provisionalism.* Dogmatic, inflexible statements create defensiveness. Openness creates a supportive environment. Rather than "I am never going to drive at Christmas again," say, "Driving at Christmas is something I'm not wanting to do. I still want to see our family, but I hate being on the highway at Christmas. Let's talk about other options."

Support neutralizes defensiveness. As you learn to recognize your own and others' defensiveness, you can practice support. Creating a supportive environment means you make it possible for the other person to be heard, and thus for the other person to hear you. Support does not mean agreement. Support means you see the other person as a worthwhile human being who deserves to be heard. Support means that you speak so the other knows she is being respected, and support means that listening takes as much time as talking. You can disagree and still be supportive.

Stonewalling Occurs When One Person Withdraws from the Interaction

Usually, when people are engaged in conversation, they give all kinds of nonverbal cues, as well as verbal cues, that indicate their involvement. They give eye contact, head nods, changes in facial expression, brief vocalizations, and so on (Gottman 1999). Turn taking is regulated in a refined dance of interaction that shows that the other person is "there." Stonewallers don't do any of this. They show in every possible way that they are not "there." They glance only to see what the other person is doing, then glance away. They maintain a stiff neck and frozen facial features. They try to conceal what they are thinking and feeling. Men consistently stonewall more than women. In fact, in Gottman's study (reported in 1999), 85 percent of stonewallers were men. The combination of

Combination of

criticism and stonewalling predicted divorce quite easily. Most women find this kind of "I'm not here" behavior on the part of men highly upsetting. Stonewalling is more than avoidance of conflict. It is an attempt to signal withdrawal from communication while, in fact, still being present in the conversation, but in a destructive way. Stonewalling also can mean a refusal to engage in a topic no matter how the other person brings it up. You can probably imagine the frustration and fury that accompanies stonewalling. A less destructive form of stonewalling might be called *holding back*. When Yankelovich (1999) asked people why they were not more forthcoming in group discussions, they said they had to be comfortable enough to speak, or that they wanted to see what developed before they got involved. Men hold back in public discussions more than women do, although women also feel reserved when trust has not been built. People hold back when they sense hostility in a group or in the other.

Taking Down the Stone Wall People stonewall when they are afraid to be influenced or when they are so angry they no longer wish to engage. Sometimes people stonewall when they have lost respect for the other person. This is a toxic situation, calling for drastic measures. Here are several ways to try to take down the wall:

> She: You aren't responding at all to me. It's as though you aren't there. Please tell me what you actually are thinking. (Note to women—when someone is stonewalling, try asking about thoughts rather than feelings!)
>
> He: I'm not thinking a blinking thing.
>
> She: How can we get back into a conversation? Would you make a suggestion?
>
> He: Just shut up.
>
> She: That's what you've done, shut up. This is not helping us solve our problem. I want you to talk to me and listen to me. I'll start by listening.

This approach may not work. The stonewaller may be so punishing and harsh that nothing works for now. Still, the approach given above might change the conversation later. If not, the relationship is functionally over. No one can stand being shut out forever. If the nastiness goes on for a while, the following might help:

> She: I feel hopeless and like going farther away. I hope you will let me in. This is a really bad situation. Please tell me what you want without making me the nag or hag.

Contempt Contributes to Destructive Conflict

"Contempt is any statement or nonverbal behavior that puts oneself on a higher plane than one's partner" (Gottman 1999). Contempt often involves a nasty kind of mockery, put-downs, hostile corrections, and nonverbal expressions of contempt. The contemptuous look (mouth pulled over to one side) is "powerfully corrosive," according to Gottman and our own experience. Many times we have heard people say the right words, but with an expression of contempt, which leads inevitably to more destructive communication. Often contempt is accompanied by sarcasm, ridicule, and outright hostile joking. In healthy relationships, contempt is almost never present. Contempt is never justified in a long-term, important relationship, since it functions as a powerful attack on the personhood of the other.

Chipping Away at Contempt Like stonewalling, contempt signals an emergency in a relationship. Whether in a marriage, friendship, or work situation, contempt calls for quick, effective action. In an architectural firm, a woman put a series of derisive, anti-management cartoons on the bulletin board outside her office. Some of the cartoons were similar to the CEO's style, and most of her co-workers saw the cartoons as a thinly veiled attack on the older, male CEO. Unfortunately, the CEO matched contempt with contempt. He compiled a set of teamwork slogans, sent them out in a group e-mail, ending with, "Which person with a bulletin board might fit exactly into these sayings?" When the consultant was called in to facilitate less destructive communication, neither person would acknowledge that they had been contemptuous. The consultant ended up saying, "I think both sets of messages are full of contempt. That means you two and others need to talk. Are you willing to do this?"

If you are the victim of contempt, you may need to say something like:

"I won't let you talk to me this way. I am being treated without respect and I can't respect myself if I continue."

"Please don't treat me with contempt. Tell me what you want/need/feel instead."

"You are so furious that I can't talk with you right now. I'll try again later." (Then leave.)

Full-blown, continuing contempt means that intervention of some kind is needed, or the relationship is over. Contempt can lead to abuse, and needs to be treated with great care. Try never to meet contempt with escalated contempt of your own. Disengage and seek counsel.

Application 1.5   Four Horsemen

Look back over the explanation of the "four horsemen." Answer the following questions, then discuss.

Which of the four communication modes has been used against you in harmful ways?

Which of the four do you use, and in what circumstances?

Choose an example of your own use of one of the four destructive modes explained above. What fear or anger underlay your use of this approach?

Can you think of a way you could communicate more honestly and constructively?

Give one example. Practice changing your communication when you are tempted to use one of the four horsemen. If you want, keep track of your attempts for a paper on your communication style.

Inflexibility Dominance

Inflexibility, or Rigidity, Characterizes Destructive Conflict

When parties are unable or unwilling to adapt to changing circumstances, instead following rules "to a T" or "going by the book," potentially constructive conflict often deteriorates. One manager refused to discuss reprimands with employees, instead recording the incidents in letters that could later be used as part of a paper trail in case an employee needed to be fired. As a result, trust plummeted to zero in the office, and employees formed coalitions to protect each other from the inflexible boss. The supervisor, in addition to creating a hostile working environment, received "pretend change" instead of genuine change in employees' behavior. Everyone lost as the cycle of distancing and inflexible communication intensified.

Spirals depend on two or more people responding to each other's behavior. In common language, spirals are referred to as "tit for tat," or "it takes two to tango." Usually, one person thinks the other has "begun" the conflict, and that he/she is simply an innocent party responding to unreasonable behavior. This leads to conflict that spirals out of control.

Soften Rigidity with Flexible Options People become rigid when they feel threatened or feel afraid of losing something important. The supervisor who refused to talk with her employees may have been afraid of the feedback she would receive. She might not know how to bring up problems in a firm but respectful way. A peer manager could suggest different ways of creating change that are more likely to work than documenting behavior. These flexible options might be:

- Call each employee in to discuss positive and negative performance. Ask for feedback about how the manager can help the employee reach the joint goals that are set.

- For a while, the manager could focus on describing what she likes. The employees may not trust her at first, but focusing on positive behavior would soften the wall of mistrust that has been built in the office.

- The manager could hold team meetings saying something like, "Our conditions have changed so much that it's clear to me that some of your jobs are changing. I would like for us to talk about what is changing in our industry, and how we might adapt to the new needs."

- The manager could ask for a meeting with the person most likely to give helpful feedback, an internal "consultant," and say something like, "I'm not getting the change I would like. I can tell people are avoiding me. Do you have some suggestions for me that might get us working as a team again? I respect your judgment."

Again, when something is not working, try a new approach, not more of the old approach.

A Competitive System of Dominance and Subordination Results in Destructive Conflict

"Authenticity and subordination are totally incompatible" (Miller 1986, 98). Dominant groups tend to suppress conflict, minimizing and denying its existence. This works reasonably well for those in power, because they can make and enforce the rules. In fact, a measure of the dominant group's success and security is often its ability to suppress conflict, to keep it hidden, unobtrusive, and unthreatening to the group's position of power. In a situation of unequal power, in which a myth of harmonious relationships is set forth, the subordinate person is put in charge of maintaining that harmony. Then any recognition of differences is treated as insubordination (Miller 1986; Jordan 1990). We will discuss how to deal with unequal power in chapter 4.

Escalatory Spirals

In the previous section we explored some of the most negative individual communication behaviors that lead to destructive conflict. Now, we will describe patterns of destructive conflict that require interaction.

Escalatory Spirals Pervade Destructive Conflict

Conflict often gets out of hand. What begins as a careful exchange of opposing views deteriorates into an emotion-laden, careless interchange in which strong feelings, usually anger and fear, are aroused. This causes the primary intentions of the parties to shift from a useful exchange to damaging the other person (Baron 1984). Escalatory conflict spirals have only one direction–upward and onward. They are characterized by a heavy reliance on overt power manipulation, threats, coercion, and deception (Deutsch 1973). In an **escalatory spiral,** the relationship continues to circle around to more and more damaging ends; the interaction becomes self-perpetuating. Its characteristics are misunderstanding, discord, and destruction (Wilmot 1987). Figure 1.2 illustrates the runaway dynamics that occur in a typical destructive conflict spiral. In this example, two roommates begin with a misunderstanding that accelerates each time they communicate. Brad begins complaining about Steve's messiness. At each crossover point in the spiral, thoughts and actions might occur as they do in this version of an actual conflict:

1.   Brad says to Steve, "Hey, why don't you do your part? This place is a hole."
2.   Steve says, "Out of my face, dude!" (He then leaves the apartment.)
3.   Brad, still upset about the messy apartment, finds Steve's ex-girlfriend and says, "Has Steve always been such a slob? I can't stand living with him."

Figure 1.2   Conflict Spiral

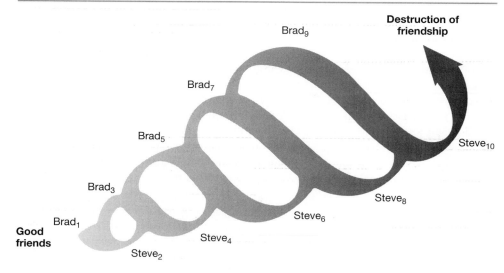

4. Steve, hearing from his ex-girlfriend that "even Brad knows that you are a slob," decides that he will get back at Brad for his meanness. So Steve begins deliberately messing up the bathroom, knowing that it will drive Brad crazy.

5. Brad comes home, sees the messy bathroom, and puts an ad in the campus newspaper that says, "If anyone sees Steve K., tell him to clean up his half of the apartment—it's a pigsty."

6. Steve, angered at the public announcement, comes home late one night and, while Brad is sleeping, lets the air out of Brad's tires.

7. Brad runs into a mutual friend the next day and hears that Steve is the one who let the air out of his tires. So Brad goes home, moves all of Steve's belongings into the hall, changes the locks on the door, and puts a sign on Steve's belongings that says, "Help yourself."

Brad and Steve's conflict escalated without much direct communication between the two of them—they let their actions speak instead of words. A destructive conflict in an intimate relationship, between spouses, for example, may be characterized by the above features, in addition to "hitting below the belt" (Bach and Wyden 1968). Each person uses hit-and-run tactics to damage the other person where it hurts most, emotionally. For instance, a woman may ridicule her husband for making less money than she does when she knows he is extremely sensitive to this issue. She may be trying to bring up an important topic, but the attempt will surely fail. The injunction "don't fight unless you mean it" is ignored in a destructive conflict, and the interlocking, damaging moves occur repeatedly. In a destructive conflict, one party unilaterally attempts to change the structure of the relationship, restrict the choices of the other, and gain advantage over the other.

Probably the best index of destructive conflict is that one or both of the parties have a strong desire to "get even" or damage the other party. When you hear a friend say, "Well, she may have gotten me that time, but just wait and see what happens when I tell some things I know about her!" you are overhearing one side of a destructive conflict in action. Wilmot (1995) observes, "if the conflict is responded to in destructive ways . . . it starts sequences of episodes that detract from relational quality" (95). The conflict continues unabated, feeds upon itself, and becomes a *spiral of negativity* (see figure 1.3). The three parts—the behaviors, the perceptions of others, and the perceptions of the relationship—mutually reinforce each other. As behavior becomes more destructive and one's view of the other and the relationship goes downhill, each person continues to perceive himself or herself as free from blame (i.e., "It is all his or her fault"). In an organization, for example, one person on the verge of firing an employee said, "Well, I'm a good supervisor. He just won't cooperate. It is all his fault. Besides, he will probably be better off if I fire him."

Escalatory spirals bring about a cascade of negative effects. Self-perpetuating dynamics create the (1) behaviors, (2) perceptions of the other, and (3) perceptions of the relationship which continue to disintegrate (with each party viewing oneself as not responsible for any of it). Beck (1988) aptly summarizes the later stages of the process:

> When a relationship goes downhill, the partners begin to see each other through a negative frame, which consists of a composite of disagreeable traits ("He's mean and manipulative"; "She's irresponsible") that each attributes to the other. These unfavorable attributions color how the offended mate sees the partner; negative actions are exaggerated and neutral actions are seen as negative. Even positive acts may be given a negative coloring. (207)

Figure 1.3   The Spiral of Negativity

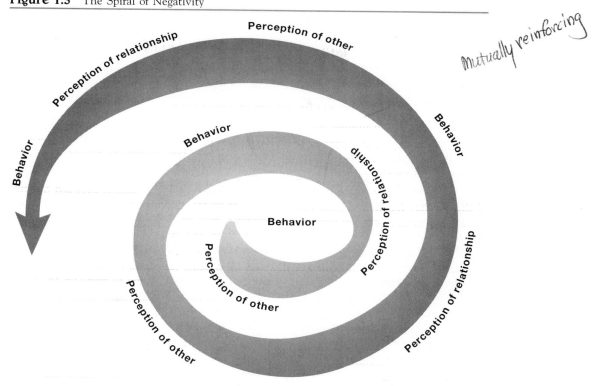

mutually reinforcing

Declines happen in all kinds of relationships—between social groups, between marriage partners, between roommates, within the work setting, and with families.

Avoidance Spirals

Avoidance Patterns Reduce the Chance for Productive Conflict

Escalatory spirals can be called "fight" patterns. Conflict parties also manifest "flight" patterns of avoidance of the conflict. For now, be aware that patterns of avoidance also create and reflect destructive conflict interaction. One form of avoidance is an active attempt to lessen dependence on each other. By making such an attempt, each party reduces the influence of the other on his or her choices. Both parties then become less invested in the relationship. Many long-term marriages, for example, become devitalized, with the spouses expecting less and less of one another. This is often the natural consequence of lessened interaction. Spouses who are prevented from enriching daily interaction by the pressure of jobs, children, and other stresses become estranged. The barrier between them becomes harder and harder to breach. **Avoidance spirals** occur in other contexts as well. The child who is not picked for the soccer team and says, "I didn't want to be on your team anyway," is withdrawing, as is the employee who says, "I don't care if they fire me—who needs them anyway?" The basic dynamics of all avoidance spirals are

Avoidance Spirals

- *Less direct interaction.*
- *Active avoidance of the other party.*
- *Reduction of dependence.*
- *Harboring of resentment or disappointment.*
- *Complaining to third persons about the other party.*

Whereas escalatory spirals are characterized by overt expression of the conflict, avoidance spirals demonstrate covert expression. At least one of the parties tries to impact the other through lack of cooperation. If you are mad at your small group, your late report may get everyone into difficulty with the professor. Any form of withholding from someone who depends on you can bring negative consequences to the other. For example, when you withdraw, the other party does not know what you want or are thinking. Often the other will say something like, "What is wrong?" Then you say, "Nothing," covering up anger, resentment, or disappointment.

Oddly enough, sometimes people want destructive conflict in their relationships (Neimeyer and Neimeyer 1985). Although escalatory and avoidance spirals may appear to be totally negative to outsiders, the conflict party may be getting something valuable from these spirals. For example, if John can stay locked in an overt struggle with Bill, the impasse may give John a sense of power and self-esteem: "I refuse to cooperate because I'll never forgive him for what he did. He was a sneak." Or, if you are in an avoidance spiral, complaining about your supervisor, employee, spouse, or friend to others builds closeness between you and your listener. For example, a husband and wife may both complain about the other to the children, each thereby building a close bond with the child who is the chosen listener. One can get locked into a position of complaining bitterly about a spouse or co-worker but not take any steps to alter the relationship directly. In short, people may be invested in not moving past the destructive conflict.

The Attack/Withdraw Pattern

This pattern is a destructive dance usually manifested in intimate relationships. It destroys chances for productive interaction. In the pursue/flee pattern, described in detail in Lerner's **Dance of Intimacy** (1989), one partner specializes in initiating conversation, commenting on the lack of closeness between the partners, bringing up feelings and issues to get them resolved, and drawing the other partner out by asking questions like "You seem preoccupied—what's going on?" or "We don't seem close these last few weeks. Is something bothering you?" Then the "dance" of distance is engaged in as the other partner minimizes the problems, denies anything is wrong, promises to do better, comments on content problems only, avoids discussion of any relationship issues, or gives excuses such as "I've just been really busy," or "I'm distracted by what's going on at work," or "I'm just premenstrual. Don't take it personally." The conflict remains frustratingly unresolved because each partner specializes in a role that is so prescribed, whether initiating or fleeing, that the issues remain unexplored. These dynamics will be addressed in chapter 5, "Styles and Tactics." For now, as you begin to watch and analyze conflicts around you, pay attention to who initiates and who withdraws, or flees.

One way to arrest this pattern is to make a comment about communication such as "I notice that I'm the one who brings up problems, and you feel defensive. We need to do something different." The one who flees can own up to the discomfort caused by the pursuit by saying something like "I feel pounced on, especially about my feelings. I need time to sort out what's going on. I will talk to you; I just need to do it at a time when I'm not exhausted or frazzled."

Gottman (1994) discovered that the avoidance sequence described as attack/withdraw, or pursue/retreat, leads to relationship breakup because of its negative impact. Avoidance, or stonewalling, comes after some preliminary episodes. As we have disscussed, for the marriages Gottman studied, the destructive sequence consisted of criticizing, defensiveness, stonewalling, and contempt. Thus, avoidance can be viewed within the overall spiral of conflict as leading to eventual dissolution of a relationship. One other feature of Gottman's work is noteworthy: If avoidance is accepted by both partners ("conflict-avoiding couples"), it can stabilize the marriage. Avoidance, coupled with dissatisfaction and disagreement, (one person pursuing and the other fleeing) is damaging.

Reciprocity of Negative Emotion Can Lead to Destructive Conflict

Three kinds of reciprocity can be identified in communication: (1) low-intensity emotion is responded to in kind (e.g., anger is met with anger), (2) high-intensity emotion is met in kind (e.g., fury is met with fury), and (3) low-intensity emotion is met with high-intensity emotion (e.g., hurt is met with rage). Gottman and Krokoff (1989) found that the escalation of negativity by husbands predicted divorce. When men refused to accept influence from their women partners, the relationship went downhill. It's important to understand just what is being reported by this finding. Gottman and his researchers are not saying that men should do what women want, but that meeting negative emotion with more negative emotion predicts relationship breakup. Why would this be? *Escalating negativity on the part of men can lead to violent interactions*. A team of researchers watched videotapes of violent men interacting with their partners. They likened the experience to that of baseball players at automatic pitching machines who bat back every pitch. These violent men refused to be influenced by anything their wives had to say. Small requests or complaints were "batted back" regardless of their merit. In a companion study of 130 nonviolent couples, 80 percent of the men who did not accept any influence from their wives ended up divorced! Most women accepted influence from their husbands, and that acceptance did not predict anything about their marriages (Gottman, 1994). The violent relationship is a one-way power struggle gone wild; the escalating spiral of negativity ends in verbal or physical violence. We will have more to say about the cycle of violence, but the important thing to note at this point is that meeting negative emotion with more, especially more destructive, negative emotion leads to big problems in relationships.

Retaliation Runs Rampant in Destructive Conflicts

Conflict participants destroy chances for change when they pile up grievances, hold grudges, and wait for opportunities to retaliate. "Don't get mad—get even!" is the watchword for this urge to get back at the other person. Retaliation often becomes paired with covert avoidance. One person acts as though everything is just fine while planning a payback move for later. You can probably think of many retaliatory moves that have either been made against you or been made by you yourself. Some examples of retaliatory moves are letters to someone's supervisor complaining about or pointing out some indiscretion that the employee committed; a snub such as not inviting someone to a function; a blatant move such as emptying out a partner's savings account, running up phone bills, and then moving out; and so on. Dirty tricks inevitably ruin the conflict atmosphere.

Humans in various cultures distinguish between the kind of aggression that can be directed against members of their own population and that directed toward other human groups. Stevens (1989) cites a tribe in Brazil, the Mundrucus, who distinguish between themselves, whom they call "people," and the rest of the world population, whom they call "pariwat." These in-group and out-group distinctions allow them to refer to others in the way they would refer to huntable animals (40–41). In North American and Western European cultures, the use of verbally demeaning and abusive communication serves a similar function (Evans 1992). Whole groups of minorities receive demeaning descriptions, and individuals in low-power positions in relationships suffer from pervasive demeaning, shaming, and blaming communication.

❧Your Opportunities

Conflict brings both danger and opportunity, and the dangerous aspects are well known. Changing our usual behavior, learning to "do what comes unnaturally," requires an examination of one's most deeply held values and spiritual beliefs. At its most effective, conflict resolution can never be simply a set of techniques, put on or cast aside at will. You will want to think and feel through your own principles as you study this subject.

If people are to survive and thrive, working together is not an option but a necessity. Principles learned at the interpersonal level lead to collaborative principles at the global level. Because of this, what you learn about collaboration within relationships will affect a much larger plane of well-being. Breggin (1992) reminds us:

> In every aspect of life . . . we need better principles for resolving conflict and promoting harmony within ourselves and others. We need approaches that make personal and political sense, that connect us in a rational and caring manner to ourselves as individuals and to the world around us, including people and nature. We need a viewpoint that helps us understand and heal the pain of human conflict. (3)

We are connected human beings who must balance our need for personal autonomy with our need for interdependence. We can no longer live by the myth that somewhere out there is a place where we can be completely independent and do what we wish. More than 40 years ago, Martin Luther King stated this imperative: "I can never be what I ought to be until you are what you ought to be, and you can never be what you ought to be until I am what I ought to be. This is the interrelated structure of reality" (King, 1989).

In conflict, no one set of principles will always work to keep you out of conflict altogether. Yet, people do change their orientation to conflict and amaze themselves with their ability to transcend formerly destructive situations. If enough of us are willing to weave webs of connection with others, all our shared hopes for the world can be realized. Long-standing stereotypes can be dissolved, mistrust can be overcome, understanding can be achieved, people previously at odds can work together on shared objectives, new levels of creativity can be reached, and bonds of community can be strengthened (Yankelovich 1999).

In order to find creative solutions, we must be willing to take our conflicts seriously. We need to find ways to manage our worst reactions and call on our best communication. When you improve your conflict skills, you will enrich your life.

Summary

Conflict happens. It is part and parcel of all our interactions—at work, with romantic partners, with friends, and with our families. Why would you want to study conflict? This study will help you learn new responses to situations that inevitably arise.

Conflict is defined as "an expressed struggle between at least two parties who perceive incompatible goals, scarce resources, and interference from others in achieving their goals."

Destructive conflict damages the parties and their relationship. In marriages, for example, the Four Horsemen of the Apocalypse destructive pattern is criticizing, defensiveness, stonewalling, and contempt. We provide specific suggestions on alternatives to each one of these destructive responses.

In addition to these destructive patterns, it is helpful to understand escalatory spirals and avoidance spirals. After describing these, we suggest that you have opportunities for productive conflict.

Key Terms

Use the text's Online Learning Center at **www.mhhe.com/wilmot8e** to further your understanding of the following terminology.

mental health   2
family of origin   2
destructive marital conflict   3
conflicts at work   4
unresolved conflict   6
emotional intelligence   6
prevention   10
definitions of conflict   11
conflict   11
perception   12
intrapersonal conflict   12
interpersonal conflict   12

intrapersonal perceptions   12
expressed struggles   13
conflict parties   13
interdependent   13
strategic conflict   14
mutual interests   14
mutual interdependence   15
gridlocked conflict   15
perceived incompatible
goals   17
perceived scarce resource   17
power   18

self-esteem   18
perceived interference   19
destructive conflicts   19
four horsemen of the
apocalypse   19
critical start-up   20
defensive climate   22
supportive climate   22
escalatory spiral   27
avoidance spiral   29
dance of intimacy   30

✒Review Questions

1. Give reasons why we need to study conflict.
2. In what contexts do conflicts arise?
3. Define conflict.
4. What are common responses to abuse in one's history?
5. What are the interpersonal expressions of conflict?
6. What is the purpose of dialogue?
7. What do we depend on others for?
8. What do they depend on us for?
9. What is the role of perception in conflict?
10. How do power and self-esteem function in conflict?
11. What is the relationship between perceived incompatible goals, scarce resources, and interference?
12. How can you create a supportive climate?
13. What are intangible resources?
14. What characterizes destructive conflict?
15. What is a "good complaint"?
16. What is a spiral?
17. What is an escalatory spiral?
18. What is an avoidance spiral?
19. Give an optimistic answer to "conflict always happens; therefore . . ."

Chapter 2

Perspectives on Conflict

⤳Your Personal History

Think of the most disturbing conflict you have experienced in the past half-year or so. What was your emotional response to this conflict? What is your usual response to conflicts? Do you generally like to get everything out in the open, even if such an effort creates tension and strong feelings? Or do you usually seek peace, harmony, and reduction of strong emotions?

Keep these recent interactions in mind as you read this chapter, reflecting on your own philosophy and experience of conflict.

In your family of origin you may have learned that to "blow up" was a normal, natural way for people to show they cared about each other. Perhaps your family was quiet, calm, and restrained. Fighting, if it happened at all, went on behind closed doors. Maybe you were punished for raising your voice, physically hurt for talking honestly to an adult, or told to keep your opinions to yourself. Maybe you learned, as co-author Bill did, that conflict was not talked about and that "actions spoke more loudly than words." You may have been taught not to dwell on problems but to just move on. Or, maybe you experienced, as co-author Joyce did, hours of sitting around the family dinner table, catching up on the events of the day, talking over what was happening, and being asked how you felt and thought. If so, you might bring a "we can work this out" perspective to conflict.

Think about how your **personal and workplace history** has taught you either to jump right into conflict or to strenuously attempt to reduce or avoid it. For most of us, the choice to avoid or confront a conflict is *difficult*. We all weigh the costs and benefits of bringing up something that may well be awkward, unpleasant, or frightening. We make choices every day about what conversations to avoid and what conversations to have. We struggle about these choices, knowing that if we avoid a tough topic we might feel taken advantage of and experience resentment. If we confront a problem, we might make matters worse.

We hope you come to terms with your own life's learning—what to keep, what to challenge, what to change, and what to discard because it no longer fits your needs. Think also about your role in your family of origin, friendships, or romantic relationships in the workplace or in class. Do you want to change your usual role? Do you need to learn more about getting along rather than automatically challenging authority?

Maybe you want to learn to speak up in your own clearly heard, authentic voice if you are usually silent or have been silenced by others.

We ask our students to choose which of the following descriptions best describes systems they have been in: (1) **avoidant,** where members avoided most conflict; (2) **collaborative,** where members used collaboration; or (3) **aggressive,** where members engaged in a lot of overt yelling, calling of names, and similar aggressive moves. While there is an artificial nature to these distinctions (for example, some people will avoid, then be aggressive, then avoid again), what emerged were "rules" for handling conflict that are quite distinct. Here are some of them:

Avoidant Systems

- Conflict doesn't exist, and if it does, don't recognize it.
- If there is a conflict, figure out what to do about it on your own.
- Don't tell anyone else if there is a struggle.
- Walk away if something starts to brew.
- Don't ever raise your voice.
- Snide comments are fine.
- Sulking and the silent treatment are necessary strategies.
- If someone has a concern, don't respond to it.
- Don't express strong feelings.

Collaborative Systems

- Have meetings or mealtime chats to discuss issues.
- Use good listening skills when someone has a concern.
- Deal with people directly.
- Say openly what you are feeling.
- Help is offered in resolving children's or employees' conflicts.
- Regular interaction is important.
- Dirty tricks such as sulking are not allowed.
- Strong feelings are seen as normal and are allowed.

Aggressive Systems

- Survival of the fittest describes the general climate.
- Be brutally honest regardless of the impact.
- Show your emotions strongly even if that hurts someone.
- Establish your position early.
- Have an audience present when you engage someone.
- Don't back down—hold your ground no matter what.
- If someone attacks you have to fight back.
- People who don't engage are weak.

While these lists will vary from group to group, notice how different the three lists are from one another. If you grew up in an avoidant family and your roommate grew up in an aggressive family, it would not be too surprising if a conflict between the two of you is difficult to resolve—each of you would break the rules of interaction the other expected you to follow. So our personal history in our families of origin will have a big impact on what we choose to do when conflict starts to rumble below the surface in our relationships.

One family exemplifies the way approaches to conflict may change over time. Karen and Len are parents of Rachel, who suffered a serious head injury while riding a horse when she was 14. Up until that time, the parents seldom raised their voices and life at home was fairly peaceful. Since Rachel's accident, Mom feels stress because of numerous medical appointments and very little time to get her work at the family business and at home completed. Len has decided that Rachel should help out more; he has begun yelling at Rachel to "pitch in and do something to help your mother," while Karen yells back, "You expect too much. She's only 14 and she's doing the best she can." Rachel alternates between placating her father by working hard, then disappearing to avoid the yelling. The family could now be described as aggressive, but this approach has developed recently because of stressors.

Our personal history also includes all of our interactions with others up to the present. What we experience as a preschooler, in school, with friends on the playground, and in all of our adult exchanges influences our expectations. Some of us have experiences of working through difficulties with others and life; thus, we willingly engage in what might prove to be a difficult talk. Others of us expect (and thus receive) constant tension, turbulence, and strife. These people are more likely than others to react to daily challenges with self-criticism and criticism of others, blame, negativity, defensiveness, irritability, or selfishness (Heitler 1990). Of course, these approaches invite a reciprocal response. Think about your current beliefs and expectations about human interaction. Are you primarily hopeful and optimistic, or cynical and pessimistic?

If you grew up in a family in which verbal, physical, or sexual abuse was part of the environment, you definitely will have very strong reactions to conflict. You may be very watchful, careful to smooth over any signs of discomfort. You may have learned to take the abuse to protect others in the family. You may feel guilt at the inevitable failure of that strategy. Maybe you waited until you were old enough and then left, to go to work, get married, or go to college, the armed forces, or a friend's apartment. Perhaps you learned to escape, either physically, or by numbing out, not caring, thinking of something else, or forgetting the conflict. Alyssa, who grew up with ongoing verbal and physical violence, learned to take her horse out for all-day rambles, coming back after dinner and making herself busy with grooming her horse and cleaning the stalls. Then she would grab a snack when no one was looking and take it to her room. Josh, now 25, started to use drugs at 11, which enabled him to tune out mentally while the yelling and hitting was going on. Some kids hung out at friends' houses until they absolutely had to go home. Children of violent homes have developed many strategies for dealing with their dangerous backgrounds. Some victims of violence learn to use violence in a "first strike capability" mode. They intend never again to be taken by surprise.

Application 2.2   My History with Violence

It is important to begin to think about the influence of violence on your life. Answer these questions in your own journal, notebook, or with a small group. What influence, if any, does violence have on your conflict responses? What experiences have you had with violence, whether verbal, physical, or sexual? If you have not experienced violence directly, what violent experiences of others have affected you?

Your particular age group is subjected to unique influences that may shape how you view conflict. If you were raised in the Great Depression you are not likely to view the open expression of conflict as positive (Krokoff, Gottman, and Roy 1988), while the younger generation is beginning to learn about constructive conflict in school—a topic not even considered a couple of decades ago.

Your current living situation certainly influences your methods of handling conflict. If you are with people with whom you feel safe and supported, you can experiment with new styles. If not, you will experience less freedom, possibly relying on what you already know how to do. Similarly, some work situations encourage constructive (or destructive) conflict, whereas others reward people for silence and withdrawal. All of these factors of our own personal history feed into our expectations and actions when we are in conflict situations.

Application 2.3   My Influences

List the 10 most important influences on your personal response to conflict, in order of importance. Keep this list for later discussion of "My Personal Style of Conflict."

We encourage you to understand yourself and your history while you are learning to change conflicts and gain confidence in your new repertoire of interpersonal conflict skills. The authors of this book often undertake a self-review of conflict influences. These influences change in importance over our lives. For Joyce, the major influences on her approach to conflict were the experience of her father being terminated because of conflict over social justice issues, and the way her parents coached the three siblings to talk things out and never fight. Her early training in leadership development quickly placed her in a coaching and teaching role as early as junior high. She gained humility when intimate relationships ended or changed even when good skills and good will were employed. For Bill, some of the major influences on his approach to conflict are that he grew up in a family that totally avoided all conflict, so he thought avoidance was the only option. Then in college, he became an intercollegiate debater and developed the ability to argue with others. Now, he practices a value of neither avoiding nor attacking—but pushing himself to collaborate with others in all situations, work and private.

Negative Views of Conflict

Prior to a training session to be held for a large corporation, a revealing dialogue took place. The agreed-upon topic was "Conflict on the Job: Making It Work Productively." Three days before the training was to take place, a worried manager called. He said the proposed topic "certainly sounded interesting," and he was "sure everyone needed help in the area," but he wondered if the leader would take a more "positive" approach to the subject. He urged a title change to "Better Communication in Business," and explained that his company didn't really have "conflicts," just problems in communicating. He felt conflict was such a negative subject that spending concentrated time on it might make matters worse. The executive's apprehensions about conflict were mirrored by a participant in a course called "Managing Conflicts Productively," who said she came to the course because she had never seen a productive conflict—all the conflicts she had witnessed were destructive. Further, her statement suggested that such a thing as a helpful conflict probably did not exist.

Several well-known cultural clichés present a fairly clear picture of how many of us were taught to think about conflict. Parents may tell their children, "If you can't say anything nice, don't say anything at all"; "Pick on somebody your own size"; "Don't hit girls"; "Don't rock the boat"; "Children should be seen and not heard"; "Act your age!" (which means act my age, not yours); "Be a man, fight back"; and "Sticks and stones may break my bones, but words will never hurt me!" All of these sayings give a bit of philosophy about conflict, regarding with whom to fight, permissible conflict behavior, when to engage in conflict, and the power of words in conflict behavior. All of the sayings make assumptions that are not helpful to persons who want to learn to carry out productive conflict behavior.

If you were asked to list the words that come to mind when you hear the word *conflict*, what would you list? People commonly give the following responses:

destruction	anxiety	threat
anger	tension	heartache
disagreement	alienation	pain
hostility	violence	hopelessness
war	competition	stress

Many people view conflict as an activity that is almost completely negative and has no redeeming qualities (Longaretti and English, 2007). Some take the attitude that "what the world needs now is good communication," that if people could just understand each other better, they wouldn't have to experience conflicts. While there is an increasing awareness of the potentially positive features of conflict when done skillfully, many widely accepted assumptions continue to work against a positive view of conflict. Some of the most common **negative views of conflict** are presented here.

1. *Harmony is normal and conflict is abnormal.* Years ago Coser (1967) and Simmel (1953) supported the idea that conflict is normal in a relationship that endures over time. They described conflict as cyclical, or rising and falling. No one expects relationships to be in a constant state of upheaval, or they would reach the "critical limit in a degenerative communication spiral and disintegrate"

(Wilmot 1995, 70). Observation of people in relationships shows that conflict is not a temporary aberration. It alternates with harmony in an ebb and flow pattern. But common expressions such as "I'm glad things are back to normal around here" or "Let's get back on track" express the assumption that conflict is not the norm. You can expect conflict, even in vibrant, enduring relationships.

2. _Conflict constitutes a breakdown of communication_. Designating conflict as a breakdown assumes that communication itself does not occur, but communication always occurs in an interpersonal conflict. Often more communication, if it is not effective, makes the conflict worse. The recipe "add communication into the breakdown" doesn't work out well.

3. _Communication and disagreements are the same thing._ Often we mistakenly assume that "we aren't having a conflict; we are just disagreeing." Sometimes this is true. As we described in chapter 1, conflicts are more serious than disagreements. The attempt to label a real conflict "a disagreement" may be an ineffective strategy to minimize the conflict.

4. _Conflict is a result of personal pathology_. Conflict is often described as "sick," and conflict participants may be labeled as "neurotic," "hostile," "whining," "paranoid," "egomaniacs," "antisocial," "dependent" or "codependent," or "enabling." Labels offer no substitute for a careful analysis of the elements of the conflict. Conflict results more often from a lack of appropriate personal power and too little self-esteem than from someone with a sick personality. In studying conflict, people's _behaviors_ should be described, _not their personalities_. Of course, people do get stuck in pathological patterns because of learning or emotional disorders. Sometimes people are so stuck in a destructive pattern that they cannot change and they cannot participate in collaboration. But the process of conflict itself should not be viewed as pathological. People engage in conflict for understandable reasons. If someone is "rigid," they may have too much or too little power. If someone is "defensive," they may be under attack or expect to be threatened.

5. _Conflict should never be escalated_. The term _conflict process_ better describes the various options in conflictual interactions than _conflict resolution_. Sometimes, the most productive choice is to temporarily make the conflict larger so it can be seen, dealt with, and given importance. Sometimes an escalation—not a runaway upward spiral but an emotionally intense expression—is unavoidable and cannot be suppressed without relationship damage (resentment, silent hostility, despair, hopelessness, and private decisions to leave). Conflict skills include learning to make enough noise to be heard and to make conflict big enough to be seen. Justice is often served by people of lower power banding together to confront higher-power people. Sometimes people with higher power take a stand to make a conflict larger because it is the right thing to do.

6. _Conflict interaction should be polite and orderly_. Overly nice communication of any kind ensures a lack of authentic interchange. Productive conflict management often is chaotic and confusing. Private arguments, especially, seldom conform to public standards of reasonableness, consistency, or relevance in argumentation. Sillars and Weisberg (1987) note that conflicts do not follow rules of polite conversation. Unlike college debaters, conflict participants do not have to respond directly, or in

order, or even with relevant expressions. "As conflicts intensify, conversations become increasingly less orderly, clear, relevant, and goal-directed, and increasingly impulsive, emotional and improvisational" (149). With intensity, communication becomes less strategic and rational and more emotionally expressive and personal. A good conflict is not necessarily a nice conflict, although the more people use productive communication, the more likely that the conflict will both solve problems and help the relationship go forward.

7. _Anger is the only emotion in conflict interaction._ Another misconception is that the primary emotion associated with conflict is anger, or hostility. Instead, many emotions accompany conflict. Many of us are familiar with the heated, angry, gut-wrenching feelings accompanying conflict. Yet people often experience loneliness, sadness, anxiety, disappointment, and resentment, to name only a few other feelings.

In our society, adults are not encouraged to acknowledge fears, loss, feelings of abandonment, and loneliness. As a result, people talk about their conflicts in terms of anger rather than heartbreak or loss. In conflict the emotional connection is altered between people. As the relationship changes to one of distance, the natural give-and-take that used to come easily is lost and they experience bitterness, anger, sadness, or other emotions. The loss of a positive emotional bond remains one of the most painful experiences of humankind. The poet Robert Frost has expressed this loss well:

Fire and Ice

Some say the world will end in fire
Some say ice.
From what I've tasted of desire
I hold with those who favor fire.
But if it had to perish twice,
I think I know enough of hate
To say that for destruction ice
Is also great
And would suffice.*

Application 2.4   Emotions in Conflict

What emotions are most common for you when you experience conflict? Think of four areas of conflict: family, roommate, romantic, and work. In each area, list your most common emotions. If there doesn't seem to be a set of common emotions, think of one conflict as an example in each area. How did/do you feel? Be sure to use words of feeling, not judgment or description. We will further explore how to work with these feelings. For now, simply identify them.

---

*From _The Poetry of Robert Frost,_ edited by Edward Connery Lathem. Copyright 1951 by Robert Frost. Copyright 1923, © 1969 by Henry Holt and Company, Inc. Reprinted by permission of Henry Holt and Company, Inc.

8. *A correct method for resolving differences can be prescribed.* Americans tend to resolve disputes, at least in public, in one of four ways: *fight, vote, litigate, or appeal to various authorities* (Stulberg 1987). These approaches assume that someone will win and someone will lose and that all will accept the process and abide by its outcome. In a local church whose members were trying to employ new forms of decision making, great disagreement arose over the idea of using collaborative, consensus-based forms of decision making. In one conflict over whether homosexual people should be given full rights and privileges in the church, the debate at the large public meeting centered primarily around whether it was possible to make decisions that were binding without a vote and how to vote without automatically creating "winners and losers." Many appeared more threatened by the change in process than by the possible outcome of the decision. In everyday life, subordinates subvert managers, children disobey parents, and coalitions form after a vote is taken, essentially changing the meaning of the vote. People assent with half a heart, then fight against the agreement with all their strength. Sometimes the best method for resolving disputes is not apparent, which leads to a struggle over how to struggle. Rather than being viewed as a waste of time, conflict should be viewed as multilayered.

Positive Approaches to Conflict

The above set of common assumptions probably reflects the predominant mode of thought in the contemporary West. However, one cannot just say "that is how people see conflict." Many societies, including our own, express contradictory views of conflict—sometimes it is bad, sometimes it is good. Therefore, we may grow up with a confusing perspective on when conflict is helpful or when it should be avoided. We learn few strategies for changing conflict situations from harmful ones into productive ones. Children may receive confusing messages about their conduct of conflict. Sports are all right, but violence outside a sports framework is not. Conflicts with peers are all right if you have been stepped on and you are a boy, but talking back to parents when they step on you is not all right. Having a conflict over a promotion is acceptable, but openly vying for recognition is not. Competing over a girl (if you're a boy) is admirable, but having a conflict over a boy (if you're a girl) is catty. And so on. Persons in power send two different messages: (1) fight and stand up for yourself, but (2) only when it is acceptable (Bateson 1972). Thus, people develop mixed feelings about conflict, and many simply learn to avoid it altogether.

Yet, there are some **positive approaches to conflict** worthy of our examination. For example, would you list the following words after hearing the word *conflict*?

exciting	intimate
strengthening	courageous
helpful	clarifying
stimulating	opportunity
growth producing	enriching
creative	energizing

One of the assumptions of this book is that conflict can be associated with all of the above words. Conflict does receive some positive endorsement in legal challenges and competition in business. In games, children learn that "hitting hard" and "fighting to win" are positive virtues. Strategizing, scheming, and maximizing your gains are also necessary. Conflict can be approached from a potentially positive perspective. Consider the following advantages and functions of conflict:

1. *Conflict is inevitable; therefore, the constructive way to approach conflict is as "a fact of life."* Too often, people blame others for conflict, assuming, as we saw above, that harmony is the norm. If you can accept that conflict is inevitable, you can calm down and use your problem-solving skills rather than expending effort in blame and avoidance.

2. *Conflict serves the function of "bringing problems to the table."* In intimate relationships, conflict can make clear that there are problems to be solved. Many times in couple relationships, conflict emerges over division of labor (Kluwer, Heesink, and Van de Vliert 1996) and over the distribution of power (Kurdek 1994). When couples report high levels of problem severity, they are more likely to divorce (Amato and Rogers 1999). One rule of thumb we have developed is that "If a conflict occurs three times it isn't about the content." It may be about power, self-esteem, division of labor, or resentments and hurts from the past.

   Don and Heather have been married for two years. They have a nine-month-old son. Heather works three days a week out of their home, running an environmental consulting business. Before their marriage, she worked for various nonprofit environmental groups. She is also an artist who sells her work to environmental organizations. Don is a mechanical engineer with a full-time job at a small firm. They reported a conflict over tasks at home. Here is a summary of their dilemma:

> Heather: Don and I have agreed that I will work three days a week, and in the other two days, take on most, but not all, of the home responsibilities. But since our child is home some of the day, every day, I often am doing many things at once—laundry, playing with or caring for Nathan, answering e-mails about work, and trying to write up reports and initiate contacts with clients. That's all right with me, since I like to have a lot going on, except for one problem. When I want to go out with my women friends some evenings, after being home all day, Don gets upset if I leave household and child care tasks for him to do. He doesn't understand that I can't just neatly divide my work into three days of business and two days of home and child care. I can't stand feeling stuck and controlled.

> Don: I thought Heather and I had worked out a good plan. I would work full-time out of the home, and she would work three-fifths' time at home, leaving her time to do most of the home tasks. I don't think she organizes very well. I resent being left with housework when she goes out in the evenings. It's not what we agreed. We need to change something.

Application 2.5   Don and Heather

What problems, specifically, do Don and Heather face? What are some of the areas that could derail them? In other words, applying the "three times" rule, what is the conflict *not* about? What is the conflict more likely to be about? How could they begin to solve the problem and make their relationship better?

3. *Conflict often helps people join together and clarify their goals.* Many times people keep on doing things "the same old way" until there is a conflict. When conflict arises, they must decide what their priorities are and how to use their resources. In one organization, a group of nurses were told they must function without a nursing supervisor. They were told by upper management to work out their own schedules and assignments as a team. As they struggled with more work and fewer paid hours available, after a period of several months of blaming and complaining, they met together as a team and worked out their problems. While the initial reduction in resources was not at all desirable, they now work effectively as a team.

4. *Conflict can function to clear out resentments and help people understand each other.* In a conflict, one cannot continue to go along as though one's own perspective is the only one. When others speak up and say what they need, want, think, and feel, the circle of understanding is often expanded beyond the individual. Even though it may be difficult, conflict can help people pay attention to other points of view.

To continue the examination of views of conflict, we will present an overview of everyday metaphors people use when describing conflict.

❧Insights from Metaphors

We try to make sense out of the disturbing, difficult experience of conflict by comparing one's current experience to something else we understand. When people compare one thing to another, we often use metaphors to create a kind of compact, vivid shorthand description of a complicated process (Ortony, 1975). Metaphors provide imaginative descriptions of emotional experiences. Our way of thinking depends on metaphoric language (Lakoff and Johnson 1980; Hayakawa 1973; Weick 1979). Conflict elicits such strong feelings that metaphors arise in everyday speech, often taking "its creator as well as its hearers, quite by surprise" (Rushing and Frentz 1983). Aristotle understood analogy or metaphor to be the source of truths, and a mark of genius. If this is true, you are a genius, because you certainly use metaphors. **Conflict metaphors** reflect and create certain kinds of communication.

In the following section, common metaphors for conflict interaction are explained. The way a conflict is expressed metaphorically creates a certain perception of what can happen, what will happen, what should happen, and with what kind of feeling behavior takes place (McCorkle and Mills 1992).

Two examples will get us started. ①Arnie, a manager, described his office as a windmill, with people going around in circles above the ground, not knowing that the pipe connecting the windmill wheel to the underground well has been severed. You can picture the pointless, aimless effort in the office, the sense of purposelessness, and even the dry, arid quality of the human interactions. Nothing lifegiving comes from the work.

② One student described her family as a melodrama—an old-time film in which a tram rushes across a bridge that is about to collapse. Father, the engineer, drives on at top speed, unaware of the crumbling bridge. No lookouts are posted, and no one else is in the engineer's cab. Disaster looms. Imagine the confidence of the engineer, the panic of the passengers (the family members) and the utter frustration at having no way to communicate with the engineer who is steering them into disaster.

Application 2.6	What Is Conflict Like?

Before you read further about metaphors and conflict, take a moment to think of how you generally describe conflict. Finish this open-ended sentence, "Conflict in my family is like . . ." Then, "conflict in my workplace is like . . ."

Win-Lose Metaphors

Many images and expressions of conflict cast such a negative tone that creativity is stifled. **Win-lose metaphors** imply that the outcome is predetermined with little possibility for productive conflict management. Conflicts viewed in this way are generally called *win-lose conflicts,* or *distributive conflicts*. In conflicts of this nature, what one person wins, the other person, by necessity, loses. A scarce amount of resources is distributed, usually unevenly, among the participants. One of the main reasons conflict brings up so much emotion is that people assume that they have so much to lose. Sometimes, that is true. Other times, as you will see, that assumption can be changed.

Conflict Is Warlike and Violent

War, with its violence, is a central metaphor for conflict. The following phrases regarding conflict reflect the metaphor of war and violence:

> Your actions are completely indefensible.
>
> He attacked me where I was most vulnerable—through my kids.
>
> That criticism is right on target.
>
> OK, shoot!
>
> I feel beaten down and defeated after our talk.
>
> He is killing me.

When conflict is envisioned as warlike, certain actions seem natural. In a staff meeting, for instance, if accusations are "hurled back and forth" as if primitives are bashing each other with stones. If arguments are felt to be "right on target," then the whole melee is structured as a battle. The scene is that of a battlefield; the actors are people of warring groups who are committed to wiping each other out. The acts aim to produce an advantage by killing or reducing the effectiveness of the opponent. The resolution possibilities are reduced to offense and defense, and the purpose is harm, or vengeance. The war metaphor influences the entire perception of the conflict. Both winning and losing sides feel incomplete; victors desire more power, and losers shore up their defenses for the next attack.

Perhaps you work in an organization whose workers act as if conflicts were large or small wars, and fights were battles in the ongoing war. If your organization uses a "chain of command," gives people "orders," "attacks competitors," "wages advertising or public relations campaigns," "fires traitors," "employs diversionary tactics," or "launches assaults," then the organization has evolved a military metaphor for conflict management (Weick 1979). If so, conflict is likely to be solved the way it would be if one were on a battlefield.

"He Is Killing Me"

In a large technological research firm, military metaphors abound. The program directors are under a lot of stress with high-stakes external negotiations, which involve millions of dollars. When they have a meeting with someone who shouts or stomps out of the room, they find it very unpleasant. Between rounds of negotiation, they might tell another program director that "he is killing me." Everyone immediately knows what this metaphor means: (1) this negotiation is very important, (2) I'm concerned that we won't "make a deal" on this contract, and (3) he is acting in ways that make me uncomfortable.

Couples talk in warlike terms, too. They may say:

I just retreat. I fall back and regroup. Then I wait for an opening . . .

He slaughters me when I cry and get confused.

When I don't want it to come to blows (laughs), I launch a diversionary tactic, like telling him the kids are calling me.

"She's Squeezing the Life out of Me"

A divorcing couple, Kent and Jeannie, were at odds over the division of their property. Most of the big items had been decided, and they were down to the smaller but more symbolic things such as music, art, family pictures, and gifts to one another. In describing their negotiations, Kent said in the mediator's office, "She's choking me," "These are my lifeblood," and "These things are my life." Jeannie saw the items as "just stuff, for heaven's sake." The metaphors the couple used revealed the degree of importance they put on the items.

Chronic use of military or violent metaphors severely limits creative problem solving. However, "other metaphors are needed to capture different realities that exist right alongside those military realities" (Weick 1979, 51).

Conflict Is Bullying

In an extensive analysis of metaphors that explain workplace bullying, vivid and painful images of being hunted, ("Everybody's fair game," experiencing abuse "(I've been "ripped," "broken," "beaten," and "eviscerated") emerged from the question, "What does bullying feel like?" (Tracy, Lutgen-Sandvik, and Alberts 2006) Respondents spoke of a "dictator" lording it over the slaves. One worker said, "You literally have a Hitler running around down there who's a mile away from the management who can't see it" (the bullying). The same researchers heard bullies described as evil demons and a Jekyll and Hyde character who was entirely unpredictable. In the extended "bully" metaphor, low power people described themselves as "a piece of property," "slaves," and "a caged animal." People referred to themselves as prisoners who were "doing time." (Tracy, Lutgen-Sandvik, and Alberts 2006).

Conflict imagined this way, as a drama of bullying, implies an extreme power difference. The "winner takes all" in a bullying scenario.

Conflict Is Explosive

Perhaps you experience "explosive" conflicts, using phrases like the following to describe the process:

> He's about to blow up. Any little thing will set him off.
>
> Larry's got a short fuse.
>
> The pressure's building up so fast that something's gotta give soon!
>
> I just needed to let off steam.
>
> She really pushed my button.
>
> Put a lid on it!

Such perceptions represent the action of igniting flammable materials (feelings), trigger issues, and setting off an explosion. Maybe the pressure builds "under the surface," like in a volcano, or "in a pressure cooker," such as an overcrowded office. People often say they "blew their stacks" in response to an event. If people act out explosive conflicts, they often see them as somehow out of their control ("He touched it off, not me"). The "exploder" may feel better after a release of pressure; the people living in the vicinity may feel blown away.

The explosion metaphor limits creativity in conflict because the only way participants can imagine resolving the issue is by "blowing up" or by avoiding "touching it off." Additionally, people with "explosive tempers" are often relieved of their own responsibility to do something about the buildup of tension before they have to blow up. Family members are taught to keep from making Dad or Mom mad, thus learning that conflict can be avoided by not provoking someone, thus keeping the peace. Family systems theorists have labeled this pattern as one of the destructive patterns of codependence—of taking too much responsibility for the actions of others.

Conflict Is a Trial

The legal system provides a regulated, commonly accepted system for managing social conflict. The system has evolved over hundreds of years and serves our culture well in many instances. However, Western society has come to rely too much on the legal system, partly as a result of the breakdown of community and personal modes of managing conflict. Thus, legal terms creep into personal or organizational conflict metaphors, since at least the legal system has firm rules and expectations. Phrases like the following indicate that legal metaphors may be shaping conflict behavior:

He's got the best case.

The jury's still out on that one.

You're accusing me.

She's the guilty party.

Don't you dare accuse me . . .

Even in conflicts between romantic partners or friends, one person might take on the role of the accusatory prosecuting attorney, one the role of the defender of the accused. Friends might get informally brought in as jury; one might say to friends, "Should I let him off on this one?" Arguments between interdependent people often go back and forth as if there will be a judgment of guilt or innocence, but often the jury stays out, no judge appears, and the case remains unresolved, to simmer through the system until another suit (interpersonally) arises. Courts maintain clearly delineated processes, basing decisions on law and precedent. Interpersonal situations, however, maintain no system of law and order to back up a decision. Few "trials" settle underlying issues in the conflict in personal relationships. Instead, romantic partners or friends keep "going back to court" (keep arguing). The legal metaphor doesn't fit most interpersonal situations, but the participants act as if it does, then remain bitterly disappointed that their case "doesn't carry the day."

Conflict Is a Struggle

People experience conflict as a hopeless or difficult struggle like "being on a sinking ship with no lifeboat," traveling "a rocky road," working with "a checkbook that won't balance" (McCorkle and Mills 1992), or "arm wrestling." Sometimes conflict is expressed as a power struggle, or a struggle to get "one up." The "conflict as a struggle" metaphor implies that the process takes a lot of emotional and physical energy and may indeed turn out to be fruitless. Sometimes people say, "It was a struggle, but we finally made it," indicating conflict resolution worked out reasonably well.

Conflict Is an Act of Nature

Conflict is expressed as a negative natural disaster, or at least an uncontrollable act of nature, such as a tornado, a hurricane, an avalanche, being swept away by a flood, a tsunami, an earthquake, or a fire raging out of control (McCorkle and Mills 1992). One telling phrase was that conflict felt like being "a rowboat caught in a hurricane." McCorkle and Mills note that those who feel powerless may "(a) take little or no responsibility for their own actions that sustain the conflict, (b) feel that the other participant has all the choices, or (c) believe that no one involved has any choices" (64). The best course of action, then, would be to avoid conflict, since no positive outcome can be expected.

Conflict Is Animal Behavior

Human animals often characterize conflict as something done by other members of the animal realm—not themselves. People may be called "stubborn as a mule" or described as "butting heads," or in a very common phrase, conflict is called "a zoo" (McCorkle and Mills 1992). You may hear phrases like "tearing his throat out," "slinking around," "stalking," or entering into a "feeding frenzy." One worker was labelled as a bully's "Chew toy." Another felt like a "caged animal" (Tracy, Lutgen-Sandvik, and Alberts 2006.)

Conflict Is a Mess

Another intriguing image is that of conflict as a mess or as garbage. You'll hear "Let's not open up that can of worms," "They got all that garbage out in the open," "Things are falling apart around here," or "Everything's disintegrating." People will ask to "tie up some loose ends." Another clear expression of the "mess" metaphor emerges when people say, "This is a sticky situation," or "Something stinks around here."

Messes are difficult to manage because they spill over into other areas and can't be contained easily without making a bigger mess. A messy conflict usually means one that is full of personal, emotional attachments. This metaphor limits creativity to the extent that feelings are judged to be messy or not amenable to rational treatment. If the opposite of a messy conflict is a clean or straightforward one, involving only facts and rationality rather than messy feelings, then only part of the conflict can be resolved. The feelings will go underground and "create a stink."

Conflict Is a Communication Breakdown

A "breakdown in communication" is one of the most popular designations of conflict. McCorkle and Mills (1992) refer to this breakdown as "one-way communication," in which people "talk to a brick wall" or "argue with someone from another planet." Referring to the process as a breakdown implies a telephone line that is down, a computer that won't communicate, a car that won't run, or a sound system that won't amplify sound. The implication that a breakdown can be "fixed," however, often turns out to be inaccurate. Many times people communicate clearly in conflict interactions—only to find out that they are in an intractable conflict. Clarity of communication sometimes improves the process of conflict management greatly, but it is a mistake to assume that clarity removes conflict.

Neutral or Objective Metaphors

A few **neutral** metaphors represent conflict not as positive or negative, but as having some potential for a positive outcome.

Conflict Is a Game

The game, especially the ball game, image is popular. While it is true that games end in victory or defeat, making the overall metaphor win-lose, the process of "playing the game" can be viewed as neutral. People "bat around ideas," "toss the ball into his court," "strike out," go "back and forth," and "make an end run."

The game image assumes rules defining the game and limiting interaction among the players. Rules define fouls, out-of-bounds behavior, winning, losing, and when the game is over. An even more intricate game is chess, which requires the players to keep in mind at all times the predicted moves of the opponent. Chess is a game that can only be won by a highly developed prediction of the strategy of the other player. If one doesn't take account of the opponent, one loses immediately. In chess, everyone plays by the same rules.

The game metaphor is limiting when people won't "play fair" or don't see the conflict as having gamelike qualities at all. Many men are raised to feel comfortable with the game image, accepting wins and losses as "all part of the game." Many women are less comfortable with the metaphor, insisting on talking about what is going on, which men see as not playing by the rules. In an extended study of women engineers, Fletcher (1999) was told again and again that solving high-visibility problems was the way to get ahead. People solving problems of this type were referred to as "hitting a home run," as opposed to being "singles hitters," who were seen as slow, steady contributors, but not the kind of team players that win the promotion game. "Real work" was defined as the kind of problem solving that involved team playing. Men consistently were ranked higher in this skill than were women (Fletcher 1999, 91). Game metaphors may be positive for men and potentially limiting or negative for women. Game metaphors work poorly in intimate conflicts, since most games provide a winner and a loser. In intimate conflicts, if anyone wins, the relationship loses.

Conflict Is a Heroic Adventure

The hero image is endemic to conflict images. The superheroes of Western movies, science fiction, and myths, and life describe scared people appointing a leader who is "bigger and better" than they are, then pledge loyalty to that leader, who is bound to protect them. The hero or heroine is one who has found or done something beyond the normal range of experience. "A hero is someone who has given his or her life to something bigger than oneself" (Campbell 1988, 123). The question is whether the hero or heroine is really a match for the task at hand, can really overcome the dangers, and has the requisite courage, knowledge, and capacity to serve.

This desire to follow a heroic leader emerges in all cultures. In social or political movements, leaders organize the energies of many people who overcome many obstacles to reach a common goal. Many contemporary films focus on the actions of a hero or heroine who saves large numbers of people (Rushing and Frentz 1995). The limit to this heroic metaphor in conflict resolution is that one can become used to passively watching events happen on TV or elsewhere. The spectator feels helpless or unimportant. And if the right leader does not emerge, a wonderful chance for change may be lost. Additionally, people often get stuck in certain roles in the heroic drama, such as damsel in distress, knight in shining armor, lieutenant or helper to the "great one," or victim.

Many of the heroic roles specify men as actors. Roles such as king, dragon slayer, the lone Western gunslinger, the sports hero, or the action hero of adventure movies are more often filled by men than women (Gerzon 1992). However, Rushing and Frentz (1995) indicate that films, especially Westerns and science fiction, are providing more and more heroic roles for women.

Conflict Is a Balancing Act

Conflict is referred to as a delicate balancing act, like that of a tightrope walker, or that of a rock climber, who must find just the right handholds or fall to sure death. Often negotiations in the formative stages are referred to as "in a very delicate" stage, in which one "false move" will scuttle negotiations. Satir (1972) refers to a family as a mobile, which can be unbalanced by one member's having too much weight or getting stirred up, thus making the whole mobile swing and sway. Working toward balance is seen as a positive process.

Transformative Metaphors

Some conflict metaphors help us envision ways to transform the conflict. By picturing conflict in a transformative way—that is, using **transformative metaphors**—we may use our imagination to move out of the negative perspective of conflict into understanding conflict as an opportunity to change the *way* interactions proceed.

Conflict Is a Bargaining Table

A collaborative approach to conflict is exemplified by the common metaphor of "the table." Diplomacy, labor negotiations, and parliamentary procedure all use this image. The conflict structure and procedure depend on the table as a central feature. Families are urged to sit down to dinner together, labor and management officials "come to the table," and diplomats struggle over the shape of actual tables at conferences. These real or imagined tables communicate information about who the conflict participants will be, how they will act, and what their placement will be in relationship to each other.

King Arthur, in historical legend, created a round table to symbolize equal discussion, with each knight having one vote. The idea of "Right makes might" substituted, for a time, for "Might makes right." When the federation disintegrated, the round table, smashed to pieces by dissident knights, became a symbol of the disintegration. Other examples of "table" imagery in conflict management include the following:

In parliamentary procedure, "tabling a motion" stops movement toward a decision.

"Bringing a motion off the table" indicates a readiness to decide.

"Under the table" refers to hidden or secretive agreements.

"Turning the tables" comes from a medieval custom of turning from one dinner partner to another to begin conversation. It was done in response to the king's or queen's gesture. If the "tables are turned," a person feels a sudden lack of contact or support, or loss of an ally.

The table metaphor continues to help us think about power, especially uneven power. Conflict resolution remains difficult if people are "negotiating at an uneven table" (Kritek 1994). People may be metaphorically seated at an uneven table if they do not have the skills to negotiate, come from the nondominant culture, hold unequal positions in an organization, or do not have the freedom to come and go from "the table."

Conflict Is a Tide

A second transformative metaphor for conflict is the tide. Tides ebb and flow within predictable parameters based on the phases of the moon, the climatic conditions, the shape of the shoreline, and the currents of the ocean. The tides are predictable only through observation and careful record keeping. They must be seriously considered by those on land and sea or they can become life threatening. Every sailor knows the folly of going out on the ocean without knowing the tidal patterns. Tides can be destructive, but they also wash in nourishment and unexpected flotsam, sometimes even treasure. Debris is washed out, exposing new features of the coastline. Tides are repetitive, powerful, and inescapable.

Thinking of conflict as a tidal rhythm in relationships may help to reduce fear. If the relationship is equal and trusting, conflict will develop its own rhythm that will not wash away the foundation of the relationship. Conflict will ebb, as well as rise. For example, many families experience more conflict than usual when a college student comes home for the summer to work. After being on their own for several years, many students experience too many restrictions at home, and parents experience what appears to be too little family involvement and accountability on the part of the student. Many times, several "high tide" conflict experiences prompt a family to reset the expectations and boundaries. Then for the rest of the summer, conflict episodes recede to "low tide." Thinking ahead about this possibility helps many family members navigate well through a potentially stormy time.

Conflict Is a Dance

Another potentially positive image is conflict as a dance. People speak of "learning to dance to the same music." In a dance, participants have to learn how close and how far to move, how to regulate distance, when to slow down and when to speed up, how to maintain contact with partners so you know where they will be, and how to end the dance (Lindbergh 1955). Different flourishes and steps can add to the grace and beauty of the dance. Dancing can be energetic, stimulating, and exhilarating. Sometimes one's partner steps on one's toes, can't dance very well, is awkward, or doesn't know the steps yet. But the whole idea of dancing with partners is to create something beautiful, graceful, and inspiring that depends on each person's skill, training, and individual expression. Dance can give collaborative images of conflict on which to build. Conflict envisioned as dance is reflected in the following statements:

> "I feel hurried. I need more time." (The person is not saying, "I need a different partner.")

> "Quit dancing around, and come over here and talk with me, please." (One person may be saying, "I don't know these steps, and I can't reach you. Please let me in.")

> "They're just do-si-do-ing [a square-dancing term] around." (The people look as though they are doing something together but really have their backs to each other and their arms folded—a fairly noninteractive way to dance!)

Conflict Is a Garden

Conflict can be like a carefully cultivated garden or farm. In creative conflict, as in good gardening, seeds are planted for future growth, pests are managed, weeds are pulled, and the garden is watered when needed. Sun and light are needed for the plants to grow, and the most fruitful outcomes occur when the conditions are carefully tended. If constructive conflict can be seen as a garden, many positive outcomes can be experienced. In good gardening, poisons are not put on the ground—thus, rage and attacks, which poison an ongoing relationship, become as unthinkable as putting dry-cleaning fluid on rosebushes. In good gardens, individual plants are given room to grow. Some plants are thinned to make room for mature plants. In human relationships, people learn to leave space for others, to give them room to grow, and to plant compatible varieties together. As a child you may have learned that no amount of watching beans or carrots in a garden would make them grow any faster. Human relationships, especially when conflict has recently been part of the environment, need time to grow slowly, to recover from stress, and to put down roots. We can "harvest" the fruits of careful labor (Kritek 1994, 275).

Conflict Resolution as Quilt Making

One metaphor that many women relate to is the vision of making a quilt (Kritek 1994) or "piecing together a solution." We may speak of putting together a "patchwork of ideas." When making a quilt, people have to decide on the basic color scheme (tone or emotional climate), the design, and what kind of fabric to use. Many individuals work together to create something beautiful and useful. While quilts can be made by individuals instead of groups, the more common experience is for women to gather together to sew and solve relational problems. Recently, quilt making has been studied as an art form pioneered by women. Not only did women gather together to make a quilt out of scraps and remnants, they also engaged in informal conciliation around the quilting activity. Such activities still flourish. Community groups have made quilts for AIDS projects, for relief activities, and have raised funds for their programs.

Conflict as Musical Improvisation

Conflict can reflect artistry, as in jazz or drumming. In certain kinds of music, individual musicians follow the lead of one soloist, picking up on the theme or the rhythm and extending the music. The solo passes around in the ensemble. In drumming circles the rhythms grow out of the shared experience of the rhythm. Interpersonal conflict can be like this. Someone gets a good idea, expresses it, and the others, rather than insisting on a different melody or rhythm, "add in" to what has begun. Dissonance and harmony make interesting music.

When Metaphors Differ

Problems occur when people envision conflict in different ways. One person may think of conflict as war, with all the attendant warlike images, while the other assumes that conflict is more like a chess game—strategic, careful, thoughtful, and planned. The case 2.1 presents an example of problems arising from different images of conflict.

Case 2.1	Is It a Mess or an Explosion?

Lynn and Bart are married to each other. Lynn sees conflict as a mess, something sticky and uncomfortable, even slightly shady or dirty. People in her family believe that husbands and wives who love each other don't have conflict very often. Conflict is distasteful to her. She is

(continued)

Case 2.1   Is It a Mess or an Explosion?

likely to say, "I don't want to talk about it now. Let's just leave the whole mess until this weekend. I can't handle it tonight." Bart sees and feels conflict as an explosion—his stomach tightens, his pulse races, and his heart begins to pound. He likes to reduce the pressure of all this emotion. He's a feelings-oriented person, while Lynn is more likely to use a reasoning process if she has to deal with an issue. Bart is likely to say, "I am not going to sit on this until Saturday morning. I'll burst. You can't expect me to hold all this in. It's not fair, you always . . ."

In addition to their specific conflict, Bart and Lynn are fighting over how to fight; indeed, they are fighting over what conflict is and how they experience it. Each assumes that the other thinks about the conflict the way he or she does. They could not be farther from the truth, as they probably will find out.

You can find your own metaphors using a structured technique to generate creative ideas for managing your conflicts.

Application 2.7   Playing with Your Conflict Metaphor

1. Class members generate *a metaphor* for an important conflict, using one of the previous suggestions. Each person writes out their own metaphoric image. ("We are a . . .")

2. One person *shares the image* with the group of conflicting parties or the discussion group. The group then asks clarifying questions of the person sharing the metaphor, using the images developed in the original metaphor.

3. The group then *brainstorms,* still using the imaginary mode, about ways to resolve the conflict. (In brainstorming, you reserve "editing" until later.)

4. The facilitator or leader then asks the group to *translate* these imaginary resolutions into practical steps for conflict management.

5. The primary party, or the group, then *chooses the options* that are most likely to lead to collaborative conflict management.

6. After all the conflict parties have repeated this procedure, a *contract* is made for selected change.

The following box presents an example of using metaphors to generate communication options.

Application 2.8   The Dangerous Minefield

Margaret, a college student, writes:

My father and I are in a minefield. The sky is blue, the sun is shining, there is green grass and sudden death underneath. Each of us is responsible for some of the mines underfoot, and we have to avoid our own mines as well as those planted by the other person. There are scattered trees and bushes around the field, which is quite large. They provide limited cover. We are each trying to get in close enough to the other to get a good look without being seen.

My father throws rocks at me to try to flush me out into the open. I back around a bush and meet him. Boom! There's a big explosion—we both flee, wounded, only to begin the standoff over again.

Here are some metaphoric solutions for "The Dangerous Minefield" translated into practical steps for conflict management:

Metaphoric Solutions	Communication Possibilities
1. Dig up my mines, or tell him where they are	Disclose myself
2. Get a metal detector, locate his mines, and	Psych him out and
a. dig them up;	a. confront him;
b. throw heavy objects from a distance to set them off;	b. backstab him;
c. avoid them	c. avoid him or "be nice"
3. Wear explosion-proof armor	Decrease my dependence
4. Throw rocks at him	Attack or goad him
5. Abandon the field; leave	Don't communicate at all
6. Hold on to him during explosion so we can't run from each other	Increase closeness and interdependence
7. Cut down the foliage to get a better view of each other	Describe our behaviors and feelings
8. Use binoculars to see each other	Get information on him from other sources; focus carefully
9. Whistle as I go around the field	Let him know "where I'm coming from"
10. Stand in the open so he can see me	Give him a chance to get information about me; write him a letter

Options 1 and 7 through 10 seem to be moves that would help productively manage the conflict. Many more exist, but these are a good start.

Other images of conflict can be detected in ordinary conversation. Listen to the way you and others talk, scrutinize news reports, and pay attention to images in public speeches. See if you can determine the metaphor that shapes a particular conflict in a family, an agency, a social group, the general public, or even the nation. What might it mean, for instance, if conflict is seen as an irritant, as in "She bugs me," or "Get off my back," or "He's just trying to get a rise out of you"? Do you think conflict takes on a life of its own, as when it "snowballs out of control" or is "a runaway train"? Many people experience conflict as an endless circle of repetition, going nowhere, as exemplified by phrases such as "We're just going round and round," "We're on a merry-go-round," or "Here we go again!" The tedium of conflict is reflected in "Same song, second verse." People refer to conflicts as "a drain," "a lot of grief," "a heavy burden," or "poison." Attending to these vivid images can unleash your creativity and help you to sort out which images of conflict are limiting and which are helpful.

Application 2.9   Reframing Your Conflict

Think of a conflict you have observed or experienced—possibly one you thought about earlier in the chapter. First, determine whether any negative conflict metaphor applies to this conflict. You can think of a negative metaphor of your own, or use one we have presented. If you stay in the negative framework, what options are available to you for resolving the conflict? List at least three. Now choose a transformative or neutral metaphor for "framing" the same conflict. List at least three options that might be available to you if you envision the conflict in this way. Discuss your results.

The Lens Model of Conflict

The metaphors we use for conflict illuminate our personal ways of viewing conflict interactions. While each conflict episode is unique, common elements underlie all conflicts.

The building blocks of conflict are represented in Figure 2.1, the **lens model of conflict.** For the sake of simplicity, the lens model will be illustrated with just two conflict parties, though many times there will be more than two parties involved. Two fundamental aspects are important in all conflicts: (1) *communication behaviors* and (2) the *perceptions of those behaviors*. Think of the study of conflict as a view through a lens, like the lens of a camera, or through prescription glasses. The lens model specifies that each person has a view of (1) oneself, (2) the other person, and (3) the relationship. These perceptual pieces form the fundamental "views" of all conflicts, and combine together to form the mosaic of a particular conflict. Figure 2.1 shows these central features.

Figure 2.1   The Lens Model of Conflict Interaction

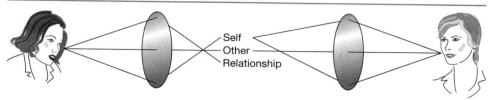

As you can see from figure 2.1, the <u>minimal features of all conflicts</u> are as follows:

- The *communicative acts* (behaviors) of each person
- The *meanings* (attributions) attached to those acts by each person:

   each person's view of self

   each person's views of the other

- The *meanings* (attributions) the two people ascribe to their relationship:

   past events

   current events

   future projections

Note that each person has a "lens" that gives that person a particular perspective, just as people use different types of glasses to see. <u>There are multiple views of conflict, yet each looks "real" to the one seeing</u> it.

In the Far East, this notion of lens is captured when people speak of two sides of seeing something. In <u>Nepal and Tibet</u>, for example, a person in conflict might say, "Well from my side, I guess I am getting tired of waiting for him, but I don't know what is going on from his side." The <u>notion of "side"</u> captures just how different two perceptions will be. <u>One side usually does not understand the other side</u>—your lens and his lens distort the events in different ways.

Have you noticed how <u>easy it is to focus on what your "opponent" does in a conflict?</u> She leaves you out of a meeting, cuts you off in the middle of an explanation, or takes a position and sticks with it even though you have perfectly reasonable grounds for what you think. How easy it is to tell your friend, "her actions say it all." However, actions "speak for themselves"—yet the impact of someone's actions depends on how the behaviors are <u>interpreted by the other people involved.</u> For example, Amber and Aaron are attorneys married to each other. At home, Amber interrupts Aaron a lot; both push for airtime.

For a lot of married people, having your spouse interrupt you signals disrespect. Yet, actions do *not* speak for themselves—our lenses determine the results. In this case, Aaron likes Amber's interruptions, appreciates her passion because he likes full involvement in the conversation. Or take the case of two small children, Sydney and Luke. When Sydney accidentally steps on Luke, he shouts to her parents, "she did that on purpose" and begins crying. <u>His perception of her intent drives his reaction.</u> Intent does *not* equal impact.

<u>intent ≠ impact</u>

So when you are in a conflict, your "intent" will not be the same as the impact on the other person. Judy, a manager in a city office, sees herself as friendly and open. She is often asking employees how they are doing, inquiring about their family members—she has a good intent. Yet, the impact is that employees feel forced to talk about personal things. The dispute escalates into a petition from the employees to have her removed as manager. When she is told about the petition, she is shocked, and says, "But I'm only intending to show interest and support for them." Intent is not equal to impact.

Behaviors do not carry meaning by themselves—meaning is created through the interactions. Intent and impact are different. All behavior is up for interpretation.

Behaviors do not occur in a relational vacuum. Perceptions of and attributions about behaviors are at the heart of the conflict process. Research on attribution theory shows quite conclusively that we make different attributions about ourselves than about others. Attribution research shows the following:

- We try to make sense out of behavior by looking for causes.

- We attribute causes of *our* behavior to external factors (e.g., "I was under extreme time pressure.")

- We attribute causes of *others'* behavior to internal dispositions (e.g., "She always wants her own way.")

Clearly, we use a different lens for viewing ourselves than we do for viewing others. When we are exposed to conflict, we tend to attribute the negative effects to the other rather than to ourselves. This tendency explains the familiar refrain of "It's his fault!" Sillars and Parry (1982) found that as the stress of conflict increases, blame of others also increases. We begin with an attribution of blame, then choose our next conflict move based on our perception that the other is at fault. Confounding the problem, we attribute our successes to our own efforts and our failures to external factors. The other party does the same thing. No wonder conflict is so difficult.

The lens model illustrates that people's views of self, other, and relationship are always, to some degree, distorted. We all have "filters" influencing our experience. As we will see in chapter 3, often in U.S. culture we "save face" for ourselves and "damage face" of the other. The other is probably doing the same thing. If you have ever known both individuals of a broken-up romance, you see the two sides very clearly. Where they once had only good things to say about the other ("she is just so perfect"), they now see only the negative features. When you talk to both of them after the breakup, their filters are so strong it doesn't even sound as though they were in the same relationship! Indeed, they were not, since each saw the relationship through his or her own lens.

The following conversation between two people occurred with two listeners present. As you can tell, the people conversing are in conflict with one another. Notice the different internal filters they automatically use that give them their opposing perspectives. The two of them work together and had just hosted a special event. They coordinated a series of public meetings for 13 people outside their organization.

Program coordinator: The executive director does not listen to me, does not include me in decisions, reluctantly agrees to include me, then goes her merry way without consulting me. This happened five times this week

during the visit of some important people. She is just too controlling. I don't see that I have a future here.

Executive director: The program coordinator is too passive and does not remember
when I talk to him. Further, he is being power hungry and want-
ing to run things himself. I specifically remember inviting him to
participate on most of these occasions. What is his problem?

The two of them then began a round of "did too," "did not." Slowly, they began to work
their way through this dispute. Both remain involved in the organization, with the program coordinator taking more responsibility and the executive director sharing more
information.

Outsiders to a dispute, whether they are social scientists or friends, also have their
own **attributions** and lenses—adding still other sides to the conflict equation. Whereas
the parties in the example above see the issues as inclusion, power, control, and
assertiveness, an outsider might focus on other issues. For example, during the exchange
between the program coordinator and executive director, one of the outsiders was thinking, "Hmmm, if the coordinator doesn't dampen this outburst, it will blow this relationship sky high, and the executive director is looking a bit smug—maybe she excluded
him on purpose and is glad she did."

These three lenses offer very disparate pictures of the unfolding dispute. Notice how
different the starting observations are for all the people present in the discussion. The
lenses are operating at full force. And when the categories become rigidly defined, you
can see how people get locked into intense struggles.

In a conflict interaction, you often hear the principal participants say, "Yeah, well that
is just your perception," as if the other's view isn't relevant. At the heart of all conflicts
are the perceptions of the parties—they fuel the dispute engine. Research illuminates the
importance of perceptions. For example, one consistent finding about married couples
is that if they believe they are similar to one another, they are happier. Whether or not
they are similar is actually irrelevant—their lenses determine their happiness (Acitelli,
Douvan, and Veroff 1993). On the other side of the coin, when you come to see your
work relationship (or personal relationship) as "having no hope," that belief alone predicts dissolution (Wilmot 1995). As a relationship declines, the individuals make fewer
joint and more individual attributions (Lloyd and Cate 1985). The dissolution of a marriage is speeded up if the two players see it as emanating from individual factors (Siegert
and Stamp 1994, 358). If during the first big fight the individuals develop a shared view
of what happened, their relationship is more likely to survive.

One study on environmental organizations and the timber industry found that each
side responds to, anticipates, and often copies the moves they think the other will make
(Lange 1993). This same dynamic is present in personal and workplace conflicts as well.
If you are not in communication with the other party, much like the environmentalists
and timber industry representatives in Lange's study, then you mull over the conflict in
your own mind. Without interaction with the other, the only "information" you have is
what is going on in your own mind—your filter doesn't have a chance to get corrected.
The result? "Prolonged thinking about disputes in the absence of communication focuses
individuals on their own perspective and enhances biases toward seeing disputes as serious and holding partners responsible for conflicts" (Cloven and Roloff 1991, 153). When

we run our own stories in our minds, then our view gets even more distorted. Cloven and Roloff found that only 1 percent of the time, individuals reported that they had thought about the conflict from the partner's view (136).

As you can see, the distorted lens can become even more warped in time. Here is an example of such thinking:

Joan

- Why is Jack late?
- He must be tied up.
- He was late last week, too.
- Hmmm, he is moving into the "irresponsible zone."
- I wonder if he wants to tell me something about our relationship.
- It has now been 25 minutes—he is so inconsiderate.
- I knew he would be like this—Sandy warned me about him.
- Jack is a real jerk.

Jack

- Hi, Joan. Sorry I'm late. I was counting on Kevin to bring my car back on time and he was late. Driving over I realized my cell phone was out of power. I am very sorry—you must have thought I was not coming.

Application 2.10   "That's Not What I Meant!"

Think back to a difficult issue that was made more difficult by perceptions that colored the experience. Remember a time when you were certain that the other person's motivation was harmful to you. How did you react as a result of this assumption? What was the outcome? Was the other ever able to say, "That's not what I meant at all. I was trying to tell you . . .?" What happened to the relationship as a result of these different perceptions?

Gender Effects and Gender Filters

Gender Effects

Membership in the "gender club" exerts a powerful, pervasive influence on your developing conflict repertoire. Your own gender and the gender of those with whom you engage in conflict affects (1) your behavior and (2) your views.

One of the primary ways to view the role of gender in conflict interaction comes from the *communication differences tradition*, made popular by scholarly work in communication and linguistics. This tradition has taken a "separate but equal" way of viewing communication differences. Rather than presenting women as deficient in "general" (male) communication skills or males as lacking important relational skills that women are assumed to possess, both gender-based preferences are studied openly. Given the scope of that work, only that directly pertaining to conflict interactions will be summarized here. (See Ivy and Backlund 2003, Wood 1997, Tannen 1994, and Pearson, Turner, and Todd-Mancillas 1991 for comprehensive reviews of gender differences and similarities.)

Gender encompasses both biological and social differences between men and women. Biologically, males and females are distinguished based on their sexual organs. Parents of a newborn will look for the presence or absence of organs. When a new parent says "It's a girl," they are referring to the biological differences. Gender also entails socially defined gender identity—when you see yourself and others as male or female. These roles are socially constructed, such as when someone says "oh, he is just a typical boy." Usually when people are talking about conflict, they see biological sex and gender identity as the same. For example, if you say, "the glass ceiling has finally been broken and a woman can run for president," you are treating biological sex and gender identity as the same. But when biological sex does not match the social expectations of female/male, we then talk about sexual orientation, gay, lesbian, bisexual, and transgender filters. If the male president of a firm undergoes a sex change operation, and becomes biologically female, this profound change alters your filter for interpreting your communication with her. Gender, both how we see ourselves and how we see others, has an impact on conflict behavior because it is so fundamental.

You see the impact of such filters when faced with a conflict driven by gender identity in real life. When Mark, a well-liked president of a firm, altered his biological sex, we worked with the human resource director on helping board members adjust. Working behind the scenes, one on one, the HR director helped the board members slowly adjust their filters. Marcia volunteered to change her role from president to president emeritus, and be an active day-to-day advisor. The organization kept her valued advice and involvement, and she was able to make the final adjustments to being female both in her identity and biologically. The conflict created by the change in both identity and biology was successfully managed.

Current research does show that in some circumstances there are female/male differences—that is, **gender effects**—in enacting conflict. In laboratory exercises, men will often exhibit dominating and competitive behavior and women exhibit avoidant and compromising behavior (Papa and Natalle 1989). In real-life observations of young girls and boys (at age 11), it has been noted that adolescent girls use indirect means of aggression, whereas the boys use more physical aggression. Interestingly, both sexes used direct verbal aggression equally (Bjorkqvist, Osterman, and Lagerspetz 1994). Tannen summarizes her research on gender differences in conflict by concluding that women are more likely to avoid conflict. Men are more likely than women to take control of the conversation to lead it in the direction they want. However, they expect their (female) conversational partners to mount some resistance to this effort, as men would be likely to do. Women often remain in the "listening" role rather than "lecturing," which puts them at a disadvantage in having their voices heard (Tannen 1994, 11). In organizations, women are more likely to leave than men are when there is ongoing, pervasive conflict. Higher status individuals interrupt more than lower status people; however, women (in one study, women doctors) provided more supportive, clarifying, and mending interruptions than male doctors did (Mentz and Al Roubaie 2008).

Before we decide that "men are like this and women are like that," we need to examine the similarities among men's and women's conflict behaviors. In a comprehensive examination of sex differences, researchers concluded that "no meaningful gender differences in positive affect behavior, influence strategies, autocratic behavior, democratic behavior communication, facilitation and leader emergence" were found. They report, "in both survey and observational studies, we discovered more similarities than differences between men's and women's conflict behaviors" (Canary, Cupach, and Messman 1995, 131). However, the question of gender differences remains highly complex. In an approach called **social learning theory,** individuals are assumed to learn to be male or female based on communication and observation. They learn gender roles in same-sex groups. Wood (1997) explains that through imitation, young children imitate almost anything they see and hear. However, only gender-consistent communication is rewarded by important others around the child. Children slowly learn how to be a girl and how to be a boy.

Culture plays an important role in gender development. Different valuing of autonomy and dependence is reflected in culturally defined gender roles (Young-Eisendrath 1997). In Western culture, girls and women are seen as valuing **connection with others**, the communication of care and responsiveness, and the preservation of the relationship (Gilligan 1982; Jordan et al. 1991). Boys and men are seen as valuing **autonomy and independence** more highly, learning to communicate in ways that preserve their independence from others (Kohlberg 1976). One of the main hopes we have as we explore conflict, gender, power, and culture is to give each of you the opportunity to choose from a wide range of communication behaviors, whether you are female or male. The more choices you have, the more likely you are to be able to resolve disputes intelligently and constructively.

Self-esteem is influenced by one's gender. Current research clearly identifies a major slump in self-esteem for girls in early adolescence (Sadker and Sadker 1994). They may not experience a major climb in their self-esteem until midlife, when family roles are less stringent and their career development is more in place. Boys typically feel more self-esteem earlier in their lives but suffer from a sense of failure and disappointment in midlife when they do not reach their (unrealistically) high personal goals (Barnett, Marshall, and Pleck 1992, 79). One of the tenets of this book is that all conflicts are about two issues: power and self-esteem. Both genders are limited by self-esteem issues, perhaps at different times in their lives. One finding seems clear on a worldwide basis, however. Men have more power culturally, even in highly educated countries such as the Scandinavian countries (Young-Eisendrath 2000). Therefore, women and men often sit at an uneven table. Later, we will discuss in detail ways to balance power effectively for long-term conflict resolution, especially in intimate relationships.

Gender differences depend partly on maturity and experience. One study shows experienced managers manifesting no gender differences in style, but "among participants without managerial experience, women rated themselves as more integrating, obliging, and compromising than did men" (Korabik, Baril, and Watson 1993, 405). Likewise, in a negotiation context, "Women are not necessarily more fair-minded or compassionate" than men (Watson 1994, 124). In the workplace, Gayle (1991) notes that on conflict strategy selection, the effects of gender are "minuscule" compared to the effects of a host of other, unidentified factors. It may well be that most of the effects ascribed to gender are due to other relationship factors such as power, gender of the opponent, prior moves of the other, and so on.

Gender Filters

In addition to potentially directing behaviors, gender often affects how one sees conflict behaviors. As we have seen, males and females tend to differ in terms of seeing self and other as connected. Even when actual behaviors may seem identical, for instance negotiating competitively, men and women often conceptualize the relationship differently. Women tend to see the **self-in-relationship,** with everyone affecting everyone else. One's self is formed and enacted in various relationships. Men are more likely to see the self as independent, not as connected to specific relationships. For effective conflict management, we must have both separate voices and a view that we are connected. When we see the self-in-relationship as a theoretical starting point, it allows us to concentrate on the following dimensions of conflict:

- Interdependence rather than power over others.
- Mutual empathy as the basis for understanding and communicating.
- Relational self-confidence instead of separate self-esteem (autonomy).
- Constructive conflict instead of domination.
- Staying engaged with others while in conflict.
- Valuing separate knowing and connected knowing.
- Utilizing both report talk and rapport talk.
- Continuing dialogue when there is disagreement.

Models of constructive conflict are built on the ideas of partnership and self-in-relationship (Tannen 1990; Young-Eisendrath 1993; Belenky et al. 1986; Jordan et al. 1991; Goodrich 1991; Brown and Gilligan 1992; Wilmot 1995; Gottman 1999). These ideas underlie the development of constructive conflict practices that are developed more in depth in subsequent chapters.

The filters based on gender have two effects on our understanding of conflict. First, many of the studies trying to pinpoint conflict behaviors are based on differences as perceived by the respondents of surveys. For example, most of the studies that find male-female differences in conflict choices ask college students to answer "in general" rather than for a particular conflict. College students have a stereotyped belief that there are gender differences, and as a result, they report "behavior" differences when they may not be present. They may also answer according to how they would like to see themselves, or how most women and men their age see themselves. Their filters for seeing self and other influence the studies looking for behavior differences in women and men.

Gender filters also affect our understanding of conflict because our filters may affect our behaviors. When feeling powerless, males tend to "state their position and offer logical reasons to support it." Women's approaches depend on the gender of their opponents (Watson 1994). As another researcher put it, "Men may use a more independent criterion for managing conflict and women a more interdependent one" (Miller 1991, 28). Women will choose responses based on interpersonal obligations, and men based on the offended person's rights. As a result of their focus on relationships, females in conflict seem to exhibit fewer self-presentational actions (Haferkamp 1991–92). In preschool children ages three to five, for example, Sheldon (1992) notes that young girls' expressions of self-interest are often meshed with "an expression of communal interests." Research also indicates that women in lesbian relationships may benefit from both being female in that they have "more optimism about conflict resolution" (Metz, Rosser, and Strapko 1994, 305). The filters we use, based on gender, affect how we enact conflict behaviors.

Cultural Effects and Cultural Filters

Who knows but one culture, knows no culture.
— Augsburger, *Conflict Mediation Across Cultures: Pathways and Patterns*

Cultural Effects

Application 2.11   Your Cultural History

The United States is culturally diverse. Think about your own cultural history and roots, whether you and your family have been in the United States for generations or whether you are recent immigrants. To gain a sense of how pervasive cultural differences are, think about the neighborhood in which you spent part of your childhood, your fourth-grade classroom, your experience making a geographical move, or your experience getting to know friends or new family members from a different cultural background from your own. Share the results of your reflections with someone from a different culture or geographical background in your class.

Each of us experiences cultural diversity at some level. About 150 different languages are spoken in the United States. The United States becomes more influenced by Hispanic cultures each year. U.S. culture is becoming less of a Western European offshoot in many ways, making the recognition of **cultural effects** essential.

Changes in the workplace demand that we become sensitive to different ways to process conflict. "Consider the increasing diversity, for instance. The often quoted Hudson Institute Report on Workforce 2000 predicts that 85 percent of those entering the workforce in this decade will be women, minorities and immigrants." Augsburger (1992) states:

What comprises a conflict in one culture is a daily difference of opinion in another. A serious insult in one setting—crossing one's legs or showing the sole of one's foot, for example—is a matter of comfort in another. An arrogant challenge in one culture—putting one's hands on one's hips—is a sign of openness in another. A normal pathway for de-escalating a conflict in one society—fleeing the scene of an accident—constitutes a serious offense in another. Human boundaries are cultural creations—social boundaries, legal boundaries, and emotional boundaries are all drawn according to each culture's values, myths, and preferences. (23)

Cultural Effects Depend on Many Factors

Conflict behavior is not easily predicted by country of origin. In general two kinds of cultures exist: **individualistic and collectivistic.** See Gudykunst and Yun Kim (2002), for an overview of intercultural communication. As these authors explain, communicating across cultures is a kind of intergroup communication. One of the problems we encounter is that communicating with "strangers" (their term for persons from other cultural groups than one's own) becomes more and more the norm as our worldwide communication becomes more rapid and frequent. Those of us in the largely Western, individualistic cultures must come to an understanding about the values and expectations of those in collectivistic cultures. For instance, prevention of serious conflict is much more likely to occur in Japan, China, and Thailand (collectivistic cultures) than in individualistic cultures (Moran et al. 1994, McCann and Honeycutt, 2006). But each culture uses a very wide variety of ways to do conflict. These ways are taught from childhood to persons in the culture, so that they become the expectations for how conflict is conducted (Tinsley 2001). Yet, these cultures—for instance, Nigeria (a non-Asian collectivist culture) and Canada (an individualistic society)—do not teach their members to take neatly predictable, opposite approaches (Gire and Carment 1993).

Westerners now understand that in many Asian cultures, self-expression is frowned upon if it does not further the needs of the group. In the West, in general, autonomy and self-expression are regarded more highly. Therefore, for Westerners to assume that individual expression is of higher value than harmony in the larger group is to remain in a Western, **ethnocentric** mode. Culturally, it may be for Westerners that harmony is achieved by explicit expression of individual emotion. Avoidance, which is prized in some other cultures, may escalate conflict in the United States.

The United States, generally, is an individualistic culture. A person is supposed to say what he or she means and resolve disagreements through the use of power (as in competition) or by working things out together (collaboration) (Wilson 1992). In this type of culture, things are discussed and spelled out, rather than supported by culturally defined, subtle nuances of interaction. This approach to resolving differences and communicating relies on assertiveness, relatively equal power, and freedom from fear of reprisal. Since these attributes are seldom present, however, U.S. culture rewards actions that are, for some people in the culture, stressful or even impossible. For example, Barnlund notes, "One of the most frequent shocks experienced by Japanese in coming to America is the resilience of friendships in the face of such strong clashes of opinion: Friends are able to confront each other, to vigorously argue contradictory views and to continue to be close friends in spite of their differences" (1989, 157). In situations in which people enjoy approximately equal power and understand the rules of interaction easily and well, the ideal of clarity and expressiveness works well. But when there is not a common base of assumptions, one's assertiveness can backfire.

In less individualistic, more collective cultures, discrepancies abound between what is meant and what is actually said. Disagreements are resolved through avoidance or accommodation, resulting in considerable face saving (discussed at length in chapter 3). Nuances of communication take on major importance, along with expected ways of behaving and working out problems. People do not confront others assertively and directly; to do so is considered rude and ignorant. In collectivistic cultures, members

Table 2.1   Characteristics of Conflict in Two Types of Cultures

Key Questions	Individualistic Cultures	Collectivistic Cultures
Why?	Analytic, linear logic	Synthetic, spiral logic
	Instrumental-oriented	Expressive-oriented
	Dichotomy between conflict and conflict parties	Integration of conflict and conflict parties
When?	Individual-oriented	Group-oriented
	Low-collective normative expectations	High-collective normative expectations
	Violations of individual expectations create conflict potentials	Violations of collective expectations create conflict potentials
What?	Revealment	Concealment
	Direct, confrontational attitude	Indirect, nonconfrontational attitude
How?	Action and solution-oriented	Face- and relationship-oriented
	Explicit communication codes	Implicit communication codes
	Line-logic styles	Point-logic style
	Rational, factual rhetoric	Intuitive, affective rhetoric
	Open, direct strategies	Ambiguous, indirect strategies

Source: Reprinted, by permission of the publishers, from W. Gudykunst and S. Ting-Toomey, *Culture and Interpersonal Communication* (Beverly Hills, CA: Sage, 1988), 158.

rely heavily on inferred meaning, whereas in individualistic cultures, members strive for an understanding of the literal meaning (Borisoff and Victor 1989, 141). Communication researchers have provided a clear summary of some of the differences between individualistic and collectivistic cultures. Table 2.1 portrays the differences in communicative strategies—direct and open compared to ambiguous and indirect. No wonder cross-cultural communication is getting more and more attention; we certainly need all the help we can get!

Similarly, Triandis (1980) notes some of the salient differences between the two orientations. In individualistic cultures

many individuals are high in internal control, who emphasize private goals, who pay attention to what the person does rather than who the person is . . . and where one finds more alienated and rootless individuals, where people think that decisions made by individuals are better than decisions made by groups . . . where going one's way and not paying attention to the view of others is acceptable, where personal enjoyment is emphasized, where friendship is a matter of personal choice. (65)

However, in collectivistic countries

there is an assumption that maintaining a strong group is the best guarantee of individual freedom, there is a strong emphasis on doing what the in-group specifies . . . shame and loss of face are mechanisms of social control, there is sometimes the tyranny of the group, interpersonal relations are an end in themselves, there are narrow in-groups, there is a concept of limited good, there are more people under external control or motivation, people tend to think that planning is a waste of time, goals tend to be group rather than individual goals, who does something is more important than what she/he does. (66)

We live in a cobweb of relationships. When you die you are finally free of this cobweb of relationships—which you leave to your children to carry on.
—Hiroko Takada, from Japan

In addition to bridging the gaps between cultures, we need much more exploration of cultural diversity within the United States. For example, many cultural groups share some of the features of mainstream U.S. culture yet are distinct in ways that make conflict management and mediation of their disputes challenging to someone from the dominant culture. Buitrago (1997) outlines some of the key features of Hispanic cultures that require careful consideration, and we need detailed exploration of many other cultural groups as well, ranging from Native American to African American cultures.

Whatever set of assumptions you choose to use, each framework places boundaries on constructive conflict management. Sometimes effective management requires people to be clear, direct, and assertive. Yet, at other times, deferring until the time is right, focusing primarily on the relationship components, and thinking of indirect ways to manage the dispute are the best approaches. To solve the most difficult problems, we cannot rely solely on the teachings of one culture. One major problem encountered in individualistic cultures is that we receive little training in the search for commonly acceptable solutions. If three people want different things, often the problem is resolved by competing to see who is the strongest ("We'll play it my way or not at all!"), or a person has to have enough power to persuade others to go along with a search for a collaborative solution. Therefore, many potentially collaborative ideas generated by low-power people are dismissed as unimportant.

In the United States, students are often taught that directness, ease in public, clarity of expression, assertiveness, and the ability to argue well are prerequisites to participation in conflict management. Indeed, in many contexts these skills are essential. However, for people who hold low-power positions in society, this is a very difficult set of skills to learn. To correct this imbalance, we need to focus also on *indirect* communication skills for people in high-power positions. Both high- and low-power people contribute to the tangles that occur in interpersonal conflict, and both must participate in better conflict management. Finally, cultural considerations include nonverbal communication; concepts of time (such as lateness or promptness); place of meetings or talks; whether content, relationship, identity, and process issues can be separated or not; and face saving (Borisoff and Victor 1989). As you begin to pay attention to the structure of conflict interactions, include these cultural and power issues in your analysis. Conflicts usually are not at all simple. If someone opens a conflict interaction by saying, "It's simple. We just have to do what makes sense . . . " you can be sure that, if the conflict is ongoing or has raised a lot of emotion, the solution is not simple at all. Even within a given culture there will be differences. In China, for example, people in the younger generation prefer more direct talk than do older Chinese (Zhang, Harwood, and Hummert 2005).

Interesting

Southern and Northern United States regions may experience conflict differently. Northerners seem to use "small doses of anger, rudeness and confrontational behavior" to send a message to someone to change their behavior. Southerners appear less likely to send "warning signals" when conflict escalates. A culture of politeness may cover escalating anger, but then anger erupts quickly. Researchers have called this the "culture of honor"—anger is suppressed and then escalates quickly (Cohen, Vandello, Puente, and Rantilla, 1999).

Cultural Filters

As you would expect, your filters based on your culture influence how you interpret others. If you come from an individualistic culture, and have a friend from Asia who rarely speaks, in public agrees with everything everyone says, and never has an overt struggle with someone else, you might see that person as having "no backbone." Or, conversely, if you come from a culture that prizes indirectness, to hear someone argue with a parent is offensive. Such a person seems rude and insensitive to you. In collective cultures "loss of face" has more serious relationship consequence (Kam and Bond, 2008). Each **cultural filter** influences our perceptions of others' behavior, and therefore is a key to attributions we make.

If we want to make more accurate attributions and meaning of others' behavior, we need to translate, interpret, and become fluent in several "conflict dialects." For instance, if you find it difficult to express hostility, then when your new friend begins to rage at the cashier, you will have difficulty dealing with it. For you he is "off the scale," yet for him he is "letting them know how to treat customers."

While this book cannot cover all facets of cross-cultural communication, some working acquaintance with your own filters absorbed through your cultural background will allow you to have more conflict management options. Without such an awareness, one remains ethnocentric and trapped within the assumptions of one's own culture and biased against people from other groups with different assumptions about behavior.

❧Summary

Conflict is an important area of study because we all face it as we move through our interpersonal, family, and work lives. Your personal history, such as your family of origin and other influences, makes a difference in how you respond to conflict. Perceptions about conflict, whether it is an activity to be avoided or sought out and whether it is a negative or positive activity, develop over one's lifetime. In this process, refined images or metaphors develop in one's imagination and language that give shape and meaning to conflict episodes. The lens model of conflict provides a framework for viewing how both gender and culture (1) shape behaviors and (2) influence perceptions of others' communicative behavior. Gender often plays a key role in the behaviors one chooses in conflict, and also influences how one sees others. Finally, one's culture (such as being individualistic or collectivistic) affects one's behaviors and one's perceptions of others in a conflict.

ᴥKey Terms

personal and workplace
history   35
avoidant system   36
collaborative system   36
aggressive system   36
negative views of conflict   39
positive approaches
to conflict   42
conflict metaphors   44

win-lose metaphors   45
neutral metaphors   49
transformative metaphors   51
lens model of conflict   56
attributions   59
gender effects   61
social learning theory   62
connection with
others   62

autonomy and
independence   62
self-in-relationship   63
gender filters   63
cultural effects   64
individualistic   65
collectivistic   65
ethnocentric   65
cultural filters   68

ᴥReview Questions

1. What is your own personal history with conflicts?
2. Is your family avoidant, collaborative, or aggressive?
3. Has your family approach to conflict changed?
4. What are some negative views of conflict?
5. Describe some positive views of conflict.
6. What do conflict metaphors tell us?
7. What are some examples of win-lose metaphors?

8. What are some neutral or objective metaphors?
9. Can you come up with a new transformative metaphor?
10. Chart the elements of the lens model of conflict.
11. What are some persistent gender effects?
12. What does it mean to say there are gender and cultural filters?
13. How does your culture affect how you view and do conflict?

Chapter 3

Interests and Goals

An American father and his 12-year-old son were enjoying a beautiful Saturday in Hyde Park, London, playing catch with a Frisbee. Few in England had seen a Frisbee at that time, and a small group of strollers gathered to watch this strange sport. Finally, one homburg-clad Britisher came over to the father: "Sorry to bother you. Been watching you for a quarter of an hour. Who's winning?" (Fisher and Ury 1981, 154).

Our interests and goals are sometimes hard to identify. Not only do outsiders usually misperceive our interests, we are often confused about them ourselves. This chapter describes the types of interests we struggle over with others. We treat "interests" and "goals" as different terms for the same things—what we want from others.

All conflicts at some level hinge upon the fact that people perceive that there are *incompatible goals* held by at least two people who are *interfering* with what the other person wants. Whether a sister and her older brother are struggling over limited parental attention, two managers are competing for a coveted promotion in the organization, or a seller and buyer are arguing over the price of a car, the perception of incompatible goals fuels the conflict. In every conflict the interdependence of the parties is built on both common and disparate goals, but the parties often perceive only the disparate goals. Conflict intensifies as people think they want different things; often the dawning awareness of conflict's existence comes when people say to each other, "What you want is not what I want." Conflict is more than a disagreement; it is when people believe that another interferes with their interests and goals.

Our goals are different in diverse relationships. In a friendship, for example, your main goal might be affinity—wanting the other to like you (Bell and Daly 1984). On the job, you may primarily want to gain information from colleagues or to persuade them about something. Our goals range from obtaining money, goods, services, love, or status to getting information. In a conversation, your primary goal might be to express your feelings (Argyle and Furnham 1983). Coleman, Fine, Ganong, Downs, and Pauk (2001) found that the majority of conflicts in stepfamilies involved resources (e.g., possessions, space, time, attention, privacy, money), divided loyalty, perceptions that the parents were showing favor to their "own" children, and conflicts with members of the extended family.

Many times, especially in emotionally charged conflict situations, we may be unaware of what goals we want to achieve. If you are angry at your roommate, you might not know whether (1) you want to punish her for being sloppy; (2) you want to have her like you, but you still want to influence her cleanliness standards; or (3) you want her to get angry and move out, so you can get a new roommate. Most conflict participants initially lack goal clarity; participants only discover their goals through experiencing conflict with the other participants. As we will see later, the goals will probably shift during the course of the conflict. What you want to achieve in the conflict also affects the tactics you choose during the conflict. For example, if you are "defending yourself," you are likely to use self-oriented tactics—being competitive and looking out only for yourself. On the other hand, if you want to improve a relationship, you are more likely to use conflict moves that are integrative—taking account of the others' needs as well as your own (Canary, Cunningham, and Cody 1988). One fact emerges from studying goals in personal and organizational settings—effectively functioning teams have a clear understanding of their objectives. The more clearly individuals or groups understand the nature of the problem and what they want to occur, the more effective they will be in solving problems (Larson and LaFasto 1989; Hilgerman 1994).

❧Types of Goals: TRIP

People in conflict pursue four general **types of goals:** (1) *topic* or *content*, (2) *relational*, (3) *identity* (or *facework*), and (4) *process*. The acronym TRIP stands for these major types of goals, which overlap and shift during disputes. These types of goals will be examined one at a time.[1]

Figure 3.1   The Four Types of Goals Pursued During Conflict

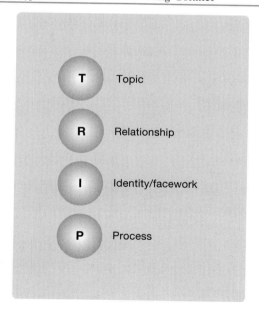

---

[1] In earlier editions of this book, we used "content" following the influence of Watzlawick, Beavin, and Jackson (1967). We have found that the TRIP acronym is much easier for students to recall; thus, we have changed the label "content" to "topic." Throughout this book, "content" and "topic" are used interchangeably.

Topic Goals: *What* Do We Want?

The key question when looking at a conflict is "What does each person want?" **Topic,** or content, **goals** emerge as different ideas about what to do, what decisions to make, where to go, how to allocate resources, or other externally objectifiable issues. Topic goals can be listed, argued, supported by evidence, and broken down into pros and cons. For example, Amanda might tell her supervisor, "I have been here six months, and I am hoping for a raise." Other examples of topic goals are

securing a student loan	a clean apartment
more free time	meaningful work
a new pair of skis	fashionable clothing
space to work	a different job
a vacation overseas	reliable transportation
to sell a house for $200,000	a digital video recorder

In different contexts, the topics change. For example, in the workplace here are some typical topics that emerge that cause disputes.

promotion	efficiency	getting to work on time
title	how hard you work	job assignments
accuracy	salary	new computer
office location		

In friendships, people might struggle over

Loaning money	what holiday plans to make
sharing a ride	how welcome friends are in a shared
where to recreate	apartment
what music to listen to	whether to share possessions
which movies to see	

Application 3.1   My Topic or Content Goals

Select three different relationship contexts such as school, work, friendship, and romantic relationship.

1.   For each relationship, list the "topics" that typically arise in disputes.
2.   Compare the list of topics across the three relationships.

Most of us have topics that are distinct in each relationship type as well as some that cross all three categories. You might, for example, have cleanliness as an important topic regardless of the situation, or it might be restricted to only your living environment.

Topic goals can be easily seen and talked about; they are external to us—we can point to them and say, "I want that." Yet, although they are objective, people often feel very deeply about them.

Topic or content struggles are of two types: (1) people want different things (I want to get the most for my car, and you want to pay the least for it); or (2) people want the same thing (same job, same romantic partner, same room in the house). In either case, what happens is a struggle over the goals. The perception that there is not enough to go around—a perception of a scarce resource—intensifies the conflict. More examples of struggles over content goals are:

- Three mid-level managers must come to agreement about which benefits to offer employees. Jill favors educational benefits, in addition to a basic benefits package, whereas Chuck favors increased insurance options, while Jim wants to increase flextime options. All three managers want to keep employees longer but disagree on how to do that.

- A divorcing couple tries to construct a visitation schedule that allows each parent access to their young children but that also fits with each parent's work schedule. The specific visitation schedule is the topic goal (at this point, separate goals) of the couple. Mom may state, "I want the kids on Sundays," or "I want to see them one night a week when they are at your house." Dad might say, "I want them on alternate weekends."

- A romantic couple talks about the pros and cons of either being together for the summer and both working in a restaurant, or one going to Glacier Park to be on a trail crew and the other to work as a biologist in the River of No Return Wilderness Area. They want to spend the summer together, but both also want to advance their respective careers.

- Mary is going to put her house up for sale because she will be moving to a different region. She asks $195,000 for the house, knowing that this price will pay for both her relocation and three months of living while she finds a new job.

Usually, when you ask people what they want in a conflict, you will hear a topic goal from at least one of the parties—"I just want a different office." For most people, topic goals are the easiest to identify and tell others about. The topic, although important and the beginning point to understanding all disputes, is just one part of the conflict mosaic. Some writers refer to topic goals as "substantive" or "realistic" goals, but we believe the following kinds of goals are also real and substantive.

Relational Goals: *Who Are We* to Each Other?

The key question when assessing the **relational goals** of a conflict is "Who are we in relationship to each other during our interaction?" Relationship goals define how each party wants to be treated by the other and the amount of interdependence they desire (how they define themselves as a unit). Additionally, the amount of influence each will have with the other is worked out through relational interaction.

Differing relational goals lead people into conflict just as differing topics do. People often experience deep disagreement about the question of who they are to each other. The following statements, expressed during actual conflicts, are relational goal statements:

How You Want to Be Treated by the Other

What I need here is some respect.

So, what happened to our collegial relationship?

What I want is for you to support me when we are in public.

I won't put up with that kind of abuse.

Well, you don't have to be nasty about it.

I want to be included on projects that affect me.

I expect professional conduct from everyone on this team.

You told Sandra the report would be in by the due date. Then you called in sick and had me handle it. This hurts my trust that you will do what you say.

I was hired at the same time Jim was, and now he's receiving extra training. I want access to training as well so I can grow in this job.

The Amount of Interdependence You Want (What Kind of Unit Are We?)

I thought we were best friends.

I can't help if I don't know if you want to stay on the project with me.

We both have our separate lives to live now, so let's get on with it.

What I do is none of your business.

I just don't know who we are to each other anymore.

Relational goals will emerge in any ongoing dispute and must be recognized and managed. For example, Donohue, Drake, and Roberto (1994) note that "the more mediators ignore disputants' relational concerns, the more difficulty they will experience in reaching agreement" (261). Yet, relational goals seldom become open, spoken messages (Wilmot 1995). Relationship definitions might instead be communicated by who talks first, who talks the most, nonverbal cues such as eye contact, and many other factors. For example, if an employee asks for a raise and is told no, the supervisor might be warning, on the relational level, "Don't push too far. I have the right to tell you what we can afford and what we cannot afford." If the employee says, "Why not? This is the best year we've ever had!" the relational message might be, from the employee's perspective, "I have a right to challenge what you say."

Much of the communication regarding relational goals remains tacit and unspoken. Productive conflict interaction sometimes requires that a third party or a participant clarify the tacit relationship definitions. The following are some examples of relational goals:

- A second wife decides not to go to a big family gathering of her husband's relatives. She resents the expectation that since his family gathers at Labor Day every year, she is expected to attend. She prefers to visit with her family at that time of year. If the husband and wife have a conflict over this issue, the content goals may be fairly clear: the husband wants the wife to go to the gathering, whereas the wife wants to visit her family and not attend the big gathering. The wife's relational goals might be varied: to establish equity in the time she spends with her family, to establish her independence from the new family group, or to protect herself from comparison to the first wife. The husband's relational goals might be to please his family, to introduce his second wife to the family in a relaxed setting, or to spend more time with his wife. Each argues about how much influence they will allow the other to have, about what kind of a unit they are, and about many other relational issues. If the couple argues about content goals only, they will get stuck on issues about plane fares and what they can afford, or the weather in Georgia around Labor Day, or the accommodations provided. In ongoing relationships such as this one, the goals surrounding who the participants are to each other need to be given priority. Most people argue content when they ought to be talking about relational goals.

- In a staff meeting, Joan insists that "before we decide on the reorganization, I need to know how committed you all are to staying with the organization." She needs some clarity on how people define their relationship to the larger group before plunging ahead with an extensive reorganization plan.

- Two teenage girls currently are "on the outs" with each other. Jennifer talks about how JoAnn is "high and mighty," then JoAnn complains to another friend that Jennifer has "an abnormal need to be in on everything." The conflict erupted the day after JoAnn canceled her plan to go shopping with Jennifer and went with another friend instead. The content, whether to go shopping together, was not the issue; the relational strain was.

Relational goals *are at the heart of all conflict interactions* yet are difficult to specify from the outside (and sometimes from the inside as well). That is because each person translates the same event into his or her own relational meaning. A conflict is interpreted differently by each participant. Just as we have no success in translating Ukrainian unless we speak the language, conflict parties must learn the relational language of their conflict partners. For example, a father and daughter fight many evenings when she comes home from school and he arrives home from work. Mother gets pulled into playing peacemaker, trying to urge them to get along better. The following example demonstrates how an event can trigger such a conflict.

Daughter scatters books, shoes, and lunch box in the living room while she gets a snack. Father comes home an hour later, sees the mess, and explodes. Daughter says, "I forgot," and Father says, "You always forget."

    Content messages: "I forgot." "You always forget."

    Daughter's translation: It's not important. I wish he'd pay attention to something that is more important to me.

    Father's translation: She doesn't listen. She is getting too independent to care what I think.

The difficulty with relational issues is that we never ultimately know the other person's translations. Just as the daughter and father have different translations for these events, usually the conflict parties cannot accurately guess what the other's translations will be, or if they can, they try to dismiss them. The friend who says "you shouldn't be bothered by not being invited to the picnic" is not accurately tuning into your translations. One technique in conflict management, therefore, is to have conflict parties *share their relational translations* of the content issues.

Other examples of incorrect or incomplete translations of each other's messages are illustrated by the following:

- Co-workers bicker each day about whose turn it is to lock up the business, which requires staying longer at the end of the day. None of the procedures developed seem to work—people have doctors' appointments, or have to pick up a child, or have a racquetball court reserved, so they have to leave early. This conflict is becoming a big issue. So far, the only way people resolve the issue is by coming up with creative excuses for leaving work. Resentments grow daily, factions are created, and pretty soon, the boss will have to step in and make a new rule, which will displease everyone. No new procedure (content solution) will work until leftover resentments are explained and attended to (relational issues). Then new, shared goals can be developed that have a chance of finally working.

- A couple argues over who should fill the car with gas each week—each feels she or he is doing more work than the other and wants credit for what is already being done. But the man argues that he shouldn't have to do all the work on the car, and the woman argues that he doesn't notice now much work she does for him, such as taking clothes to the cleaners. Not only are they arguing about content, but they are mistranslating the crucial relational goals (which remain unstated).

Relational goals are often reactive. What I want from you is the result of what I think you think about me. Once a conflict is triggered, each party reacts to what he or she thinks the other is doing or wanting. When Sandy says, "I won't take that kind of treatment from Jason," she is reacting to her guess about how Jason will act in the future, too. Once the conflict spiral begins, each person responds to an image of the other that may not be accurate. When Jason replies, "You are just trying to control me," he states his relational reaction to Sandy. In this manner, relational goals escalate into polarized states.

Application 3.2   My Relational Goals

Take two important relationships to you, for example, a parent, romantic partner, life-long friend, or other personal relationship. Think of a time you were upset at how he or she treated you. Then, list the "relational issues" that arose. For example, look at the samples of relational issues and amount of interdependence examples we gave above and see if you can identify your key relational issues.

Let's summarize some principles about relational interests and goals.

- Every statement carries a relational message.
- We each translate or interpret relational messages differently.
- Relational interests carry more urgency than topic interests.
- Our relational interests are triggered in reaction to our interpretation of the other's behavior.

Good relationships make the topic issues much easier to resolve, bring synergy to a conversation and enhance our positive identity.

Identity, or Face-Saving, Goals: *Who Am I* in This Interaction?

The key question in assessing **identity,** or **face-saving, goals** is "Who am I in this particular interaction?" or "How may my self-identity be protected or repaired in this particular conflict?" As conflicts increase in intensity, the parties shift to face saving as a key goal (Ellis 2006; Rubin 1996). Face saving, or identity protection, occurs throughout the conflict but will be highlighted more at certain times than at others.

In addition to content and relational goals, interaction goals include specific desires to maintain one's sense of self-identity. Identity needs have been extensively discussed as face work or saving face (Folger, Poole, and Stutman 2004; Wilson 1992; Goffman 1967; Brown and Levinson 1978). Often people will say, with frustration, "What are we fighting about?" or "I don't know what is going on!" Many times, a puzzling or maddening interaction can make sense if one analyzes whether one or more of the parties is primarily trying to present a positive face by claiming one's need to be approved of, to be included, and to be respected (Lim and Bowers 1991). When face saving becomes an issue, people are less flexible and engage in destructive moves (Ellis 2006; Folger, Poole, and Stutman 2004). According to Brown (1977), "In some instances, protecting against loss of face becomes so central an issue that it swamps the importance of the tangible issues at stake and generates intense conflicts that can impede progress toward agreement and increase substantially the costs of conflict resolution" (175).

Many times we express our identity or face-saving goals openly. The athlete who says, "I don't use drugs because I'm not that kind of person" or a friend who says to you, "I'm really good with verbal retorts" is telling you about their preferred identity. Or the teenager who says, "I don't have premarital sex because it violates my beliefs" is giving a clear identity statement. Simply listing the answers to "who am I" will be a good start for identifying your identity. These identity statements often arise when people are talking about themselves.

competent	likeable	responsible	trustworthy
best friend	logical	enthusiastic	well-organized
reliable family member	friendly	expert	leader

Another way to find your identity concerns is the exercise in Application 3.3.

Application 3.3   My Criticism Log

Keep track of all the negative thoughts you have about people in your world over a few days and jot them down in your notebook or diary. You don't need to track the type of relationship, who the other is, or anything else—just list the negative thoughts you have or comments you make. Some examples are "he is so stupid," "I can't believe how incompetent she is," "he is so mean to everyone," and "she is just power hungry."

1.   List all these criticisms of others, then in groups of three or four, just read them aloud to others (don't worry about how you sound; just say them even though they are sometimes difficult to share).

2.   Members of your group help you identify your two or three main "themes" for your criticisms of others. Most of us have two or three main identity dimensions that arise in criticisms of others. Put these "themes" in nonjudgmental or positive terms.
      For example, medical doctors often say things about their colleagues such as "he isn't the sharpest knife in the drawer," "she didn't do very well in medical school," "I just don't know how he became a doctor given his inability to process all the details," and "he isn't very bright." The theme of "intelligence" is clear.

3.   Discuss with the group your main identity "themes" and how they predict with whom you will have conflict or struggles.

The importance of identity, or saving face, can be seen when large corporations or individuals are sued in court. In some circumstances, they can enter an "Alford Plea," which means "I don't admit guilt, but based on the evidence presented I think I would be convicted." Thus, we read news reports of organizations saying, "we didn't do it, and we paid the plaintiff $15,000,000." On one hand this seems absurd, but on the other it helps sensitize us to the importance of saving face. The issue is no longer "did I break the law," but "how can I protect how I see myself and others see me?"

In each conflict interaction, individuals either save face or lose or damage face. Self-esteem has been discussed as a scarce resource. This is another way of saying that people's sense of self is often tenuous, not fixed. Few people are so full of self-esteem that they do not care about looking good in conflicts, or being seen as intelligent, honorable, correct, or justified. Likewise, when your opponent begins to perceive that you are damaging his or her sense of self, the stakes get higher. Face work occurs for each party throughout the conflict (see Figure 3.2). In face-saving conversations, people often give accounts of what has happened, or what the interaction meant, as a way to "repair" one's identity after a personal attack (Buttny 2000).

Since people often act out of self-interest, what normally happens as a dispute progresses is that people protect their own face, or identity, while damaging the other's face, or identity. Productive conflict management demands that we attend to neglected quadrants. One study analyzed communication in three cases of hostage negotiations. The cases involved three different people: (1) an armed, suicidal man barricaded inside a TV station; (2) a man suffering extreme emotional instability who was barricaded in a house; and (3) an armed man holding his children hostage. What emerged in the taped FBI

Figure 3.2   Dimensions of Saving and Damaging Face

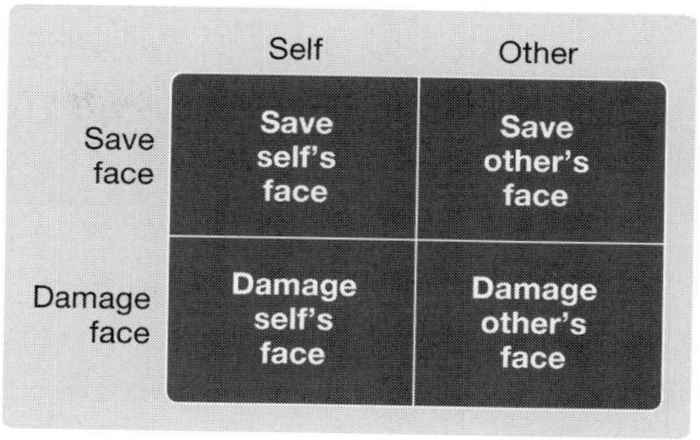

	Self	Other
Save face	**Save self's face**	**Save other's face**
Damage face	**Damage self's face**	**Damage other's face**

transcripts was the necessity to let the men save face while working to get the hostages released. The outside negotiators had to restore the armed men's face, by saying such things as "I think you are an extremely strong person for how you have handled this so far," "You've got a whole lot of people who care about you," and "The people you are trying to help, they need you" (Rogan and Hammer 1994). Sometimes face is saved ahead of time, and other times it is restored after there has been some loss, like in the hostage situation.

Figure 3.2 also shows how someone can damage one's own face. Though it seems unlikely, people often say negative things about themselves. When you say, "I'm just a terrible parent," or "I'm a lousy student," or "What does someone my age think he/she is doing going back to school?" those statements are damaging to one's own face, or identity. In the hostage situation, the armed men were, in effect, saying, "I'm just crazy," and the job of the outside negotiators was to get the men to start to see their own behavior as not quite so damaging to their view of themselves. Once face is restored, one is more free to give up extreme defensive tactics, such as holding hostages.

People try to avoid loss of face by defending their self-images against humiliation, embarrassment, exclusion, demeaning communication, or general treatment as unimportant or low-power individuals. Attempts to solve a problem or stop a conflict by causing another person to lose a sense of dignity and worth never work in the long run. Remember the four horsemen discussed in chapter 1, and how many destructive conflict cycles result from this kind of destructive communication. Overuse of power may temporarily solve a problem. When losers are created, however, the losing group or individual waits for a time and place to "make it right," either by getting back at the winners, by subverting the ongoing process, or by leaving the relationship, work setting, or group. Demeaning communication creates ongoing pain and dissatisfaction, and the conflict remains unresolved at a deep level.

Face saving and giving others face are extremely important in all cultures but often take precedence over topic issues in Asian cultures. It is now well known in the business community that entirely different kinds of negotiations are required in Asian cultures. Attempt to support the others face and avoid at all costs the loss of face of the other requires attention to face are part of the requirements of polite interaction among many Pacific Rim cultures. One would never pin an opponent down or attempt to prove him or her wrong.

The box labeled "Going Public," from a newspaper column about mediation in different types of disputes, briefly treats the necessity of saving face, even in Western cultures.

Going Public: Like Dirty Laundry, Gripes Are Best Aired in Private

"Ask a Mediator"

by William Wilmot, PhD, and Roy Andes, MA, JD

Reader: I'm an employee of a business that's falling apart. We have a high profile in the community and could easily pressure the management by going public with our complaints. Should we?

Mediators: We are a society addicted to two values at odds with one another: privacy and public disclosure. Nowhere more than in conflicts do those values collide. Although the public likes to know what's going on, and the press likes the pizzazz of conflict, people whose relational dirty laundry gets hung out in public suddenly become more positional, more intransigent and more likely to use lawsuits and other formal or hostile procedures.

Why? The answer is privacy and face saving. We all want people to feel good about us, to like us, and to give us strokes. We feel that if we are completely open about our dilemmas and conflicts people are less likely to give us the things we want. How many of us tone down, postpone or even entirely avoid family arguments in public? How many of us in conflicts with friends or co-workers prefer to talk "privately" rather than in the presence of strangers? ALL of us, of course, do so. It's only natural. It's just as true for public officials and corporate executives as for the rest of us. People want privacy when they have to confront strong feelings and disagreements.

Destroying that privacy is as much an escalation of a conflict as throwing a bomb into the room. In response to such a "bomb," most people respond aggressively. They are certainly less likely to be cooperative, and less willing to try to work collaboratively to help you get what you want and need.

If you want to solve problems rather than preach about them, do it in private. If you want sincerity and openness, privacy is the best way to go. This is why mediators provide absolute confidentiality of mediation discussions. It's also why good negotiations take place out of the glare of press attention. Collaboration and problem-solving take mutual commitment, safety, patience, and thoughtfulness. None of those virtues emerge in a 30-second sound bite.

You can tell that attempts to save face are being employed when you or others engage in the following kinds of communication (adapted from Folger, Poole, and Stutman 1993):

1. *Claim unjust intimidation.* Topic goals take second place to this specific kind of relational goal—to stand up to another's attempt to take over. People accuse others of taking advantage, declare their resistance to unjust treatment, and often seek support from outside parties when they are being treated unjustly.

2. *Refuse to step back from a position.* A person who no longer feels comfortable with an earlier position may choose to stay with it, even in light of new information, because looking foolish or inconsistent results in losing face. Thus, topic and larger relational goals are set aside to avoid looking weak, ill informed, or incompetent. In a community in a Western mountain state, water rights became a major conflict for a group of summer home owners in the mountains. A city tried to claim water rights to a small creek that flowed through the home owners' property. One man resisted the efforts of a majority to build a legal defense fund because he had said at a meeting, "I'm not going to pay some lawyer to fritter away my money on something we can't stop anyway!" As several summers wore on, this embattled individual refused to step back from his position of "no money to lawyers" and "we can't make any difference anyway." He wrote letters to others in the home owners' group, bitterly protesting the intimidation by the majority group in assessing a fee for each home owner to build the legal fund. Clearly, as new information came in strongly supporting the efforts to fight the city's water claim, as when the district court judge supported the summer-home group, the man who was fighting to avoid losing face found himself in a dilemma—to fight further might be to lose face even more. Eventually, he pretended he had supported the legal efforts all along but just thought the fees were too high. This was a face-regaining effort, and the home owners' group wisely dropped the issue so the man could be part of the community again. For him, the content and relational goals had become temporarily unimportant.

3. *Suppress conflict issues.* People also try to save face by refusing to admit that a conflict exists, since to acknowledge the conflict might mean that events are out of control, which might make people feel uncomfortable and incompetent. In the water rights conflict discussed previously, several longtime friends of the dissident home owner said things like, "Well, Kent is just cantankerous. He'll get over it," or "Well, these things bring up strong feelings." The association had few effective means of conflict resolution. Many felt that to acknowledge conflict at all would mean that their group was in danger of losing a sense of camaraderie and community spirit. One board member tried to schedule a meeting that the dissident individual could not attend because of his travel schedule—an attempt to suppress or avoid the issue of face, or identity, needs.

In productive, ongoing relationships, several kinds of communication will help people restore their lost face or prevent further loss of face. You can increase flexibility and problem solving if you

1. *Help others increase their sense of self-esteem.* Treat others with goodwill, giving them the benefit of the doubt even when they have been belligerent or unproductive. You might say things like "Everyone gets upset sometimes. We can get past this," or "You must not have had all the information I had. You couldn't have known about the Grandview project yet, as I did." Even saying something like "I know you were doing what you thought was best" gives the other person the benefit of the doubt and is usually true. People do tend to do what they think is best at the time.

2. *Avoid giving directives.* Parents can tell their teenage children, "I want you to honor the house rules we've discussed. I want to be able to trust you and not worry about monitoring you—you're almost grown and can make decisions for yourself." This approach is much better than "If you don't follow the rules we've set up you can find somewhere else to live!" As will be discussed later, it's better to avoid direct threats and to use persuasion and face-saving communication instead. No one wants to be pushed around. Even if you have "right on your side," it may not always be wise to be "right," as this creates winners and losers.

3. *Listen carefully to others and take their concerns into account.* Even when you don't have to listen because you have the power to make a decision independently, listening and taking care of others' concerns as best you can helps them feel included, approved of, and respected.

4. *Ask questions so the other person can examine his or her goals.* By asking questions instead of attacking, you give the other person a chance to change in the interaction instead of entrenching or digging in (note the warlike metaphor).

In conclusion, helping others protect their self-identity as a good, worthy and competent human being goes far toward helping resolve conflict by allowing people to focus on goals other than self-protection.

Process Goals: *What Communication Process* Will Be Used?

The key question when assessing **process goals** is "What communication process would work best?" Many times people disagree about how to formally or informally conduct a conflict. A group might argue over the merits of consensus versus voting. Intimates often disagree about whether strong emotions hurt the process of conflict or not, or whether the partners should stay up and talk when one is sleepy or wait until morning. Work groups go back and forth about whether to send out opinion questionnaires, talk informally in a series of meetings, delegate certain decisions, or put off deciding certain issues. All these relate to the process of conflict interaction and will impact content, identity, and relational goals.

Some examples of process goals are

giving each one equal talk time	talking informally before deciding	not allowing the children to speak
consensus	having high-power person decide	voting
decisions made by subgroup	secret ballot	

Different processes of communication may change the relationships involved. For instance, minorities may be given more power with a free flow of communication, whereas higher-power people might maintain their power with a more tightly organized form of interaction, such as one that relies heavily on written communication.

One of the current trends in the workplace is that people want processes that enhance equality and open participation. People struggle in organizations and small groups over the pros and cons of consensus, informal discussion, information gathering, delegated decisions, written summaries, voting, and parliamentary procedure. Women, more so than men, are more comfortable soliciting everyone's opinion (Brown and Gilligan 1992).

Process goals also vary in different cultures, with some being quite authority oriented and others relying on equal participation. In Native American tribal politics, a long process of consensus building is often required before a decision is considered valid by the tribe. The tribal members delegate less to their elected officials than do Western European cultures.

In addition to changing the levels of influence, different processes encourage or discourage creative solutions. Quick, well-defined processes help you move forward but may decrease creative, innovative solutions. Longer, sometimes confusing processes that build in time for reflection and evaluation improve the chances for creativity. Thus, different processes affect the outcome of a conflict interaction as well. For instance, one couple began to struggle over when to buy a house. The wife wanted to buy a house in the next few months, whereas the husband wanted to save more money before they looked seriously. The husband suggested that they first discuss with each other their financial goals and then talk about the house. This discussion resulted in the wife's decision that she, too, wanted to wait at least a year so that they could better their financial situation. By changing from content issues, such as the interest rate, the availability of houses in the desired neighborhood, or the likely tax consequences, to a different process, such as talking about other goals, the couple changed the relational conflict ("I've got to get her/him to listen to me") to a mutually acceptable process.

Large public meetings are arenas for process conflict. People who know they are in the minority or low power often argue over correct parliamentary procedure, which provides more options for hearing from the minority than does, for instance, informal large-group discussion followed by voting. Often, process conflicts change as individuals are heard. People drop their obstruction to a certain process if they are assured of being heard and counted (face/identity issues) and when they see that their content and relational goals are being protected. As in struggles over differing content, relational, and identity goals, process conflicts blend into the other conflicting goals. Shifting from one level to another often helps parties avoid becoming stuck in an unproductive conflict.

❧The Overlapping Nature of TRIP Goals

Now that each type of goal has been explained and illustrated, we can deepen our analysis of goals in conflict. A number of features about conflict goals need to be highlighted.

Feature 1: Not all types of goals emerge in all disputes. Disputes go on in which no process, or procedural, issues emerge. In the workplace, for example, there may be a heated disagreement between two supervisors, yet neither wants to change any of the processes used, how frequently they meet, or who is included. Similarly, many examples of conflicts can be cited in which there are no content issues. Two friends may be locked in a struggle over how responsive they are to one another, a relational issue that doesn't involve content. It is often puzzling to parents how their children can fight for hours over "nothing"—no identifiable content issues. But rest assured, if there is a struggle and no content issues are apparent, the struggle is about something. The dispute rests on identity, process, and/or relational grounds.

Feature 2: Interests and goals overlap with one another and differ in primacy. When you begin a dispute over your grade (the topic goal), you also want to be treated well by the professor (the relational goal) and want to think that you tried hard (the identity, or face-saving, goal). Figure 3.3 demonstrates how this might look from your side.

Figure 3.3   Content Goals Paramount

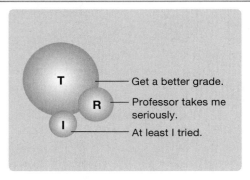

As you can see, you begin a discussion with the professor with the topic issue paramount in your mind; the relational and identity issues are there but not as important to you. Note therefore that even though they differ in prominence, different goal types emerge. The professor, on the other hand, may be most concerned that she be seen as a fair and kind person, so a diagram of her goals at the beginning of the conversation might look like Figure 3.4. She may be most concerned about relational issues, such as others seeing her as a fair person who treats students equally, and identity issues ("I'm doing this job the way it should be done; I like how I respond to student concerns"). Her primary goals, then, are relational and identity goals. The topic goal of the student's grade is much less significant, unless the student feels he or she is being treated unfairly.

A second example illustrates how a process or procedural goal might be utmost in one party's mind. You are a member of a departmental student group and would like to run for president. You were out of town last weekend, and this Tuesday in class someone said, "Hey, what do you think about Stan being president of the student club? We had an election last night." For you, the procedural issue of not being notified of a meeting when others knew you wanted to run for president is the paramount issue, as shown in Figure 3.5. Note that in this case, the procedural issue looms largest, followed by identity and relational issues of equal weight.

Figure 3.4   Relational and Identity Goals Paramount

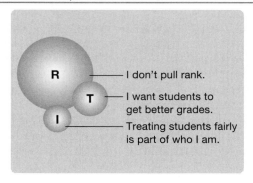

Figure 3.5   Process Goals Paramount

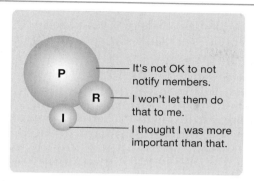

The examples illustrate that for each party, the paramount interests probably differ from those of another person in the same situation. Notice that all of these examples included relational and identity goals because it is rare to have a conflict that does not involve identity and relational issues.

Feature 3: Identity and relational issues are the "drivers" of disputes; they underlie topic and process issues. As you listen to people describe conflicts, you begin to notice a pattern—at the core of the disputes are their concepts of who they are and how they want to be treated in relationships. In most business disputes, for example, regardless of the topic issue, someone is concerned about trust, treatment, or communication—relational issues. Further, the face saving discussed earlier is a key element in all disputes. Because we are human beings, our inherent subjectivity drives disputes. Think back to when you were not chosen to play as a kid or were excluded from some high school activity, and you may remember just how important relational and identity issues are. As discussed under Feature 1, relational and identity concerns will almost always overlap—*who you are* with others is related to *how* the relationship is conducted. Figure 3.6 illustrates which goals are almost always present and, in fact, drive almost all disputes.

Figure 3.6   Relational and Identity Goals Propelling a Dispute

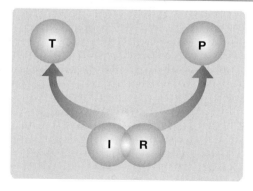

Note that the relational and identity issues are the subjective forces that propel the topic and process issues into focus.

Even though the identity and relational issues are the most difficult to talk about, they are the most potent issues in conflicts. One interesting feature of how people operate, given that relational and identity issues are the foundations of all conflicts, is that sometimes identity and relational interests may be met indirectly. For example, it may not be common in your family to say, "I feel excluded," but rather, family members may watch others at the family picnic, see who is left alone, and seek them out for a talk. In an organization, it may not be within the cultural norms to say, "I don't feel very valued here," but the president may give you access to the boardroom for meetings if he or she guesses that you are feeling pushed aside. Similarly, watch little kids at play. One of the kids may be left out, and another may turn to that child and say, "Want to play dolls with me?" Such a move is both a relational and identity tactic. Another example of meeting issues indirectly was when Bill, one of the coauthors of this book, was 12 and not getting any time with his dad. Bill was hyperactive and on the verge of delinquency. An observant neighbor, Francis Cowger from Upton, Wyoming, noticed him, and offered him a summer job driving his tractor. Many relational and identity needs were filled for Bill on the John Deere tractor. If Francis had approached Bill's dad and said, "I think your kid needs some attention, but I know you are working 14 hours a day, so how about I give him a job on my ranch this summer?" Bill's dad would have been insulted. But the indirect offer to help, by giving Bill a job, avoided a conflict with the father and allowed Francis to give neighborly assistance.

By being alert to the "relational translations" someone else might make, you can serve both relational and face-saving needs indirectly through content. Indirect, topic-only solutions do not work in intense conflict situations, however. The more severe and strained the conflict, the less satisfying the content approaches will be. This leads to the fourth feature of conflict goals.

Feature 4: In a serious dispute, topic-only solutions are rarely satisfying to conflict parties. If you know someone who has ever won a lawsuit, ask him or her, "How do you feel about the other party and the process you went through?" You probably will hear anger, frustration, and exasperation, with the person usually launching into a tirade about both the other party and the other party's attorney. That is because (unless it is a very unusual case) only topic issues have been addressed, and the needs to save face, to be listened to, and to be told that you aren't crazy have not been attended to. During the dispute there is often so much threat to each person's identity that content solutions alone are not satisfying. In this type of situation, if an outsider says, "You got $150,000; what more do you want?" the plaintiff will usually answer, "An apology."

Feature 5: Conflict parties often specialize in one kind of goal. Conflict parties in ongoing struggles often highlight one type of goal and limit themselves to it, as in the following dialogues:

In the Organization

Faculty member: This is a ridiculous place to work. I put in a lot of hours and no one notices. I'd just once like to get some credit for what I do here. (relational specialization)

Chair of department: Dr. Samuels just doesn't do a very good job in the classroom. I can't support him for promotion until he begins to get higher marks from the students. I'll have to have some hard-hitting sessions with him outlining how a professional person does a job like his. (topic specialization)

In the Family

Grandfather: My daughter is just not a good mother to her kids—she needs to learn how to be a better mother. The kids need to be cleaner, and they are always late to school. Those kids need a better mom. (topic specialization)

His daughter: [the mother of two small boys] I am just not willing to have the kids spend time at their grandparents' house until Dad learns how to treat people better. He only criticizes me and the kids and never says anything positive. (relational and identity specialization)

In these conflicts, the participants separate and specialize—one party on topic goals and the other on relational goals. This split tends to keep the conflict going—as the topic specialist continues to expect better "performance" from the other, the relational specialist becomes more and more critical of the treatment he or she receives.

Specialization in either topic or relational goals often reflects the parties' relative power. All too often, high-power parties are the ones who focus exclusively on topic. Failure to acknowledge relational goals may be due to a lack of skill or can show hostility, lack of caring, or even a desire to compete. Focusing only on topic devalues the other person and his or her concerns. The most powerful group member usually wins by structuring the conflict and ignoring troubling relational issues from lower-power people. Topic discussion is simpler and requires less investment in the other person. Similarly, lower-power members may wish to bring in goals other than topic goals as a powerbalancing mechanism. If a lower-power person can get the higher-power person to agree that relational process, and identity goals, are important, the lower-power person is "empowered" and becomes a legitimate party in the conflict.

Feature 6: Goals may emerge in a different form. Sensitivity to the different types of goals allows you to recognize when one type of goal is being acted out in terms of another. Any one of the four can come to the surface in a different form. Topic goals emerge as relational, identity, or procedural goals. Relational goals can emerge as topic, identity, or procedural goals, and so on—there are 12 possible substitutions. One of the most common is illustrated in Figure 3.7: a relational goal carried by topic.

Many times conflict parties are simply unable to identify their relational goals. Instead, they act them out at the topic level. For example, you may feel devalued by your boss, so you wage an ongoing, persuasive campaign to change the performance evaluation system used by the organization. Or you think your brother does not respect you, so you argue that he doesn't have the training to handle your aging mom's finances. In "Stay for Dinner," notice the shift in goals.

Figure 3.7   Relational Goals Emerging in Topic Form

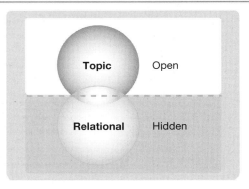

"Stay for Dinner"

Connie, Sharon, and Janene, seniors at a university, share an old house near campus. They have known each other for years; they grew up in the same town. Their roommate relationship has, thus far, been fairly smooth, although recently an issue has emerged. Janene eats two meals a day on campus at the food service. Connie and Sharon like to cook, so they prepare their meals at home. They have invited Janene to share their evening meal several times, and Janene has occasionally accepted. It's Thursday night, Janene is rushing to get to the food service before it closes, and the following dialogue takes place:

Connie: Hey, Janene, you might as well stay and eat with us. It's late—you'll never make it.

Janene: No big deal. If I miss it, I'll get a hamburger or something. [She rushes out the door.]

Connie: [to Sharon] That's the last time I'm going to ask her to eat with us. She thinks she is too good to be bothered with staying around here with us.

A few weeks later, Connie and Sharon find someone who is willing to room with them, share cooking, and pay a higher rate. So they approach Janene and say, "We are struggling with finances, and we have someone who will eat here, share expenses, and save us all money on food. Would you rather pay a higher rate or move out?"

As you can see, this dispute began with two people feeling excluded and quickly degenerated into a topic-only conflict. Because relational issues were ignored, a long-time friendship was lost.

Identity conflicts, as well, often erupt on the topic level, as shown in Figure 3.8.

"I'm right/Are not/Am too" is an example of an identity-driven dispute that gets played out on the topic level. Each person starts by wanting to feel right (identity, or face saving). Watch what quickly happens.

Figure 3.8   Identity Goals Emerging in Topic Form

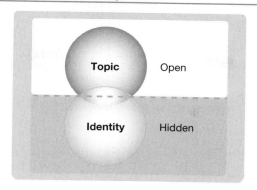

"I'm Right/Are Not/Am Too!"

Duane and Kathy are going to a movie. Duane is driving, and they both notice a red car passing them.

 Duane: That's a Subaru, like the kind I was telling you about.

 Kathy: No, I think it was a Toyota. But it's pretty.

 Duane: No, it was a Subaru!

They argue back and forth about the rightness of their claims. Neither is a car expert, but both are adamant, using sarcasm and biting humor.

 Kathy: Well, you may be right, but I still think it was a Toyota.

 Duane: Look, I know I'm right!

 Kathy: You never think I know anything!

 Duane: You don't know anything about cars. Blow it off. It's not important.

Kathy sits silently for 10 minutes.

The couple will continue to argue about identifying cars, but both have stated relationship concerns. Kathy feels she is not given credit as a knowledgeable person. Duane states that he needs to be right on things he knows more about. The couple appears to be negotiating about who has preeminence in certain areas of expertise. They haven't worked out how to "call off the conflict" or how to ask for more respect from each other. They are likely to find other topics to fight over until the relationship is addressed directly. The following box presents two openings that might start them off more productively.

> Duane: I get bothered when you challenge me about something I know a lot about. I start thinking you don't think I'm very smart.
>
> or
>
> Kathy: Duane, I'm not that interested in Toyotas, or Subarus either. But I've been thinking that you get the last word on most topics we discuss. It makes me want never to give in—even if I know I'm wrong.

Goals Change in Interaction

TRIP goals are like a lava lamp, glowing, changing, altering, and always moving.
—Leanne Eleff, 2001

Goals don't stay static but undergo transformation before, during, and after disputes. They will emerge as one type and, during the course of the dispute, change into another type. Even after the struggle is over, goals will shift and change.

Take the case of Eleanor, a senior in a class. She felt the grade on her last essay was too low.

The Bad Grade	
Eleanor to her friend:	That instructor has it in for me. He continues to ignore me in class and on the last assignment, he really cheated me. I'm simply not going to put up with that any longer.
Eleanor thinking to herself as she waits to see the instructor:	Ok, when I go in there, I'm going to get him to apologize to me for causing me such grief. I want him to see just how much he has ruined my senior year.
Eleanor in the office:	Mr. Jones, I would like it if you would re-grade the first essay question. I don't think you understood what I was trying to write.
Mr. Jones:	Sure, glad to. I'll give it back to you on Tuesday after class.

Note how her goals changed. She began with bad treatment and being ignored (relational goals) and a content goal (being cheated) to a relational goal (I want him to apologize to me) to a pure content goal (reevaluate one question). Such change and flow are typical in conflict situations.

One way to look at this flow of goals is to specify how goals change across time from (1) prospective (before interacting with the person), to (2) transactive goals (during the interaction itself), to (3) retrospective (after the conflict). It is important to be able to track the changes in both your and the other person's goals—they continue to evolve over time.

Prospective Goals

The word *goals* most commonly connotes intentions people hold before they engage in conflict. For instance, Sally might say to Dorothy, "What do you hope to accomplish at the board meeting? The last one was awful—so much confusion and disorganization." Dorothy might reply, "I want to sort out who's in charge of the budget decisions and how we're supposed to come up with $5,000 more next year than we took in this year. I don't want to take responsibility for more fund-raising." Dorothy has stated her **prospective goals**—those she can identify before the board meeting begins. Simply stated, she hopes that the board will decide who makes budget decisions and delegate fund-raising to some responsible party. Most of the other board members will come to the meeting with their own prospective goals. An effectively managed meeting will take account of all the prospective goals members bring, whether they are readily stated or not.

Taking the time to clarify what you want from a particular interaction lays the groundwork for more effective conflict. The expectation of collaboration establishes a positive tone for the discussion.

When you clarify your prospective goals, you

- Gain clarity about what you want from a meeting.
- Prepare yourself for a discussion.
- Get a sense of "I can do this."

Of course, as we have the actual conversation with the person, we usually change in their presence. During the discussion, your goals continue to shift and change during the transaction itself.

Transactive Goals

In many conflicts "goals are quite complex and ephemeral" (Sillars and Weisberg 1987), and they only become clear as the conflict unfolds. For example, during a struggle with your housemate over financial misunderstandings, you discover that what you really want is to move—which you did not know you felt until the argument began. You have just stumbled onto a **transactive goal**—one discovered during the conflict itself.

Transactive goal development takes place during conflict episodes rather than before or after. You may have been absolutely certain that you wanted an assistant to carry out the new project your boss assigned to you, but during a staff meeting you may change your demand for an assistant. You now say that you can do the work without an assistant for at least six months. What happened? Did you back down? Did the boss win? Did you have "no guts"? More likely, you became aware of the interdependent nature of your work team and decided to change your demand, given the needs of the entire group. You may have been given recognition for the difficulty of your job. Maybe your boss said in front of the group, "I'd like to give you an assistant, but I don't have the money in the budget and don't know where I can get it" (a face-saving message). Your conflict goals changed because of the communication event.

A school board member was trying to decide how to handle her strong opposition to the closed, or "executive," sessions of the board that her colleagues on the board supported. She discussed the incipient conflict with friends ahead of time, rehearsing what she was going to do (prospective goal). When the next board meeting arrived, she did not give her prearranged speech. She compromised and agreed with her colleagues that some closed meetings, in limited circumstances, were acceptable. This change is an example of transactive goal development.

The concept of transactive goals developed from the conviction that communication, itself, is transactional. To describe communication accurately, we must look at what happens when people are together instead of looking at each person's separate experiences (Wilmot 1987; Laing, Phillipson, and Lee 1966). Relationships are interpenetrative, with each person influencing and being influenced by the other (Wilmot 1995). To say that the board member in the example was persuaded by the other board members is simplistic. Neither did she persuade them to adopt her point of view. They all influenced each other, creating new, transactive goals through the process of a board meeting.

You may have noticed that your goals change in conflicts as you get a chance to express your feelings, be heard, and talk through your opinions and wishes (while the other party does the same). If you are a person who says, "I don't know what I want until we get a chance to discuss it," you understand transactive goals. The following box exemplifies the way new goals develop as a conflict progresses. Note that the two friends see themselves as interdependent and that they value their relationship as well as solving the immediate topic issue (finding the lost silver pendant).

Verbal Communication	Goal Analysis
First phone call:	
Amy: You know that silver star pendant I loaned you? I guess you didn't return it with the rest of the jewelry, because I can't find it.	Amy's #1 prospective goal is to *get the pendant back from Janice.*
Janice: I don't have it. I remember that I didn't borrow it because I knew it was valuable to you. You must have misplaced it somewhere. But I'll look.	Janice's #1 prospective goal is to *convince Amy that she is not responsible for the disappearance of the necklace,* a goal that is incompatible with Amy's prospective goal.
Second phone call:	
Amy: I still can't find it—I'm getting panicky. I'll stay on the phone while you go look. Please check everywhere it might be.	Amy maintains prospective goal #1 by escalating her previous goal statement. Amy and Janice still have incompatible goals.

(continued)

Verbal Communication	Goal Analysis
Janice: You're upset about the necklace, and I don't know what I can do since I honestly don't think I have it. But what really concerns me is that you are upset with me. You mean a lot to me, and this hurts.	*Transactive goal #2: Affirm the relationship in spite of the loss of the necklace.*
Amy: I know. I really don't want to put it all on you. I'm glad you understand, though. You know, John gave me that necklace.	Amy reaffirms transactive goal #2, making it mutual. She agrees to discuss, affirming the relationship as a new, additional goal.
Janice: Well, what can we do to get this solved? I feel awful.	Janice restates transactive goal #2 and offers transactive goal #3: *Find the necklace together without damaging the relationship.*
Amy: I'll hang up and we'll both go look everywhere and then report back.	Amy advances transactive goal #4: *Share the responsibility with a new plan of action.*
Janice: OK. And then we'll come up with something if we don't find it right away. Cross your fingers.	Janice accepts transactive goal #4 and advances transactive goal #5: *We will keep working until we solve this problem.*

We shift to negative goals when we can't "get what we want." It is when we get frustrated that we belittle, injure, or try to damage the other. This shift from the original topic or content goal to a negative relationship or identity goal characterizes the destructive conflict. In diagram form, the goal change occurs as follows:

1. You want a promotion:
    You ——————————→ Promotion

2. When you ask her for a promotion, your supervisor says, "No way. You aren't going to get a promotion as long as I'm the boss here. Your work has been substandard, not worthy of promotion." Your boss interferes with your original goal, and you begin to focus most of your attention on her interference and your attempts to gain power.

3. You then begin to lose sight of your original goal and spend energy trying to get even with the boss. You talk to people at home and at work about her, tell others how biased she is, spread rumors at work, and do other things to undercut her authority.

This example describes a typical pattern of goal shifting in a conflict. What began as a topic goal, getting a promotion, turns into a relational contest between the two of you—you shift from a positive topic goal to a negative relational goal.

Such shifts occur often and can be either spontaneous or strategic (Infante and Wigley 1986). Two business partners, for example, who begin by wanting to help each other earn sizable amounts of money, experience a misunderstanding over a contract and then spend the next two years trying to one-up each other during board meetings and to get others in the organization to side with them. The partnership begins to flounder as each member thinks the other is more trouble than he is worth.

One other type of goal shifting occurs in conflicts. Often, a person who is frustrated over the content of a conflict (the vote doesn't go your way; you can tell the outcome of the discussion will be unfavorable) will shift from content to process. Concerns about fair process, equal treatment, and other process issues often surface when one has not been successful at attaining a desired content goal. The teenager who launches an appeal to use the family car and is turned down may resort to arguing that "you listened to Steve, but you didn't let me tell you why I needed the car. You treated me unfairly." She is switching from the unsuccessful content attempt to a discussion of process. Similar process concerns arise in many conflicts after the participants realize their content goals have been thwarted.

A change in any type of conflict goal spills over to the other types of conflict goals. Often, as in previous examples, identity issues become intertwined with relational goals. When you feel powerless in relationship to another person, your sense of effectiveness or worthiness is challenged. Thus, identity goals rise in importance.

Conflict parties also *sacrifice content for relationship goals* or relationship goals for content. When the spouse never argues, avoids expressing any disagreement, and always says, "whatever you want, dear," he or she is sacrificing content goals in order to maintain the relationship. Acquiescing to others and never telling them what you really feel are types of content goal sacrifice. Alternatively, if you are intently set on your content goal (making money, negotiating the best possible contract, or always winning), you may be sacrificing the relationship in order to win the content. If you never consider the wishes of the other and always try to win, you are probably destroying valuable relationships in order to accomplish your goals.

In conclusion, conflict goals change over time. As one goal is frustrated, others assume more importance. You may not know which goals, topic, relational, identity, or process, are the most important, for they are in flux. Goals change during the transactions we have with others.

Retrospective Goals

Retrospective goals emerge after the conflict is over. People spend a large part of their time and energy justifying decisions they have made in the past. They need to explain to themselves and others why they made the choices they did. This process often happens with intimates who, for example, have an intense conflict over discipline of the children. After the first triggering comment, they may say, "Let's decide what's best for the children, not just what fits our own upbringing" (prospective goal). During subsequent conflicts over specific instances of discipline, they discuss everything from how the individual children react, to whether Mom and Dad should support each other's choices, even if they don't agree. If they decide that discipline is to be handled differently from the way it was in past episodes, Mom might say retrospectively, "I mainly wanted to see whether you would begin to share the discipline with me." Dad might say, "All along I was really trying to get you to see that you need to loosen up with the kids." Assuming that the couple comes up with a wise agreement they can follow in future episodes, the retrospective sense making helps them to define who they are and to make meaningful statements about the place of the conflict in their lives. Monday morning quarterbacking is important in ongoing relationships as well as in sports.

Since we do not know the implications of a conflict until we look back on it, retrospective goals give us clarity. Weick (1979) explains this sense-making process as the reverse from the usual way of looking at goals. He explains organizational behavior as "goal interpreted." People act in an orderly fashion, coordinating their behavior with each other, but with little notion of how this is accomplished until after the fact. Then they engage in retrospective meetings, conversations, paper writing, and speeches to explain why they did what they did. Talking about what happened after an important conflict is as important as talking about what will happen before a conflict episode. In these retrospective accounts, your prospective goals for the next episode are formulated. Thus, we learn from experience.

Retrospective sense making also serves the function of face saving. Visitors to the United States often comment on our lack of face-saving social rituals as compared to Japan, China, and other countries. Even if you have been involved in a competitive conflict and have won, rubbing it in or gloating over the loser will only serve to alienate and enrage the person, perhaps driving him or her to devious actions in retaliation. If you give respect to the person, even if you did not agree with the position, the person's "face" will be saved, and you will lay the groundwork for collaboration in the future. Following are some face-saving comments:

> Employer to job applicant: We looked very highly on you and your application. Our offer to Ms. Shepherd was based on her experience in our particular kind of operation. Even though you and I have been at odds for some time over organization of the new program, I want you to know that your new ideas are always sound and well organized. I just have different priorities.

> Mother to teenage daughter: I know you didn't want to cause us worry. You couldn't have known how upset we'd be that you were four hours late. But since you did not follow our agreement, we are grounding you for a week, as we said we would if the rule was not followed.

❧Goal Clarity

As noted above, how conflict parties formulate, alter, and explain their goals in a conflict determines to a large degree the success of the conflict experience. This section gives suggestions for better articulating and working with goals to improve your conflicts.

Clarify Your Goals

Goals that are unclear or hard to specify usually produce more conflict. One study demonstrated that in organizations, unclear and ambiguous goals produced more conflict between employees (Schnake and Cochran 1985). A careful specification of everyone's goals lets you decide which ones to abandon, which ones to trade, and which ones to maintain (Hermone 1974). Further, as Papa and Pood (1988) demonstrated, **goal clarity** before the conflictual interaction results in increased satisfaction with the discussion with the other party.

Sometimes, however, a discussion of goals in interpersonal conflict elicits the same avoidance reaction mentioned in earlier chapters: "I don't want to be manipulative. If I figure out what I want ahead of time, I'm being pushy and presumptuous—I'll let the chips fall where they may." However, all effective communication is goal directed (Phillips and Metzger 1976). This means that communication is purposive, not that it is manipulative, and that people communicate for reasons and to reach goals. Since no one can avoid being goal directed, especially in conflict communication, productive conflict management depends on parties' taking open responsibility for their goals. In other words, know what your goals are, state them clearly to yourself, and communicate them in a flexible manner to your conflict partners. Advantages of clarifying your goals follow:

1. *Solutions go unrecognized if you do not know what you want.* If parents are not clear about whether they want their 18-year-old to live at home or to board in the dorm at a local college, they will not know how to manage the conflict with the son who wants to live in the dorm but does not have a job. If saving money is the primary goal, the parents might allow the son to live in the dorm and get a job. If the parents have decided that they do not want him to live in the dorm under any circumstances, the son's offer to get a job may trigger a covert conflict that is unclear and unproductive for all parties.

2. *Only clear goals can be shared.* Since people cannot read your mind, you must clearly communicate your goals. An example of this kind of goal sharing occurred in an academic department. The chairperson complained that the faculty was not paying enough attention to university politics. He made several statements over a period of a week or so, urging more attendance at meetings, more discussion of long-term budget and curriculum plans, and voluntary participation in activities around campus. Since all this happened at the beginning of a semester, when the rest of the faculty were feeling busy, hassled by bureaucratic demands, and underappreciated, the response from the faculty was negative. A genuine conflict began to brew. Finally, the chairperson said, "Since keeping us involved in the university is my job, I feel really down when nobody supports what I'm doing. I need some feedback on what you think so I'm not just floundering around." Because he changed his goal statement from "Why don't you people work more?" to "I need support for what I'm doing," the conflict was reduced and productively managed.

3. *Clear goals can be altered more easily than vague goals.* One agency was embroiled in conflict over whether to fund and provide staff support for a new program to aid recently unemployed families. The three staff members who had been charged with setting up the new program did not know whether the agency director

wanted to support that particular new program or whether he wanted to demonstrate to the funding sources that the agency was committed to being responsive to families in general. When the director clarified that the specific program should serve an underserved population, the staff members altered their previous goals so that the new program would assist with community problems of child abuse that were receiving little funding at that time. The change in staff goals was possible because the larger goals were clarified for the staff members, along with their important role in reaching the goals.

4. *Clear goals are reached more often than unclear goals.* Having a map helps travelers reach a destination. Similarly, Raush et al. (1974) found that 66 percent of the conflicts in which the issue was clearly stated were successfully resolved, whereas only 18 percent of the conflicts in which the issue remained vague and nonspecific were resolved. For example, a couple is considering where to move after college. If they choose the first option, "We will stay in the same city no matter what," they will have made a significantly different choice than if they choose the second option, "We will both get the best jobs we can." Those with shared individual and relational destinations are more likely to arrive at some desired point together. Clarifying goals has one risky outcome: it may make seriously incompatible goals apparent. However, they will become apparent sooner or later. Additionally, when goals are "stated explicitly and directly there is control of escalation" (99). When one's goals are unclear, they often promote overreaction from the other person, who misjudges the nature of the conflict. We are remarkably poor at second-guessing the goals of our conflict partners.

Often people create difficulty by assuming that their goals cannot be attained—that the other party will stand in their way. How many times have you planned and schemed for days, only to find that others were perfectly willing to give you what you wanted? A friend was miserable because her children would not give her any free time on the weekends. She began to believe they did not respect her needs. Finally one night she said in tears, "If I don't have some time alone, I'll go crazy." The teenagers were glad to make plans to give her time with no responsibilities. She simply never had asked. Even if the goal is a difficult one, allotting time to accomplish a clear goal allows for its attainment (Neale and Bazerman 1985).

In conclusion, clarifying goals is a key step in conflict management. People assess the conflicts in which they participate by making decisions about which goals are worth pursuing. In common language, they get a "grip" on the situation before deciding how to proceed.

Estimate the Other's Goals

Once a destructive conflict begins spiraling, *all our behavior is* **reactive.** We make choices based on what we think the other is thinking and intending. While not as elaborate as chess moves, all conflicts share a structure similar to chess—knowing the other has "moves," you try to counter his or her moves. Our **estimate of the other's goals**—about "what the other wants"—propels our own choices.

When you talk to two parties to a dispute individually, you will be struck by their misjudgments of the other's goals. Here are some samples from real disputes:

Party #2 Estimate of #1's goals	Party #1 Goals
He wants to control me	I need some predictability
She is trying to fire me	I want to restructure the unit
He wants favored treatment	I want to be recognized
He doesn't value our input	This crisis demands action
She is getting ready to break up with me	I need just a little more space

One of the patterns in disputes is that as you get more convinced you *know* what the other wants, you are less accurate. Figure 3.9 demonstrates this relationship.

Becoming convinced we know absolutely what the other wants sets the stage for misinterpretation. As Sillars (2002) notes in his research on married couples in conflict, "I have been struck by how confident people seem to be when making very tenuous inferences about others" (8). One dramatic example comes from Catholics who were abused. They had this to say about their goals:

> Most survivors do not want to receive money from the church as compensation for what was done to us. Most of us merely want to ensure that our perpetrators are removed from being able to abuse others in their position as trusted priests. We'd like some apology for what we've endured. Sometimes we want an apology or acknowledgement given to our parents (Survivors 2004).

Now, of course, this doesn't mean that the legal system will respond to these goals. In American culture we often substitute money for other goals, since legally it is easier to do that and also pay for your lawyer.

In most personal conflicts where you have known the other for a long time, your inferences about the other are "well informed but also quite biased" (Sillars 2002, 2). We all assume we "know" someone well, but the research is quite clear that we don't! For one thing, when individuals are asked to report their thoughts during a video recall, only 5 to 7 percent of the time are they thinking about their partner's perspective (Sillars 2002).

Figure 3.9   Confidence and Accuracy about the Other's Goals

Confidence and accuracy about
the other's goals

Your confidence   Your accuracy

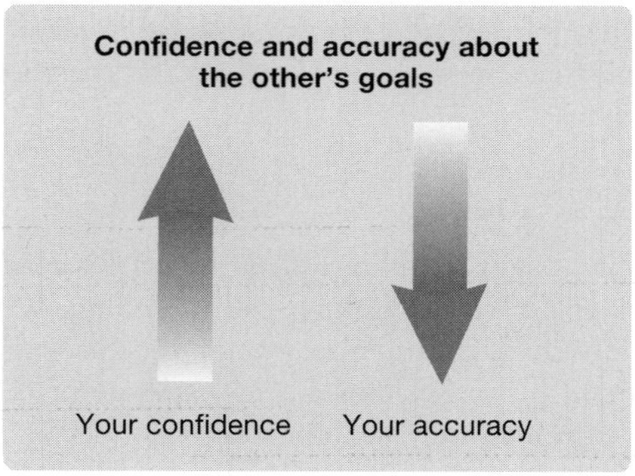

Further, while one person focuses on the topic (content), the other focuses on the relationship—they tend to see only their part of the TRIP issues and not the other person's.

Given that there is misunderstanding about the other, this by itself feeds negative conflict spirals and the descent into destructive conflict. In addition, however, *both parties feel misunderstood by the other.* They somehow know the other is misunderstanding their goals, and, in fact, feeling misunderstood then moves the conflict to a more destructive level. As you feel misunderstood, you will choose destructive conflict moves to get back at the other.

No wonder we get into such difficulties in conflict. We misunderstand the other, react to what we think he or she is intending, feel very confident in our assessments, and then justify our damaging moves.

No magic process untangles these intertwining misperceptions. Communication itself is fraught with difficulties, but one revolutionary thing to do is ask the other what he or she needs. Many years ago, Bill, one of the coauthors, had an ongoing struggle with a colleague. Finally, after many days of tug-of-war in meetings, Bill stomped into Wes's office and said (not in a good tone of voice), "Wes, what do you want?" Wes calmly replied, "For you and me to go to lunch." Bill, taken aback, said, "What are you saying? We are arguing about a tenure case." Wes said, "Well, that is what I want." So, against his better judgment, Bill went to lunch with Wes and survived it. Not only that, but their relationship began to slowly transform. What was driving the dispute from Wes's side was feeling that Bill didn't value him. They had lunch every three weeks from then on, and as a result, their conflicts subsided. Sometimes all you have to do is (1) ask and (2) listen!

Collaborative Goals

The best goals are clear, as explained previously, and help conflict interactants collaborate on resolving the conflict while protecting their ability to work, live, or interact with each other in important ways. The following statements characterize **collaborative goals** and may be used as a checklist for "good goals":

1. *Short-, medium-, and long-range issues are addressed.* Many times people engage too forcefully with others at the beginning of a conflict because they are afraid their ideas will not be heard. Collaborative goals build in ways for people to be involved in the process as it unfolds. To form collaborative goals, plan for evaluations along the way. Give as much attention to a few weeks or months from now as to "right now." Looking at longer-range goals helps de-escalate the importance of initial, prospective goals. One city council, meeting in a retreat, specified which goals, over a time line, were important to them. They set up a plan to specify who would do what by when and with what evaluation process. A year later, only those goals that had been broken down into a specific time line were achieved. Goals that are set up on a time line are less overwhelming than global goals such as "Let's change the way we get along as a family" or "I want more say about the financial structure of our family."

2. *Goals are behaviorally specific.* Doable goals (Phillips and Metzger 1976) can be checked. "I'll try to do better" might become a doable goal with specification; at present, it is a positive statement but not a collaborative goal. Terms used in

intimate relations are often more vague than statements in business relationships. A corporate vice president could not get away with telling the president, "I will try the best I can to remember to turn the monthly reports in on time," but intimates make such vague promises frequently. Specificity helps the parties know when a goal has been accomplished. The following examples illustrate how to make vague statements more specific:

- Instead of saying, "Please respect my things more," say, "I want you to ask me before you borrow any of my clothes. I'm usually glad to oblige, but I want you to ask me, all right?"

- Instead of saying, "Let's get this show on the road" (and then showing non-verbal impatience during a meeting), say, "I need to leave this meeting at 5:00 sharp."

- Instead of saying, "This time, young lady, you're going to listen to what I say!" a parent might say, "Last time we talked about your messy room I wasn't pleased with where we got. This time, I want you to listen to me, and I will listen to you, and then I want us to decide on what is reasonable. OK?"

3. *Statements orient toward the present and future.* The language of change uses what can be done now instead of what should have been done in the past. Hopeful statements instead of blaming statements set the expectation that agreements can indeed come about. A department head might say, "I want our program group to increase services to clients without increasing hours worked by our counselors," instead of, "We have got to be more efficient than we were last year."

4. *Goals recognize interdependence.* In all conflicts, tension arises between serving self-interest and serving the interests of the other party. In Western cultures we have overemphasized self relative to community interest, whereas Eastern cultures tend to focus on the interests of the group, or community (Dien 1982). Research consistently indicates, however, that when conflict parties operate with both concern for self and concern for others, the agreements that emerge serve the parties best (Tutzauer and Roloff 1988; Holloway and Brager 1985). This does not mean that you give in to the other; you can remain firm in achieving solutions that work for you while simultaneously seeking to please the other (Tutzauer and Roloff 1988). When one has low concern for the other coupled with a high demand for one's own goals, however, coercion and manipulation result (Kimmel et al. 1980). High concern for self and the other coupled with high demand that one's own goals remain important gives the parties an opportunity to develop creative, integrative solutions to the conflict.

5. *Collaborative goals recognize an ongoing process.* An overriding goal of constructive conflict is to remain committed to the process of constructive conflict. The particular content can be transcended by adhering to a collaborative process.

Fisher and Ury (1981) remind conflict managers that goal setting begins with the participation of all conflict parties. "Give them a stake in the outcome by making sure they participate in the process" (27). For collaborators, "the process is the product" (29).

The outcome of constructive conflict should be wise agreements on each of the TRIP interests. Wise agreements are fair and durable and take the interests of all parties into account (Fisher and Ury 1981, 4). The struggle for wise agreements is exemplified by a couple with children that goes to court for a divorce. The agreement should be representative of both sides; should be fair to all parties, including the children; should keep the couple out of court in the future; and should set up care for the children if they are too young to care for themselves. The process should be efficient, involve all parties' interests, and improve or at least not damage the relationship between the parties.

When conflict parties work together to clarify goals and specify what the conflict is and is not about, destructive conflicts subside. Collaboration is a high-energy alternative to avoidance, violence, coercion, frustration, despair, and other forms of destructiveness. Collaboration is not always possible, but when it is, destructive conflict is transformed into constructive problem solving.

The participants can come to see themselves as working side by side on a problem, attacking the problem instead of each other. The overarching process goal is "We, working together, can solve this problem that is confronting us." Part of the self-interest of conflict parties is preserving a workable relationship, focusing on the problem instead of each other. Relational preservation becomes a superordinate goal, as in the classic Sherif and Sherif (1956) study where groups of boys were placed in situations that aroused conflicts of interest between the two groups. The researchers then introduced a common enemy, thus stimulating the two groups to work together, which reduced their intergroup hostility. In interpersonal conflicts, long-term relational, process, and identity goals can reduce conflict over short-term topic goals.

❧Summary

As a conflict unfolds, topic, relational, identity, and process goals emerge (TRIP). Topic goals are the "objective," verifiable issues that people talk about. Relationship goals are those pertaining to the parties' influence on each other. Who gets to decide, how they treat one another, and other aspects of their communication are relationship goals. Identity, or face-saving, goals have to do with the needs of people to present themselves positively in interactions and to be treated with approval and respect. Process goals refer to parties' interests in how the interaction is conducted. Although most conflict parties center their discussions on content and process goals, the relationship and identity components fuel the feeling in a given conflict.

Goals change in the course of a conflict. Prospective goals are those identified before interacting with the other parties. Transactive goals emerge during the communication exchanges. Transactive goals often shift; a destructive conflict is characterized by a shift from original goals to a desire to harm the other party. Retrospective goals are identified after the conflict episodes have occurred. Unregulated, unplanned, fast-paced conflicts keep many people from understanding their goals until they later have time to reflect on the transactions.

Productive conflict management is enhanced by clarifying your goals, better estimating the other's goals, and working to build collaborative goals. Working against or without consulting the other party often sets destructive forces in motion that preclude integrative management of the conflict.

⌒Key Terms

types of goals 71
topic goals 72
relational goals 73
identity, or face-saving,
goals 77

process goals 82
prospective goals 91
transactive goals 91
retrospective goals 94
goal clarity 96

reactive behavior 97
estimating the other's
goals 97
collaborative goals 99

⌒Review Questions

1. Define the four types of goals (TRIP).
2. How do goals shift over time?
3. How do goals overlap and influence one another?
4. When do conflict parties shift their goals?
5. What does it mean to sacrifice one kind of goal for another?
6. What happens to goals in interactions with others?
7. What happens when we experience change in prospective goals?

8. Give an example of a transactive goal.
9. What are common identity themes?
10. How do retrospective goals change?
11. What does it mean to "specialize" in a type of goal?
12. What are the advantages of goal clarity?
13. Do conflict parties accurately estimate the other's goals?
14. What determines if goals are collaborative?

Chapter 4

Power: The Structure of Conflict

The stick, the carrot and the hug may all be necessary, but the greatest of these is the hug.
—Kenneth Boulding, *Three Faces of Power*

What Is Power?

Just as energy is a fundamental concept in physics, **power** is a fundamental concept in conflict theory. In interpersonal and all other conflicts, perceptions of power are at the heart of any analysis. Hundreds of definitions of power tend to fall into three camps. Power is seen as (1) *designated* (power given by your position), (2) *distributive* (either/or power), or (3) *integrative* (both/and power). *Designated* power comes from your position, such as being a manager, the mother or father of a family, or the leader of a team. Your power is conferred by the position you hold.

Distributive power comes from your ability to achieve your objective "over the resistance of another . . ." (Dahl 1957, p. 3). Distributive power focuses on power over or against the other party. For example, if you see dominance as the key to power, you see power as distributive. You would see the situation as either "I dominate you or you dominate me" (Burgoon, Johnson, and Koch 1998).

Integrative definitions of power highlight power *with* the other. Integrative views stress "joining forces with someone else to achieve mutually acceptable goals" (Lilly 1989, 281). Integrative definitions focus on "both/and"—both parties have to achieve something in the relationship. As we shall see, it is not what outsiders say about power, but the views the conflict parties have that determine the outcomes of their conflicts.

This chapter examines the role of power in conflict by examining common assumptions people have about power. We then further develop orientations to power, analyze currencies or resources that lead to power, and propose a relational theory of power. We conclude with ways to assess power, and give ideas about how to rebalance power so constructive conflict can take place. Sometimes all we can do in conflicts is keep the destruction from spiraling out of control, or negotiate an uneasy "balance of terror." Often, thankfully, alternatives to the top-down exercise of power emerge when people commit themselves to finding them. Constructive use of power solves problems, enhances relationships, and balances power, at least during interaction. When that happens, the hard work that goes into learning about conflict management is worth it!

Orientations to Power

Power is the ability to achieve a purpose. Whether . . . it is good or bad depends upon the purpose.
Dr. Martin Luther King, Jr.

In chapter 1, we outlined the lens model of conflict. You learned that your particular views of self, other, and relationship are the key ingredients in a conflict (along with the other's perceptions of these). When a dispute occurs between two people, they often talk about power, and their perspectives will predispose them to engage in certain communicative moves. People feel passionately about power—who has it, who ought to have more or less, how people misuse power, and how justified they feel in trying to gain more power for themselves. This orientation toward power seems to be true for many reasons.

We each need enough power to live the life we want. We want to influence events that matter to us. We want to have our voices heard, and make a difference. We want to protect ourselves against perceived harm. We want to hold in high esteem ourselves and those we care about. We do not want to be victimized, misused, or demeaned. No one can escape feeling the effects of power—whether we have too much or too little.

When people struggle with each other, they almost never agree on anything having to do with power. For example, if you are a student intern in a real estate firm and you feel that brokers have all the power, you are likely to keep silent even when you disagree—giving the impression that you agree when you don't. If, on the other hand, you feel that both you and the brokers have sources of power, you will be more likely to engage in discussion to work through issues. As an intern, you may have sources of power such as your close connection to others in the office, your ability to help the brokers do their jobs, and your knowledge of the real estate business you gained working last summer. If you think of yourself, however, as "just a lowly intern," you may miss many opportunities to be a team member because you have assessed your power incorrectly. We will discuss these issues later in this chapter.

You probably have an emotional response when you hear the word *power*. Kipnis notes, "Like love, we know that power exists, but we cannot agree on a description of it" (1976, 8). The following exercise will help you think about how you respond to the *idea* of power.

Application 4.1   Meaning of "Power"

Respond quickly to the word *power,* as you did with the word *conflict* in chapter 2. What comes to mind? The following are common associations: Mark the ones that fit for you, and add connotations of your own:

power play	power source	power corrupts
high powered	power behind the throne	devious
bullheaded	run over	authority
power politics	powerhouse	overpower
low powered	sneaky	strong-arm
bulldozed	powerful	influence

(continued)

Application 4.1   Meaning of "Power"

Discuss what you were taught about the use of power. List three explicit or implicit "learnings" about power from your personal history, then discuss these with your small group. Some examples from students include

"When people gang up on you, there's nothing to do but get away. You can't go up against a group."

"The most important kind of power is your own character."

"Stay connected to people in power; they can help you."

"Using power with those you care about is despicable."

"We don't talk about power. Power isn't nice."

"Your father/mother has the say around here. Don't cross him/her."

"It's safest to get in a coalition with someone older and stronger."

"I learned to gain power by manipulation, deception, sneaking, or lying."

"As a pretty young girl I learned to gain power by flirting and playing with boys and men."

John P. Kotter

Most of us, to be blunt, are remarkably naive when it comes to understanding power dynamics in complex organizations.

As reflected by this list, people have different views of power, some positive and some negative. One group of researchers (Cavanaugh et al. 1981a, 1981b; Goldberg, Cavanaugh, and Larson 1983) classified views of power. Using samples of salespeople, government employees, corporate executives, and law enforcement personnel, they concluded that the prime *orientations toward power* were varied. Some people viewed power as good—that the responsibility and challenge of power are exciting and that they would like to be powerful. Others saw power as instinctive—something we all possess innately. Still others saw power as consisting of valued resources, such as political skill; as a charismatic thing that people have within themselves; or as being reflected in control over others and autonomy of the self. We respond to conflict differently based, in part, on our different orientations to what power itself consists of, and whether it is a positive, negative, or benign characteristic.

Either/Or Power

Take a look at the list of words associated with power—most show an either/or association. You have power in order to move others against their will; it becomes a contest of the wills when you are in a "power struggle." When you examine typical newspaper stories about power, you read about the either/or (distributive) notions of power. In fact, it is difficult to even find examples of any other orientation toward power in the popular press. Many people think that power is only "force"—pushing others around against their will. When you read about nations using military might against other nations, you see **either/or power** in operation.

Once a relationship begins to go downhill, concerns with power increase. As any relationship deteriorates, the parties shift to a more overt focus on power—and this shift is reflected in their discourse (Beck 1988). In fact, a characteristic of destructive conflict is that parties start thinking and talking about power. Almost no one thinks that he or she has more power than the other, at least when emotions run very high. We think the other has more power, which then justifies dirty tricks and our own attempt to gain more power. We often see ourselves as blameless victims of the other's abuse of power. When partners are caught in this destructive cycle of either/or power, their communicative interactions show a lot of "one up" responses, or attempts to demonstrate conversational power over each other (Sabourin and Stamp 1995). Partners might say, "She is just trying to control me," or "I'm not going to let him push me around." People, whether married couples or work colleagues, try to "keep score"— watching the "points" they have vis-à-vis the other party (Ross and Holmberg 1992). When partners develop an overt concern with power, their struggles over power are directly related to relationship satisfaction (Kurdek 1994). Figure 4.1 demonstrates how concerns rank in a distressed relationship.

As Ury, Brett, and Goldberg (1988) so aptly note, the focus for a dispute becomes power—who has the right to move the other. The teenager who says, "You can't boss me around," the spouse who shouts, "Just who do you think you are?" and the co-worker who states, "Well, we'll see who the boss is around here!" are all highlighting power and giving it center stage in the dispute. These struggles often escalate. Dissatisfied couples are more than three times as likely to escalate episodes and focus on power than satisfied couples (Alberts and Driscoll 1992). Using the terms we developed in

: "boss"

Figure 4.1   Power Emphasized in a Distressed System

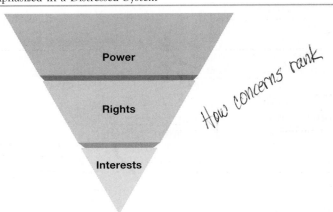

How concerns rank

Distressed system

Source: From William Ury, Jeanne M. Brett, and Stephen B. Goldberg, *Getting Disputes Resolved: Designing Systems to Cut the Costs of Conflict.* Copyright © 1988 Jossey-Bass Inc., Publishers, San Francisco, California. Reprinted by permission.

Figure 4.2 Power De-emphasized in an Effective System

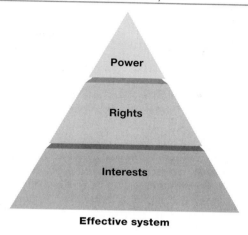

Effective system

Source: From William Ury, Jeanne M. Brett, and Stephen B. Goldberg, *Getting Disputes Resolved: Designing Systems to Cut the Costs of Conflict.* Copyright © 1988 Jossey-Bass Inc., Publishers, San Francisco, California. Reprinted by permission.

chapter 3, power becomes the overriding relationship concern. Getting more power becomes the overriding *relationship issue*. We are not suggesting that power shouldn't be an issue. Rather, we suggest that when power itself becomes the main focus of thinking and discussion, parties are likely to be involved in an escalating power struggle, and may well have temporarily lost sight of their original interests.

Notice in figure 4.1 that disputes also involve "rights" and "interests." Rights, similar to our idea of core concerns, include not being discriminated against, being free from physical harm, and other constitutional and legal guarantees we have as citizens. Sometimes it is more appropriate that disputes get settled on the basis of rights rather than power or interests. For example, if the famous *Brown v. Board of Education* case in 1954 outlawing segregation in public schools had been settled on the basis of power, it would have resulted in a struggle in the streets. If, on the other hand, it had been settled on the basis of interests, Brown might have negotiated her way into school, but the country's social policy would not have changed.

When we solve a dispute based on interests, the goals and desires of the parties are the key elements. For instance, if you don't want your teenage son to use the car, you can (1) tell him it is not OK as long as you pay the bills in the house (power); (2) let him know that you own the car (rights); or (3) let him know that you are dissatisfied with how he drives, and until you are convinced he will be safe, you will not lend the car (interests). Thus, disputes can occur on any one of the three levels. When power becomes the only personal goal, the dispute is harder to resolve.

Figure 4.2 illustrates an effective system in which the emphasis is on interests with rights and power playing smaller but still important roles. As you can see by comparing figure 4.1 with figure 4.2, an overemphasis on power is symptomatic of a distressed system.

Both/And Power

Rather than always seeing power as distributive, you can view it as "both/and." Boulding (1989) notes that "the great fallacy, especially of political thinking in regard to power, is to elevate threat power to the position of dominance" (10). Interpersonal relationships reflect the same fallacy—many people just can't envision power in terms other than "either/or," or "win/lose." Yet a study of the dynamics of successful disputes and ongoing relationships reveals that power functions on a broader basis than either/or thinking. Disputes become power struggles if the parties allow them to be defined as such. Conceptually, the alternative to framing disputes as power struggles is to place power in a position subordinate to rights and needs.

To help us understand the cultural basis of our assumptions, Augsburger (1992) details the lack of verbal fighting in some other cultures. In these cultures, power is activated as both/and or designated power, discussed in the next section. In Japanese and Javanese cultures, for instance, to name two obvious examples, harmony and cooperation are basic values, and verbal contradiction is not the automatic first choice in conflict. A more accepted process is to affirm the strengths of each other's position, let them stand without attack, and then join in exploring other options. Both parties search for superior options (59).

Both/and power is often the first choice of women in our culture. Researchers at the Jean Baker Miller Center at Wellesley have spent three decades explicating "relational theory" in an attempt to balance the traditional male orientation that permeates United States culture. In their view, relational theory is a belief system that describes how growth and effectiveness occur (Fletcher 1999). Masculine theories, which until the last 20 years or so have been accepted as the only psychologically sound theories, often assumed that maturity and competence depend on autonomy, or separation from constraints, other people, and group identity. Boys, for instance, learn to relate to power through games and competition more than girls do. Boys learn to be comfortable with the hierarchy of teams, captains, coaches, and bosses. Girls learn to play with less focus on hierarchy. Many girls' games are cooperative in nature, with girls taking roles to play out, after discussing together what to do. As Heim and Galant (1993) note, "There's no boss in dolls." For boys, conflict means competition, which often enhances relationships. For girls, competition is often painful and damages relationships. Girls often prefer to look for a win/win situation (Heim and Galant, 1993, 27).

Relational theory and practice offer the idea that maturity and competence depend on growth-in-connection and mutuality. The ability to develop relationally depends on mutual empathy, mutual empowerment, responsibility to both oneself and others, and the ability to experience and express emotion, to experience and learn from vulnerability, to participate in the development of another, and to enhance each other's efforts (Fletcher 1999; Jordan et al. 1991). This approach does not need to be seen strictly as a female approach. Weeks, for example, calls it "share positive power" (1992). Many effective forms of conflict resolution depend on a relational approach. Some situations in which power is heavily unbalanced also require a level of competition and assertiveness that does not come naturally for many women. If competition remains the dominant approach, however, constructive conflict resolution is unlikely to occur, except temporarily.

For instance, when people work in teams, a major skill required is the ability to use the kind of mutual power described above. Making the project work, moving toward mutual goals, and getting a new effort up and running require skills very different from those used with either/or power. Yet, this kind of mutuality often is not valued as much as the more masculine either/or power. Fletcher (1999) explains how relational work disappears in organizations since it is not categorized as "real work." For instance, preventing problems is not seen as being as important as solving problems in some work environments. Mothers who coordinate highly complex family activities sometimes are seen as "not working" because their efforts involve interaction among all the family members instead of major attention being given to their own schedules and needs. (Fletcher's (1999) research with engineering firms showed that in a culture of independence and self-promotion, which prizes individual achievement and winning at competition—coming out on top—voluntarily helping others was seen as naïve and powerless (95). The following case illustrates the difference between either/or and both/and power.

*[handwritten margin note: wow * Voluntarily helping others—seen as naïve & powerless]*

Application 4.2   **The Case of Lynn and Daniel**

Lynn and Daniel are a married couple in their 30s. Daniel is employed as a smoke jumper supervisor. This work requires him to be ready literally at a moment's notice to get in a plane and direct safety activities for firefighters from various regions when a fire breaks out. Lynn and Daniel have two small children, ages two and four. They have decided that for now, the family needs are best served by Lynn's being the primary parent, and taking care of the children, especially since Daniel is sometimes gone for weeks during fire season. Here's where the problem comes in. Daniel was raised in a family in which the person making the money had the power. He believes that since Lynn is not making much money (she works part-time as a piano teacher), she should not make major purchases without his permission. He expects Lynn to pay the necessary bills, but to ask him for money, when she needs it, for household expenses. Lynn is angry and sometimes feels defeated since, in her view, Daniel does not know the needs of the household. She thinks she should be able to make expenditures as she sees fit. When she wants to plan a trip, or buy something out of the ordinary, Daniel says, "Make the money, then. I'm working as hard as I can." Lynn believes that Daniel completely devalues her work at home.

How Might Lynn and Daniel Talk About Their Conflict?

What Lynn Feels and Thinks Lynn feels furious some of the time; she often feels misunderstood and devalued. She sees herself as extremely careful with household expenses. She shops when needed items are on sale, watches for good grocery values, and buys the kids' clothes at consignment shops. She swaps clothes and toys with other mothers of young children. Lynn often feels competent and powerful in her role. She loves her children, is glad to be home with them, and experiences her mothering as a chosen job. Truth be told, she is often glad when Daniel is gone on a fire, because she can make decisions without "going through Daniel." She loves Daniel, but is often angry with him, and feels sad because her affection diminishes when they fight.

Lynn grew up in a family in which money was always very tight, and she is proud of her skills at stretching a small budget. Her mother did the same kind of good job that

Lynn does, and her father appreciated her efforts. Her father worked as the manager of a small town store, so he was present in the home and often complimented Lynn's Mom on her homemaking skills.

Lynn has a college degree in communication with a minor in child development. She is upset that she and Daniel have not been able to solve their chronic, ongoing conflict about expenses. Lynn now sees Daniel as "just wanting to have all the power" and lording it over her since she doesn't make money. Lynn sees herself as making money by saving the family money.

Then a trigger event arises. Daniel is gone for six weeks on a major fire. During that time, Lynn's mother develops breast cancer. Daniel is out of cell phone contact much of the time. Lynn decides to fly herself and the kids to the Midwest to be with her mother for the period when Mom is deciding what kind of treatment to pursue. Lynn puts the tickets on their credit card.

"Nothing is more important than being with my family at this time," Lynn thinks. "Daniel will be upset, but he has to understand my values. I'll let him know how important this is to me and Mom. She hasn't seen the kids in over a year and it's the right thing to do."

What Daniel Thinks and Feels Daniel agrees that it is important for Lynn to be home with the young kids. He agrees that she should go to graduate school, if she wants to, when the kids are in school. He loves Lynn and feels fortunate to have found her. He thinks she is an excellent mother. Daniel is very concerned about his job. His major concern is his safety, and the safety of his crew. He has to make very tough judgment calls that affect their safety. He has a degree in forestry and resource management. While he has had a chance to move out of active firefighting, since he trains and supervises during non–fire seasons, he likes the challenge of making good judgment calls. He is popular with his crew. They trust him and like working on his crew, because he is skilled and fair. He is a quick thinker, a no-nonsense leader, who nevertheless feels his responsibilities deeply.

At home, Daniel loves to be a father to his kids. He misses them when he is gone, as he misses Lynn. Daniel worries about money since he is, for now, the sole earner. His ability to earn extra money depends on his hardship pay, which means being gone for more than a few days. His father and mother argued about money. His father made most of the money, while his mother worked part-time while raising five children. His father was a school administrator who was an alcoholic, although most of the people in their community did not know it. He was occasionally abusive to the kids, and demeaning to their mother. Daniel made a decision when he first left home never to be abusive, as his father was. He has made his own peace with his father, who admires Daniel's work. He is close to his mother.

Daniel thinks he and Lynn are doing a good job of raising their children and getting along as young parents. However, Daniel becomes angry when Lynn spends more than a budgeted amount of money without checking with him. He does not see it as "Lynn has to ask me." Rather, he feels it is a matter of respect. He is not interested in what he considers "frills," and disagrees with Lynn's choices about some of the ways to spend money, especially on trips, vacations, and family visits. He thinks those expenditures can wait until they are both working. He has not seen his parents and younger siblings in three years; they communicate infrequently, although he calls his mother often when he comes back from a fire since she worries about him.

When Daniel was able to call Lynn he found out that she was leaving the next day to see her mother. He was furious and told Lynn he wanted her to cancel her plans.

The Communication Possibilities Lynn and Daniel will not be able to see each other for at least two weeks. They have never been more at odds with each other in their eight-year marriage.

Here are some **ineffective** ways for Lynn to begin resolving their conflict.

Lynn's Ineffective Communication Strategies

- "We may not have the money in the bank, but that's what emergency credit cards are for. We can deal with the expenses later."
- "You cannot tell me when to see my own mother when she is scared and sick."
- "Sure. You couldn't possibly understand a normal relationship with a parent, given how sick your family is."
- "If you try to stop me, I'll go any way and maybe I won't come home."
- "My Dad sent the money." (This is not true. She thinks she'll deal with the problem later.)
- "You are breaking my heart. I'll never, forgive you."
- "I've already told the kids we are going to see Grandma."
- "You can't possibly understand how I feel."

Daniel's Ineffective Communication Strategies

- "You do not have the right to make this decision without me."
- "You care nothing for how hard I am working. It will take a year to pay off this trip."
- "Can't you talk to her on the phone every day?"
- "Leave the kids with your friend. She owes you some babysitting time."
- "You are being unreasonable. Wait until you know what is going to happen, then maybe we can work out a trip."
- "Don't you care what I think? Is this all up to you?"
- "You have no sense of what the limits are to what I make. If you want to go, get a part-time job."

In small groups, (1) identify what's wrong with these approaches; (2) specify ways that might work to open up communication. Role play some of the best ideas you have learned so far, without "caving in." Lynn and Daniel both have reasons for their opinions and feelings. Identify your biases, and use the best communication skills you can—without abandoning the issues and concerns under this power struggle. The class should give feedback on how realistically the "Lynn team" and "Daniel team" play their roles. During the role play, class members can come up and give new suggestions about what might work. Remember that Lynn and Daniel are interdependent; they love each other, and a lot is at stake.

Designated Power

The third kind of power is **designated power,** giving *power* to some other group or entity. In earlier editions of this book, we referred to this kind of power as being similar to a "relational savings account." People place "power" into an "account" that they can then draw on when their individual reserves are not sufficient to solve a problem. Many examples of designated power can be noted. As citizens, we delegate power to law enforcement officers, elected politicians, heads of regulatory agencies, teachers, administrators, and even employers. We do not assume that we have or should use our independence without restraints in our civil society. At work, by agreeing to work in a retail outlet, agency, or other organization, we delegate power to others. For instance, someone else may be in charge of your schedule, place of work, tasks, and pay. Yet, you are not powerless, since the employer needs your services and, we hope, wants to create a productive work environment. Even though power is inherently unbalanced in an employer–employee dyad, the low-power person has delegated personal power to the employer. They still maintain interdependence. In a couple situation such as the case of Lynn and Daniel above, the couple could designate power to "the needs of the family," which both would then define. In a marriage, threat power works poorly, since threats build resentment and distance. When people designate power to a greater entity, they are giving up power over, or distributive power, for the larger good of the interdependent relationship.

Application 4.3	Types of Power

List as many kinds of designated power (*"power to"*) relationships as you can. Think of educational, family, couple, work, friend, and recreation contexts. See if you can think of several *either/or* power relationships that could be improved by being made a *"power to"* relationship. Not all distributive power relationships can be changed in this way; we are, however, urging you to think creatively at this point. Many of the later conflict resolution strategies in this book depend on creative thinking about power.

Power Denial

Some people are so "antagonized by any discussion of power" (Madanes 1981, 217) that they may deny that power and influence are appropriate topics for discussion and say that control is not part of our interpersonal patterns. One student wrote that in her relationship with her boyfriend, "No one has to have power—we just listen to each other, try to respond with love, and always put the relationship and each other first." She seemed to think that acknowledging any use of power would destroy her perfect relationship with her boyfriend.

Many people view power as negative and find "explicit references to power . . . in bad taste" (Kipnis 1976, 2). Cahill (1982), conducting research on married couples, encountered this view when he interviewed them about their relationships. When he asked them about decision making, persuasive techniques, and disagreements, the discussion flowed smoothly. But when he asked about their relative amounts of power, he encountered long silences, halting answers, obvious embarrassment, and reluctance to speak of the topic. Similarly, McClelland (1969) noted that when people were told they had high drives to achieve or affiliate, they derived great satisfaction from the feedback, but people who were told they had a high drive for power experienced guilt.

In its extreme form, reluctance to talk about power emerges as **power denial.** Haley (1959) listed four common attempts people use to deny that they exercise power. These four forms of denial are presented in the following box.

Denying Power Use

1. Deny that you communicated something.
2. Deny that something was communicated.
3. Deny that you communicated something to the other person.
4. Deny the situation in which it was communicated.

The speaker can deny *he or she is communicating* by using a number of common ploys, such as saying, "I'm not myself when I drink," or "It's just the pressure I'm under that's making me act like such a grouch." You may hear the claim "I can't help it. I told you I was jealous. I'm not responsible for what I said." To say that you are not responsible for your communication lets you exercise control (if others accept your claim) while denying that you are doing so.

Denying that a *message was communicated* is another way to ignore the existence of power. The simplest way to deny communication is to say, "I did not say that." Since this kind of denial usually gets you in trouble after a while, another form develops, such as, "I forgot I said that. Did I really say that? I didn't mean to." For example, a supervisor might consistently forget to include the new members of a staff in the e-mail lists. As a result, the newer, less powerful members are often late for meetings or miss them totally, having to reschedule other meetings at the last minute. When confronted by those left out, the supervisor said, "Oh, my administrative aide is responsible for scheduling meetings."

Denying that a message was communicated *to a particular person* is another way of expressing discomfort with the exercise of power. For example, a salesperson rings the doorbell of an apartment complex, and the following dialogue ensues:

Salesperson: Hello, I'd like to take this opportunity . . .

Apartment dweller: People are bothering me too much! Oh, I'm not talking about you. It's just that everyone bugs me day in and day out. I get no peace of mind. I wish the world would calm down and leave me alone.

Salesperson: Maybe I can see you another time. I'm sorry I bothered you . . .

The person who was bothered is exercising considerable control in the communicative transaction and also denying that the remarks are not meant for that particular salesperson. Another common way of denying that your comments were addressed to the other person is to claim that you were "just thinking out loud" and did not mean to imply anything toward the other person. For instance, a boss might say, muttering under his or her breath, "If I could count on people . . ." Then when a subordinate asks what is wrong, the boss might say, "What? Oh, nothing—just a hard day."

The last way to deny communicative power attempts is to _deny that what has been said applies to this situation._ Saying, "I'm used to being treated unfairly by others; I probably always will be" denies the clear implication that you feel the other is treating you in a demeaning manner. One employee left work without notifying her supervisor. She had been working extra hours in order to finish a report due to their funding agency. As she left, she was heard to say, "Let's just see how everyone can get along without my help since they seem to ignore my suggestions." When her supervisor confronted the employee on the overheard statement, she said, "Oh, I was just under stress from working all weekend. I didn't mean anything about the rest of the team. They're doing the best they can." The employee who left denied that she used her power to withhold her expertise under deadline pressure. She also denied the importance of what she said.

All of the preceding examples are ways that people can deny exercising power in a relationship when, in fact, they really are exercising power. Whenever you communicate with another, what you say and do exercises some communicative control—you either go along with someone else's definition of the conflict, struggle over the definition, or supply it yourself. Even if you would rather be seen as a person who does not exert power, you exercise influence on how the conflict interaction is going to be defined.

We have noticed that people who hold high power positions are particularly prone to denying that they have or use power. We now say to directors, presidents, CFOs, doctors, teachers, managers, and some parents, "You have more power than you think. You may not see yourself that way, but here are some of the communication consequences of being in your position:

- You don't know what people don't want you to know.
- You hear about one-tenth of the "grapevine" information.
- People are more cautious/afraid/nervous/withholding than you think they are.
- The "Open Door Policy" that you talk about is not effective.
- People want to please you.
- Your supervisees cover up what they don't know.
- Your team may express agreement and approval of your ideas, then talk among themselves about problems with your ideas.

People in high power positions must take specific communication steps to address the natural outcomes of unequal power. The most common ineffective message we see in organizations is one sent by e-mail, to "everyone," which invites people to come talk when there is a problem. More effective ways to balance power can be used. We will write about this later in the chapter. For now, remember, if you are in a position of designated leadership or organizational power, the communication around you changes. Lower power people cannot balance the power without the help of the higher power people.

The fact that power is central to the study of conflict does not mean that people are always sneaky and try to get power illegitimately. Rather, the productive exercise of personal power is crucial to your self-concept. Without some exercise of power in your interpersonal relationships, you would soon feel worthless as a person. As you read this chapter, do a "power profile" of your own behavior—the way you really communicate, not just the way you might want to be seen. Sometimes there is a difference! Remember that just as one cannot not communicate (Watzlawick, Beavin, and Jackson 1967), one does not have the option of not using power. We only have options about whether to use power destructively or productively for ourselves and relationships.

✧A Relational Theory of Power

A common perception is that power is an attribute of a person. If you say, "Lynn is a powerful person," you may, if she is your friend, be referring to such attributes as verbal facility, intelligence, compassion, warmth, and understanding. Or you may refer to a politician as powerful, alluding to her ability to make deals, call in favors, remember names and faces, and understand complex economic issues. In interpersonal relationships, however, a **relational theory of power** explains status more effectively. Excluding situations of unequal physical power and use of violence, power is a property of the social relationship rather than a quality of the individual. Lynn, for instance, has power with her friends because she has qualities they value. When she suggests something to do, like going on an annual women's backpacking trip, her friends try to clear their calendars because they like her, have fun with her, and feel understood by her. Lynn has a way of making a group feel cohesive and at ease. But if an acquaintance hated backpacking, did not like some of the other people going on the trip, and was irritated at Lynn because of a misunderstanding that had not yet been cleared up, Lynn's power with the irritated acquaintance would lessen considerably.

Power is not owned by an individual but is a *product of the communication relationship* in which certain qualities become important and valuable to others (King 1987; Rogers 1974; Harsanyi 1962; Deutsch 1958; Dahl 1957; Soloman 1960). Deutsch (1973) states the case well: "Power is a relational concept; it does not reside in the individual but rather in the relationship of the person to his environment. Thus, the power of an agent in a given situation is determined by the characteristics of the situation" (15). Rather than residing in people, "power is always interpersonal" (May 1972, 23). In the strictest sense, except when violence and physical coercion are used, power is given from one party to another in a conflict. Power can be taken away when the situation changes. Power dynamics are fluid, changing, and dependent on the specific situation. Each person in a conflict has some degree of power, though one party may have more compared to the other, and the power can shift during a conflict.

Power is based on one's dependence on resources or currencies that another person controls, or seems to "possess." Emerson (1962) specified that a person's power is directly tied to the nature of the relationship. In terms of two people, A and B, person A has power over person B to the extent that B is dependent on A for goal attainment. Likewise, person B has power over person A to the extent that A is dependent on B. The following box expresses this simple formula.

$$PAB = DBA$$

(the power of A over B is equal to the dependence that B has on A), and

$$PBA = DAB$$

(the power of B over A is equal to the dependence that A has on B).

Your dependence on another person is a function of (1) the importance of the goals the other can influence and (2) the availability of other avenues for you to accomplish what you want. As Emerson (1962) states, "The dependence of Actor B upon Actor A is directly proportional to B's motivational investment in goals mediated by A, and inversely proportional to the availability of those goals to B outside of the A-B relation" (31). In a mutually beneficial relationship, power is not fixed, but shifts as each becomes dependent in a positive way on the resources the other person may offer. This process builds a relationship and takes time to accomplish (Donohue and Kolt 1992).

Defining Interpersonal Power

Building on the ideas of power, dependence, and resource control, we offer this definition of interpersonal power:

> Interpersonal power is the ability to influence a relational partner in any context because you control, or at least the partner perceives that you control, resources that the partner needs, values, desires, or fears. Interpersonal power also includes the ability to resist the influence attempts of a partner. (Thanks to Mike Monsour, University of Colorado, for this classroom-tested definition.)

When we write about power in relationships, this is the kind of power we mean. Often, it's difficult to hold on to the idea of interpersonal power. Under stress, we go back to "she has power because she has a supportive family," or "I have power because I don't care" (when the person really does care). Of course it is true that certain areas of expertise can bring power. Some people may be valued by others because of excellent cooking skills, or because they have taken an Emergency First Responder course, or because they know their way around a large city. However, if their conflict partners do not value these areas of expertise, they do not have power because of the expertise. Power in relationships depends on control of resources that are valued by a partner.

Many conflicts go awry because one person believes that their own expertise in, for instance, childrearing, Spanish, or map-reading gives them power in certain situations. And it may. Take this situation as a negative example. A group of women friends visited Costa Rica. One of the leaders spoke Spanish. She developed a good conversational relationship with several local guides who wanted to take the women on a zip-line tour of the tropical canopy. However, when the women saw the height of the platforms, and the length of the zip-lines, they opted out. No matter how hard the leader tried to convince the women that the guides thought the activity was perfectly safe, translating the Spanish with great skill, the group had already made up their minds—reassurance or no reassurance, they were not climbing to those platforms.

Increasing another's dependencies on you can be constructive or destructive. In the following case, we see an example of mutual dependence at the beginning of the case, but in the end, a destructive outcome based on too much dependence that was not worked out to the parties' mutual satisfaction.

Application 4.4   Power Play

In a medical clinic in a rural town, a conflict over flextime had been brewing for several months. Many of the staff wanted the option of flexible time. The doctor in charge of the clinic traveled frequently since she often had to give presentations elsewhere. The administrative assistant especially wanted the option of flexible time. She was unhappy with the way the office policies were set up, believing them to be unfairly weighted toward professional staff and against hourly employees. When the assistant had problems with child care or needed to go to an appointment, she was not allowed to leave if the director was gone. The physician in charge also was a working mother, but she was able to work out her own schedule. The administrative assistant used tactics that a person stuck in a low-power position would typically use—calling in sick, forgetting, making mistakes, losing files, promising and then not following through, and complaining to other staff members. The director had begun a process of documenting her poor work. When the doctor went to a professional meeting in another state, she discovered that no hotel reservations had been made, the conference fee had not been paid, and the materials for her presentation to the conference had not arrived. When the doctor arrived back at the office, ready to fire the assistant, she found that the assistant had resigned without notice.

Destructive way of trying to balance power

In "Power Play," a seemingly unequal power situation was suddenly balanced by the resignation of the assistant—a classic "got you now" move on the part of the low-power person. Each of the participants in this conflict attempted to exercise power. When the administrative assistant assured the physician that she would take care of the arrangements for the conference and then did not, she destructively increased (temporarily) the doctor's dependence on her. If the physician had rethought the flexible-time needs of the office staff and then given desired resources (flexible time off), this change would have been an example of constructively increasing dependencies.

One way to reduce power others have over you is to change your goals. If after a few years in a job a person is not valued by an organization, a change of goals is likely to occur. The disenchanted employee might remark, "It is not important to me what they pay me for this job. I'll just do the minimal amount of work and expend all my creative energy on my hobbies." By altering the importance of the goal, you reduce the power the other has over you. The often-heard remark "There are other fish in the sea," used when a person has been dropped in a love affair, is just another way of saying that you have alternative sources for accomplishing your goals. (Or at least you hope you do, and you want other people to think you do!)

"other fish in the sea"

Communication plays a very important role in working out interdependence. People try to persuade others that they are valuable, that they need to be connected, and that the other's needs can be met best in a constructive relationship with the person doing the persuading. Communicating about the value you offer another is one way of increasing your power; the other becomes more dependent on you, and thus you have more power in that relationship. For example, recently Cheryl moved to a new state, and she immediately began going out with Jon, who had lived there for a long time. Jon took Cheryl on trips, introduced her to his wide circle of friends,

Communication— Interdependence

and introduced her to cross-country skiing, rafting, and rock climbing. When Cheryl became disenchanted with Jon and made one attempt to break up with him, he reminded her of all the plans they had made for the future, and that he was going to include her on a big rafting trip Cheryl wanted to do. Jon was attempting to persuade Cheryl of the importance of what he provided her—he tried to influence her perception of his positive power. Unfortunately for Jon, Cheryl was unhappy enough that she had already investigated other ways to raft and climb, and decided a mediocre relationship was not what she wanted. His influence attempt failed, and they broke up.

Individual Power Currencies

You may have had the experience of traveling in a foreign country and trying to adapt to the use of different currencies. Drachmas, used in Greece, are worthless in India, where rupees are used to buy items of value. A pocketful of rupees is worthless in France unless you exchange it for the local currency. Just as money depends on the context in which it is to be spent (the country), your **power currencies** depend on how much your particular resources are valued by the other persons in *a relationship context.* You may have a vast amount of expertise in the rules of basketball, but if your fraternity needs an intramural football coach, you will not be valued as much as you would be if they needed a basketball coach. Power depends on having currencies *that other people need.* In the same manner, if other people possess currencies you value, such as the ability to edit your term paper or give you a ride, they potentially maintain some degree of power over you in your relationships with them. Conflict is often confusing because people try to spend a currency that is not valued in a particular relationship.

Power currencies are classified in many different ways by researchers. Raven and French (1956) label the bases of power as reward, coercive, legitimate, referent, and expert. Kipnis (1976) maintains that influential tactics are best classified as threats and promises, persuasion, reinforcement control, and information control. May (1972) notes five types of power: exploitative, manipulative, competitive, nutrient, and integrative. Folger, Poole, and Stutman (1993) supply this list: special skills and abilities, expertise about the task, personal attractiveness and likability, control over rewards and/or punishments, formal position in a group, loyal allies, persuasive skills, and control over critical group possessions. Regardless of the various labels, everyone has potential currencies that may be used to balance or gain power in a relationship. Even when you devalue your own currency, a careful analysis can show you areas of wealth. The following box presents a list of general interpersonal power currencies.

The acronym *RICE* will help you recall the power currencies.

R

Resource control: Often comes with one's formal position in an organization or group. An example is the controlling of rewards or punishments such as salary, number of hours worked, or firing. Parents control resources such as money, freedom, cars, and privacy for teenagers.

(continued)

I

Interpersonal linkages: Your position in the larger system, such as being central to the communication exchange. If you are a liaison person between two factions, serve as a bridge between two groups that would otherwise not have information about each other, or have a network of friends who like each other, you have linkage currencies.

C

Communication skills: Conversational skills, persuasive ability, listening skills, group leadership skills, the ability to communicate caring and warmth, and the ability to form close bonds with others all contribute to interpersonal power. All people need to be related to others, to matter to others, and to be understood by others. Those who communicate well gain value and thus interpersonal power.

E

Expertise: Special knowledge, skills, and talents that are useful for the task at hand. Being an expert in a content area such as budget analysis, a process area such as decision-making methods, or a relational area such as decoding nonverbal cues may give you power when others need your expertise.

Resource control often results from attaining a formal position that brings resources to you. The president of the United States, regardless of personal qualities, will always have resources that go along with the job. Leadership and position, by their very nature, place a person in a situation in which others are dependent upon him or her, thus bringing ready-made power. Whatever your position—secretary, boss, chairperson, teacher, manager, or volunteer—you will be in a position to control resources that others desire. Many resources are economic in nature, such as money, gifts, and material possessions. *Economic* Many people try to be close and supportive to those around them by buying gifts. They trade on economic currencies in order to obtain intimacy currencies from others. Their gifts are not always valued enough to bring them what they want, however. As Blau (1964) writes, "A person who gives others valuable gifts or renders them important services makes a claim for superior status by obligating them to himself" (108). People with little money usually have limited access to these forms of power. College graduates who cannot find jobs must remain financially dependent on parents, thus limiting independence on both sides. Elderly people whose savings shrink due to inflation lose power; mothers with children and no means of support lose most of their choices about independence, thus losing most of their potential power. Economic currencies are not the only important type of power currency, but they operate in personal conflicts as well as in larger social conflicts.

Economic—NOT the only important kind of power currency— but do operate micro-mezzo-macro

Another cluster of power currencies comes from one's *interpersonal linkages*, a set of currencies that depend on your interpersonal contacts and network of friends and supporters. People often obtain power based on whom they know and with whom they associate. For instance, if you have a good friend who has a mountain cabin you can

Linkages

share with others, then you have attained some power (if your family or friends want to go to the cabin) because of your ability to obtain things through other people. Young children try to trade on their linkage currencies when they say such things as "My Aunt Kate is a park ranger, and she will give us a tour of the park."

Interpersonal linkages help one attain power through coalition formation. Whenever you band together with another (such as a good friend) to gain some sense of strength, this coalition can be a form of power (Van de Vliert 1981). The small boy who says, "You better not hit me, because if you do, my big sister will beat you up" understands the potential value of coalitions. Similarly, Jason, a four-year-old boy, invented a friendly ghost, Karsha, who would come and help him in times of difficulty. After one particularly trying day with his younger sister (who was two years old), Jason recited to his father the virtues of Karsha. Karsha was "bigger than a mountain, a giant, who comes in the mornings and kills spiders with his hands. Karsha also makes electricity and has long hair. And Karsha is mean to babies that bite little boys." Interpersonal linkages are a source of power when people check out their network for what classes to take, where jobs might be available, where rentals might be found, and other kinds of information. "Who you know" is often a source of power.

One's *communication skills* also serve as potential power currencies. If you can lead a group in a decision-making process, speak persuasively, write a news release for your organization, serve as an informal mediator between people who are angry with each other, or use tact in asking for what you want, you will gain power because of your communication skills. Many times, students who have developed their communication skills are sought by employers because of their skills. Likewise, if you can facilitate the social process of a group, serve as the fun-loving joker in the family, or get conversations started at work, others typically will value you. It is not only the qualities, per se, that bring power but that these currencies are valued by others.

Communication skills also include the ability to form bonds with others through love, sex, caring, nurturing, understanding, empathic listening, warmth, attention, and other characteristics of intimate relationships. If a father provides genuine warmth and understanding to his teenage daughter who is going through a tough time at school, his support is a currency for him in their father–daughter relationship. Some people draw others to them because they listen attentively, remember what is important to others, and ask questions that show the importance of the others. These qualities should not be viewed as manipulative because if one's words and actions are not sincere, the phony quality of the communication becomes evident and power is not enhanced. Conflict management skills depend on a thorough grounding in communication skills. One cannot become an effective conflict manager without excellent interpersonal communication skills. These skills provide a positive base for the exercise of power with others, or relational power.

Expertise currencies are involved when a person has some special skill or knowledge that someone else values. The worker who is the only one who can operate the boiler at a large lumber mill has power because the expertise is badly needed. The medical doctor who specializes in a particular area has expertise power because her information and skills are needed by others. Almost all professions develop specialized expertise valued by others, which serves as a basis of power for people in the profession. Family members develop expertise in certain areas that others within the family come to depend on, such as cooking, repairing the car, or babysitting.

We limit our own power by developing some currencies at the expense of others. For example, women have traditionally been most comfortable providing more warmth and affection than men do (Johnson 1976). If this particular communication skill is developed at the expense of the ability to clarify a group discussion, a woman unnecessarily limits her power potential. The person who trades on currencies of interpersonal linkages, such as access to the boss, may neglect the development of expertise. The person who gains power by controlling resources, such as money or sex, may neglect the development of communication skills, resulting in a relationship based on coercive instead of shared power; withdrawing warmth in intimate relationships too often substitutes for good communication skills. A worker who focuses on the development of expertise in computer programming and systems analysis may ignore the power that can be developed through interpersonal linkages, thus furthering a tendency toward isolation in the organization. The most effective conflict participant develops several forms of power currencies and knows when to activate the different forms of power. A repertoire of currencies is a better base for sharing power than exclusive reliance on one form of power, which too often leads to misuse of that power.

Clarifying the currencies available to you and the other parties in a conflict helps in the conflict analysis. People are often unaware of their own sources of productive power, just as they do not understand their own dependence on others. Desperation and low-power tactics often arise from the feeling that one has no choice, that no power is available. Analyze your power currencies when you find yourself saying, "I have no choice." Usually, you are overlooking potential sources of power.

Application 4.5   My Sources of Power

Think of a particular relationship in which there is conflict, strain, or the potential for struggle. List your own sources of power, using the *RICE* acronym explained above. Then list sources of power that the other person has in this particular relationship. Are there any that you (1) might be overlooking or (2) have under- or overdeveloped? What did you learn from looking at your own and the other's sources of power?

Assessing Your Relational Power

Since power is a dynamic product of shifting relationships, the amount of power parties have at any one time cannot be measured precisely. One maxim to remember when you are in the middle of a conflict is this: "*Each person firmly believes that the other person has more power.*" Many of the pathologies or misuses of power arise because the image people have of their power (and others') is unrealistic (Boulding 1989, 65). Because each person in the conflict so often believes that he or she is in the low-power position, the conflict escalates. People use devious and manipulative tactics, since they truly think they have no choice. This **perception of power** is almost always inaccurate. In this section, ways of assessing power more accurately are presented. Remember that in emotionally involving conflicts, we usually feel out of power. Therefore, feelings are not the only, or even a very accurate, guide. *Feeling* out of power may not mean you have no currency.

What might be a better way to assess the various power issues when your emotions are involved? Thinking about power, with the use of concepts and assessment instruments, can help engage your objectivity instead of subjective feelings only. As you think through what is happening, what has happened in the past, and what you would like to have happen in future interactions, you can gain a healthy distance on a current conflict.

The most common way to measure power is to compare the relative resources of the parties in a conflict (Berger 1980; Galvin and Brommel 1982; McCall 1979). For instance, in organizational work, it is generally agreed that power accrues to "those departments that are most instrumental in bringing in or providing resources which are highly valued by the total organization" (McCall 1979).

People have power in the organization when they

- are in a position to deal with important problems;
- have control over significant resources valued by others;
- are lucky or skilled enough to bring problems and resources together at the same time;
- are centrally connected in the work flow of the organization;
- are not easily replaced; and
- have successfully used their power in the past (McCall 1979).

This method of assessing power places high reliance on the resources controlled by a person or group on whom the organization is dependent. Although it provides a useful starting point, this method has two limitations:

1. It defines resources too narrowly (Berger 1980).
2. It puts too much emphasis on the source of the influence. Overemphasis on the source is characteristic of most studies of power, such as the "bases of power" work of Raven and French (1956) and the research of Kipnis (1976). Most assessments of power view the relationship as one-way. Person A is seen as exerting influence on person B. In diagram form, the relationship looks like this:

$$A - - - - - - - - - \rightarrow B$$

The relational perspective presented thus far characterizes the communication as two-way: each participant has power *with the other*. The relationship looks like this:

$$A \leftarrow - - - - - - - - - \rightarrow B$$

As power is designated to a partnership or other entity, the relationship might look like this:

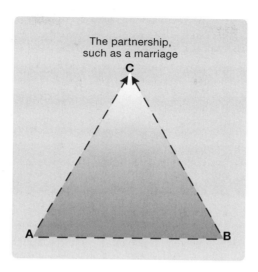

Most research presents power as a static property and disregards the dynamic elements of power. Resources are treated as possessions rather than as a changing part of the relationship process. One would assess power, using this perspective, by examining the resources that one party possesses. Many popular books on power take this individualistic approach. We have already discussed the serious limitations of this "one-way" approach.

Research on power has also focused on decision making or conversational control within the family unit. Decision-making approaches began with the classic Blood and Wolfe (1960) study of Detroit housewives. They asked wives questions such as "Who decides where the family will take a vacation?" and "Who decides what job to take?" Researchers in subsequent years tried to analyze power similarly by asking "Who has the last say about spending money?" (Safilios-Rothschild 1970), "Who is the real boss in the family?" (Heer 1963), and "Who would decide how you would spend $300?" (Kenkel 1957). It seemed reasonable that the most powerful member of a family would be the one who made most of the important decisions; unfortunately, there were difficulties with this popular method of measuring power. First, the researchers did not ask both spouses the questions. They might have received different answers if they had asked each partner separately. Second, the questions asked for "perceived authority"—who the participants thought made most of the decisions rather than who actually did (Bochner 1976; McDonald 1980). As a result, the participants may well have answered according to who they thought *should* have been making decisions. Given the sex-role stereotypes of that time period, a woman may have not wanted to tell a researcher that she was "the real boss." Whether it was accurate or not, women usually reported that their husbands made most of the decisions (Turk and Bell 1972).

At one time or another, you have probably judged someone as powerful because he or she controlled the conversation. Many researchers have studied conversational control in couples (Mishler and Waxler 1968; Rogers and Farace 1975; Millar & Rogers, 1987, 1988). Assuming that conversational control and power were the same thing, these researchers studied who talked the most, who interrupted the most, who changed topics the most, and who engaged in more "one up" moves. These two measures of power, decision making and conversational control, do not measure the same concept.)) If you look at different measures of power, you will probably reach different conclusions about who is most powerful (Olson and Rabunsky 1972; Turk and Bell 1972; Bochner 1976; Berger 1980; McDonald 1980).

Application 4.6

Who Has the Power?
An Observation and Assessment

With a group of people serving as the audience, try this experiment: watch a movie, role-play, or video presentation of two people in conflict. Or have two class members take on a problem-solving task or role-play an argument. They might argue about where to go for spring break, whether to ask a roommate to leave a living arrangement, or how fairly to assign grades to a group project. The audience makes notes throughout the conversation about who has the most power, and why. Then discuss your observations and your assessment.

You will probably find that almost everyone in the audience has a different way of deciding who really is more powerful. For some it may be nonverbal dominance; for others, vocal quality; for still others, amount of time spent in overt argument, or who "wins" at the end, or who appears to "let the other win." In essence, no single validating criterion for assessing power has been discovered by researchers; such a specific technique does not exist (Gray-Little 1982; Berger 1980).

Power is especially difficult to assess when influence is exercised covertly, or in hidden ways. Most of us have trouble deciphering covert power, or choices made based on another person's potential influence. For example, Will is an outdoorsman who would like to take a weeklong fishing trip, but he knows that his wife will not like being left alone for such an extended period of time since she works and would have to assume all the care of the children. Will proposes a two-day trip and, in the process, talks more and controls the discussion. An observer might guess that Will was in control of both process and outcome, since he and his wife agree that he will go on the two-day trip. Yet Will's conversation was structured around his estimate of his wife's reaction. Her power was important to his decision, yet an outside observer could not have known that without asking.)

People who look the most powerful to outsiders often are less powerful than they appear. In fact, without knowing the structure of a relationship, you cannot guess who has the most power, since people balance their power currencies in complex ways. For instance, if one person "lets" the other do the talking for the group, the person who gives tacit permission for the other to talk is actually controlling the situation. Gender issues come into play, since women in our culture cannot usually become the powerful aggressor without facing social disapproval or physical danger. Many women learn to seek safety and power by hiding, becoming invisible, or becoming relationally oriented. Whereas a woman's safety and power needs are often met by becoming smaller and less visible, the traditional masculine style of seeking safety is by becoming the feared individual, by becoming bigger and more visible (Kaschak 1992, 126). A woman's overt use of power often exposes her to denigration and attack, whereas a man's overt use of power may be viewed as evidence that he is a good leader. Overt use of power by men at home is judged differently than in some work situations.

Women

Power is exercised in ways that look weak. Sometimes the most powerful behavior is to appear to submit, yet resist, or act in a nonresistant way. An example of this form of power was Martin Luther King Jr.'s civil rights tactics, based on Gandhian principles, in which civil rights workers were trained to sit down when confronted by powerful persons, to protect their bodies if attacked but not to attack in response, and to use nonaggressive verbal responses. As happened in India, weakness in the face of strength made stronger persons question their use of force and coercion. A less productive "weak" way of exercising power is that of the apocryphal Army private who, when ordered to do KP duty, does as sloppy a job as possible while asking constantly, "Is this the way? Am I doing it right?" This "reluctant soldier" example can be seen in offices, in families, and on work crews where one person is "trying" (but failing) to get it right. The supervisor, parent, or crew boss then gets disgusted and does the job himself or herself.

Another indirect way to gain power is to refuse to cooperate when other people are depending on you. When this tactic is used in conjunction with unexpressed anger, it is labeled *passive aggressive behavior*. In passive aggression, a person acts aggressively (in one's own self-interest, without much regard for the other) by being passive, or unconcerned, when the other person needs a response. Passive aggression is displayed when people feel they have a low level of power, whether they do or not, since it appears to be a safer way of expressing anger, resentment, or hostility than stating such feelings directly. Additionally, "nice" people (Bach and Goldberg 1974) may use passive aggression instead of direct conflict statements because they have been taught that it is not nice to engage in conflict. Bach and Goldberg's (1974) list of common passive aggressive behaviors has been expanded to include the following:

Interesting

- Forgetting appointments, promises, and agreements.
- Slipping and saying unkind things, then apologizing.
- Acting out nonverbally, such as by slamming doors and banging objects, but denying that anything is wrong.
- Getting confused, tearful, sarcastic, or helpless when certain topics come up.
- Getting sick when you've promised to do something.
- Scheduling two things at once.
- Evading situations so that others are inconvenienced.

The following case presents an example of passive aggressive communication.

Application 4.7	Deteriorating Roommate Relationship

Two college roommates have a practice of borrowing each other's possessions. When Jan and Cheryl first moved in together, they decided it would be inconvenient to ask each time they wanted to use a CD or borrow an article of clothing. Cheryl has been keeping Jan's things longer than Jan wants her to, however, often causing Jan to have to look for her CDs, textbooks, car keys, sweaters, skis, and gloves. Recently, Jan lost several of Cheryl's possessions, including a CD she took to a party. She feels justified since Cheryl has been misusing the privilege, too. They are avoiding the issue and spending time away from each other. Role-play a direct instead of indirect way for Jan to ask for change. Remember to verbalize content and relationship concerns, specific goals, and face-saving techniques. Show listening and problem solving. Try the role-play two ways: (1) Both people cooperate and (2) Cheryl does not cooperate at first. She instead becomes defensive, attacks, withdraws, or acts in any other way you want to play out a destructive conflict. Show how she and Jan might finally resolve the conflict (realistically!).

A better strategy would be to confront angry feelings directly instead of indirectly. The college professor who double-schedules may feel overloaded and underappreciated but could tell people directly that too many appointments are interfering with the rest of his or her work.

Power Imbalances

Power is a product of the relationship.

In most relationships, there are times when the participants become aware of discrepancies in their relative power with one another. If one party has more power than the other, the conflict is unbalanced; many of the choices the parties then make are attempts to alter these imbalances. Keep in mind that who has power is always a relative judgment— each party has sources of power even during times of **power imbalance.** Such power asymmetries have predictable effects on both the higher- and lower-power parties, and the imbalance produces systemwide effects on the relationship. (Cromwill and Olson, 1975).

Strong emotions accompany different levels of power. Think of times when you have felt yourself to be in a position of low power. People often feel hostility or hatred, saying "I simply cannot stand his attitude. If I never had to deal with him again I'd be glad." Or you may feel helpless rage or helpless lethargy. When you are low power in a relationship that matters, you may feel a sense of low self-esteem, of feeling worthless or unable to influence your situation. You may feel sad, defeated, or depressed. When people hold the high-power position in an important relationship they may not feel universally pleased at all. People who have a lot of power often feel burdened with decision-making responsibilities, worry about being blamed, and feel responsible for doing more than is good for them. Many type A, over-working people with high power do not report feeling happy. Instead, they feel misunderstood, resentful of how much responsibility they feel, and unhappy with the attitude or performance of others. Neither high of low positions automatically brings about certain feelings. But you can be sure that an imbalance of power does bring about strong feelings. These feelings become part of the conflict communication and affect the overall conflict.

High Power

The exercise of social power for most people in Western culture is satisfying and even produces joy (Bowers and Ochs 1971; May 1972). **High power** is often a goal that people strive for; those with less power often feel, "If I were just the boss, things would be a lot better around here." The major difficulty with having a higher power than someone else is that it may corrupt you. Corruption is more than a word that describes a crooked politician. Corruption means moral rottenness, and inability to maintain the integrity of the self. A constant high level of power may "eat into" one's view of self and other, forming a perceptual distortion that may take on monstrous proportions. Higher-power persons, organizations, or nations may develop altered views of themselves and other parties. Constant feelings of higher power can result in these consequences:

1. A "taste for power" and the restless pursuit of more power as an end in itself.

2. The temptation to use institutional resources illegally as a means of self-enrichment.

3. False feedback concerning self-worth and the development of new values designed to protect power.

4. The devaluing of the less powerful and the avoidance of close social contact with them (Kipnis 1976, 178).

The undesirable consequences of a power imbalance can take many forms. For instance, studies show that if a teacher uses strong power over a student, the relationship disintegrates into the exclusive use of coercive strategies (Jamieson and Thomas 1974; Raven and Kruglanski 1970). Or the person highest in power may claim benevolence, that harmful actions are actually "for the good of the other person," thereby dismissing the negative consequences to the lower-power person. When someone is fired from an organization, it is common to hear, "It was for her/his own good—he/she will be better off spending time doing X." According to Guggenbuhl-Craig (1971), persons in helping professions, such as ministers, teachers, health workers, and others, can lose touch with their need to exercise power in order to feel valued and needed. Although helpers undoubtedly are in their professions in order to help, they also must have "helpees," or they have no function. How can a physician be a physician without people who need healing? How can teachers teach if no one values learning? If helpers do not understand that helping also contributes to their own sense of self-worth and personal fulfillment, the act of helping can become a high-power move (Just as during the Inquisition, when the learned scholars were sure that they were helping the persons accused of heresy, an unrestrained high power may make the powerful party blind to the havoc wreaked on the less powerful party.) You may have had times in your personal relationships when power became unbalanced; if so, you know the harm that unrestrained power can bring, whether you were the one with too much power or the one without enough power.

Teacher-Student → Coercive

Striving for higher power can destroy even the best of relationships. For example, in intimate relationships, the person who is least invested in the relationship has the most power (the "Principle of Least Interest," Waller 1938). Paradoxically, decreasing the investment for the purpose of gaining higher power is ultimately self-defeating, since you have to continue your decreasingly fragile investment in order to remain more powerful. And the lessened dependence can lead to the demise of the relationship. If you convince yourself that "I don't have to put up with this," then you don't usually stay in the relationship.

Finally, persons or nations with higher power can deny that power is exercised; they may deny that there is a conflict (it is a "minor disagreement") or use any of the other forms of denial mentioned earlier. Unrestrained higher power can corrupt the power holder's view of the self and view of the other, and it can set the stage for continued unproductive interaction.

Low Power

If absolute power corrupts absolutely, does absolute powerlessness make you pure?
—Harry Shearer

Just as power can corrupt, *powerlessness can also corrupt* (May 1972). If lower-power people are continually subjected to harsh treatment or lack of goal attainment, they are likely to produce some organized resistance to the higher-power people. When one reaches the stage where "nothing matters" (one cannot attain his or her goals through accepted means), violence or despair is spawned. It is the person who feels powerless who turns to the last resort—giving up, aggression, or violence (Richmond et al. 1984; Kipnis, Schmidt, and Wilkerson 1980; Falbo and Peplau 1980).

Too much losing does not build character; it builds frustration, aggression, or apathy. A typical example of how perceived unequal power results in aggression is the relationship between students and teachers. In one study, when students were asked what they considered doing to resolve conflicts they had with more powerful teachers, they replied on paper, "Use a .357 magnum," "Blow up his mailbox," "Sabotage him," and "Beat him up" (Wilmot 1976). At the very least, asymmetry in perceived power can lead to coercion in an attempt to "get even" (Jamieson and Thomas 1974; Raven and Kruglanski 1970). Most examples of retaliation occur because the person doing the retaliating perceives himself/herself to be in a low-power situation.

In severe, repetitive conflicts, **both** parties feel **low power,** and they continually make moves to increase their power at the other's expense. Since, as noted, the assessment of power is problematic, it is very difficult to determine the exact levels of power in a conflict. However, if each party believes she or he has less power than the other, a destructive, escalating spiral of conflict usually results. Each party attempts to increase power at the other's expense, with the next round bringing yet more destructive moves. Each person feels "behind" and justified in engaging in dirty moves because of what the other did.

Jake and Julie are a couple in their early 40s who have been divorced for two years. They share custody of their 14-year-old son, Tom. Julie works as a nurse in a highly stressful clinic. Jake works as a seasonal construction worker. Jake and Julie both feel that the other received more of the marital resources than they should have. Feeling low power and taken advantage of by the other, they have continued a bitter argument about who should pay for Tom's school expenses, even his food and clothes. Both say, "Ask your mother/father" when Tom needs anything extra. Because each feels lower power than their former partner, they are communicating to Tom that he has no power with them. They are in a high-power position with their son. Tom, not surprisingly, is alternately furious and depressed, since he cannot get either parent to pay attention to his needs. He has started hanging out at his grandmother's house (Julie's mom). Grandmother feeds Tom and takes him shopping for clothes. Jake takes this as further evidence that he does not need to provide anything extra. The school counselor has asked all the adults to come in for a session to talk through how to keep Tom in school (he has been skipping school). How might the counselor talk in a productive way about recognizing the needs of each person, especially Tom? What constructive approach might get the parents to focus on their son instead of their own perceived low power? (*Hint:* shame will not work!)

Often, as with Jake and Julie, even if both people want to act aggressively, there are restraints against that person's doing so. The powerless will try to restore equity, and if that fails, they have few options; one option is to use passive aggressive behavior, as discussed previously. In addition, Madanes (1981) notes that developing severely dysfunctional behavior is an exercise of power that affects all close associates. Lower-power parties will sometimes destroy a relationship as the ultimate move to bring about a balance of power. Jake and Julie are perilously close to destroying their relationship with their son.

The combination of denigration from the higher-power person and destructive power-balancing moves from the lower-power person contributes to a system of interactions that is not productive for either party. A cyclical, degenerative, destructive conflict spiral characterizes the ongoing interactions. The power disparity promotes struggles over power, increases the underlying bases of the conflict, and leads to lessened involvement in the relationship for both parties. When the conflict parties enter a spiral, nobody wins.

Application 4.8   **Nobody Wins**

Craig is a supervisor in a community agency, and Marilyn is a staff member who works part time. Craig coerces Marilyn into taking on a community volunteer program—a job she neither wants nor has time to develop at a competent level. Marilyn resists working on the program, and deadlines are looming. Craig, noticing her avoidance, humiliates her in a public meeting by pointing out what has not been done, and asking her to agree to work hard on the program. Marilyn accedes (on the surface) but talks to her friends about how poorly she is treated. After two months of Craig's disapproval of her progress and of her seeking social support and a new job elsewhere, she brings Craig her resignation.

(continued)

Application 4.8   Nobody Wins

Internally, Marilyn might have some of these thoughts and feelings:

Craig should not have put me in the position to work with all these community volunteers. I am still learning my other work, and this is a job for a more experienced person. He manipulated me by telling me how important the work is. I agree, but I'm not the person to do it. I'm 20 years younger than most of the volunteers and I don't have the history with the agency to know their jobs. I feel foolish; I'm trying to do something I don't know how to do. When I ask Craig or the others for help, they brush me off. I think they want the volunteers, but don't want to put in the time to train them. And they don't want to train me. I don't want to resign, but I can't take this. Being asked at the staff meeting if I would "work harder" was insulting. If I can find another job, I'm going.

Internally, Craig may have had some of these thoughts and feelings:

Marilyn is a smart young staff member. I wish we could hire her full time. She's perfect for the volunteer program because she is enthusiastic and inspiring. I'm disappointed at how many people she's signed up, though. I thought she would really jump on this chance. If she succeeds in setting up 20 or 30 well-trained volunteers, I'm sure I can get the funding for a full time job for her. But lately she's seemed to me to be whining and not really trying. She's asking for help that none of us has time to give. Doesn't she know how important this task is? When I brought it up at the staff meeting, I was trying to encourage her, but I could tell she was upset. I guess I'd better talk to her. I don't want to lose her.

Answer the following questions about Craig and Marilyn:

How might Marilyn have changed her low-power stance into a constructive one?

How might Craig have changed his "power over" stance into a constructive one?

What might a beginning dialogue that is constructive sound like?

Craig did not accomplish his original goal of starting the community program, and Marilyn is leaving her job. They achieved a power balance in an unproductive manner, much like in a game of leapfrog. When one person is behind, he or she then jumps into the lead, and the other person, sensing that he or she is "losing," does the same. Pretty soon the relationship is suffering, and neither person has achieved any of the original goals. In cases of power disparity, agreements are "basically unstable since they are grounded on unilateral threats rather than on mutually established norms" (Apfelbaum 1974, 151). The ever-accelerating unproductive moves are the result of attempts at power balancing through counterproductive means. The alternative is to balance the power through productive avenues and recognize that with extreme power asymmetry, effective long-term management is not likely.

A concise visual summary of our view of power and its effects is in Figure 4.3. Cameron and Whetten (1995) inspired this graph, which we adapted to an interpersonal orientation. As you can see, both lack of power (low power) and excessive power (high power) lead to ineffective communication behaviors. When you have sufficient power, your interpersonal behaviors are at their best.

Figure 4.3   Interpersonal Power

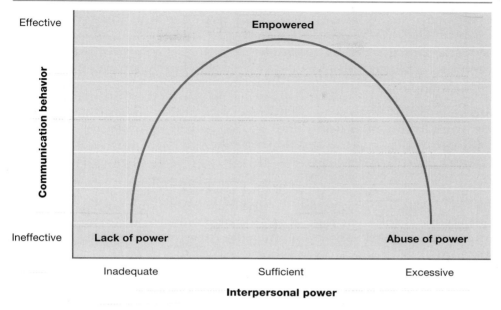

Constructive Power Balancing

> Integrative power depends very much on the power of language and communication, especially on the powers of persuasion.
> —Kenneth Boulding, *Three Faces of Power*

Up to this point, various words have been used almost interchangeably—*integrative power, both/and power, power with, power to a partnership, collaboration,* and *sharing power.* What is the rationale for viewing power in such terms? Is it actually possible to develop practices in which power isn't used against people but is used for mutual benefit?

We believe that *collaboration and the constructive realignment of power* is usually best for all concerned, with the following conditions:

- The high-power person is not abusing power in a way that takes away all possibility of influence by the lower-power person or persons.

- One person is not lying, distorting, or suffering from a disorder of character, such as sociopathy. A sociopath is a person who has no conscience and is not moved by the plight of others.

- The long-term gains are worth the expenditure of energy.

Competitive power has its place, too. We view competitive power as being useful when the following conditions are in place:

- Crucial needs of one party are at stake—needs the person is not willing to compromise about unless no other option exists. These might be economic or personal survival, protection of children, avoidance of harm, or protection of a crucial sense of self.

- Competition can lead to collaboration—when the playing field becomes more level.

Since destructive conflicts are often set off by struggles over power, and given that power is relational, power always is in a state of change. The only question is how one goes about changing power. If you struggle with someone because "you won't give in," you are trying to block their exercise of power—and they are probably doing the same thing. The paradox is that the more you struggle against someone, the less power you will have with that person. From a both/and perspective, the more powerful we feel, the more we are setting ourselves up for resistance from the other party. Put bluntly, power against is usually eventually blocked and diminished. Boulding (1989) says it well: "Power over human beings is very complex. Other human beings can answer back, fight back, obey or disobey, argue and try to exercise power over us, which a tree never does" (53). We must recognize that while we need to exercise appropriate power and influence, the other person needs to exercise influence as well, so we might as well cooperate with each other so we can both be effective. The both/and perspective as well as the "power to the partnership" perspective assumes that you all want to accomplish your goals and that you need each other to do that. Since it is the other who is blocking you (and you blocking him or her), integrative power moves beyond the tug-of-war and to a new plane of relationship.

Whereas destructive struggling for power leads to a downward spiral of more thwarting and interference and to a lessened ability to accomplish your goals, shared power leads to a synergy of power creation through productive communication. As you work with each other, each of you stops directly interfering with the other and actively assists the other in getting what he or she wants, and the communication between you serves a transcendent function (Wilmot 1995). With cooperation you actually *create more power* than the two of you could have created separately. Shared power is not a weak, tentative approach—it is powerful and energetic, and it requires great skill.

Collaboration depends on a model of shared power. Rarely will you be in a life situation in which all the power resides with the other, so collaboration is almost always possible. Research makes this clear. Alberts and Driscoll (1992) demonstrated that satisfied couples will "pass, refocus, mitigate or respond" to the other rather than struggle over power. The sense of "we-ness," of working together, pulls romantic couples through their first big fight (Siegert and Stamp 1994). Gottman (1999) makes it clear that successful couples work together to "repair" their relationship instead of making the other wrong. If they do not learn to seek repairs as a matter of course, they do not stay together. Any relationship in which power is not shared ultimately will end, in divorce, abandonment, withdrawing, retreat into mental illness, or the continuation of a grim, joyless relationship.

Application 4.9   It's Their Fault

Bruce is the production manager of a large electronics manufacturing facility, and Lenny is the engineering manager. Each supervises a five-person team of managers. Lenny's engineers are responsible for (1) designing systems for production and (2) quality control.

(continued)

Application 4.9	It's Their Fault

Bruce's production employees are responsible for output—they have to get the product out the door and shipped to customers. Over a two-year period, the two teams seemed gridlocked. Engineering staff members complained, both in their staff meetings and to the plant manager, saying, "Those production people—we design good systems for them to follow; they don't follow them, and then quality slips. What is their problem?" Meanwhile, production employees openly criticized the engineers on the manufacturing floor by saying, "They think they are so hot—yet their elaborate designs don't work, they treat us like slaves, and they don't know or care how we are being held to a minimum number of units produced." Finally, the plant manager had to ask for outside help. The production and engineering managers met, as did the work teams. They agreed to (1) shift quality control to the production side, (2) have the engineers provide training to the production employees so they could enforce quality control, (3) not make any more negative public comments about the other team, and (4) require the production and engineering managers to attend each other's staff meetings. What was a "power-against" situation became, over a period of a month, a "power-with" situation. The plant manager was very pleased that his two key players in engineering and production were now helping each other accomplish their goals rather than interfering with one another. Production output and quality both improved. A new system of rebalanced power made collaboration possible.

Analyze the success of the change described in this case. What made the change possible? Specify how the power-against model changed to a power-with model. Take these steps and apply them to another power-against situation. What are some general principles you can use in the future?

Conflict participants are more likely to make a long-range relationship work if they move toward equality in power. Models for productive power balancing, although scarce, do exist. In everyday life, individuals can learn to cooperate and to reach agreements if power is distributed equitably, or fairly (Apfelbaum 1974, 138). For relationships to work over time, people must continually realign the power balance as the situation warrants.

What can friends, co-workers, family members, or intimates do when they discover power asymmetry in their relationships? They can (1) work to make the relationships more equal, (2) try to convince themselves and their partners that the relationships are more equal than they might seem (by restoring psychological equality), or (3) eventually abandon the unbalanced relationships (Hatfield, Utne, and Traupmann 1979). For instance, family members negotiating household tasks may say, "I should get more credit for taking out the garbage than you do for cleaning the counters because I hate to take out the garbage and you don't mind doing the counters." The person who hates taking out garbage is trying to balance power by restoring psychological fairness. We are all too familiar with friendships that fail because of inadequate power balancing.

An interpersonal relationship with a power disparity between participants can achieve a more productive focus by moving toward balance. The destructive attempts by lower-power parties to balance power are a move toward balance, but power must be balanced productively to lead to effective management. Power must be realigned in order for sharing to exist.

❧Techniques for Balancing Power

Dialogue

Balancing power usually starts not with outside intervention (as in the design/engineering case mentioned), but with a skill we all already possess.

> **Conversation is one of the most important ways of establishing equality.** Young-Bruehl and Bethelard 2000, 209.

Face to face conversation remains the starting point for enacting the internal desire to balance power. You may have thought and felt through the issues in a particular conflict. You may be fairly clear about what you want, what the other person's issues might be, and what the stakes are. The best first step is to talk directly with the people involved. We continue to witness conflicts that are worsened by broadcast e-mails, policy changes, announcement at meetings, memos, any other forms of avoidance—it seems hard for people to talk with each other when feelings are strong.

One of us has been consulting for many years with a government agency. Here is a typical phone call. Director calls Joyce. She describes a difficult person and asks for counsel on how to proceed. Joyce listens, then says:

> Joyce: I think you should talk to him directly. You could go down the hall and ask for a brief conversation/pick up the phone and call him/ask for time at the conference next week.
>
> Director: I knew you'd tell me to do that. I guess I still find it hard.

When Bill, for instance, is coaching executives, after they give all of the details about a co-worker who is interfering with them, Bill asks, "Have you told him that and had a conversation about it?" The answer is always "no."

The basic form of conversation that helps to balance power involves:

- *Speaking to the other with a positive tone.* For instance, your opening words should communicate respect, should be *clear*, should *show compassion for the perspective of the other,* and should be *direct.*

- *Listen.* Pay close attention, ask open-ended questions, and let the other person know you've heard what they have said. Avoid saying, "I understand you, but it's just that. . ." This assures that the other will not feel understood. Instead, say, "I think what you are saying is that you are uneasy about my plan." When you use "but" the person hears nothing you've said before that one word.

- *Reflect feelings.* In addition to listening and reflecting content, reflect the feelings of the other person. This is harder than it seems. Often, we miss the feeling tone of the other. Reflecting feelings might sound like this: "You are too pressured to take on a new project now, although you like the sound of it."

- *Clarify what you have heard.* You might say, "Let me be sure I understand what you are saying. . ."

- *Question when needed.* Ask questions for which you do not know the answer; avoid asking questions as a way to slip into your opinion. A good question would sound like this: "Tell me more about your concern for your son. What are you worried about?"

- *Summarize*. You can help track and orient the conversation by summarizing what you have both/all talked about so far. Avoid adding your own opinion—that comes later. Summarizing might sound like this: "We've identified the problems about scheduling the family reunion. People have a lot of different ideas about where to meet. Some feelings have been hurt already, and many of the family members have strong opinions. We've decided to ask Carolyn to contact everyone giving the best options the three of us have come up with. Is this right?" (This approach was first pioneered by Carl Rogers in the 1950s and has been adapted and expanded by many others.)

In addition to opening a dialogue, the following techniques can be used to balance power.

Restraint

Higher-power parties can limit their power by refusing to use all the currencies they have at their disposal. A militarily powerful nation that refuses to invade a neighboring country and a physically powerful spouse who refuses to inflict damage on the other spouse are examples of a higher-power party limiting power usage. If the high-power person refuses to engage in "natural" responses, this restraint can alter the automatic nature of a destructive cycle. In this self-regulating approach, power is given to a higher partnership or unit, instead of being used as an individual right. Art, a college teacher, refuses to use punitive power when students present last-minute pleadings for more time to write final papers. Instead, Art simply says, "Why don't you set a deadline for the final paper that you can meet, and it will be fine with me? What day and time do you want to hand it in?" A married couple found a way to lower one member's economic power, thereby providing more balance in their relationship. They valued monetary equality and were used to having separate accounts and almost the same disposable income. The husband got an unexpected raise, however, and suddenly had more money to spend. They started arguing frequently because he would propose expensive weekends for recreation and his wife had difficulty paying for her half. In response to their increasingly destructive arguments, they decided to set up an automatic savings withdrawal from his monthly paycheck, to be put in a joint long-term savings plan. Then they would use this money occasionally for a "lost weekend." Even though he still earned more money than his partner, the negative effect on them as a couple was lessened, while he gained the long-term advantages of saving more money. He limited his immediate use of his higher monetary power, with positive effects on the couple's balance of power.

Focus on Interdependence: Power to the Unit

One way to balance the power in a relationship is for lower-power individuals to focus on ways the people involved in the conflict are dependent on each other instead of demanding attention to their own individual needs (Donohue and Kolt 1992). Higher-power individuals usually try to minimize interdependence; therefore, lower-power individuals need to point out how the conflict parties are more related than it might appear. (The strategy of searching for overlapping interests will be discussed in detail in chapter 8, "Interpersonal Negotiation.") When individuals are scared and feeling powerless, they often angrily demand that their own needs be met or begin to use threats. These are ineffective approaches, since the higher-power person has the ability to move away or lessen the interdependence.

A thorough understanding of interdependence clarifies power relationships. People are interdependent because of their emotional, behavioral, and cognitive dependence on each other. We need affection and regard certain tasks to be accomplished, and for ideas to be freely shared. If John and Sarah are dating and decide to live together, they both increase their dependence on the other. Following Emerson's formula of **power-dependence relations,** as John becomes more dependent on Sarah, Sarah's power increases. Likewise, Sarah becomes more dependent on John, thereby increasing his power. When two people elevate their dependence on each other, both increase their sources of power. Each one expands his or her currencies that are valued by the other. Therefore, power in enduring relationships is not finite—it is an expandable commodity. The focus shouldn't be the singular amount of power each one has but the balance of power between them. John and Sarah may have little power with each other at the beginning of their relationship. Later, as each develops more power, the other's power rises approximately equally. The absolute amount of power may change, but the crucial issue is the comparative dependence that John and Sarah have on each other.

Application 4.10   Quick! It's an Emergency!

Conflict Parties: Tom, a midlevel manager in an office; Helen, the secretary for four people in the office.

Repetitive Conflict: Often when Helen is too busy to get all her work done immediately, she will set priorities and plan her schedule based on known deadlines. Tom's work makes up the largest share of Helen's work. Tom and the other three supervisors rank equally on the organizational scale. However, when Tom is busy and pressed, he rushes to Helen's desk with work that needs to be done immediately. Following is a typical exchange:

> Tom: Helen, I have just this one little thing that has to go out today.
>
> Helen [sighing]:   Yes, Tom, I know—just one little thing. But I have to get this out for Joe today, and it must be done first.

Tom puts more pressure on Helen to do his job first by saying that it won't take long and that just this once she needs to respond to the emergency pressures. Helen gets angry and tries to persuade him that it can wait one more day. Then she pouts a bit.

> Helen: I am only one person, you know. Just put it there and I'll try to get it done.
>
> Tom: Helen, you're a sweetheart. When this madhouse calms down, I'll take you out to lunch. I knew I could count on you.

(continued)

| Application 4.10 | Quick! It's an Emergency! |

Helen then stays late to finish the work, but she asks her office manager to speak to Tom again about interfering with her ability to manage her work. Tom apologizes a few days later.

Tom: I didn't mean to make you mad. I didn't think that one report was going to tick you off so much.

Helen: It's OK; it's just that I can't please everybody.

In the "Quick! It's an Emergency!" case, the power may appear to be organized such that Tom has more because he is the boss and Helen has less because she occupies a lower position in the organization. A closer look reveals that the parties are fairly well balanced in power. The balancing act is, however, taking a toll on their relationship, and the work could be managed more creatively. Tom is dependent on Helen for getting his work out error free, quickly, and with the benefit of Helen's experience. He depends on Helen to respond to his needs before those of the others in the office, since he is carrying more of the work in the office than the other three at his level. He sees himself as a pleasant and noncontrolling person whose employees work because they want to. He depends on Helen to view him as a reasonable and professional person because this is how he views himself. Helen, meanwhile, depends on Tom for some of her self-esteem. She prizes her ability to skillfully organize her work so that it gets done on time. She wants to be treated as a valuable decision-making employee. She knows, too, that if Tom becomes dissatisfied with her work, he will complain to her immediate supervisor in the office, and she might be overlooked for promotions or might even lose her job. So Helen depends on Tom for positive ratings, a good work climate, and self-esteem. Restructuring their interactions could allow them to achieve more of their independent and interdependent goals. Helen could ask Tom to help her respond to disparate pressures; Tom could ask Helen how to set up a way to take care of emergencies. A problem-solving approach to conflict management would allow both to balance their power more collaboratively.

The Power of Calm Persistence

Lower-power people in a conflict often can gain more equal power by persisting in their requests. Substantive change, when power is unequal, seldom comes about through intense, angry confrontation. Rather, change results from careful thinking and from planning for small, manageable moves based on a solid understanding of the problem (Lerner 1989, 15). When intensity is high, people react rather than observe and think. We overfocus on the other instead of an analysis of the problem, and we move toward polarization.

Lower-power parties cannot afford to blow up. One source of power the lower-power person has, however, is careful, calm analysis that directs attention to the problem. If lower-power people have patience and avoid giving up out of frustration, they gain "nuisance value," and the higher-power person or group often listens and collaborates just to get them to go away. Persuasive skills become crucial. The low-power person must analyze the situation well, taking into account what will be judged appropriate, effective, credible, and practical. (The lower-power person *must* shown respond.) ?,?

Several examples of **calm persistence** illustrate this strategy for increasing one's power. Ellen is the head of a large, successful consulting organization. She travels a lot and has a tightly organized schedule. A few years ago her daughter, Linda, whined and pouted about not being able to go horseback riding alone with her mother. This was ineffective since Ellen hates whining. Finally, Linda, at age 8, hit upon a solution. She asked her mother for a "management meeting," in which she pointed out her complaints and asked for what she wanted. This approach so impressed her mother that, with affection and humor, they broke through an avoid-pursue spiral. Linda gained power, and Ellen felt much better about how the two of them were spending time.

Individuals in conflict with institutions often experience frustrating, demeaning powerlessness as they are shunted from one person to the next. Phone calls are not returned and frustration rises dramatically. Sometimes only calm, clear persistence increases an individual's power enough for him or her to be heard and dealt with. Some suggestions for dealing with large, impersonal institutions are as follows:

- Identify the individuals on the phone by name and ask for them when you call back.

- Stay pleasant and calm. State clearly what you want, and ask for help in solving the problem.

- Follow the rules even if you think they are ridiculous. If they want five copies of a form, typed and folded a certain way, give it to them. Then point out that you have followed the rules and expect results.

- Write simple, clear memos summarizing what you want, what you have done, and when you expect a response.

- Tell them all the steps you took to try to get a response from them.

- Avoid taking out your frustration on low-power individuals in the organization. They may respond with "I'm just following the rules," avoiding personal responsibility—and who could blame them? Instead, be courteous and ask for help. Humor always helps if it is not at someone else's expense.

Stay Actively Engaged

Remaining in a low-power position, assuming that one's weakness is a permanent instead of a temporary condition, and adopting low-power tactics set up a dangerously unbalanced situation that benefits no one, not even the high-power person. The higher-power person, who has the power to define the terms of the conflict in his or her own favor, often understands only one side of the conflict. Therefore, the higher-power person may not be able to find a constructive solution. People who perceive themselves as powerless usually do not talk effectively about their own needs and, after a while, may adopt a self-defeating, accommodating style that becomes fixed or they may use passive-aggressive tactics. When one person believes that the other person can go elsewhere for whatever is needed, the lower-power person tends to avoid conflict (Folger, Poole, and Stutman 1993). If the fixed power position becomes intolerable, the lower-power person may act out of desperation, doing something such as resigning, leaving a romantic relationship, blowing up and antagonizing the high-power person so that he or she ends the relationship, or threatening self-destructive behavior, such as by saying, "Just do what you want. Just tell me what to do. I'm tired of fighting. You win." This unstable situation invites escalation on the other person's part and may lead to the end of the relationship.

Rather than remaining in self-defeating spirals, Lerner (1989, 35) suggests that people in low-power positions adopt the following moves:

- *Speak up and present a balanced picture of strengths as well as weaknesses.* One might say, "It's true that I am afraid to ask my boss for a raise, even though you want me to. But I earn a steady paycheck and budget and plan well for our family. I want some credit for what I do already contribute."

- *Make clear what one's beliefs, values, and priorities are, and then keep one's behavior congruent with these.* An entry-level accountant in a large firm was asked by the comptroller to falsify taxable deductions, hiding some of the benefits given to employees. The accountant, just out of school and a single parent, said, "When you hired me I said I was committed to doing good work and being an honest accountant. What you are asking me to do is against the code of ethics and could result in my losing my license. I can't afford to take that risk. I'm sure you'll understand my position."

- *Stay emotionally connected to significant others even when things get intense.* It takes courage for a low-power person to let another person affect him or her. One teenage son was furious and hurt when his father decided to remarry, since the son did not like the wife-to-be and felt disloyal to his mother. After some tough thinking, he decided to tell his father honestly how he felt, what he did not like, and what he feared about the new marriage instead of taking another way out, such as angrily leaving his father's house to live with his mother in another state. This conversation balanced the power between father and son in an entirely new way.

★ Good example

- *State differences, and allow others to do the same.* The easiest, but often not the best, way for a low-power person to manage conflict is to avoid engagement. Again, courage is required to bring up differences when a power imbalance is in place. Brad, a college freshman, worked at a fast-food place during school. He was unhappy because the manager kept hiring unqualified people (without checking their references) and then expected Brad to train them and provide supervision, even though Brad was barely making more than minimum wage. Finally Brad told the manager, "I have a different way of looking at whom you should hire. I try to do a good job for you, but I have to try to work with people who have no experience and maybe don't have the personality to pitch in and work hard as part of the team. Would you consider letting me sit in on interviews and look over applications?" The manager was pleased with Brad's initiative and said yes.

Empowerment of Low-Power People by High-Power People

Sometimes it is clearly to the advantage of higher-power groups or individuals to purposely enhance the power of lower-power groups or individuals. Without this restructuring of power, working or intimate relationships may end or rigidify into bitter, silent, passive aggressive, and unsatisfactory entanglements. Currencies valued by higher-power people can be developed by lower-power people if they are allowed more training, more decision-making power, or more freedom. For instance, in one social service agency, Sharon was not doing well at directing a grant-funded program on finding housing for homeless people. Jan, the director of the agency, realized that Sharon was a good fundraiser but not a good program director. By switching Sharon's job description, the agency gained a good employee instead of continuing a series of negative job evaluations that would have resulted in Sharon's eventual termination.

Empowerment also occurs when third parties are invested with the power to intervene on the behalf of less powerful persons. For instance, children who have been abused by their parents or caretakers can be empowered if their plight is reported to the proper agency. The legal system will provide attorneys, caseworkers to monitor the situation, counselors to work with the parents, judges to arbitrate decisions involving the children, and free services to help the children recover from the effects of the abuse. Our society has decided, by passing certain laws, that extreme forms of power imbalance, such as abuse, will not be allowed to continue when they are discovered. Children are empowered by laws that give them rights and give responsibilities to others.

Metacommunication

Another way to balance power is to transcend the win/lose structure by jointly working to preserve the relationship during conflict. By metacommunicating during or before conflicts (talking about the relationship or about how the parties will handle their conflicts), the parties can agree about behaviors that will not be allowed (such as leaving during a fight).

Metacommunication focuses the parties on the process of their communication with each other. They talk about their communication, and if that fails, they can agree to bring in outside mediators or counselors. They can agree that whenever a serious imbalance occurs, the high-power party will work actively with the low-power party to alter the balance in a meaningful way. Usually romantic partners, friends, family members, and work partners can accomplish such joint moves if they agree that the maximization of individual power, left unrestrained, will destroy the relationship. They see that individual power is based relationally, that dependence begets power, and that successful relationships necessitate a balancing of dependencies and therefore of power. The lack of a balanced arrangement is a signal to reinvest in the relationship rather than a clue that the relationship is over. The person temporarily weaker in the relationship can draw on the relationship currencies, as if the relationship were a bank and the currencies were savings. The weaker party can claim extra time, space, money, training, empathy, or other special considerations until the power is brought back into an approximation of balance. The following case presents an example of an interpersonal peacemaking agreement.

Application 4.11   I'm Not Your Slave!

Cheryl and Melissa are two teenage girls who share a room in a foster home. Cheryl is more outgoing and friendly than Melissa, who is shy in groups but demanding of Cheryl's time and attention. Recently, Melissa increased small demands for Cheryl to shut the door, turn down the radio, bring her a drink of water, include her in phone gossip, and lend her clothes, records, and other items. Cheryl, after discussing the situation with several helpers, decided she did not want to continue to respond to Melissa in anger and disdain (e.g., "Get your own water—I'm not your slave!"). She then took the following steps to restore the balance of power:

1. She reminded Melissa that they had agreements about chores in the room, made at a family meeting, that Cheryl wanted to follow.

2. She voluntarily began to fill Melissa in on happenings at school that involved people whom Melissa admired.

3. She complied with Melissa's requests, such as getting her a drink of water, the first time they were made, but then said, "I'm glad to get it this once, but remember we agreed to be equal in who does what in the room. So you're on your own now."

4. She asked Melissa to go to basketball games with her and her friends. Melissa became sociable, made new friends of her own, and needed Cheryl's assistance less.

Granted, Cheryl was a remarkably compassionate teenager. But she reported that her life was better, too, since she got along so much better with her roommate.

What to Say When You Are Low Power

We end this chapter with some specific low-power statements that can be used to balance power. Since a power imbalance brings destructive behavior, these are offered in the spirit of helping bring a sense of balance into relationships. The assumption is that they will be used for productive ends to help work through relationship issues. When you are feeling low power, you might try

- Validating or acknowledging the other: "Noah, I appreciate how you . . ."

- Using "I" statements: "What I would like is . . ."

- Asking the higher-power person what he or she needs: "Sara, I'm wondering what would work for you in this situation?"

- Letting the other person know what they can gain from helping you: "Kathy, if I'm included in the discussions, I'll be able to support the decisions more fully."

- Announcing all intended escalation and looking for a way out: "Patricia, I really don't want to go to the union on this problem. I want to reach some understanding so we can put this to rest."

- Expressing optimism: "Juan, I know that if we just sit down together and talk we can resolve this pretty easily."

Slow the Process.

- "I feel like a tidal wave of reasons why we can't try my idea are washing over me. Could we slow down the discussion and take my ideas one by one?"

Show Concern for the Relationship.

- "I feel like we're digging ourselves deeper and deeper into a hole. How can we get out of this?" (Fisher and Shapiro 2005, 48)

Use a Metaphor.

- "I feel like I'm trying to swim upstream. How can we make this easier for both of us?" (Fisher and Shapiro 2005, 48)

Say Something True and Affirming About the Other Person, Then Make a Request.

- "Noah, you've been open to new ideas from interns in the past. I remember how pleased I was when you let us try out a staff meeting just for interns. But now we're pretty isolated since you aren't coming to our meetings. What would make it possible for you to be involved in our internship year more fully? We all value your mentoring a lot."

Describe the Situation.

- A 13-year-old girl to her mother: "Mom, this one week with Dad and one week with you worked okay when I was younger. But now it's impossible for me to plan and see my friends and keep doing my extracurricular activities. You and Dad don't communicate with each other except through me. I've had it. Something needs to change—please!!!"

Balancing power requires courage and creativity.

Most of us are caught in a paradox of power. To be effective people, we need to maximize our abilities, take advantage of opportunities, and use resources at our disposal so we can lead the kind of lives we desire. Yet within the confines of an ongoing relationship, *maximization of individual power is counterproductive* for both the higher-power and lower-power parties. The unrestrained maximization of individual power leads to damaged relations, destructive moves, more destructive countermoves, and the eventual ending of the relationship. Since people are going to take steps to balance power—destructively, if no other means are available—we can better manage conflict by working to balance power in productive and creative ways. Equity in power reduces violence and enables all participants to continue working for the good of all parties, even in conflict.

❧Summary

In this chapter we discuss what power is and note that people usually have negative connotations of power. We compare and contrast three different views of power—either/or power, both/and power, and designated power. Also, many times people deny power in various ways.

Power is presented as a relational concept rather than as an attribute of the individual. Our power currencies are described as "spendable" energy that can be used in conflictual relationships. Power imbalances often impede conflict management; the various ways to deal with too much or too little power are described, with specific suggestions on how to balance power in positive ways. Suggestions for people in low power end the chapter.

ꙮKey Terms

Use the text's Online Learning Center at **www.mhhe.com/wilmot8e** to further your understanding of the following terminology.

power 103	power currencies 118	high power 127
either/or power 106	resource control 118	low power 128
both/and power 108	interpersonal linkages 119	power-dependence relations 136
ineffective 111	communication skills 119	
designated power 112	expertise 119	calm persistence 138
power denial 113	perception of power 122	empowerment 140
relational theory of power 115	power imbalance 126	metacommunication 140

ꙮReview Questions

Go to the self-quizzes on the Online Learning Center at **www.mhhe.com/wilmot8e** to test your knowledge of the chapter concepts.

1. Define power.
2. Describe your own orientation to power.
3. How does power operate in a distressed system?
4. Clarify the difference between either/or power and both/and power.
5. What are the ways people deny their use of power?
6. Explain the relational theory of power.
7. What are power-dependence relations?
8. Define and give examples of power currencies.
9. What does the acronym RICE stand for?
10. What makes power difficult to assess?
11. What behaviors does feeling high power lead to?
12. What behaviors does feeling low power lead to?
13. List some approaches to balancing power.
14. What is metacommunication?
15. If you are low power, what can you do?

~Chapter 5

Styles and Tactics

Style preferences develop over a person's lifetime based on a complicated blend of genetics, life experiences, family background, and personal philosophy. By the time you are an adult, your basic orientation to conflict is in place. Your preferences for either harmony and calm or high-energy engagement are apparent. For instance, if you traditionally go on a final, end-of-summer backpack trip involving 10 friends, and the main goal is a wonderful time, it would make no sense for you to stubbornly insist on going where you want to go. Instead, you cooperate to find a place to go that fits the goals of the group.

Developing a repertoire of diverse styles and tactics may require some stretching of your comfort zone. However, having a choice of styles you can use will enhance your chances for productive conflict. This chapter will introduce you to a variety of styles and tactics used in conflict situations and will show you the impact of each style or tactic.

~The Nature of Styles and Tactics

Conflict styles are patterned responses, or clusters of behavior, that people use in conflict. **Tactics** are individual moves people make to carry out their general approach. Styles describe the big picture, whereas tactics describe the specific communication moves of the big picture. While "tactics" makes it sound like each move is planned, as in a war, most people do not plan their moves—they just act. Unfortunately, there is not a better word to represent these "moves," "behaviors" or "communication choices." When you use a tactic numerous times, it becomes a style—a patterned response. Conflict styles have been researched more than any other in interpersonal conflict management, and one can classify styles a number of ways. The classification schemes range from the two-style approach to the five-style approach and are as follows:

- Two styles: Cooperation and competition (Deutsch 1949; Tjosvold 1990).
- Three styles: Nonconfrontation, solution orientation, and control (Putnam and Wilson 1982).
- Four styles: Yielding, problem solving, inaction, and contending (Pruitt 1983b); accommodating/harmonizing, analyzing/preserving, achieving/directing, and affiliating/perfecting (Gilmore and Fraleigh 1992); aggressive/confrontive, assertive/persuasive, observant/introspective, and avoiding/reactive (Robert 1982); exit, voice, loyalty, neglect (Rusbult, Zembrodt, and Gunn 1982).
- Five styles: Integrating, obliging, dominating, avoiding, and compromising (Rahim 1983; Rahim and Magner 1995); collaboration, accommodation, competition, avoidance, and compromise (Thomas 1976; Kilmann and Thomas 1975).

Most trainers and researchers are currently using a five-style approach; therefore, this approach will be emphasized for the remainder of the chapter. Kilmann and Thomas (1975) most clearly defined the five styles when they located them on a graph according to two dimensions: (1) **assertiveness** and (2) **cooperativeness.** The five styles are presented in figure 5.1.

Figure 5.1   Conflict Styles

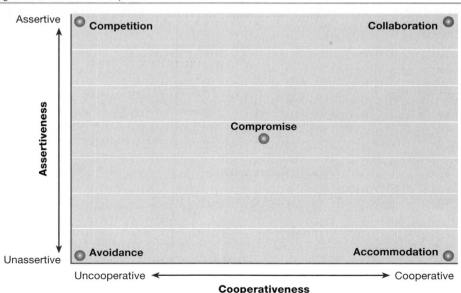

Because of the differences between various writers in labeling styles, this one set of labels is being used throughout this chapter. The original Kilmann and Thomas graph has been slightly modified, and Rahim and Magner's (1995) style questions and labeling have been modified for consistency in this presentation.

Notice that avoidance represents low assertiveness and low cooperativeness. Accommodation represents a low level of concern for yourself but a high level of concern for the other (you give them what they want). The opposite of accommodation is competition— you are highly concerned for yourself but have only a low level of concern for the other (you "go for it" regardless of the desires of the other). Collaboration factors in both your concerns and the other's concerns. Compromise is a middle ground, where there are moderate degrees of assertiveness and cooperativeness.

Measuring Your Styles

Before we proceed, take the style measure in the following box. This measure is adapted from Rahim and Magner (1995) and will give you scores on each of the five styles of avoidance, accommodation, competition, collaboration, and compromise.

As you will see later, our styles often vary according to different contexts or relationships. As a result, we would like you to fill out the style measure for two different situations, situation A and situation B. For situation A describe a personal relationship—with a friend, romantic partner, or close family member. Then, for situation B, pick a less personal relationship—someone you are doing a class project with, someone you don't know well at work, or some other less personal close relation. The key is to pick specific people for situation A and situation B. Do not fill out the scales "in general."

Application 5.1   Measuring Your Conflict Style

STYLES

Think of two different contexts (A and B) where you have a conflict, disagreement, argument, or disappointment with someone. An example might be someone you live with and a work associate. Then, according to the following scale, fill in your scores for situation A and situation B. *For each question, you will have two scores.* For example, on question 1 the scoring might look like this: 1. 2 | 4

Write the name of each person for the two contexts here:

Person A _____   Person B _____

1 = never   2 = seldom   3 = sometimes   4 = often   5 = always

Person | Person A | B

1. ___|___ I avoid being "put on the spot"; I keep conflicts to myself.
2. ___|___ I use my influence to get my ideas accepted.

(continued)

Application 5.1   Measuring Your Conflict Style

3. ___|___ I usually try to "split the difference" in order to resolve an issue.

4. ___|___ I generally try to satisfy the other's needs.

5. ___|___ I try to investigate an issue to find a solution acceptable to us.

6. ___|___ I usually avoid open discussion of my differences with the other.

7. ___|___ I use my authority to make a decision in my favor.

8. ___|___ I try to find a middle course to resolve an impasse.

9. ___|___ I usually accommodate the other's wishes.

10. ___|___ I try to integrate my ideas with the other's to come up with a decision jointly.

11. ___|___ I try to stay away from disagreement with the other.

12. ___|___ I use my expertise to make a decision that favors me.

13. ___|___ I propose a middle ground for breaking deadlocks.

14. ___|___ I give in to the other's wishes.

15. ___|___ I try to work with the other to find solutions that satisfy both our expectations.

16. ___|___ I try to keep my disagreement to myself in order to avoid hard feelings.

17. ___|___ I generally pursue my side of an issue.

18. ___|___ I negotiate with the other to reach a compromise.

19. ___|___ I often go with the other's suggestions.

20. ___|___ I exchange accurate information with the other so we can solve a problem together.

21. ___|___ I try to avoid unpleasant exchanges with the other.

22. ___|___ I sometimes use my power to win.

23. ___|___ I use "give and take" so that a compromise can be made.

24. ___|___ I try to satisfy the other's expectations.

25. ___|___ I try to bring all our concerns out in the open so that the issues can be resolved.

Scoring: Add up your scores on the following questions:

A	B		A	B		A	B		A	B		A	B
1. ___	___		2. ___	___		3. ___	___		4. ___	___		5. ___	___
6. ___	___		7. ___	___		8. ___	___		9. ___	___		10. ___	___
11. ___	___		12. ___	___		13. ___	___		14. ___	___		15. ___	___
16. ___	___		17. ___	___		18. ___	___		19. ___	___		20. ___	___
21. ___	___		22. ___	___		23. ___	___		24. ___	___		25. ___	___

(continued)

Application 5.1   Measuring Your Conflict Style

__	__	__	__	__	__	__	__	__	__
A | B	A | B	A | B	A | B	A | B
Avoidance Totals	Competition Totals	Compromise Totals	Accommodation Totals	Collaboration Totals

Source: Adapted from M. A. Rahim and N. R. Magner (1995), "Confirmatory Factor Analysis of the Styles of Handling Interpersonal Conflict: First-Order Factor Model and Its Invariance across Groups," *Journal of Applied Psychology 80,* no. 1, 122–132.

Now that you have scores for the five styles, across two different contexts, you can see what "styles" are. You may have different styles across the contexts (slightly more than 50 percent of people do), or you may be consistent across the relationships.

Application 5.2   Styles in Your Group

Compare your scores on the styles measure for situation A and situation B. In small groups, address these questions:

1. How many people of your group have relatively consistent styles in different contexts?
2. For those who have different answers, answer this question: "What is it about the two situations that prompts me to use different styles?"
3. As a group, discuss the advantages of using the same style across two different situations.
4. What are the advantages of using different styles across the two situations?
5. Do personal situations and less personal situations call for different styles?

Before we examine the five styles in depth, we look at our most fundamental orientation to conflict—**avoidance** or **engagement.**

Will You Avoid or Engage?

Recall a conflict in which you felt intense emotion. In such a situation you may not have been aware of making a specific choice about whether to engage or not, yet that choice defined all future interactions. Earlier we noted that destructive spirals occur when one person pursues and the other distances. This preference for engaging or avoiding the other can develop into a rigid style, and when this happens, constructive conflict becomes difficult. One needs to choose when to disengage and when to engage. Neither style is always the right choice. As Kaplan (1975) writes, one chooses "maintenance-by-*suppression*" or "maintenance-by-*expression*." People who have experienced trauma, whether the trauma has been physical violence, sexual abuse, observing violent events, or trauma from separation from caregivers, traumatized people tend to avoid conflict (Johnson 2002, 42). For example, the following couple is struggling over how much engagement they will have:

Application 5.3   **Avoid or Engage?**

Brent: There is something bothering me.

Janette: I'm way too stressed out to talk about anything right now.

Brent: I'm upset about what you said about me at the party.

Janette: You're picking on me. Leave me alone! Another time!

Brent: When are we going to talk about things that bug me? You never want to talk if I'm upset.

Janette: You aren't respecting what I told you about my stress. I'm going for a walk. See you later.

Role-play the couple portrayed above. What could each have done to

- Assert his/her needs even more articulately, while
- Working with the stated needs of the other person?

Brent wants to engage in the conflict and Janette wants to protect herself by avoiding it. Each time an issue surfaces, they will have to reach agreement on avoidance/engagement, or this metaconflict will override any other emerging issues. Their fundamental issue is "How much conflict am I willing to risk to get what I want?" (Stuart 1980, 295). Of course, during the next conflict on a different topic, she may push for engagement and he may avoid, but usually people in a relationship specialize in one approach or the other. This overriding preference limits their ability to resolve their conflicts well.

Application 5.4   **Thinking about Styles**

Which is the best style for use in conflict? Read the four statements below and put a check mark by the one that you feel is the most accurate:

1. Avoidance of conflicts leads to unhappy marriages and work relationships—it keeps important issues buried.

2. Avoidance of unnecessary conflict helps promote harmony and keeps people from getting involved in unnecessary upsets.

3. The only way to really manage conflict is to work through it by engaging the other person.

4. Engagement in conflict leads to escalatory spirals and hurt for all parties.

Both avoidance and engagement are workable options in different circumstances (Canary and Spitzberg 1987; Canary and Cupach 1988). Recall the example of the couple struggling over their level of engagement. The woman's avoidance may have prompted the man to examine his reaction, decide that he was too reactive in social situations, and back off to reduce the conflict. Or her avoidance may have signaled to him that she did not care for his feelings and that he should start exiting the relationship. Avoidance and lack of overt conflict may indicate that the participants are unable to reach accommodation, that they cannot work through problem areas, and that they will gradually drift apart.

Avoidance of conflict often leads to a cycle that is self-perpetuating. Here is a typical pattern that occurs when one avoids conflict:

- We think of conflict as bad.
- We get nervous about a conflict we are experiencing.
- We avoid the conflict as long as possible.
- The conflict gets out of control and must be confronted.
- We handle it badly (Lulofs 1994, 42).

Avoidance is designed to protect the self and other from discord, yet the avoidance may lead to lack of clarity, set the stage for later uncontrollable conflict, and, lead back to even more avoidance (Bullis 1983).

There are times when avoidance can also be productive for a relationship. Avoidance serves as a defense against engagement, or confrontation, with the partner (Raush et al. 1974, 65). Spouses who practice avoidance within a bond of mutual affection often describe their marriage as happy. On the other hand, if the relationship is not important to you, avoidance can conserve energy that would be expended needlessly. We cannot invest equally in all relationships. Similarly, when someone attempts to engage you in conflict over an issue that is of trivial importance to you, your best choice is avoidance (Thomas 1976).

The tension between avoiding and engaging can be seen in the following dialogue:

Application 5.5	Should I Bring Up the Problem or Let It Go?

Marjorie:	Hi, Terry, what's going on?
Terry:	Oh, not much. [He is thinking, "If I say how upset I am, we'll get into it, and I just want to cool out."]
Marjorie:	You don't look very happy. [She's thinking, "I know you're upset about my mother's criticism of your job search plans. We might as well talk about it."]
Terry:	No big deal. ["I hope she just lets it go."]
Marjorie:	Are you mad at my mother? ["He must be more angry than I thought. This doesn't look good. Uh-oh."]
Terry:	Why do you always have to blow everything out of proportion?

(continued)

| **Application 5.5** | Should I Bring Up the Problem or Let It Go? |

The conflict then escalates as they struggle tacitly over whether to engage or avoid. In Application 5.3 we asked you to role-play better options that preserved both individual needs and relational needs. In the case of Marjorie and Terry, discuss how more self-disclosure could help this couple keep from getting stuck in avoidance, or contain their escalation so the relationship is preserved.

In the following section, avoidance *as a style* with specific tactics will be presented.

Avoidance

We have discussed the basic choice of whether to avoid or to engage. In this section we will explore the dynamics of *avoidance as a style* characterized by denial of the conflict, changing and avoiding topics, being noncommittal, and joking rather than dealing with the conflict at hand. The avoider may sidestep an issue by changing the topic or simply withdrawing from dealing with the issue. Just as use of the competitive style does not mean that one will get what one wants (because of interdependence with the other party), the use of avoidance as a style does not mean that the avoider will be ineffective. For instance, if a person is having a conflict with a large organization, the organization can enhance its position by not responding to correspondence on the matter. By pretending that the conflict does not exist, the high-power party is freed from dealing with the low-power party.

Avoidance can serve similar functions in interpersonal conflicts. If two roommates are both dating the same woman, they may refuse to discuss the subject openly, even if both of them are aware of the problem. Furthermore, in intimate relationships the style of avoidance is often invoked during conflict over sensitive matters. If a couple is having some difficulty in dealing with each other's families, they may not feel free to discuss the problem. Avoiding a conflict, however, does not prevent it. Conflict occurs when parties have the perception of incompatible goals, regardless of the style they choose to use in responding to this perception. Avoidance is simply an alternative mode of conflict expression. Some of the advantages and disadvantages of avoidance are presented in the following box.

Avoidance

ADVANTAGES

Avoidance can supply time to think of some other response to the conflict, as some people cannot "think on their feet." It is useful if the issue is trivial or if other important issues demand one's attention. If the relationship itself is unimportant to one person or if others can manage the conflict without his or her involvement, avoidance is a wise choice. Avoidance can also keep one from harm if he or she is in a relationship in

(continued)

Avoidance

which anything other than avoidance will bring a negative response from the other party. If one's goal is to keep the other party from influencing him or her, then avoidance helps to accomplish that goal.

EXAMPLE:

Shirley is a 23-year-old graduate who has recently broken off a long relationship with a man her parents like very much. They ask her to tell them "what went wrong" and offer to pay for a trip to visit him. Shirley decides not to take them up on the trip offer and says, "Many things happened to make us want to break up. Thanks for caring about me." She avoided a discussion that she felt would end in conflict.

DISADVANTAGES

Avoidance tends to demonstrate to other people that one does not "care enough to confront" them and gives the impression that one cannot change. It allows conflict to simmer and heat up unnecessarily rather than providing an avenue for reducing it. It keeps one from working through a conflict and reinforces the notion that conflict is terrible and best avoided. It allows partners each to follow his or her own course and pretend there is no mutual influence when, in fact, each influences the other. It usually preserves the conflict and sets the stage for a later explosion or backlash.

EXAMPLE:

Professor Lane has recently made several sarcastic comments about low class attendance. Chuck has missed three classes. Upon receiving a midterm grade of C, Chuck decides to wait for a while before asking for the reasons for the low grade. Later he decides to forget trying to get a B and instead to concentrate on geology, in which he has a higher average.

In marriages, avoidance of conflict relates to lower satisfaction in general. Be aware that stonewalling and avoidance are different approaches—stonewalling is a hostile tactic (see chapter 1). In one study, partners who believed in their first year of marriage that conflicts should be avoided also reported lower levels of happiness in the first three years of marriage than those who believed that conflicts should not be avoided (Crohan 1992). In some traditional marriages, however, stability and predictability are emphasized and continual renegotiation of what the spouses expect of one another is not useful. As Pike and Sillars (1985) found, "Satisfied couples used conflict avoidance to a greater extent than dissatisfied couples" (319). Similarly, for couples who are not traditional and who lead somewhat independent lives, "Avoidance may be a satisfying style of communication" (321).

Avoidance also can cycle back and affect the one avoiding. Studies show that a lot of avoidance (1) tends to result in health problems and (2) affects well-being (Nicolotti, el-Sheikh, and Whitson 2003; Braman 1998).

Finally, older couples in our culture who avoid conflict can often be characterized as happy, although inexpressive (Zietlow and Sillars 1988). Avoidance can be useful and appropriate when (1) open communication is not an integral part of the system (family or organization); (2) one does not want to invest the energy to "work through" the conflict to reach accommodation with the other—he or she wants to stay at arm's length and not get close; (3) the costs of confrontation are too high (Van de Vliert 1985); or (4) one simply hasn't learned how to engage in collaborative conflict management.

Avoidance and Culture

Whether avoidance is productive or destructive generally depends on the cultural contexts. Cultures differ in their valuing of avoidance. The Japanese avoid conflict in order to preserve congeniality and consensus and out of sensitivity to others' feelings. When one avoids, the implicit social hierarchy is reinforced—so avoidance makes sure the social bonds are not disrupted. In one study, Japanese students avoided a potentially conflictual relationship 80 percent of the time (Barnlund 1989).

In such collectivistic cultures, if you avoid a conflict, others will talk to you about how to heal wounds, make amends, and solve the conflict in indirect ways. In individualistic cultures, like the United States, on the other hand, if you avoid someone as the result of a conflict, your friends might cheer you on, suggesting that you "don't have to take that junk" and making other escalatory suggestions. Depending on the culture, those around you push you either to reconciliation or into continual fighting. In collectivistic cultures, one is "more concerned with the group's needs, goals and interests than with individualistic-oriented interest" (Trubisky, Ting-Toomey, and Lin 1991, 67). Thus, avoidance serves different functions in collectivistic cultures than in individualistic ones. In collectivistic cultures, avoidance represents "indirect working through," but in individualistic cultures, avoidance represents "indirect escalation."

The Avoid/Criticize Loop

When Mira says, "I can't talk to him, he is just so uncaring," she is both avoiding and arguing that no other response is possible with this type of avoidance.

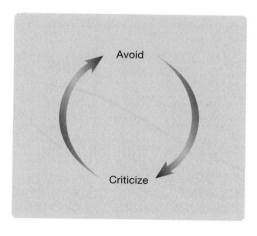

In the **avoid/criticize loop,** you avoid bringing up an issue to people directly but spend a lot of time talking about them to others. Viola owned a mountain cabin in Wyoming. Each of the cabin owners had horses and there was a general caretaker who took care of the horses. Each summer as Viola would return to live there for two months, she would stand on the front porch and say, "Can you believe that Mike (the caretaker) parks those horse trailers out there? They are in plain sight and really ugly—he should move them." When asked by her son Bill, "Mom, have you ever asked Mike to move them?" she said, "No, I shouldn't have to ask him; he should know they are ugly and need moving." The son, wanting to see her get some relief from the negative energy of criticism, said "Well Mom, he doesn't know what you are thinking, and I bet if you make a direct request, there's a good chance he will move them." Her response was, "If he were a *good* caretaker, he would know what I want." Thus, the avoid/criticize loop was kept in motion summer after summer and the horse trailers are still being parked there.

The avoid/criticize loop is quite common in professional circles and the business world. One talks about others, but doesn't join with them face to face and solve the problem. Especially if you are good at your job, you can really get involved in criticizing others—"he doesn't understand the new initiative," "she hasn't the training to see this accurately," "he is just so negative I can't stand to be in meetings with him." Critical statements substitute for a constructive request that keep us from directly asking for what we want. We make the other wrong, keeping ourselves in avoidance and continuing the criticism.

[handwritten margin note: Common in professional circles and the business world]

Avoidance Tactics

The lists of tactics presented in table 5.1 are from the work of Sillars et al. (1982), Sillars (1986), and Zietlow and Sillars (1988). This coding scheme has been applied in various forms to conflict between college roommates and between marital couples. The codes have been rearranged for this presentation. Readers wishing to pursue the scheme in greater detail should consult Zietlow and Sillars (1988) and Sillars (1986).

Avoidance tactics form distinct categories. For example, a person in a low-power position may refuse to engage the other by using both topic management and noncommittal remarks. Often avoidance takes the form of what Brockriede (1972) termed "seduction," which Sillars would classify as a combination of joking, evasive remarks, and topic avoidance. The low-power person using seduction tries to charm or trick the other conflict party into going along with what he or she desires. Argument tactics vary from classical reasoning, such as "ignoring the question, begging the question, the red-herring appeal, and appeals to ignorance or to prejudice" (Brockriede 1972, 4). The clash between issues is not direct; the issues are circumvented in a sometimes deceptive or charming way. It is not important to the seducer to appeal to the other party's sense of free choice. She or he wants what is wanted, no matter what, but is not willing (or perhaps able) to ask for it directly.

For instance, Liz asked friends of hers to help her find a job for the summer. She appeared weak, took little initiative, and became stuck in a low-energy period in her life. She frequently dropped in on her friends, politely asking for "any suggestions" they might have on finding a job, but was evasive and seemed confused when friends suggested that she needed help from an employment service. It appeared that she was trying to "seduce" her friends into taking responsibility for her but that she needed to

Table 5.1   Avoidance Tactics

Conflict Codes	Illustrations
A. Denial and equivocation	
1. *Direct denial.* Statements that deny that a conflict is present.	"That's not a problem."
2. *Implicit denial.* Statements that imply denial by providing a rationale for a denial statement, although the denial is not explicit.	"We've never had enough money to disagree over" (in response to a question about disagreements over money).
3. *Evasive remarks.* Failure to acknowledge or deny the presence of a conflict following a statement or inquiry about the conflict by the partner.	"That could be something that a person might resent but I don't know."
B. Topic management	
4. *Topic shifts.* Statements that terminate discussion of a conflict issue before each person has fully expressed an opinion or before the discussion has reached a sense of completion.	"Okay, the next issue is . . ." (the preceding statement occurs before each person has disclosed his or her opinion on the topic).
5. *Topic avoidance.* Statements that explicitly terminate discussion of a conflict issue before it has been fully discussed.	"I don't want to talk about that."
C. Noncommittal remarks	
6. *Noncommittal statements.* Statements that neither affirm nor deny the presence of conflict and are not evasive replies or topic shifts.	"The kids are growing up so fast I can't believe it."
7. *Noncommittal questions.* Unfocused and conflict-irrelevant questions.	"What do you think?"
8. *Abstract remarks.* Abstract principles, generalizations, or hypothetical statements that are not also evasive remarks.	"All people are irritable sometimes."
9. *Procedural remarks.* Procedural statements that supplant discussion of conflict.	"You aren't speaking loudly enough."
D. Irreverent remarks	
10. *Friendly joking.* Friendly joking or laughter.	"We need to either clean the house or torch it" (stated with friendly intonation).

Source: Reprinted, by permission of the publisher, from A. L. Sillars, "Procedures for Coding Interpersonal Conflict," rev. (Department of Communication Studies, University of Montana, 1986), 7–16.

preserve her own self-concept to avoid any direct clash with her friends. Finally, her choice of the avoidance strategy became a great disservice because her friends got tired of trying to help her and started avoiding her in return. All of the avoidance tactics in table 5.1 involve refusing to engage in the conflict. Note, however, that postponement of a conflict may not be avoidance per se but rather temporary avoidance with a promise to engage in the future. Bach and Wyden (1968) suggest that setting a time for a later conflict is a productive tactic. They suggest "fighting by appointment." Here are two examples of a conflict—the first using simple avoidance and the second using postponement:

Gloria is upset. She wants to talk to her husband, Sam, late at night. Sam, however, has an appointment at eight o'clock in the morning.

Gloria: I am so upset that I can't sleep. Whatever possessed you to talk about our summer plans to the Carters at the party? You know we've been trying to get free of doing things with them. You said last week—

Sam: Can't we talk about this in the morning?

Gloria: It's fine for you to say that. You don't have to deal with Sandra when she calls tomorrow to decide where we'll take our families for a joint vacation. I have to talk to her and tell her we changed our minds.

Sam: I'm sorry I brought it up. But I'm sleepy, and I don't want to talk about it.

At this point, the avoidance tactic Sam is using—"Maybe if I close my eyes all this hassle will go away"—is certainly not productive. His twin goals—to get some sleep and to avoid further antagonizing his wife—are not likely to be met. By this time Gloria is probably angry not only about his lack of discretion at the party but also about his refusal to talk to her about it. An example of a productive postponement tactic follows:

Sam: Gloria, I know you're upset. I also feel foolish. But I am exhausted, and I really don't want to deal with all the issues now. When Sandra calls tomorrow, tell her we haven't had a chance to talk yet and you'll call her back. Then when I come home from work tomorrow, we'll discuss the whole thing.

Gloria: You always say that, and we never talk.

Sam: This time we will. We'll sit down before dinner, banish the kids, and the two of us will talk. I know you're upset.

Gloria: OK, if we really will. I know it's hard to know what to say in public like that. They presume so much . . .

Postponement as a tactic works best when several conditions are present. First of all, the emotional content of the conflict needs to be acknowledged while other issues are deferred to a later time. Sam said, "I know you're upset," acknowledging the depth of Gloria's feelings. She would not have been likely to go along with the postponement if he had said, "It's stupid for you to be upset. We'll work it out later." After the emotional content is acknowledged, all parties have to agree on a time that is soon and realistic. If Sam had said, "We'll talk about it sometime soon," that would not have been precise enough. The other party has to believe that the postponer really means to bring up the issue later. Postponement does not work well as a tactic if the other people involved think they are being put off, never to return to the issue. Vague statements such as "We'll have to work on that sometime" or "Let's all try harder to get along" are often giveaways that the person wants avoidance rather than genuine postponement.

As you study the avoidance tactics in table 5.1, note that although avoidance comes in many costumes, its function is always to deflect, avoid and not engage in the conflict. Whether a professor who is confronted about a grade says, "That's an interesting point. It brings up an interesting question" (abstract remark), or a supervisor says, "That's enough complaining. Let's get back to the job" (topic shift), the basic dynamic is the same—to avoid the conflict.

ᴥ Competition

A competitive, or "power over," style is characterized by aggressive and uncooperative behavior—pursuing your own concerns at the expense of another. People with competitive styles attempt to gain power by direct confrontation, by trying to "win" the argument without adjusting to the other's goals and desires. A person with a competitive style is one who usually thinks it necessary to engage the other participant in overt disagreement. The conflict is seen as a "battleground," where winning is the goal, and concern for the other is of little or no importance. Someone who adopts a competitive style in conflicts would probably agree with statements such as, "Once I get wound up in a heated discussion, I find it difficult to stop," and "I like the excitement of engaging in verbal fights."

Competitive tactics can be employed in an **assertive** rather than an aggressive manner. Usually, however, aggression creeps into a competitive style. Whereas nonassertive people deny themselves and inhibit their expression of feelings and open striving for goals, assertive people enhance the self, work toward achieving desired goals, and are expressive. The aggressive person, however, carries the desire for self-expression to the extreme. Goals are accomplished at the expense of others. The aggressive style results in a put-down of others while the aggressor actively works against their goals. The assertive person can be competitive without berating, ridiculing, or damaging the other. The aggressive person is competitive primarily by trying to destroy the opponent's options.

The competitive style of managing conflict is productive if one competes to accomplish individual goals without destroying the other person. The relationship focus is maintained even while the topic is debated. Competition can be productively used in conflict, especially if the participants agree about the amount of aggressiveness that can legitimately be used in their conflict. The following box summarizes the advantages, as well as the disadvantages, of **competition.**

Competing

ADVANTAGES

Competition can be appropriate and useful when one has to make a quick, decisive action, such as in an emergency. Competition can generate creative ideas when others respond well to it or when one is in a situation in which the best performance or ideas are rewarded. It is useful if the external goal is more important than the relationship with the other person, such as in a short-term, nonrepeating relationship.

(continued)

Competing

Competition also informs the other of one's degree of commitment to the issue and can be used to demonstrate to the other party the importance of the issue. Competition can be useful in situations in which everyone agrees that competitive behavior is a sign of strength and in which such behavior is treated as a natural response, such as in games and sports or in a court battle. In these cases, other styles may confuse the resolution of the conflict.

EXAMPLE:

A human services agency competes with others for grant money from United Way. A limited amount is available, so the best proposal for solving a human services problem will be funded. The director of the agency competes with other directors for funding. The larger good of the community is served by the best program's gaining support.

DISADVANTAGES

Competition can harm the relationship between the parties because of the focus on external goals. Competition can be harmful if one party is unable or unwilling to deal with conflict in a head-on manner. Conflict waged competitively can encourage one party to go underground and use covert means to make the other pay. Competition tends to reduce all conflicts to two options—"either you are against me or with me," which limits one's roles to "winning" or "losing."

EXAMPLE:

Greg and Marcie, both young, competitive salespeople for the same company, live together. High sales, naturally, are rewarded by their manager. The couple keeps track of who's ahead of the other by placing a chart on the refrigerator. The week's loser has to do the laundry for the week. However, when Marcie's sales are low because she has been ill and has missed a lot of work, she angrily proclaims to Greg, "I'm not your slave! Do your own damn laundry!" Their relationship and her identity suffered from the "loss."

A competitive style is useful to show the other party how important an issue is to you. Especially when both parties agree that a competitive style is the norm, the style can be useful. Competitiveness can be a sign of strength or commitment. For example, two attorneys who one-up each other during negotiation are each attempting to persuade the other to alter his or her position.

On the other hand competitive tactics can damage a relationship, lock the participants into round-robin sequences of attack on each other, and deprive the participants of cooperative solutions to their problems. In severe cases a competitive style can become self-encapsulating—the participants can't give up or stop because they get too caught up in winning at any cost. When people launch never-ending court challenges against one another or continue to verbally abuse their ex-spouses for many decades, such approaches indicate a frozen position of competitiveness. The ever competitive combatants lose all perspective on the original goal, and they dedicate their energies to triumphing over the other.

Destructive Competition

Competitive tactics involve "verbally competitive or individualistic behavior" (Sillars et al. 1982, 83). These tactics focus on a win/lose orientation and often reflect a belief that what one person gets, the other loses (Thomas 1976). As a result, the party using competitive tactics will try to one-up the other party to gain an advantage (Rogers and Farace 1975). Table 5.2 displays various competitive tactics (Sillars et al. 1982; Sillars 1986; Zietlow and Sillars 1988).

Confrontational remarks summarized in table 5.2 are the essence of unhelpful competitive tactics. If someone personally criticizes you, rejects your statements, or acts in

Table 5.2   Destructive Competitive Tactics

Communication Category	Illustrations
1. *Personal criticism*. Remarks that directly criticize the personal characteristics or behaviors of the partner.	"Sometimes you leave, and you don't say goodbye or anything. You just walk right out."
2. *Rejection*. Statements in response to the partner's previous statements that imply personal antagonism toward the partner as well as disagreement.	"Oh, come on." "You're exaggerating."
3. *Hostile imperatives*. Requests, demands, arguments, threats, or other prescriptive statements that implicitly blame the partner and seek change in the partner's behavior.	"If you're not willing to look for a new job, then don't complain to me about it."
4. *Hostile jokes*. Joking, teasing, or sarcasm that is at the expense of the partner and that is accompanied by hostile intonation.	"It's very easy to say, 'Gee, I *really* appreciate you' [said mockingly], but that doesn't mean anything." "Every time you send me flowers, two days later I get the bill."
5. *Hostile questions*. Directive or leading questions that fault the partner.	"Who does most of the cleaning around here?"
6. *Presumptive remarks*. Statements that attribute thoughts, feelings, motivations, or behaviors to the partner that the partner does not acknowledge.	"You're purposely making yourself miserable."
7. *Denial of responsibility*. Statements that minimize or deny personal responsibility for conflict.	"That's not my fault."

Source: Adapted, by permission of publisher, from A. L. Sillars, "Procedures for Coding Interpersonal Conflict," rev. (Department of Communication Studies, University of Montana, 1986), 7–16.

a verbally hostile manner (with threats, jokes, or questions), you become vividly aware of the competitive nature of the exchange. Confrontational remarks are at the heart of "I win–you lose" perspectives on conflict. Just as with avoidance tactics, competitive tactics are often used in combination. Denial of responsibility for the conflict ("I didn't cause it!") is usually linked with presumptive remarks ("It's your fault"). Whatever the specific tactical move, a competitive approach demands that the other give in, take responsibility for the conflict, and solve it.

Most of us know that drugs and alcohol makes conflict worse. We often hear stories about someone being drunk and "going after the other." Research on this is quite clear—there is a definite link between substance abuse and harmful competitive tactics. Alcohol especially makes conflict episodes much more damaging (MacDonald, Zanna, and Holmes 2000; Edelgard and Colsman, 2002; Huang et al. 2001). It is so common that in some classes we have given the admonition *never engage in a conflict when you or the other has been drinking*. Of course, other drugs have even more dramatic effects. The recent surge in methamphetamine use is often correlated with violent interpersonal aggression. So, if you want your conflicts to be less damaging, avoid trying to work through difficult issues when you or the other is under the influence of a substance.

When one person has chosen, however tacitly, the rapist strategy, the other person functions as the victim, even though most people certainly do not want to be victimized. Often, the person who feels powerless and victimized escalates the conflict to a point, then gives up, thinking, "There's nothing I can do to win anyway." In effect, the participants cooperate in the escalation. A very angry person was once observed trying to take over the microphone and the floor at a convention. He shouted loudly, disrupted the proceedings, and was finally given five minutes to state his case. He did so, supporting with vehemence the pullout of his church group from a large national group, which he perceived as being too liberal. He chose the rapist style to escalate the conflict—soon he and the chairman were yelling back and forth at each other.

Threats

The most commonly used competitive tactic is the **threat.** We rush to use threats because we believe they are effective (Johnson and Ford 1996; Rubin, Pruitt, and Kim 1994). Many parents are too quick to say, "Do your homework or you're grounded." Supervisors too often say "get off at the next stop," in a misguided attempt to build a team.

Table 5.3 shows that a threat has to meet two criteria: the source of the threat must control the outcome and the threat must be seen as negative by the recipient. If you (the source) control the outcome ("If you don't go to bed in three minutes, I won't read you a story") and the sanction is seen as negative, then it is a threat. Similarly, if the professor says, "If you don't get your paper in on time, I will dock your grade," it is a threat. However, if the source does not control the outcome (a friend says, "If you don't get your paper in on time, it will hurt your grade"), the comment is not a threat—it is a **warning.**

Many parents get confused between warnings and threats. For example, "If you drink too much, you'll never graduate" seems like a threat, but it is not because the parent does not control the outcome. (If, on the other hand, the parent says "stop partying so much or I won't pay for next semester" it *is* a threat.) Or, if you say to a friend, "If you cheat on your boyfriend, he will leave you," you are issuing a warning. If you say, "I wouldn't challenge her on that topic," you are recommending a course of action to your friend.

Table 5.3   The Nature of Threats

	Source controls the outcome	Source does not control the outcome
Negative sanction	Threat	Warning
Positive sanction	Promise	Recommendation

Small children understand the difference between a positive and a negative sanction. If the parent says, "If you don't do the dishes, you'll have to spend the evening in your room," and the child has a computer or TV so that going to the room is not negative, the child may well retort, "Is that a threat or a promise?" As you can see, if the source controls the outcome and the recipient sees the outcome as positive, the threat is, instead, a **promise.**

A threat is credible only if (1) the source is in a position to administer the punishment, (2) the source appears willing to invoke the punishment, and (3) the punishment is something to be avoided. Often the other party is able to administer a threat but not willing to follow through. A co-worker who threatens to tell the boss that someone's work is not up to par may not carry out the threat if the boss dislikes "whistleblowers." Similarly, in an intimate relationship, one intimate might say, "If you want to make your summer plans alone, go ahead. But if you do, then don't expect to find me here when you come back." Such a threat (relational suicide) is effective only if the person who makes the threat is willing to lose the other person over this one issue. The perception that the other party is willing to carry out the threat makes it effective. As a result, intimates often avoid testing the willingness of the other party to invoke the threat and instead live under the control of the other person for years. In poker, a "bluff" is the ability to convince the other party that you are willing to bet all your winnings on a single draw of cards. The only successful bluff is one that the other party believes is true.

Finally, threats are effective only if the sanction is something the threatened party wants to avoid. One faculty member was offered a job at a competing university; when he went to the department chair and threatened to leave unless his salary was raised, the chair replied, "I hope you enjoy the climate down South."

As you have seen, threats can be either constructive or destructive. They can be used constructively to highlight the importance of the conflict topic to you, to get the attention of the other party, and to clarify one's perceptions of the power balance. On the other hand, threats tend to elicit the same behavior from the other, starting escalatory conflict spirals. They also block collaborative agreements and undermine trust in the relationship. Worse, we can become enamored of them (Kellermann and Shea 1996). If two dormitory roommates have been getting along well except for the issue of sweeping the floor, then a threat of "If you don't sweep more often, I'll process a room change!" might damage the trust in an otherwise good relationship. The recipient of the threat is likely to respond with a feeling of "OK, then go ahead. Who needs you anyway?" Unless trust can be regained, forging agreements will be extremely difficult. Once a threat has damaged the trust in the relationship, it often leads to further destructive tactics. Threats are overused, used too quickly, destroy trust, and tend to promote retaliation.

Application 5.6

Threats in Personal Relationships

Think of a time when you were threatened, or you used threats. What happened? Looking back, do you think the threats were effective in solving a problem and keeping the relationship intact? Were they harmful? What have you learned about your personal response to using threats or being threatened verbally?

Which of the following was true for you when you were the recipient of a threat or when you used a threat?

- I felt justified and right.
- I could not think of anything else to do.
- I wanted to hurt the other person.
- I wanted to get even after I was threatened.
- My feelings for/with the other person changed to fear, contempt, humiliation, rage, helplessness, or vengeance.
- I managed to avoid the other person.
- I broke the relationship, finally.
- I didn't like myself for issuing the threat.
- I didn't like myself for changing my behavior when someone threatened me.
- I felt hate/hated.
- I felt regret or remorse.

Can you think of positive outcomes of giving or receiving a threat? Discuss these with your small group.

As we have seen, threats present a risk in a relationship. Even if a credible threat is carried out, with the resulting win-lose negative sanction, what is gained? The immediate problem may be temporarily resolved, but the main goals (1) to solve the problem and (2) to preserve the relationship for work or closeness have not been met. The use of the threat automatically damages the second goal, "preserve the relationship."

⚜Compromise

Compromise is an intermediate style resulting in some gains and some losses for each party. It is moderately assertive and cooperative. A compromising style is characterized by beliefs such as "You can be satisfied with part of the pie" and "Give a little and get a little." When compromising, parties give up some important goals to gain others. Compromise is dependent on shared power because if the other party is perceived as powerless, no compelling reason to compromise exists.

Compromise is frequently confused with collaboration, which requires creative solutions and flexibility. Compromise differs, however, in that it requires trade-offs and exchanges (Folger, Poole, and Stutman 1993). Many times people avoid using compromise because something valuable has to be given up. While North American norms, especially in public life, encourage compromising, the style is not often the first choice in personal relationships. When power is unequal, compromising is usually giving in or giving up. The following box summarizes the advantages and disadvantages of compromising.

Compromising

ADVANTAGES

Compromise sometimes lets conflict parties accomplish important goals with less time expenditure than collaboration requires. It also reinforces a power balance that can be used to achieve temporary or expedient settlements in time-pressured situations. It can be used as a backup method for decision making when other styles fail. Further, it has the advantage of having external moral force; therefore, it appears reasonable to most parties. Compromise works best when other styles have failed or are clearly unsuitable.

EXAMPLE:

Mark and Sheila, ages 10 and 8, both want to play with the new computer game they received for Christmas. After a noisy argument, their parents tell them to work something out that is fair. They decide that if no one else is using the game, they can play without asking, but if they both want to play at the same time, they have to either play a game together or take turns by hours (every other hour). The compromise of taking turns works well as a conflict reduction device. The parents can intervene simply by asking, "Whose turn is it?"

DISADVANTAGES

Compromise can become an easy way out—a "formula" solution not based on the demands of a particular situation. For some people, compromise always seems to be a form of "loss" rather than a form of "win." It prevents creative new options because it is easy and handy to use. Flipping a coin or "splitting the difference" can be a sophisticated form of avoidance of issues that need to be discussed. These chance measures, such as drawing straws or picking a number, are not really compromise. They are arbitration, with the "arbiter" being chance. True compromise requires each side giving something in order to get an agreement; she is selling a bike and I pay more than I want to and she gets less than she wants for the bike.

(continued)

Compromising

EXAMPLE:

Two friends from home decide to room together at college. Sarah wants to live in Jesse dorm with some other friends she has met. Kate wants to live in Brantley, an all-female dorm, so she can have more privacy. They decide that it wouldn't be fair for either one to get her first choice, so they compromise on Craig, where neither knows anyone. At midyear, they want to change roommates since neither is happy with the choice. Sarah and Kate might have been able to come up with a better solution if they had worked at it.

Research has not clarified compromise tactics to the extent that it has avoidance and competition, but the tactics shown in table 5.4 have been compiled to exemplify compromise.

Table 5.4   Compromise Tactics

Communication Category	Illustrations
1. Appeal to fairness	"You got what you wanted last time."
	"It's not fair to ask me to do all the writing. We both are getting the grant support. Why don't you do your part and I'll do mine?"
	"I don't make as much money as you do. It's not fair to make me pay half of all the expenses."
2. Suggest a trade-off	"How are we going to pay for all that summer help? Are you willing to wait to start the staff development program for half a year or so?"
	"I won't give on my expectations that you pay me back for the car accident, but I will consider your working off some of the money by doing jobs for me."
3. Maximize wins/minimize losses	"I'll give up the idea of going to my folks' for Christmas if you'll take a real vacation so we can spend some time together."
4. Offer a quick, short-term solution	"Since we don't have time to gather all the data, how about if we do it my way for a month and then reassess when the data comes in and you get a chance to see how you like it?"

Source: Adapted, by permission of publisher, from A. L. Sillars, "Procedures for Coding Interpersonal Conflict," rev. (Department of Communication Studies, University of Montana, 1986), 7–16.

One's view of compromise is a good litmus test of how you view conflict in general. Think about the famous "the cup is half empty" versus "the cup is half full" aphorism that applies to compromise. Some see compromise as "both of us lose something" and others see it as "both of us win something." Clearly, compromise means a middle ground between you and the other and involves a moderate and balanced amount of concern for self and concern for other. "Compromises" can result from good-faith efforts, and may be very effective solutions. Compromise as a *style* sometimes shortchanges the conflict process, while at other times it effectively deals with the reality that not everyone can get everything they want.

Accommodation

One who practices **accommodation** does not assert individual needs and prefers a cooperative and harmonizing approach (Neff and Harter 2002). The individual sets aside his or her concerns in favor of pleasing the other people involved (this relational goal may be the most important goal for the accommodating person).

One may gladly yield to someone else or may do so grudgingly and bitterly. The accompanying emotion can be highly divergent for those using accommodation, from gentle pleasure at smoothing ruffled feelings to angry, hostile compliance because one has too little power to protest what is being done. The accommodating person may think that he or she is serving the good of the group, family, or team by giving in, sacrificing, or stepping aside. Sometimes this is true; often, however, the accommodator could better serve the needs of the larger group by staying engaged longer and using a more assertive style. Sometimes people who habitually use this style play the role of the martyr, bitter complainer, whiner, or saboteur. They may yield in a passive way or concede (Folger, Poole, and Stutman 1993).

The following box summarizes the advantages and disadvantages of accommodation.

Accommodating

ADVANTAGES

When one finds that he or she is wrong, it can be best to accommodate the other to demonstrate reasonableness. If an issue is important to one person and not important to the other, the latter can give a little to gain a lot. In addition, accommodation can prevent one party from harming the other—one can minimize losses when he or she will probably lose anyway. If harmony or maintenance of the relationship is currently the most crucial goal, accommodation allows the relationship to continue without overt conflict. Accommodation to a senior or seasoned person can be a way of managing conflict by betting on the most experienced person's judgment.

EXAMPLE:

A forest service manager asks the newest staff member if he is interested in learning about land trades with other federal agencies. The new employee knows that the manager must assign someone from his office to help the person in charge of land trades. The employee

(continued)

Accommodating

says, "It's not something I know much about, but I wouldn't mind learning." The manager, who could have assigned the new employee anyway, thanks him for his positive attitude about new responsibilities. The new employee's goals would not have been well served by his saying, "I have no interest in getting into that area. There is too much red tape, and it moves too slowly."

DISADVANTAGES

Accommodation can foster an undertone of competitiveness if people develop a pattern of showing each other how nice they can be. People can one-up others by showing how eminently reasonable they are. Accommodation of this type tends to reduce creative options. Further, if partners overuse accommodation, their commitment to the relationship is never tested, since one or the other always gives in. This pattern can result in a pseudo-solution, especially if one or both parties resent the accommodation; it will almost surely boomerang later. Accommodation can further one person's lack of power. It may signal to that person that the other is not invested enough in the conflict to struggle through, thus encouraging the low-power party to withhold energy and caring. A female student wrote the following example of a learned pattern of avoidance and its resulting accommodation.

EXAMPLE:

"In our home, conflict was avoided or denied at all costs, so I grew up without seeing conflicts managed in a satisfactory way, and I felt that conflict was somehow 'bad' and would never be resolved. This experience fit well with the rewards of being a 'good' girl (accommodating to others), which combined so I was not even sensitive to wishes and desires that might lead to conflict."

Table 5.5 presents tactics that accompany an accommodating style.

Accommodation is one of the most common responses to conflict between people but it is the least noticed or studied. One of the reasons is that when someone accommodates, you may not even be aware of it. If you say, "I want to go sledding" and your brother says, "whatever," accommodation has occurred. If it were more overt, like competitive moves, it would be easier to see and classify. As a result, few communication studies look intensely at accommodation—they just don't see it.

Another reason that accommodation is not noticed is that it becomes such a patterned response that even the accommodator doesn't know he or she is doing it. If you automatically agree with everything your romantic partner suggests, it is usually such a patterned response that you don't even realize you are accommodating him or her. In a traditional marriage, if the husband comes home for dinner and says, "How about turkey tonight?" an accommodating wife will say, "OK, I bet I have some frozen we can thaw out, and I can make gravy." While she was planning on beef stroganoff, she automatically adjusts to his preferences and accommodates.

Table 5.5   Accommodation Tactics

Communication Category	Illustrations
1. Giving up/giving in	"Have it your way." "I don't want to fight about this."
2. Disengagement	"I couldn't care less." "I won't be here anyway. It doesn't matter." "I don't need to be involved in this." "I don't have time to be working on this issue."
3. Denial of needs	"I'll be fine here. You go ahead." "It's OK. I can stay late and do it."
4. Expression of desire for harmony	"It's forgotten. Don't worry about it" (referring to a previous discount or hurt). "It's more important to me that we work together on this than that I do what I want." "I am miserable when we fight. Let's put all this behind us and start over. I don't even remember what we are hassling each other about."

Source: Adapted, by permission of publisher, from A. L. Sillars, "Procedures for Coding Interpersonal Conflict," rev. (Department of Communication Studies, University of Montana, 1986), 7–16.

Accommodation may be linked to **codependence.** In codependent relationships, what one person does, thinks, or feels is dependent on what someone else does, thinks or feels. Codependent relationships often result from a person growing up in an alcoholic or abusive family. The extreme escalation of the alcoholic or abusive person causes the spouse or child to become hypervigilant, to tune in with exquisite attention to the moods, needs, feelings and predicted behavior of a powerful other. Ultimately, the vigilant person does not know what she/he thinks, feels or needs, except to feel safe. One of the hardest questions a counselor asks many women and some men is, "What are you feeling?" For the person who has lived with a system of accommodation or codependence, the answer is usually, "I don't know."

As you read back over Sillars's categories of accommodation in table 5.5, you can see why such responses are hard to identify and study. They are often seen as just being kind, as being responsive to the partner, or as moves that keep things from coming up. Certainly it is true that not every issue needs to be addressed, and accommodation can be a kind and helpful part of anyone's repertoire. The problem as we search for effective conflict management styles can be that accommodation can reflect a position of "I have no choice." That power imbalance, as we have discovered, harms ongoing relationships. As we become more sensitized to accommodation moves, we should be able to expand our understanding of them and their role in conflict events.

❧Collaboration

Collaborative processes unleash this catalytic power and mobilize joint action among the stakeholders.
—Barbara Gray, *Collaborating: Finding Common Ground for Multiparty Problems*

Collaboration demands the most constructive engagement of any of the conflict styles. Collaboration shows a high level of concern for one's own goals, the goals of others, the successful solution of the problem, and the enhancement of the relationship. Note that collaboration, unlike compromise, involves not a moderate level of concern for goals but a high level of concern for them. Collaboration is an "invitational rhetoric" that invites the other's perspective so the two of you can reach a resolution that honors you both (Foss and Griffin 1995).

A collaborative conflict does not conclude until both parties are reasonably satisfied and can jointly support a solution. Relationships are better, not worse, than when the conflict began. No one person ends up feeling justified or right. The style is cooperative, effective, and focused on team effort, partnership, or shared personal goals. It is also sometimes called mutual problem solving. It is the style that calls on all your best communication skills.

Collaboration involves making descriptive and disclosing statements and soliciting reactions from the other party. One makes concessions when necessary and accepts responsibility for one's own part in the conflict. Collaboration does not mean taking total responsibility, such as saying, "It's all my fault. I shouldn't have gotten angry." Rather, collaboration is a struggle with the other to find mutually agreeable solutions. Parties engage at an exploratory, problem-solving level rather than avoiding or destroying each other. Collaboration is the search for a *new* way.

Collaboration is characterized by statements such as "When I get in conflict with someone, I try to work creatively with them to find new options," or "I like to assert myself, and I also like to cooperate with others." Collaboration differs from compromise because in compromise, the parties look for an easy intermediate position that partially satisfies them both, whereas in collaboration, the parties work creatively to find new solutions that will maximize goals for them both.

Application 5.7   Salary, Public Regard, and Secret Agreements

Both Lillian and Greg had been working in a hospital, Lillian as the Vice President for Financial Affairs, and Greg as a program director for financial campaigns. Both Lillian and Greg reported directly to the CFO, who retired. Both applied for his job, but were disappointed when someone from another state was hired. However, both Lillian, the VP, and Greg came to like and respect Karen, the new CFO. Lillian had the higher position, although Greg also reported to the CFO, not to Lillian. The conflict arose when time for pay raises and performance reviews came around. Karen told Greg that she valued him,

(continued)

Salary, Public Regard,
and Secret Agreements

and did not want to lose him. He had been looking for another job. So she promoted him to "Vice President for Financial Growth," with a salary increase slightly above Lillian's. Lillian retained her position as Vice President.

What were they thinking and feeling?

Karen: I am so new here that I don't want to train another campaign director. Greg knows everyone in town. When he told me he was thinking of going back to his previous hospital as CFO, I believed him. He is a competitive, aggressive person who wants to be at the top. I couldn't afford to lose him. However, I don't quite trust him. He is doing a lot of public forums where he says he speaks for the hospital, without checking with me. He is a lone ranger. And now I have alienated Lillian who, while quiet, is really the heart and soul of this office. She has years of institutional history and everyone trusts her. She is willing to do the hard, daily work of financial oversight. I should not have caved in to Greg's request without talking it over with Lillian and my President. I can see that I put her in a one-down position with Greg. I'm going to have to fix this, and quick. She could easily retire early and then we'd all lose.

Lillian: I am sure Karen does not know how much Greg upstages me. He never includes me in the conversation when we are with higher-ups or big donors. He treats me like the secretary. I didn't mind so much, because I know Karen values me and after all, I was second to her. Now she has effectively raised Greg above me, although I don't have to report to him. And I heard from someone I trust that he wants Karen's job. I am upset, but more with Greg than Karen. Karen, I think, got bullied, and I'm paying the price. It's not ok with me. We need to talk. I do not want to retire, but I will never put myself in the position to report to Greg.

Greg: I am pleased that Karen sees my worth. I have brought a lot of money to the hospital, and I'm developing a good public presence. I don't respect Lillian's quiet style. She lets a lot of opportunities go by without telling donors what we need. She's more of an accountant than a vice president. I don't like it that Karen goes to her for everything. I really dislike the team meetings when nothing gets done. Karen's always talking about a "team plan," but I just want to be left alone to make connections with donors and then let the President figure out what the priorities are. I do fine on my own.

Of the following options, pick the one that you think has the best chance of getting all three people to come up with a collaborative (win-win) solution. Then role-play your preferred option with all three people.

(continued)

Application 5.7 — Salary, Public Regard, and Secret Agreements

Option 1.   Karen calls a meeting with Greg and Lillian and says that she has made a mistake in raising Greg without including Lillian. She calls for a team decision about how to rectify the relationship, content, identity, and process issues.

Option 2.   Karen talks with Greg and Lillian separately, asking Greg to change some of his public behavior, and telling Lillian that Karen made a mistake and wants to brainstorm how to resolve the issue.

Option 3.   Karen calls a meeting with the President and Lillian and Greg and explains that Greg is extremely valuable to the team, but no more so than Lillian, so she is going to raise Lillian's salary to Greg's level. She asks them to collaborate more in public.

Option 4.   None of the above. Develop a plan that you think might work, including beginning language, based on what the three parties think and feel. The object is a collaborative outcome.

Research on the effect of collaborative styles is quite consistent—when one learns how to use them, they are successful tools for conflict management (Kuhn and Poole 2000). Collaboration results in "high joint benefit for the bargainers" (Tutzauer and Roloff 1988) and provides a constructive response to the conflict (Rusbult, Johnson, and Morrow 1984). Collaborative styles in a variety of contexts result in better decisions and greater satisfaction with partners (Sillars 1980; Wall and Galanes 1986; Tutzauer and Roloff 1988; Pruitt 1981; Gayle-Hackett 1989a). Cooperative styles allow conflict parties to find mutually agreeable solutions, whether the conflict occurs in an intimate or work situation.

One of the downsides to collaboration is that one party sometimes tries to use it exclusively and denigrates the other conflict party for not using it. For example, if one party is trying to collaborate and the other party is avoiding or competing, the first party might say, "I tried to solve the conflict, but he wouldn't." Negative views of the other's chosen style can become a sophisticated form of "one up"—in other words, if what I did was fine, the other person must be the cause of the continued conflict. The collaborator gives up too soon.

The following box summarizes the advantages and disadvantages of collaboration.

Collaborating

ADVANTAGES

Collaboration works well when one wants to find an integrative solution that will satisfy both parties. It generates new ideas, shows respect for the other party, and gains commitment to the solution from both parties. Because collaboration incorporates the

(continued)

Collaborating

feelings of the concerned parties, they both feel that the solutions are reality based. Collaboration is a high-energy style that fits people in long-term, committed relationships, whether personal or professional. Collaboration actively affirms the importance of relationship and content goals and thus builds a team or partnership approach to conflict management. When collaboration works, it prevents one from using destructive means such as violence. It demonstrates to the parties that conflict can be productive.

EXAMPLE:

Anne, an intern at a hospital, has been given a "mission impossible" that requires that she diagnose and keep charts on patients under the supervision of four different doctors. Her fellow interns work collaboratively to relieve her of some of the work. They want to demonstrate the need for more reasonable assignments, support Anne as a friend, and avoid being assigned Anne's work if she gets sick or resigns.

DISADVANTAGES

As with any style, if collaboration is the only style used, one can become imprisoned in it. If investment in the relationship or issue is low, collaboration is not worth the time and energy consumed. Further, people who are more verbally skilled than others can use collaboration in very manipulative ways, which results in a continued power discrepancy between the parties. For example, if one party uses collaboration, he or she may accuse the other of being "unreasonable" by choosing a different style. Often, high-power persons use pseudocollaboration to maintain the power imbalance. These latter cases are not really collaboration because at least two people are required to collaborate. However, one avoider can frustrate the intentions of four collaborators.

EXAMPLE:

Members of a small group in a communication class are under time pressure to finish their project, due in one week. They overuse collaborative techniques such as consensus building, brainstorming, paraphrasing, and bringing out silent members. Quickly breaking up into subgroups would better serve the individual and relational goals of the group, but the group clings to a time-consuming method of making decisions long after they should have adapted their style to meet the deadline.

The collaborative tactics presented in table 5.6 induce, or persuade, the other party to cooperate in finding a mutually favorable resolution to the conflict. They reflect a "mutual versus individual" orientation (Canary and Cupach 1988). Collaboration involves both parties working together for solutions that not only end the conflict but also maximize the gains for both parties. The term *integrative* can be used to describe collaborative tactics, since the tactics help people recognize their interdependence (Walton and McKersie 1965). Collaborative tactics also have been labeled prosocial (Roloff 1976; Sillars 1986). The goals of the individuals and the relationship as a whole are paramount.

Table 5.6   Collaborative Tactics

Conflict Codes	Illustrations
A. Analytic remarks	
1. *Descriptive statements*. Nonevaluative statements about observable events related to conflict.	"I criticized you yesterday for getting angry with the kids."
2. *Disclosing statements*. Nonevaluative statements about events related to conflict that the partner cannot observe, such as thoughts, feelings, intentions, motivations, and past history.	"I swear I never had such a bad week as that week."
3. *Qualifying statements*. Statements that explicitly qualify the nature and extent of conflict.	"Communication is mainly a problem when we're tired."
4. *Solicitation of disclosure.* Nonhostile questions about events related to conflict that cannot be observed (thoughts, feelings, intentions, motives, or past history).	"What were you thinking when you said . . . ?"
5. *Solicitation of criticism*. Nonhostile questions soliciting criticism of oneself.	"Does it bother you when I stay up late?"
B. Conciliatory remarks	
1. *Supportive remarks*. Statements that refer to understanding, support, acceptance, positive regard for the partner, shared interests, and goals.	"I can see why you would be upset."
2. *Concessions*. Statements that express a willingness to change, show flexibility, make concessions, or consider mutually acceptable solutions to conflicts.	"I think I could work on that more."
3. *Acceptance of responsibility*. Statements that attribute responsibility for conflict to self or to both parties.	"I think we've both contributed to the problem."

Source: Adapted, by permission of publisher, from A. L. Sillars, "Procedures for Coding Interpersonal Conflict," rev. (Department of Communication Studies, University of Montana, 1986), 7–16.

Collaborative tactics involve a stance toward conflict management that is very different from that of competitive tactics. A competitive tactic assumes that the size of the pie is finite; therefore, one's tactics are designed to maximize gains for oneself and losses for the other. Collaborative tactics, however, assume that the size of the pie can be increased by working with the other party. Both can leave the conflict with something they value.

Some people experience only avoidant or competitive attitudes toward conflict and have a difficult time visualizing a collaborative approach. If each time you have conflict you immediately say to your conflict partner, "You are wrong," you are likely to receive a competitive response in return. Collaboration calls for a willingness to move with rather than against the other—a willingness to explore and struggle precisely when you may not feel like it. You do not give up your self-interest; you integrate it with the other's self-interest to reach agreement. Usually, a collaborative approach to conflict management involves the use of multiple tactics listed in table 5.6.

You need not like your co-collaborators, but you do have to communicate respect. Collaboration does require "we" language rather than "I" language. Because parties work together for mutually desirable outcomes and protect their own as well as each other's interests, many times respect and caring develop as by-products of the collaborative effort.

In table 5.6, the first major classification of collaborative tactics is "analytic remarks," which allow one to collaborate by making descriptive, disclosing, or other types of statements. The following examples reflect descriptive statements, which are the first category of analytic remarks (Yarbrough 1977):

- Describe without interpretation. Describe what you feel, see, hear, touch, and smell instead of your guesses about the behavior.

    Example: "You're so quiet. Ever since I said I didn't want to go out tonight and would rather stay home and read, you haven't spoken to me," not "You never understand when I want to spend some time alone!"

- Focus on what is, instead of what should be.

    Example: "You look angry. Are you?" not "You shouldn't be angry just because I want to stay home."

- Describe your own experience instead of attributing things to the other person.

    Example: "I'm finding myself not wanting to bring up any ideas because I'm afraid you will ignore them," not "You are getting more critical all the time."

One makes disclosing statements by saying such things as "I am having trouble tracking this issue" or otherwise reporting one's feelings while in the conflict. The flip side of the coin is to solicit disclosure from the other party, such as by saying, "What makes you so upset when I bring up the summer plans?" As table 5.6 illustrates, one can also make qualifying statements and solicit criticism as ways to move the conflict toward collaboration.

The final three categories of collaborative tactics, classified as conciliatory remarks, are (1) supportive remarks ("I can see why that is difficult—we have all been ganging up on you"); (2) concessions ("OK, I agree I need to find new ways to deal with this problem"); and (3) acceptance of responsibility ("Yes, I have been acting uncooperatively lately"). All conciliatory remarks acknowledge one's own role in the conflict and offer an "olive branch" of hope and reconciliation to the other, paving the way to successful management of the conflict. All of the collaborative tactics move the conflict into a third dimension where partners neither avoid nor blame but grapple with the conflict as a joint problem to be solved.

Collaborative tactics are associated with successful conflict management. Although non-intimate conflict participants use collaboration infrequently (Barnlund 1989), participants who do use collaboration report "relational intimacy" (Cupach 1980); "perceived communicator appropriateness, effectiveness and attractiveness" (Canary and Spitzberg 1987); "satisfaction with the partner and relationship" (Gottman 1982; Sillars 1980); and "satisfaction with the conflict outcomes" (Canary and Cupach 1988, 306; Wall and Galanes 1986). Similarly, popular prescriptions for conflict management specify that one should work with the partner to establish mutual gain and to preserve the relationship and should engage in neither avoidance nor verbal aggressiveness but try to find mutual solutions to the problems (Fisher and Ury 1981; Fisher and Brown 1988) Fisher and Shapiro, 2005.

～Cautions about Styles

Although considerable research has been done on individual conflict styles, there are limitations to the research. Especially when one decides to pursue partnership, collaborative, and mutual-influence approaches, purely individual styles do not exist. One is always influenced by others, and should be, when striving for cooperative goals. For instance, if you want to practice constructive partnership approaches, you will not automatically respond to a sarcastic threat (competition) with a counterthreat or by backing down (accommodation or avoidance). You will, instead, look for ways to reframe what has happened and for more constructive options, even if you feel justified in blasting back at what feels like a threatening opponent. You will find it useful to thoroughly understand the styles and their supporting tactics so you can make educated choices about moves that are available to you during conflict.

One limitation of the research on conflict styles is that most studies are based on participants' "perceptions" of their conflict styles. One's vantage point can significantly alter the given response. Various instruments measuring conflict style have been administered to hundreds of people experiencing conflict in the workplace. When participants fill out the conflict style scales on themselves and on others, two predominant findings emerge:

- People most often see themselves as trying to solve the problem (using integrative styles) (McCready et al. 1996).
- People most often see others as using controlling or aggressive styles.

These results indicate that one's perception of conflict style depends on *whether one is rating oneself or others*. People tend to see themselves as trying to solve the conflict and the other as blocking the resolution of the conflict. Although no large-scale studies have been completed on the differences between self and other perceptions of conflict styles, Thomas and Pondy (1977) asked 66 managers to recall a recent conflict and state which style was used by each party. Overwhelmingly, the managers saw themselves as cooperative, and the other party as primarily competitive, demanding, and refusing. Gayle (1991) found a similar social desirability bias (giving answers that "look good"). Unfortunately, your perception of what you did will probably not be corroborated by the other person. In conflict, we tend to see ourselves in a positive light and others in a negative light. Human beings tend to value their own individual approaches to life. All too often we assume that our choices about behavior, values, and goals are the right ones. There-fore, we are right if we are "aggressive," "cooperative," "polite," "fair-minded," or "real-istic." Since we evaluate styles depending on whether they are ours or someone else's, our vantage point determines our perceptions.

A second limitation to styles research is that it demonstrates mixed results—some studies show differences between the genders and some show no differences (Gayle-Hackett 1989b). When style studies are done on high school and college students, women report themselves as being more collaborative than do men, who report them-selves as being more competitive. However, when studies are done in the workplace with older adults, male–female differences disappear (Gayle-Hackett 1989a; Rahim 1986; Bell, Chafetz, and Horn 1982; Renwick 1977; Rossi and Todd-Mancillas 1987; Shockley-Zalabak 1981; Portello and Long 1994; Korabik, Baril, and Watson 1993; Gayle 1991). In real-life settings, conflict styles are more closely related to location in the structure (as supervisor, employee, or owner) than to gender.

A third reporting bias is the underreporting of the amount of avoidance people actu-ally use (Gayle-Hackett 1989a; Gayle 1991). When a questionnaire asks you about an ongoing conflict, you answer about conflicts that are important to you. Those you have avoided and have no interest or investment in are most likely not even remembered; thus we underreport the amount of avoidance we actually use.

A fourth limitation of conflict style research is that *measures are not process oriented.* Some individuals develop preferred sequences of styles; for example, one may begin a conflict by avoiding, then move to competing, then finally collaborate with the other party. Most measuring instruments treat personal styles as if they are traits belonging to one person—something one always does or something that describes the person instead of the behavior. The accurate assessment of one's conflict style should presuppose some change over time to reflect the variability that most people enact in their lives. Baxter (1982), for example, demonstrated that conflict expressions of small-group participants differ depending on the phase of group decision making in which the group is engaged. The following chart illustrates predominant styles with fluctuations across time. Note the variability within the styles used by the two people, both of whom predominantly avoid conflict.

	Time 1	Time 2	Time 3	Time 4	Time 5	Time 6	Time 7	Time 8	Time 9
Person A:	avoid	avoid	compete	avoid	avoid	avoid	compete	avoid	avoid
Person B:	avoid	avoid	accommodate	avoid	avoid	avoid	accommodate	avoid	avoid

Both would score as "avoiders" on a general style measure, yet over time, each one demonstrates a distinctly different pattern. Measuring general styles does not reflect overtime differences between people.

Not only do our styles change with the progress of the conflict, they also change as a result of our life experiences. A young man who is always competitive learns from his romantic partner how to collaborate—thus changing his style. Alternately, someone who avoids conflict learns through trial and error to engage in the conflict earlier, thus changing her predominant mode. One can change a preferred conflict style, especially if the old style ceases to work well.

A fifth limitation of conflict style research is that measures give the impression of consistency across settings, relationships, and time. Most of the instruments, in fact, ask you to respond "in general." Of course, for many people, "in general" doesn't capture the changes they experience from relationship to relationship. When people respond to style measures "for a particular relationship" or conflict, about 50 percent of the people report disparate styles in different contexts. For example, many people compete at work but avoid conflict at home. Similarly, many avoid conflict at work but collaborate at home. Yet most instruments don't account for these differences. Some research is beginning to assess conflict styles across contexts and is confirming that many people have disparate styles in different contexts (Marin, Sherblom, and Shipps 1994). For example, as Sun and Payne (2004) show, "situational characteristics play a strong role in determining police actions during conflict resolution" (516).

Even within one setting, such as work, we use different styles with different partners. Putnam and Wilson (1982) demonstrated that employees prefer nonconfrontation when in a peer-related conflict in an organization, but they choose forceful communication to manage conflict with subordinates. Eric, a college debater, uses different styles in different contexts when he is in public; he competes every chance he gets. He loves to match wits with others, push hard for what he wants, and win arguments. He is a good-humored and driven young man in public situations. Yet in private with his wife, he avoids conflict as though it were a dreaded disease. When Joan brings up conflictual issues, Eric either avoids or completely accommodates—he cannot stand conflict within an intimate relationship. Yet if Eric were to fill out a widely used style instrument, he would be asked to report how he acts in conflicts, without a specific context designated. It is easy to watch someone in conflict and assume that the chosen style reflects some underlying personality dimension. But since most people adapt to different situations, with a preferred choice in one context and another choice in a different context, to give them a single label, such as a "compromiser," is a gross oversimplification.

As you might expect, our styles change over time. One study showed, for instance, that married couples who were confrontational early in their marriage tended to "mellow" and become more collaborative across time (Mackey and O'Brien 1998).

A sixth limitation of conflict style research is that one's style of conflict is assumed to be a clear reflection of an underlying motivation—a stable personality trait. Competers, however, may not want to "run over you," and avoiders may actually care about their relationships. For example, in Ellen's first marriage, she developed the pattern of occasionally throwing dishes when she was intensely angry. Her first husband would then leave the house. A few years later, after she had married Mick, they got into a screaming argument. Ellen threw a dish at Mick, who promptly went to the kitchen, picked up most of the available dishes on the counter, smashed them on the floor, shouting that she would not throw dishes at him! As a result of this aggressive interaction, Ellen realized that what she wanted was someone who would stay and fight out the problem instead of leaving the scene. Neither has thrown a dish since. At first glance, one could say that Ellen's aggressive style was an attempt to get her own way, stifle all opposition, and dominate Mick. The "true" motivation emerged in the interaction—which was a desire for intimacy.

A seventh limitation of current research is that it ignores the interactive dynamics in a conflict situation. As noted previously, our choices are not just the results of some personality quirk—they are responses to many elements of a conflict. This issue is of such fundamental importance that the next section will examine it in detail.

❧Beyond Styles: Harmful Conflict Approaches

Of the five styles we present in detail in this chapter, each can have its place in a reasonable approach to conflict management. While we maintain a bias toward collaboration when that high-energy style is appropriate, the others serve helpful functions, as we have demonstrated. We will now discuss approaches to conflict that are not appropriate, lead to negative outcomes, and violate the core principles of a communication approach to conflict resolution. These are not styles as such, but practices and approaches that rest on a win-lose belief about conflict.

Verbal Aggressiveness

Verbal aggressiveness is a broader category of communication than threats. Verbal aggressiveness is a form of communicative violence. Rather than just telling someone what might happen to them, when you use verbal aggression you "attack the self-concepts" of other people (Infante and Wigley 1986). Character attacks ("You are just a rotten wife"), insults ("Well, I suppose someone with your intelligence would see it that way"), rough teasing, ridicule, and profanity all are forms of verbal aggressiveness. Many conflict parties, when engaged in struggle, immediately begin attacking each other. Once one focuses on the other as the sole cause of the difficulties, it is easy to slip into disparaging personal remarks. Therefore, whether you label it as "personal criticism" or "verbal aggressiveness," this competitive tactic involves attacking the other person. The following are examples of verbal aggressiveness:

> You're so stupid.
>
> You're an imbecile.
>
> You're ugly.
>
> You're low class.
>
> I wish you would die/get hit by a car/fall off the face of the earth.
>
> No one else would have you.

In individualistic cultures, aggressive talk is common. It attacks the other's character, background, abilities, physical appearance, and the like (Carey and Mongeau 1996). The more important your relationship with someone, the more verbal aggression within the relationship hurts (Martin, Anderson, and Horvath 1996). In a collectivistic culture, on the other hand, the most damaging verbal abuse is directed toward a person's group, clan, tribe, village, or family, such as when you say, "He's a drunken Irishman" (Vissing and Baily 1996), or "You people are all animals."

One study examined the use of verbal aggression in college-age couples and found that based on 5,000 American couples, men and women engage in equal amounts of verbal aggression (Sabourin 1995). Yelsma (1995) found that 70 percent of partners in dating relationships reported some form of verbal abuse. If an occasional lapse into verbal aggression occurred, partners seemed able to absorb it, but in distressed relationships, verbal aggression was associated with ineffective conversation skills and was much more frequent than in satisfactory relationships.

The negative impact of verbal aggression is felt by most of us. When we hear someone in public verbally abusing another, we cringe. The person engaging in verbal aggression most often doesn't perceive their communication as aggressive. People who are **"high verbal aggressives"** claim that 46 percent of their verbally aggressive messages are humorous (Infante, Riddle, et al. 1992). But others view verbally aggressive people as less credible and as having fewer valid arguments than those who don't aggress (Infante, Hartley, et al. 1992). If a couple is verbally aggressive, they tend to infuriate each other and lack the skill to undo the relationship damage (Sabourin 1995). As shown in the following list of **abusive** versus **nonabusive talk,** verbally abusive couples differ from nonabusive couples in how they talk:

Abusive Talk		Nonabusive Talk
vague language	vs.	precise language
opposition	vs.	collaboration
relational talk	vs.	content talk
despair	vs.	optimism
interfering with interdependence	vs.	facilitating interdependence
complaints	vs.	compliments
ineffective change	vs.	effective change

Verbal aggression is closely associated with physical abuse. Verbal aggression is a precursor to and predictor of physical aggression in adolescents (White and Humphrey 1994). Similarly, verbal aggression in marriage is correlated with marital violence (Sabourin and Stamp 1995). Adding injury to insult, verbally aggressive couples sometimes do not see their aggression as a problem (Vivian and Langhinrichsen-Rohling 1994).

Sometimes, researchers label verbally aggressive tactics as **harassment.** A direct verbal attack on another can have serious consequences. In Sweden, for example, an estimated 100 to 300 people each year commit suicide as a result of harassment by work colleagues (Bjorkqvist, Osterman, and Lagerspetz 1994). One study found that in a Finnish university, women were more often harassed than men, and women holding administrative and service jobs were harassed more than female professors (Bjorkqvist, Osterman, and Hjelt-Back 1994). Making negative comments about appearance or clothing is considered harassment if the speaker is in a high-power relationship with the "target" person. Additionally, if a high-power person ridicules a low-power person's mode of speech or makes sexually explicit suggestions or observations, harassment is occurring. Finally, when a high-power person negatively labels a low-power person's personality, using words such as "brain-dead," "loser," "whiner," "bitch," or "wimp," the target person is being harassed. Such comments, whether labeled "harassment" or "verbal aggression," can occur at home, on the job, in public, or in any type of relationship. And sometimes, these destructive verbal tactics escalate to the next level—physical violence.

When verbally abusive tactics are extreme, they can be characterized by the "rapist" style. In the rapist style (this metaphor is not meant to imply only sexual behavior but all kinds of dominating communicative behavior), participants "function through power, through an ability to apply psychic and physical sanctions, through rewards and especially punishments, and through commands and threats" (Brockriede 1972, 2). The conflict or argument is often escalated, since participants are interested in coercion instead of gaining assent through carefully reasoned argument. The intent of those using the rapist style is to manipulate and violate the personhood of the "victims," or other parties in the conflict. In some situations, such as the courtroom, legislative hearings, political debates, and forensic tournaments, the structure of the conflict encourages the coercion, or rapist, strategy. Verbal aggression feels like, and is, violation of the humanity of the other, like rape.

Bullying

Bullying is "ongoing, persistent badgering, harassment and psychological terrorizing . . . that demoralizes, dehumanizes and isolates those targeted" (Tracy, Lutgen-Sandvik and Alberts 2004; Lutgen-Sandvik, Tracy, and Alberts: 2005). **Bullying** can occur in any social setting, including the Internet. The Berkman Center for Internet and Society at Harvard concluded, for example, that online bullying of peers is the number one threat to juveniles using the social networking sites such as Facebook and Myspace (Palfrey et al. 2009).

Workplace bullying also occurs. Defining bullying as "repeated and persistent patterns of negative workplace behavior that is ongoing for six months or longer in duration," 23 percent of the over 1000 respondents had experienced bullying in a university setting (Keashly and Neuman, 2008). And a full 45 percent experienced bullying as either a victim or a witness to it. In respect to the U.S. as a whole, a random survey of 7000 individuals, 37 percent reported a direct experience with bullying (Workplace Bully Institute & Zogby International, 2007). Such bullying is four times more prevalent than illegal forms of "harassment." And as you might guess, most bullies are bosses (72 percent). Women are affected more than men. Further, while we hear about the U.S. being "lawsuit happy" only 3 percent of those affected filed lawsuits. Those targeted are the ones most often who lose their jobs. Abroad, one Denmark study found that bullying in the workplace negatively affected both the organizational climate and the psychological health of those bullied (Hogh et al. 2005).

Communication researchers have also begun studying bullying in the workplace. The effects of workplace bullying everywhere are clear—the "target's psychological, occupational and family functioning decline" (Leymann 1990). Job performance slips and the organization's reputation, is damaged (Tracy, Lutgen-Sandvik, and Alberts 2004). Bullying at work can take many forms—"supervisors abusing subordinates, same-level workers tormenting peers, and coworkers 'ganging up' on an individual" (Tracy, Lungen-Sandvik, and Alberta 2004, 1; Einarsen 1999). When asked about his or her experience, the recipient of bullying feels vulnerable and tortured, that it is a "fixed fight," and has nightmares (Tracy, Lutgen-Sandvik, and Alberts 2004). Targets of bullying suffer long-term—sometimes permanent—damage (Einarsen 1999; Einarsen and Mikkelsen, 2003; Leymann 1990).

If you attended U.S. schools, you know that bullying occurs there also. Children do recognize it when it occurs (Murray-Close, Crick, and Galotti, 2006), and it is strongly linked to other aggressive behaviors (Aslund, Starrin, Leppeert, and Nilsson, 2008). Take the case of Will, the smallest boy in his class. In his rural town, all boys went out for sports and Will was harassed on a daily basis in the locker room—being shoved, snapped with towels, and called demeaning names. Such persistent acts continued until he quit trying out for sports altogether.

Schools have begun anti-bullying programs because bullying is so common and harmful (Jones and Compton, 2003). For example, the Olweus Bullying Prevention Program is gaining traction in many school systems (see the Olweus web site), and many other programs have been implemented (Jones, 2001; Jones and Kmitta, 2000). One study found that with elementary school children, their bullying prevention program yielded a large decrease in bullying (Heydenberk et al. 2006). This study used a number of activities, but of particular note is the STAR approach—Stop, Think, Act, and Review. The elementary students learned how to recognize emotions, consider other's emotions, act as a Peaceful Being, and chose a response rather than an angry reaction (62).

Bullying usually starts as incivility. As Lutgen-Sandvik, Tracy, and Alberts (2005) write, "Workplace bullying does not arise out of a vacuum. Rather, it is often a consequence of **unmanaged incivility,** rudeness, and injustice that contaminates the workplace. Incivility, over time, can develop into bullying as repeated, long-term acts wear down, demoralize, stigmatize, and isolate those targeted" (7). Bullying, then, is one of a group of aggressive acts that have serious consequences for the recipient.

Violence

Violence consists of any verbal or physical strategy that attempts to convince, control, or compel others to your point of view. Some forms of verbal coercion often lead to violence:

Controlling: Coercing others to your way of thinking by forcing your views on other or dominating the conversation. Methods include cutting others off, lying or overstating, speaking in absolutes, changing subjects or using hostile, directive questions to control the conversation. Verbal coercion often leads to physical violence; certainly it is a form of emotional violence.

Labeling is putting a name on people or ideas so we can dismiss them under a general stereotype. Labeling has been discussed earlier under Gottman's "four horsemen." Labeling is related to contempt and ridicule; it affects the personhood of the other.

Attacking needs little explanation. When you attack, you've moved from winning the argument to making the person suffer (Paterson, et al. 2002, 54). Nothing good can come from attacks—ever—in the world of interpersonal communication. We may feel justified, but attacks lead to destruction or revenge and further the cycle of violence.

The ultimate harmful approach is physical violence—when conflictual interactions move beyond threats and verbal aggressiveness.[1] We are faced with an epidemic of violence in

---

[1]If you or someone you know suffers from physical or sexual violence, help is available both locally and nationally. Contact local programs that help victims of violence and/or contact the National Domestic Violence Hotline at 1-800-799-7233 (1-800-799-SAFE) and the Web site www.ndvh.org.

the United States, with much of it occurring in the home and the workplace. Violence can occur in many forms. One scale measuring such physical aggression (Straus et al. 1996) lists these items:

- Threw something at my partner that could hurt.
- Twisted my partner's arm or hair.
- Pushed or shoved my partner.
- Grabbed my partner.
- Used a knife or gun on my partner.
- Punched or hit my partner with something that could hurt.
- Choked my partner.
- Slammed my partner against a wall.
- Beat up my partner.
- Burned or scalded my partner on purpose.
- Kicked my partner.

The more severe forms of violence occur less frequently (Deal and Wampler 1986). However, although we will never know the precise rates of violence, it is more common than we usually assume. Ponder for a moment these rates of incidence found in various surveys:

- Almost 20 percent of people reported experiencing a violent episode in the prior year of their romantic relationship (Marshall 1994).
- Premarital violence is a serious social problem that affects more than 30 percent of the young people in the United States who date (Sugarman and Hotaling 1989).
- In unhappy marriages, 71 percent of the couples reported physical aggression in the prior year (Vivian and Langhinrichsen-Rohling 1994).
- Men commit about 13 million violent crimes each year, with only half being simple assaults, while women commit about 2.1million violent crimes a year, with three-quarters being simple assaults.

In another study of dating relationships, 23 percent of students reported being pushed, grabbed, or shoved by their dating partner (Deal and Wampler 1986). Studies of college students have indicated that rates of physical aggression against a current mate are between 20 and 35 percent, with all forms of physical assault decreasing dramatically with age. The most common forms of physical aggression practiced by both men and women were pushing, shoving, and slapping (O'Leary et al. 1989). Additionally, 16.3 out of 1,000 children were reported to have been abused and/or neglected, and in 16 percent of homes, some kind of violence between spouses had occurred in the year prior to the survey (Gelles and Cornell 1990).

In summary, most researchers conclude that "violence is indeed common in American families" (Gelles 1987). Further, "These incidents of violence are not isolated attacks nor are they just pushes and shoves. In many families, violence is patterned and regular and often results in broken bones and sutured cuts" (192). Violence spans all social and economic boundaries, though it is more prevalent in families with low income, low educational achievement, and low-status employment.

Another working definition of violence is "an act carried out with the intention or perceived intention of causing physical pain or injury to another person" (Gelles and Cornell 1990, 22). In conflict terms, violent behavior is an attempt to force one's will on the other—to get him or her to stop doing something or to start doing something. Clearly, it is a one-sided tactic designed to force the other to do one's bidding.

Patterns of Violence

The following are some tenets of violence, based on research (adapted from Lloyd and Emery 1994):

Tenet 1: Physical Aggression Is Almost Always Preceded by Verbal Aggression Small, insignificant acts lead to verbal sparring, which then escalates into physical aggression or abuse. For instance, you burn the toast, your spouse screams at you, "Why can't you even do simple things right?" you shout back, "So what makes you think you are so high and mighty?" and the cycle continues unabated with the two of you shoving each other around the kitchen. The spiral of destruction continues until the physically stronger one, usually the man, gets an upper hand. The important feature here is that the physical abuse does not just arise out of nowhere—it follows hostile, competitive verbal acts (Evans 1992; Lloyd and Emery 1994). The partners engage in an "aggression ritual" that ends in violence (Harris, Gergen, and Lannamann 1986).

Tenet 2: Intimate Violence Is Usually Reciprocal—Both Participate Aggression and violence are reciprocal—once one partner engages in violence, the other is likely to respond in kind. In intimate male–female relationships, the woman is more likely than the man to engage in violent low-power tactics: the woman is 14 times more likely than the man to throw something and 15 times more likely than the man to slap (Stets and Henderson 1991). However, 40 percent of all women who are murdered are killed by someone close to them. Major differences in male and female violence show up in the seriousness and the effects of violence. There is no question that women are seriously victimized much more often than are men. Both participants are likely to report being both victims and perpetrators of physical aggression; 85 percent of couples report that the aggression is bidirectional (Vivian and Langhinrichsen-Rohling 1994). These statistics suggest that there is an attack–counterattack sequence to the majority of violent episodes (Deal and Wampler 1986). Once violence begins, both people tend to participate—it is a dyadic, interactive event.

Tenet 3: Women and Children Suffer Many More Injuries Violence, regardless of the cycle of interaction leading up to it, damages women and children more than men. Advocates for battered women point to a "cohesive pattern of coercive controls that include verbal abuse, threats, psychological manipulation, sexual coercion, and control of economic resources" (Dobash and Dobash 1979). Additionally, many women learn not to confront, and remain unskilled in effective verbal defense. Many women try to placate rather than leave the scene. Socialization of women that teaches them to be forgiving also leads to women staying in abusive relationships.

All you have to do is volunteer at a battered women's shelter or read in the newspaper about child abuse to see who loses. As Gelles says, "When men hit women and women hit men, the real victims are almost certainly going to be the women"

(1981, 128). Even when women use weapons as a way to gain the upper hand, they are still injured more often (Felson 1996). Throughout history, women have been the victims of violence.

Tenet 4: Victims of Abuse Are in a No-Win Situation Once the cycle of abuse begins, the victim of the abuse has few good options (Lloyd and Emery 1994). For example, it is fruitless to try to use aggression against a stronger and more violent person. Yet, on the other hand, it is extraordinarily difficult to leave because the perpetrator is trying to control all your actions. The complexity of abusive relationships is evidenced by the fact that nearly 40 percent of victims of dating violence continue their relationships and that most women who seek help from a battered women's shelter return to their spouses (Sugarman and Hotaling 1989). Many women go back to abusive situations because with children they cannot make a living. Many women feel guilty about the failure of the relationship and go back believing the abuser's promises to change. One study documented that 70 percent of fathers who sought custody of their children were successful, so many women, especially poor women, are afraid of losing their children if they stay away (Marano 1996). Tragically, abusers escalate their control tactics when victims try to leave. More domestic abuse victims are killed when they try to leave than at any other time. It is difficult for women with children to flee when they are so dependent on the very person who is violent with them.

Tenet 5: Perpetrators and Victims Have Discrepant Narratives about Violence (Moffitt et al. 1997) One of the reasons that it is so difficult to decrease violence is that perpetrators of violent acts see their behavior as something "that could not be helped or as due to external, mitigating circumstances. Thus, they may cast themselves as unjustly persecuted for a minor, unavoidable, or nonexistent offense" (Baumeister, Stillwell, and Wotman 1990, 1003). One provocative study asked the participants to recall situations where they were perpetrators of violence and then write about the events. They also were asked to recall situations where they were victims and reflect on those events. What emerged was that "perpetrators apparently see the incident as a brief, uncharacteristic episode that has little or no relation to present circumstances whereas victims apparently continue to see harmful consequences and to feel lasting grievances" (1001).

The **discrepancies in accounts of violence** extend to the underreporting of violence. Husbands are more likely than wives to minimize and deny their violence (Browning and Dotton 1986). Furthermore, husbands are more likely than wives to count choking, punching, and beating someone up as self-defense rather than violence (Brygger and Edleson 1984), but what abusers often report as "self-defense" is in reality violent retaliation.

Even though violence from women to men occurs (Ridley and Feldman 2003), it is far less common. In any event, the accounts of the abuser and victim will be discrepant.

Explanations for Violence

Why does violence occur in personal relationships? One explanation is that violent responses to conflict are learned—those who experience violence have experienced it before, have witnessed it in their family of origin or in previous relationships (Yexley and Borowsky 2002). Studies find that perpetrators of violence were often victims of violence in their childhood and in their earlier relationships (Straus, Gelles, and Stein-metz 1980; Deal and Wampler 1986; Bernard and Bernard 1983). Yet, saying that "vio-lence is passed on" is not a totally satisfying answer. We need to know much more about people who do not continue the patterns. Why do some people who are exposed to violence and aggression in childhood stop these patterns in adulthood (Lenton 1995a, 1995b)? Patricia, for example, suffered both verbal and physical abuse at the hand of her father. He said and did terrible things to her when she was a child, and she ran away from home at age 17. Yet, in raising her children, she did not once ver-bally or physically abuse them. We need much more research on people like this who break the intergenerational transmission of aggression. Similarly, what about people in families and romantic relationships who stop escalating sequences of verbal aggression that might lead to violence? And, on the other hand, why do some people who were not previously exposed to violence and aggression develop violent and aggressive behaviors?

A second explanation for violence centers on the elements of a patriarchal culture that insists the man is always right. It has been found that the more discrepant the power between the husband and the wife, the greater the violence (Kim and Emery 2003). In "asymmetric power structures" (husband-dominant or wife-dominant mar-riages), there is "a much greater risk of violence than when conflict occurs among the equalitarian couples" (Coleman and Straus 1986, 152). When the power is "asymmet-ric," conflict episodes more often trigger violence. Similarly, one study demonstrated that the more dependent a wife is, the more tolerant she is of violence against her (Kalmuss and Straus 1982). Research shows multiple factors leading to abuse and that patriar-chal explanations, while part of the picture, are too simplistic (Lenton 1995; Greene and Bogo 2002; Bell and Forde 1999). For example, incidences of violence are higher in the U.S. than Hong Kong—seen as a patriarchal culture as well (Kam & Bond 2008).

A third explanation for violent tactics is that violence is the result of lack of com-munication skills in a situation of powerlessness. It has been found that physically aggres-sive wives and husbands display rigid communication patterns, automatically responding in kind to their partner rather than with an alternative response (Rosen 1996). If you can effectively argue (without being verbally aggressive), then you have a sense of power and impact. If you feel that you can have an impact on your spouse, there is no need to resort to physical aggression, even in the heat of conflict. Yet, there are also people who are both verbally skillful and physically violent.

Clearly, no one explanation can account for the complexity of violence. For example, why does a strong belief in pacifism correlate to fewer violent behaviors for Quaker women but not for Quaker men (Brutz and Allen 1986)? Why do surveys indicate that men are more often the recipients of violence than women? Is it because males are more likely to see any violence as a violation and report it? And why do people in marriages with a lot of physical aggression often not see it as a problem (Vivian and Langhinrichsen-Rohling 1994)?

Regardless of one's explanation of violence, it is time for us as a culture to take a firm stand on it. We desperately need to approach violence from a variety of platforms—in the home; in the schools; in the churches, synagogues, Zendos and gompas; and in the work-place. We are in need of programs to teach us how to stop violence in all contexts. We need to give assistance to both perpetrators and victims so the cycles of destruction can be stopped.

☙Interaction Dynamics

Whether we are looking at an isolated tactical move or the overall conflict style of an individual, we cannot understand conflict dynamics by examining the individual in isolation. The interaction of two or more people determines the outcome of the conflict. No matter how hard one person tries to resolve a conflict, the outcome will not be constructive unless the other person is involved in working things out, too. Figure 5.2 shows two very different outcomes of conflict even though Curtis uses exactly the same tactics throughout. In one case the conflict escalates between the two participants. In the other, Pam's alternative tactics reduce the conflict. The outcome is the *joint product of both choices,* not the result of some inherent personality trait of either participant.

One chooses his or her conflict tactics and styles based on "attributions about the partner's intent to cooperate, the focus of responsibility for the conflict, and the stability of the conflict" (Sillars 1980, 182). Analysis must shift from the individual to the relationship level, viewing conflict preferences as resulting from a system of interlocking behaviors rather than as a function of personality (Knapp, Putnam, and Davis 1988). Relational variables (whom you interact with, how congruent your perceptions are with those of the other party, what intent you think the other party has, and the mirroring of each other's responses) explain conflict style choices better than does personality (Putnam and Poole 1987; Knapp, Putnam, and Davis 1988). When you are a party to a conflict, it is your perception of the other's choices that accounts for the choices you make (Rogers, Castleton, and Lloyd 1996).

Even though each conflictual interaction is unique, two patterns of interlocking behaviors are worthy of note. They are (1) *complementary patterns* and (2) *symmetrical patterns.*

Complementary patterns are tactics or styles that are different from one another but mutually reinforcing. For example, if one person tries to engage and talk about the conflict and the other avoids, each one's moves reinforce those of the other. The engager begins to think, "If I don't force the issue, he will never talk to me," while the avoider thinks, "If she would just leave me alone, it would be all right." The more she engages, the more he avoids; the more he avoids, the more she engages; and they produce a "communication spiral" with each one magnifying his or her chosen response (Wilmot 1995).

Such complementary patterns occur in many contexts. In business settings, for example, supervisors and subordinates use different styles (Richmond et al. 1984), and in personal relationships, one person is often conciliatory and the other coercive. Raush et al. (1974) found that there was a "Jekyll-Hyde" quality to spouses in unsatisfactory marriages. In the first interaction, one person would be coercive and the other conciliatory, and then they would reverse roles. The individuals changed styles, but the overall interaction pattern was the same.

Two people can engage in complementary interactions that are not causing serious relationship difficulties. For example, nine-year-old Carina, when confronted by her father about being responsible, says, "Who cares?" (with a giggle). But, if the patterns persist for years, they can keep the two parties in recurring conflict.

Symmetrical sequences occur in conflicts when the participants' tactics mirror one another—both parties escalating, for example. One type of symmetrical pattern occurs

Figure 5.2   Tactics in an Interaction Context

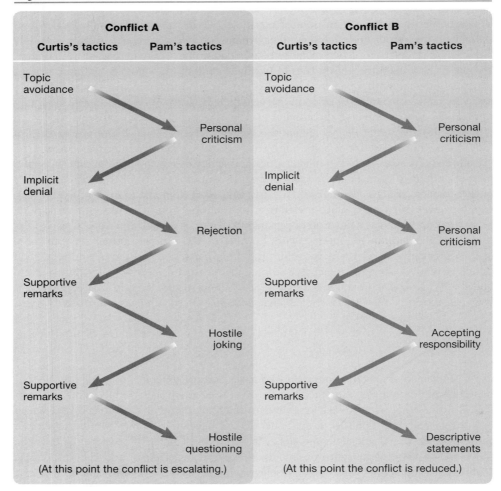

when the parties both avoid a conflict, refuse to engage in the conflict overtly, and create a devitalized spiral. As a result, the relationship loses vitality and the partners become so independent of each other that the relationship withers away. Gottman (1982) noted that there is a "chaining" of identical tactics in distressed marriages. Distressed spouses get stuck in cycles of competitive tactics. For example, a sequence might occur as follows:

Husband: threat

Wife: counterthreat

Husband: intensified threat

Wife: intensified counterthreat

John: Don't even think of walking away from me when I'm talking.

Anita: I'll walk away, and I'll walk right out of the marriage if I do. You can't stop me.

John: Try it, and see how you get to work without a car. It's in my name, so you don't have a car!

Anita: And you don't have children. We're history!

People match their spouses' competitive tactics with an increase in their own. Such escalatory spirals lead the couple into irresolvable conflicts. In organizations, what starts as an "attack-defend" pattern evolves into symmetrical "attack-attack" patterns, with each party trying to one-up the other (Putnam and Jones 1982b). These patterns have been characterized in the following ways:

- attack-attack
- retaliatory chaining
- negative reciprocity
- cross-complaining
- threat-counterthreat
- round-robin attacks
- escalatory spirals

Other conflict tactics and styles, then, are best seen in the context of the relationship. Based on available research, the following conclusions are warranted:

1. If the conflict parties both want to avoid the conflict and, as a norm, do not generally work through conflicts, joint avoidance can be functional (Pike and Sillars 1985; Raush et al. 1974).

2. Once a conflict is engaged, dissatisfaction can be caused by either fight-flight or threat-threat patterns. Either the complementary pattern or the symmetrical pattern can be dysfunctional for the parties, especially when they get rigidly locked into habitual tactics and styles.

3. Once engagement has occurred, the conflict is best managed by moving to collaborative, integrative tactics (Pike and Sillars 1985; Raush et al. 1974). One useful sequence is (a) the agenda-building phase, (b) the arguing phase, and (c) the final, integrative negotiation phase (Gottman et al. 1976).

In summary, to preserve a good relationship while pursuing a goal that appears incompatible with that of the other person, collaborative tactics are needed. You may begin the conflict by avoiding, accommodating, compromising, or escalating, but at some point collaborative engagement is usually necessary. Competent communicators are those who use constructive, prosocial, collaborative tactics at some stage of the conflict (Cupach 1982). As Schuetz (1978) says, "In situations of conflict, as in other communicative events, the competent communicator engages in cooperative interaction that permits both persons (factions) involved to achieve their goals" (10). Sillars's work (1980) demonstrates that roommates who engaged in conflicts characterized by collaboration, rather than by avoidance or competition, were more satisfied with each other and more likely to successfully resolve conflict. Furthermore, various family researchers have clearly demonstrated the link between collaboration and relationship satisfaction (Gottman 1994; Noller et al. 1994). Collaborative tactical and stylistic choices depend on a certain level of cognitive complexity (Applegate 1982; Delia and Clark 1977). Collaborative tactics involve supporting a positive, autonomous identity for the other while working toward your own goals. Such multiple demands, although difficult to master, lead to productive results for both parties, for in the end you are working with rather than against the other for mutual collaborative gains.

Whatever communication moves you make, the basic question is whether those choices lead to the effective management of the conflict over time. No one set of moves at any point will guarantee productive conflict, but collaborative tactics at least set the stage for the containment and management of the conflict if both parties move toward a problem-solving perspective. When in doubt, collaborate.

❧Flexibility Creates Constructive Conflict

People often get "frozen" into a conflict style rather than developing style flexibility. Each time they are in a conflict, they make the same choices. The work associate who always avoids any conflict, smooths over everyone's feelings, and habitually refuses to talk about the difficulties between herself and others is frozen in a particular style. Individual lack of adaptation can occur in many forms. For example, a person might always avoid conflict until a situation heats up, at which point he or she engages in violent behavior. The pattern is self-sealing and difficult to alter. The person who competes on the job and is unable to relax off the job is just as stuck as the person who is unable to openly admit that conflict exists. People who are inflexible in their style selection are often unaware that their choice of style is an important contributor to the conflict.

People often get stuck in behaviors from their "golden age." The golden age is that period in which you felt best about yourself and from which you possibly still draw many positive feelings. The 45-year-old history teacher who fondly recalls participating in high school athletics might operate from the rule that "the way to handle conflict is to get out there and give it everything you've got, fight to win, and never let anything keep you from your goal." This rule probably worked beautifully in a football game, but it may cause real havoc if the principal does not want to work with aggressive teachers and recommends this teacher's transfer to another school.

Often people are stuck in a personal style because of early family experiences and gender identity (Neff and Harter 2002; Dumlao and Botta 2000). Young girls may have been taught to smooth others' feelings and not "make waves." If you were raised with such prescriptions and bring them to a conflictual situation, you will accommodate the other and fail to assert your own desires. In the following excerpt, a woman details some of the disadvantages of this particular lack of flexibility:

As a child, I was forbidden to "talk back." As a result, I stifled all my replies until I was of sufficient age to walk out and did so. That was fifteen years ago—I have never been back . . . Thus, my strategy has been one of avoidance of a conflict to which I can see no resolution. Because I was raised by my father and stepmother, I scarcely knew my mother. When I was seventeen, I went to live with her. She wanted a mother-daughter relationship to which I could not respond. Legally bound to her, my attempts at confrontation ended in failure. Once again I walked out—this time into marriage. After seven years of marriage and abortive attempts at communication, I again walked out—this time with two children.

Likewise, many men are taught to compete regardless of the situation, learning that accommodation, compromise, and collaboration are all signs of weakness. Although the competitive style might be appropriate for certain business situations in which everyone understands the tacit rules making competition functional, carrying competition as one's only response into an intimate relationship can often result in the destruction of that relationship. Gender conditioning, whatever its particular form, is just one kind of learning that helps keep people stuck in conflict styles that may not work in certain situations.

Problems with Rigidity

How can you tell if you are *stuck in a conflict style?* Use the following diagnostic aid to determine if you are stuck in patterns that do not work well for you:

1. *Does your current conflict response feel like the only natural one?* For example, if your friends or family members suggest that you "might try talking it through" rather than repetitively escalating conflict, do such new options seem alien and almost impossible for you to enact?

2. *Does your conflict style remain constant across a number of conflicts that have similar characteristics?* For example, in every public conflict, do you accommodate others regardless of the issues at hand or your relationship with the others involved?

3. *Do you have a set of responses that follow a preset pattern?* For instance, do you "go for the jugular" then back off and accommodate the other because you fear you have made a "scene"? If you follow regular cycles of behavior, whatever the particulars, you may be in a process that could be altered.

4. *Do others seem to do the same thing with you?* If different people engage in similar behavior with you, you may be doing something that triggers their response. For instance, has it been your experience that in public conflicts, others are always competitive? If so, their behavior may be a reaction to a competitive posture that you take toward public conflict. If you were more conciliatory, others might not feel the need to respond competitively to you.

5. *Do you carry a label that is affectionately or not so affectionately used to describe you?* If you grew up as "our little fireball," you may not have learned how to collaborate. If you are referred to as a "powerhouse," a "mover and a shaker," or "a bulldog," your conflict style might be overly inflexible. If you're known as "the judge" or "the dictator," you may need to take notice of an overly rigid style. Labels, although they often hurt and overgeneralize, may carry embedded grains of truth.

Application 5.8	Your Responses

Answer the above five questions, privately first, then with your small group. What did you learn? Is there anything you want to change about your style across various contexts? Maybe it's time for a change.

Individuals who can *change and adapt* are more likely to be effective conflict participants, accomplishing private and group goals better than people who avoid change. Hart and Burks (1972) discuss the concept of **rhetorical sensitivity,** the idea that people change their communication style based on the demands of different situations. The following five communication characteristics describe people who are rhetorically sensitive:

1. They are comfortable altering their roles in response to the behaviors of others.
2. They avoid stylizing their communication behavior, so they are able to adapt.
3. They develop skills to deal with different audiences and are able to withstand the pressure and ambiguity of constant adaptation.
4. They are able to monitor talk with others to make it purposive rather than expressive. They speak not so much to "spill their guts" as to solve problems.
5. They adapt and alter behaviors in a rational and orderly way.

In other words, effective interpersonal communicators expect change and adapt to change in their communication with others. They avoid getting "stuck" in certain conflict styles.

One reward for developing a repertoire of conflict styles is that we are then able to see the behavior of others in a different, more objective light. When we have a wide repertoire of conflict behaviors, we assume that other people do, too. We are far less likely to judge the behavior of others automatically as having evil intent, being childish, or being improper. After all, if we are reasonable and justified in our choices, we will probably be able to judge others as being reasonable when they choose different styles.

Another reason for actively working to widen one's repertoire of conflict styles is that many styles were developed from rules for children. Although it may be appropriate to "respect your elders" when you are eight years old, overgeneralizing that rule to include avoiding conflict with respected elders when you are an adult is much less appropriate. Learning to seek permission to speak might be fine behavior in the third grade, but waiting for permission to speak in a bargaining session, whether formal or informal, will assure that you will never be heard. As an adult, raising one's voice may not be as great a sin as stifling it.

Your choices of conflict styles are vitally important. By unfreezing your style options, you can adapt to conflictual situations depending on the goals you have for yourself and the relationship with the other person. Most of us learn retrospectively that our natural styles are dysfunctional. We examine our past conflicts and see that we have been stuck in a particular style or style sequence. Developing a repertoire of style choices opens the way to productive management of our conflicts.

❧Summary

Conflict participants face the basic choice of avoiding or engaging in a conflict. This choice leads to the five individual styles of conflict management: avoidance, competition, compromise, accommodation, and collaboration. An assessment instrument was included to measure conflict styles.

The specific advantages and disadvantages of styles were discussed.

One must be cautious about overinterpreting individual styles. Measures of styles depend on whether you are rating yourself or someone else, are affected by gender, and suffer from "social desirability" biases. Further, style measures are not process oriented and give the impression of more consistency in behavior than there is across contexts. Finally, the measures give an impression of measuring an underlying trait (which they don't), and, finally, style measures ignore the interaction dynamics—one of the key determiners of what style someone will use.

Verbal aggression bullying, and physician violence are more than "styles" of conflict. They are damaging choices.

We discussed the interaction dynamics in some detail and concluded by noting that flexibility in style choice enhances your chance for productive conflict.

Key Terms

> Use the text's Online Learning Center at **www.mhhe.com/wilmot8e** to further your understanding of the following terminology.

style preferences 144
conflict styles 144
tactics 144
assertiveness/cooperativeness graph 145
avoidance 148
engagement 148
avoid/criticize loop 154
postponement 156
assertive competition 157
competition 157

threats 160
warnings 160
promises 161
compromise 163
accommodation 165
codependence 167
collaboration 168
verbal aggressiveness 177
high verbal aggressiveness 178

abusive talk 178
nonabusive talk 178
harassment 178
bullying 179
unmanaged incivility 180
violence 180
discrepancies in accounts of violence 183
rhetorical sensitivity 190

Review Questions

> Go to the self-quizzes on the Online Learning Center at **www.mhhe.com/wilmot8e** to test your knowledge of the chapter concepts.

1. Define *styles*.
2. Distinguish styles from tactics.
3. Reproduce the graph showing styles varying in assertiveness and cooperativeness.
4. Define *avoidance*.
5. Give an example of the avoid/criticize loop.
6. How does avoidance function differently in diverse cultures?
7. Give examples of avoidance tactics.

8. What are the advantages and disadvantages of competitive tactics?
9. Define *threats* and give examples of them.
10. Distinguish between threats, warnings, promises, and recommendations.
11. What is verbal aggressiveness?
12. Give examples of abusive talk.
13. What is bullying and what effects does it have?
14. Give examples of types of violence.

15. What different explanations are there for the incidence of violence?

16. Define *compromise*, listing its advantages and disadvantages.

17. How does accommodation differ from avoidance?

18. What are the advantages and disadvantages of accommodation?

19. Clarify collaboration and specify its advantages and disadvantages.

20. What are some cautions we should keep in mind when discussing styles?

21. Specify how styles are linked in interaction sequences.

22. Discuss the gender differences and effects in violent communication.

23. Discuss differing accounts of violent behavior.

24. What do you gain by having a flexible set of styles?

25. How can you tell if you are stuck in a style?

26. Describe rhetorically sensitive people.

Part Two

Intervention

Chapter 6

Emotions in Conflict

Introducing Emotion

Emotions are **states of feeling**. When our feelings and sensibilities are triggered, we experience emotions. When something personally significant happens to you, your feelings respond, along with your thoughts and physiological changes. Emotion sets actions "into motion," leading to your own unique subjective experience. This is what makes reflecting others' feelings so important, and so challenging. You may say, with all the best intentions, "So you are feeling dismissed and disrespected by Walt's assignment of project teams." Then your team member says , "No, not exactly. I feel invisible and unimportant." Her subjective experience is a little different from what you imagined.

Emotions are like moving water. Water that is dammed up with no inlet or outlet becomes stagnant, dries up, becomes toxic, or freezes. Emotions are designed by evolution to move through the body. We feel them, they change, they transform. Constructive conflict resolution depends upon our ability to work with and transform, not close off or repress, normal human emotion. We cannot remember a genuine conflict situation that did not involve feelings. Can you?

We teach that "feelings are facts"; they aren't right or wrong, they simply exist. What you do with those feelings is a key element in managing conflict. This chapter will explore emotion and help you prepare ahead of time for the inevitable storms of feeling that arise in conflicts.

Finding Feelings

People sometimes find it difficult to talk about feelings, so let's explore **feeling words** in more detail.

Here is an exhaustive list of feeling words. Choose words that might be clustered with anger, fear/anxiety, sadness, shame, or disgust to describe how Darlene and her father might be feeling. In the next section, we will discuss the helpful use of positive emotions. For now, expand your feeling-words repertoire by studying the words that describe what the two parties might be feeling. Then compare your responses with someone in class.

Application 6.1   List of Feeling Words

affectionate	cut off	grateful
afraid	defeated	grieving
aggressive	defensive	grudging
agonized	dejected	guilty
alarmed	demure	gutless
alienated	dependent	happy
alone	depressed	hateful
angry	deprived	homicidal
anxious	desperate	hopeful
apathetic	determined	hopeless
apologetic	disappointed	horrified
appreciated	disapproving	hostile
arrogant	disbelieving	hot
ashamed	disgusted	humorous
attractive	distasteful	hungover
awkward	domineering	hurt
bashful	eager	hyperactive
beaten	easygoing	hysterical
beautiful	ecstatic	idiotic
bewildered	embarrassed	ignored
blissful	enraged	immobilized
bored	envious	impatient
brave	evasive	inadequate
calm	evil	incompetent
caring	exasperated	indecisive
cautious	excited	indifferent
closed	exhausted	inferior
cold	exhilarated	inhibited
comfortable	fatalistic	innocent
committed	fearful	insecure
compassionate	feminine	insincere
competent	flirtatious	interested
concentrating	friendly	involved
concerned	frightened	isolated
confident	frigid	jealous
confused	frustrated	joyful
contented	generous	judgmental
cowardly	genuine	lively
creative	gentle	loaded
cruel	giddy	lonely
curious	glad	lovable

(continued)

Application 6.1   List of Feeling Words

loved	protective	superior
lovestruck	proud	supported
loving	prudish	supportive
lovely	puzzled	surly
masculine	quarrelsome	surprised
masked	quiet	suspicious
masochistic	regretful	sympathetic
meditative	rejected	tender
melancholy	relieved	terrified
mischievous	remorseful	thoughtful
miserable	repelled	threatened
misrepresented	repulsed	tolerant
misunderstood	repulsive	torn
mysterious	restrained	touchy
needy	reverent	triumphant
negative	sad	two-faced
obstinate	sadistic	ugly
old	satisfied	undecided
optimistic	secure	understanding
out of control	seductive	unresponsive
overcontrolled	self-pitying	unsupported
oversexed	self-reliant	unsupportive
overwhelmed	sexy	unsure
pained	shallow	unwilling
paranoid	sheepish	uptight
passionate	shocked	useful
peaceful	shy	useless
perplexed	silly	vindictive
persecuted	sincere	violent
pessimistic	sinful	weary
phony	sluggish	weepy
pitiful	smug	wishy-washy
playful	soft	withdrawn
pleased	sorry	youthful
possessive	stubborn	zany
preoccupied	stupid	zealous
prejudiced	suicidal	zesty[1]
pressured		

[1] Thank you to Jacquie Gibson for this expanded list of words.

Case 6.1	How to Help a Difficult Father

Darlene's father lives across the country from her. Darlene's two brothers, Hal and Mark, live in neighboring towns from their dad, a popular doctor in his community. Darlene's dad, commonly called "Doc," has been diagnosed with cancer. Darlene is a social work student, with excellent communication skills. After several conversations with her brothers, Darlene talks on the phone with Doc.

Darlene: Dad, I am so sorry your cancer has come back in this form. I want you to know that I want to help. I can talk with my professors and get some time away from my classes. This is really important and you are going to need some help (Darlene's parents have been divorced a long time).

Doc: Oh, Fred (one of his sons) is going to take me to the surgeon's consultation, and I imagine he'll help out.

Darlene: But if you go through chemo, you are going to need some help at home, especially at first. I can come for that first week or more.

Doc: Well, nobody thought my prostate cancer (five years ago) was a big deal, so I don't know what everyone is getting so upset about now.

Darlene: Dad, we all cared about your cancer, and we care now. Will you stay in touch with me and let me know what your plans are? I will be glad to help coordinate home health care, and help you get set up with your treatment plans.

Doc: Oh, I think I'll be all right. You have your school.

Darlene: Dad, you're telling me that last time you felt that we didn't care, and I want you to know that's not the way I feel. I would like to be involved.

Doc: Don't worry about me. I'll be fine.

What do you think Darlene is feeling?
    What is Doc feeling?
    As you answer these questions, avoid any interpretation, or statements of what they should do. Now put yourself in Darlene's role. What feeling words describe how *you* would be feeling? Discuss your answers with a small group.

❧Principles of Emotions in Conflict

In conflict, a tension of opposites is presented—do we open up or to close down? This basic tension can also be framed as:

- Soften or harden (Welwood 1990; Sanford 2007)
- **Move toward or against**
- Tighten up and turn away or relax and turn toward (Cloke and Goldsmith 2000)

- Follow curiosity and attraction vs. defensiveness and withdrawal
- Learn or defend (Paul and Paul 1987)

For the purposes of conflict resolution, we care about whether feelings open, broaden, and help people come toward each other for problem solving, or whether feelings shut us down, close us off, and lead us to withdraw from the person or the problem that arouses our feelings. Do we respond to emotions with communication that leads to healing and movement, or constriction of self, other, and relationship? Hard emotions lead to blame, criticism, threats—tearing the fragile fabric of the web of connection—whereas softer emotions lead to openings for transformation. We will provide a "map" of feelings so you can learn to *think while feeling*. While difficult, this maneuver can be learned.

Emotions Defined

Emotions are both intrapersonal and interpersonal phenomena. In addition, specific emotions lead people to particular tendencies to act or behave in certain ways (Frijda, Manstead and Bem 2000; Bell and Song 2005; Guerrero & Valley, 2006).

Conflict is always emotionally arousing—one cannot be "in conflict" and not experience emotional upheaval (Bodtker and Jameson 2001; Jones 2004). Human beings experience emotion in their verbal and nonverbal communication behavior, their physiological response, (Hein and Singer 2008) and in their thinking (Gottman 1994). When we are attacked or perceive a threat to our identity or goals, we will feel some kind of strong emotion. Often people feel many different "layers" of emotion at the same time.

Conflict depends upon enough feeling to "get the job done." Without enough feeling to engage people in interaction, avoidance seems like an easy alternative. When you are unhappy, distressed, excited about a possibility, or angry, you may exert enough energy to resolve a conflict. In this book, we highlight the importance of solving problems while maintaining relationships.

Emotional events trigger responses. We realize we are in conflict when we begin to feel something uncomfortable. We become agitated on the bodily level; this bodily response takes on a label as a certain emotion. For instance, Patricia, a junior, has just become engaged. She realizes that she is feeling distress and discomfort around her fiancé's family. Josh's family is large, gregarious, and warm. They often invite Josh and Patricia to join family events. Yet recently Patricia has noticed that she feels resentful and hurt, and is making up excuses to keep from seeing them. In a conflict with Josh, Patricia realized that she feels left out or "blotted out" by the large, enthusiastic family. Her feelings alerted her to a problem.

Intensity of emotion varies through the conflict process. You may feel very strongly at the beginning of a conflict, then less intensely as resolution or processing continues. For instance, you may begin by feeling fury, move to irritation, then realize you are feeling relief. It is a mistake to make a prediction based on an early emotion—to describe someone as "an angry person who can't be reasoned with." Feelings change in intensity.

Self-protective emotions tend to be associated with the **right hemisphere of the brain**. The right brain regulates raw conflict, competition, and fighting. *Prosocial or "soft"* *emotions tend to be associated with the* **left hemisphere of the brain** and with certain levels of brain chemicals of well-being. The left side brain specializes in preserving interpersonal relationships, attachment, and cooperation (Sanford 2007). Indeed we are "made" or "hard wired," to use the popular phrase, to process conflict a certain way. Conflict resolution depends on overcoming raw emotion (right brain/amygdala) and developing left-brain functions. As brain research develops further, we will learn even more about the physiological functions of conflict resolution.

We experience emotion as good or bad, positive or negative (Sanford 2007), pleasant or unpleasant, and helpful or destructive. We humans *evaluate* our emotions; we don't experience emotions from a distance, or objectively. Not many people enjoy fury, resentment, anger, or fear, but prefer the positive emotions. We will explore the role of both positive and negative emotions in greater detail later.

We become emotional because *something is at stake for us—our identity* (see also Fisher and Shapiro 2005). Often one person in a couple will say, "I can't discuss this while you are so emotional." Yet when important identity and relationship issues are at stake, emotion is simply part of the picture. We can regulate our expression of emotion, but should never require ourselves or others "not to feel." Older adults may feel that less is at stake in conflict, since they report fewer conflicts than do young adults (Almeida 2005; Almeida and Horn 2004) and when they do have conflict, they report lower overall distress (Charles and Carstensen 2008). Older adults even reported fewer negative emotions in conflicts than did middle-aged adults (Carstensen, Gottman, and Levenson 2004). We could draw the conclusion that for most people maturity increases options for putting conflicts into perspective. With maturity we define ourselves less by the outcome of each conflict because we simply have more of a sense of who we are.

★ *Elders*

Relationships are defined by the kind of emotion expressed. Two acquaintances are working on a project in class. One person feels upset because the quality of work done by the other is disappointing and the due date is coming up soon. When she expresses disappointment, the project partner says, "If you don't like it, do it yourself. I am overwhelmed by work." The relationship has been defined as one in which even moderate emotion (disappointment) cannot be safely expressed. These two will not remain friends after the project is turned in—and they may not even be speaking at that point!

The most intense conflicts if overcome, leave behind a sense of security and calm *that is not easily disturbed. It is just these intense conflicts and their conflagration which are needed to produce* valuable and lasting results.
—C. G. Jung

Just as conflict itself often is experienced subjectively as negative (as we discussed in chapter 1), "emotions" in conflict often are experienced with a negative slant. You may be familiar with someone saying, "I can't talk to you when you are emotional. Calm down and then we can discuss this whole situation reasonably." You may have felt enraged by this comment, or misunderstood. In fact, if you are in the conflict, you are "emotional." Negative beliefs about emotions might include the following. Which resonate with you?

Negative beliefs about emotion

Misconceptions of Emotion in Conflict

- Emotions are irrational.
- Emotions can't be controlled and will escalate if expressed or released.
- One should ignore emotions to resolve conflict well.
- Emotions hinder good decision making.
- Emotions are for the powerless (women, children, and marginalized people).
- Emotions are not to be expressed at work.
- Good, well-developed people should be beyond emotions.
- I can express emotions if I can justify my feelings logically.
- Emotions should be saved for "later."
- If I "let go" of emotions I will lose control.
- People will avoid me if I express emotions (except "nice" feelings).
- Other people should not burden me with their emotions.
- If other people express emotions, I have a responsibility to do something about them.
- If I express anger, it means I don't love or respect the object of my anger. The same is true for others toward me. (Adapted from Cloke and Goldsmith, 2000.)

Functions of Emotions

Emotions can be described in a variety of ways. Researchers at the Harvard Project on Negotiation have succinctly summarized various ways of looking at emotions (Fisher and Shapiro 2005, 216–218). Emotions can be seen as hard or soft, positive or negative, prosocial or selfish, open or closed, autonomous or vulnerable (Jordan 2008), fast (anger) or slow (sadness) (Rivers et al. 2006). However emotions are described, they evolved with specific purposes related to human survival (Izard and Ackerman 2000).

Emotions Help Us Adapt

Evidence abounds that discrete emotions evolved to help human beings adapt to specific kinds of challenges. Adaptive functions of emotions can be summarized by the following six principles (Izard and Ackerman 2000):

1. *Motivation depends on emotions.* Our behavioral goals depend on feelings. When our primary concern is, for instance, to avoid destructive conflict with a powerful supervisor, we may be motivated by fear and self-protection. When we want to "close the gap" with a loved one with whom we have argued, we are moved by love and attachment. We don't simply "act without reason." The reason for our actions is rooted in our feelings.

2. *Each discrete emotion serves different functions in organizing perception, cognitions, and actions for coping and creative endeavors* (Ackerman, Abe, and Izard 1998). Conflict resolution certainly calls on both coping and creativity. Different emotions help us accomplish different tasks in conflict resolution.

3. *Significant personal situations trigger organized patterns of emotions.* One emotion
    regulates other emotions. (For instance, we may desperately want to avoid an apology
    to a partner when we have betrayed them. We can think of many reasons why the
    betrayal occurred, we aren't over being angry at the way our betrayal was
    discovered, but at the same time we feel afraid of losing the relationship. Fear
    interacts with resentment and shame, mediated by love, to move us to a specific
    action—in this case, apology. If we were only afraid, we would avoid. If we were
    only resentful, we might escalate.) Emotions interact in coherent ways. Conflicts are
    difficult and complex because feelings and thoughts are complex and often mixed.

    Emotional intelligence depends on being able to understand and interpret
    many layers of feelings and thoughts. When someone says, "Look, it's simple.
    You either love me and support me or you don't," the speaker is oversimplifying
    a complex set of feelings and thoughts. It's usually "not that simple." (When people
    say, "It's simple," you can decode that wishful statement as a persuasive appeal,
    not a statement of emotional fact.)

    Emotional Intelligence

4. *People develop emotion-behavior patterns early in life and build on them.* The sad crying
    child becomes an older child with a sad face. That older child becomes an adult who
    manages sadness by learning other coping skills and developing other emotions and
    cognitive abilities. (The adult looks sad, and is sad, but also learns which people are
    understanding and nurturing, and uses love and affiliation to mitigate real sadness.)

5. *Individual personalities are built upon the blocks of emotion-behavior patterns.* For
    instance, consistently high levels of joy or positive emotions often lead to
    positive social relationships and ease with people (Abe and Izard 1999). We bring
    our personality structures into conflict resolution activities. (People differ, for
    example, in how long they can tolerate anger, or uncertainty, or hostility from
    others before they are motivated to do something about the unhappy situation.)

6. *While emotions help people adapt to community life, they also trigger difficult behavior
    in response to certain triggers.* Aggression may quickly follow anger and fear, for
    instance, if the desire to act on anger is not regulated by something else, such as
    shame or altruism.

Functions of Negative Emotions

Emotions fit, although not "neatly," into two main categories: (1) *Hard, closed or negative* emotions and (2) *positive, vulnerable or prosocial* emotions. People who can distinguish
between and know more about discrete emotions are better able to regulate negative emotions than those who made fewer distinctions and remain less knowledgeable (Rivers
et al. 2007). The good news about research on emotions in conflict resolution is that
finally the positive emotions are receiving the attention they deserve. However, since
anger and fear remain the emotions most people think of when they imagine or experience conflict, we will start with these troublesome and common feelings.

Positive emotions

* Anger & Fear - most significant emotions in conflict

The Functions of Anger

Angry emotion threatens most people; few healthy people enjoy feeling angry or having others direct anger at them. Anger differs from aggression in that aggression is an
attack, whereas "anger is the feeling connected to a perceived unfairness or injustice"

Aggression = an attack
Anger = perceived unfairness or injustice

(Young-Eisendrath 1997, 26). In this sense, anger helps people set boundaries when they need to be set, and to right wrongs. When we believe that we are the victim of an injustice, our usual response is anger (Mikula, Scherer, and Athenstaedt 1998). People who have an unrealistically high sense of self-esteem ride the horse of angry aggression more than people who are also motivated by the desire to solve problems, not seek vengeance, and avoid negative consequences (Baumeister, Smart, and Boden 1996).

Interesting

Anger can be a wake-up call, a motivator, and an energizer—a source of empowerment (usually) for the person who feels it (Planalp 1999). Anger can mobilize and sustain energy at very high levels. Anger has no direct bodily expression in behavior, only indirect avenues for expression such as heightened blood pressure, flushed face, sweating, muscle tightness, fast breathing, and a loud or high voice. When anger is expressed directly, the person to whom it is directed is warned—change or face the consequences (Planalp 1999). Self-responsibility calls for understanding our anger well enough so we don't justify ineffective and harmful behavior "because she made me mad." We can use anger to act, and we can question which actions will be most helpful, effective, and will avoid backfiring into a spiral of hostility and revenge.

Anger was termed "the moral emotion" by the ancients because it is based on a fast, reflective judgment that we have been wronged or threatened. We feel anger when our safety or our core values are threatened. Anger is "rooted in reason; it is equally of the heart and the head" (Young-Eisendrath 1983, 154). When an offense is real and important, the desire for revenge makes sense. The problem is that when we are angry, we may exaggerate an offense, plan revenge, and then lead ourselves and others into unproductive conflict (Planalp 1999). Yoshimura's research shows that while thinking about revenge can make people feel better as they imagine vengeful acts, remorse sets in when people commit acts that may come back to shame or sanction them (Yoshimura 2007).

Revenge

Expressing anger in an unrestrained way simply makes people angrier and does not discharge the emotion in a way that helps reduce the feelings (Tavris 1989). The "catharsis" view of emotion originally developed when people in Greek audiences experienced "pity and fear" while experiencing the tragic stories of the characters in early Greek drama. Catharsis functioned to help citizens identify with and learn from the flaws in character and the power of outside influences set into motion by earlier actions of the main characters. Somehow the idea that "anger is cathartic" gained prominence—that discharging anger would make anger lessen. Researchers now know that talking anger through in a way that does not escalate can be helpful; escalating verbal or physical anger usually escalates the anger emotion. Anger remains or grows rather than lessens with unbounded expression.

Catharsis of anger - Not usually helpful

Fear and anxiety

Fear and anxiety figure heavily in conflict resolution activities. Fear leads people, first, to avoid. Fear does not have to involve "flight" in the commonplace "fight" or "flight" choice. Just as anger does not necessarily lead to fighting, fear does not necessarily lead to fleeing. Fear sometimes disables the physical and emotional system as we "freeze," not able to mobilize ourselves to do anything for a while. The threat often is personal and psychological. We feel threats to our integrity, or our sense of well-being, or the painful threat of loss of a person, position, or role that we value. Fear can create "tunnel vision" as we focus only on the threat and forget to look around and assess what else might be happening (Izard and Ackerman 2000). Fear is the key emotion in anxiety. When we worry about what may happen, we are *anxious or afraid.*

Figure 6.1   Anger-Fear Sequence

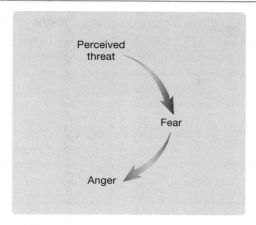

Fear and anger often interact in a patterned way. When one focuses on the "target" of anger, the person or situation that may threaten something valuable, the **anger-fear sequence** is set into motion.

Consider the list of the dynamics of anger and fear below. Fear and hurt underlie most emotions of anger. Fear makes human beings experience **vulnerability** that we then experience as anger, which is more socially acceptable for adults than is fear. The following list gives some examples of interpersonal anger situations along with possible intermixed fears/anxieties. Study these, then list a few angry situations of your own and see if you can determine how fear/anxiety might be mixed in with your own anger.

[handwritten margin note: Fear & hurt - Underlie most anger. Anger- More socially acceptable than fear]

Anger Situations

1. A woman is angry at her friend for calling her a name in public. (She is fearful of not being accepted by others.)

2. A newly promoted employee is angry because his secretary didn't get the final report to him on time. (He is afraid that his own supervisor will think he is not working hard enough, and he really needs this job.)

3. A husband is furious that his wife has disclosed their private life to others in a hurtful way. (He is frightened that their bond is no longer strong and that their relationship is ending.)

4. A single parent overreacts to a child's misbehaving at a family reunion by raising his voice and ordering the child into a time out. (He is afraid that other family members will criticize his parenting.)

5. An intimate partner casually indicates that she might change her plans and not visit when she had planned. Her partner says, "Well, if you have better things to do than honor your commitments, go ahead." (He has asked an old friend to visit to meet his significant other and fears looking foolish after speaking in glowing terms about the wonderful woman he wants his friend to meet. He is afraid he is unimportant to her, and he doesn't want to lose face with his friend.)

Sadness and Depression

Sadness and depression influence conflict resolution. Sadness can strengthen social bonds. For instance, when loved ones come together around the death of a friend or family member, the values of community and friendship are reaffirmed. Averill (1968) suggests that in the course of evolution, grief increased the probability of surviving because of the ways that enduring bonds are formed. Sadness slows a person down. This may give a chance for deeper reflection on what is happening, giving the sad person more choices to take care of him/herself and others. Sadness communicates that there is trouble (Tomkins 1963) so the person should pay attention to one's circumstances. Sadness is adaptive as well, because it may create a bridge of empathy to another person. Unrelieved sadness may create anger over a long time; this may turn into depression. In addition, many clinicians report elevated feelings of anger, along with sadness and anxiety, when people are depressed (Rutter, Izard, and Read 1986). Extreme sadness causes an almost total loss of pleasure and interest in one's surroundings, and leads to dejection and withdrawal.

Sadness and depression may help in conflict resolution because the feelings are so unpleasant that we are moved to find new solutions to problems. When we are so depressed we can hardly get out of bed to function normally, we may ask, "What is wrong and what can I do about it?" For example, Pamela found herself very sad every time she turned into her driveway after work. Even though the day might have gone well enough at work, when she came home she found herself feeling sad. One day she went to her friend's house after work and told her she just didn't want to go home, then burst into tears. Pamela's mother had died a few months before. Her husband Baird went to the farthest end of the house and turned on the TV when Pamela cried. Several times Pamela told Baird that she needed comfort when she was so sad. Baird, however, felt extremely uncomfortable with Pamela's tears. He said once, when she asked for comfort, "But there's nothing I can do. I am sorry your mother is gone but I can't change anything." Pamela felt more sorrow and loneliness at this point. Finally, after talking with her friend, Pamela decided to talk with Baird. After explaining how she felt about coming home, their dialogue sounded like this:

Handwritten margin notes:
Unrelieved sadness → anger → Depression

Depression - Often also more feelings of anger, sadness, anxiety

Excellent example

Application 6.2	Sadness Leads to a Different Solution

Pamela: Baird, I know you care that my mother died and that I am so sad. But when you go to the den and turn on the TV when I'm crying, I feel more lonely than ever. I start to tell myself that you don't care.

Baird: I care a lot but there's nothing I can do.

Pamela: There is a lot you can do. You can listen to me, hold my hand, tell me you are here for me, and that you are sorry I'm feeling so awful.

Baird: But that's not doing anything. I can't change anything and I feel helpless.

(continued)

Application 6.2	Sadness Leads to a Different Solution

Pamela: You could change a lot for me. I wouldn't feel so alone. I didn't know you felt helpless.

Baird: Yes—I see you so miserable and feel awful that I can't do anything.

As this conversation progressed, both Pamela and Baird softened instead of hardened. Pamela had been hardening into the perspective that "He doesn't care." Baird had been hardening into the story that "Nothing I do makes any difference." They found different ways to stay together through Pamela's sadness.

Some **gender differences** *occur in the expression of sadness.* Women are more likely to express sadness and cover up their anger, whereas men are more likely to express anger and cover up sadness (Timmers et al. 1998). In the case above, Pamela moved from sadness to anger at her husband's inability to comfort her. Baird felt angry at himself that he didn't know what to do. Then he retreated into sadness. Both misunderstood the emotions of the other until they talked through their dilemma.

(margin note: Women – express sadness cover up anger. Men – express anger cover up sadness)

Too little sadness expression leads to distorted emotional expression; too much sadness expression can burden others. One function of sadness is that people experiencing sadness are more likely than others to attempt to change their situation by cognitive reappraisal ("I don't think he meant to hurt me in the way he did; he was busy and distracted") or by apologizing or listening to music or doing other activities to change their mood (Rivers et al. 2007). Women have been found to be more skillful at emotion regulation in general (Rivers et al.). This gender-skill difference brings many challenges to couple relationships.

(margin note: Women – more skilled at emotional regulation)

Disgust, contempt, and revulsion are emotions that move to expel something noxious or repulsive. In an adaptive sense, it makes sense to think that humans who learned to "spit out" or expel bad food or water were more likely to survive. In interpersonal communication, we may be trying to "get rid of" something (someone) repulsive when we use disdain, contempt, condescension, and demeaning comments. We explored earlier in the book how damaging contempt is in intimate relationships. Disgust is one of those emotions to feel, reflect upon, and not communicate about until we understand and process the raw emotion.

Shame and guilt play an important role in regulating conflict. When people break social norms, and receive formal or informal social sanctions ("How could you have done that?!") they may be feeling shame, guilt, embarrassment, regret, or remorse (Nugier et al. 2007). When you act in a way that is incompatible with your own standards, your ideal self, or your own sociocultural values, you may feel these uncomfortable emotions (Frijda 1986; Fisher and Shapiro 2005). Shame acts as a force for social cohesion. We try to avoid shameful situations because we lose face, lose self-esteem, and generally feel miserable (Izard and Ackerman 2000, 260). Shame may also be present in fear and anxiety. "Shaming" others usually leads to defensiveness, and works poorly as a conflict resolution tactic.[2] When we recognize that others feel shame or embarrassment, we can further the cause of good conflict management by remaining gentle and considerate. Shame hurts.

The Value of Positive Emotions in Conflict Resolution

The adaptive theory of discrete emotions also relates to positive emotions. Many times we do not think of positive emotions in relation to the effective management of conflict. Recent research, especially the ideas of Seligman when he was president of the American Psychological Association, Isen (1987), Frederickson (2003), and Fisher and Shapiro (2005), points out the creative value of positive emotions.

Joy, love, and laughter may have had a helpful adaptive role in human development. For instance, altruistic individuals were more likely to "tend and befriend," and therefore survive catastrophes. Positive emotions broaden an individual's mindset, allowing one to "broaden and build." Whether in the lab or in everyday life, when people feel positive emotions such as interest, joy, altruism, hope, sympathy and empathy, they are more likely to think creatively. When people feel good they are more likely to integrate new ideas, be flexible, and remain open to information (Fredrickson 2003.)

Some organizations use these ideas for team building. When colleagues are able to play together, they are more likely to clarify their life priorities, strengthen social ties, and build skills to express love and care. In work-related conflicts, colleagues are more likely to choose cooperative modes of conflict resolution when they like each other and have shared positive emotional experiences (DeSilvilya and Yagil 2005). When students were asked to think of positive meaning in their daily lives, at the end of a month they scored higher on psychological resilience than those who focused on some neutral task (Fredrickson 2003). Interest and joy in play interacts with affiliation (Izard and Ackerman 2000). Rituals such as eating and playing games help people engage their feelings rather than just their cognitive abilities (Maiese 2006). Eating a meal together helps people relax and think of their opponents as people who want to solve problems. Many cultures signal the end of hostilities by having a meal together, giving gifts, and sharing greetings and apologies. Non-hostile joking helps people see each other as friendly others rather than enemies (Maiese 2006). Positive feelings (induced by watching positive-emotion films) help boost broadened thinking, and vice versa (Fedrickson and Joiner 2002).

Community conflict resolution and transformation create a "positive spiral" in an important way—people who give help can feel proud of their good deeds, and people who receive help often feel grateful. Even people who simply witness good deeds can feel elevated and more joyful (Fredrickson 2003).

Interest in the other person and the problem, as well as in oneself brings us closer to the other so we can solve problems. Interest is the only emotion that can sustain long-term constructive or creative endeavors (Tomkins 1962). As a student of conflict resolution, you can notice that paying attention and taking interest in a problem, with a positive, "we can solve this together" attitude may carry you into solutions you could not have thought of alone.

---

[2] Unless, of course, one's entire community that you cannot escape from engages in shame-based behavior. When this happens you must make a decision about adapting to the community or trying to change what your community is doing.

Joy, happiness, serenity, and contentment contribute greatly to resolving conflicts. When you approach a problem with interest and a positive attitude, you communicate these feelings to others involved, and they, too, are motivated to work with you (Deci 1992; Izard and Ackerman 2000).

Positive emotions lead to empathy and sympathy. Throughout the first part of this book we emphasized the importance of taking the other's perspective while holding fast to your own thoughts and feelings. When we assume that others want essentially what we want, we can join with them to solve problems instead of seeing the other person as the problem. Effective conflict resolution draws on feelings about and for the other person, and for oneself.

⇜Work in the Mid-Range: The Zone of Effectiveness

Conflicts that are worked out in the middle of the level of intensity are more effectively resolved than those that are left unexpressed or are handled with unrestrained emotion. See figure 6.2 for a graphic depiction of regulated conflict. Aristotle wrote about the Golden Mean and the Buddha preached about the Middle Way. Low productivity occurs when interpersonal conflicts are either not identified (but the emotions leak out anyway) or when people indulge in unrestrained emotion (thus leading others to fight or flee). A lack of regulation in personal conflicts damages the process. For instance, a divorcing couple attempting to share the custody of their two children were close to agreement when the (ex-)wife exploded in a mediation session, saying, "He's selfish! He always was and always will be!" Her unregulated outburst ruined the chance for collaboration on their problem.

Figure 6.2   Continuum of Conflict Intensity

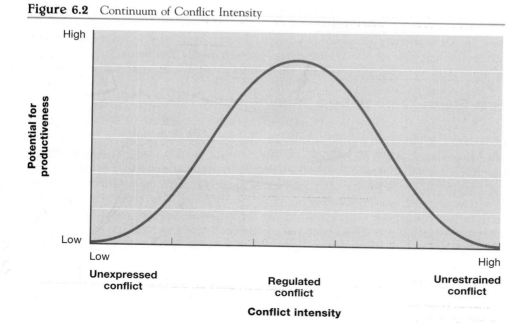

Regardless of the specific content, after an episode has passed, the other person will recall what you said and did during the conflict. *People have long memories for bad treatment.* Even if you feel perfectly justified for blowing up, your "bad behavior" will remain in memory even if the conflict outcome works out reasonably well. You may lose a relationship while solving a problem.

Venting does nothing to help the conflict process. We will be exploring how to work with one's own emotions so venting does not remain your only option for expression. If you feel the need to vent, do it with a safe friend, a counselor, or designated third party—not the conflict partner with whom you are attempting to work. Venting can feel wonderful for a while—but the price is usually too high to warrant the "Yes!" feeling of telling the other person off.

Unthinking avoidance of a conflict—pretending you don't have strong feelings when you do, will ultimately fail. Your feelings will come through, and the problem will remain unresolved. Lines from a poem by William Stafford challenge us to be clear and "wake up" with honest and direct communication:

> *If you don't know the kind of person I am*
> *and I don't know the kind of person you are*
> *a pattern that others made may prevail in the world*
> *and following the wrong god home we may miss our star.*
> *For it is important that awake people be awake,*
> *or a breaking line may discourage them back to sleep;*
> *The signals we give—yes or no, or maybe—*
> *should be clear: the darkness around us is deep.*

William Stafford, from "A Ritual to Read to Each Other"

Moderated emotions in conflict bring many advantages. The escalatory spiral will be halted, you will learn something with self-restraint, and you will be able to be more creative in your options when you don't create a bitter enemy. You will not take actions, such as revenge, that you would later regret or have to justify (Yoshimura 2007). Restraint of your emotions, but not suppression, allows trust to build when trust has broken down.

First Steps: Learn to Be a Warrior—of the Heart

How do we learn to manage the raw emotions that make up conflict? As Welwood (*Journey of the Heart,* 1990) writes in his helpful book on love and relationships, we try to manage our lives so we avoid "raw" feelings, but in fact we are human partly because we feel so deeply. He refers to feelings as "raw" because we feel tender and vulnerable, but also because our emotions, at the beginning of a conflict, are "uncooked." They have not been processed. When we approach conflict as a **"warrior of the heart,"** we draw on some of the metaphors from earlier in the book. Conflict is a dance, or is like martial arts, and is like stepping along an unfamiliar path. Since we cannot avoid conflict, we can learn to move skillfully.

Welwood suggests three first steps. Starting out on the difficult path of working with strong emotions, you will find these ideas helpful. **Awareness** is "by far the most essential, powerful resource we have for effecting change and working with life's challenges" (Welwood 1990, 23). Awareness draws not on "knowing about something," but on *clarity.* We are clear when we can use all our senses to tell what is actually happening, when we can move with *fluidity,* as though we are a zoom lens that can move in and out to change perspective. When we stay clear and fluid, we can stay stable instead of being blown around or thrown off our path.

The final requirement is to *remain compassionate toward ourselves and others.* **✱** *Remain compassionate toward selves & others*
Compassion makes us strong and expanded as conflict managers, since when we are compassionate we make space for our own feelings and the feelings of others. Making space is like stepping out of the flames (of emotion), but rather than running from the fire, we sit "next to it," look into the fire, and reflect on what is hurting. We have freedom to think, feel, move and choose actions (Welwood 1990, 24).

Often, instead, when strong emotions toss us around, we feel so miserable or anxious or furious or scared that we begin to *tell ourselves stories*. These stories become bad mental habits that lead us to take shortcuts to action/reaction instead of thinking and feeling our way along a new path in a conflict. These "stories" become dramas that we believe are true, as was the case for Pamela and Baird as they told themselves stories about each other regarding Pamela's grief and Baird's response. Stories filter what we are able to think and feel.

Finally, the "warrior of the heart" needs *courage*. Courage is ordinarily depicted as a characteristic of "the lone, separate person who defies vulnerability and fear" (Jordan 2008). Jordan, one of the pioneers of the Relational-Cultural Model of therapy, founds her ideas, as does Welwood, on a different model of courage. Courage derives from the Latin root "cor" meaning heart, "the seat of feeling, thought" (Jordan 2008). Courage involves bringing even painful truths into a relationship. It often involves courage to come into conflict. We have thoroughly explored the lures of both avoidance and escalation. Courage of the heart and feelings involves finding the truth with awareness, resisting the tried and true stories that propel us to act in habituated ways, and the true bravery required to act in an honest and compassionate manner. *Courage*

bringing even painful truths into a relationship

Jordan suggests that we redefine vulnerability as an emotion and position that requires courage. Vulnerability means that "we are open to the influence of others at the same time that we are open to our need for others" (Jordan 2008, 213). In a dominant, power-over culture, we are not safe when vulnerable. In a connected, relational culture, we can be moved by our feelings, express them with care, and continue to resolve our differences.[3] *Vulnerability requires courage -*

We will practice some of the "first steps" ideas for dealing with feelings by studying the following case and applying the ideas we've just discussed.

Case 6.2	It's Not Yours to Loan!

Jackie and Tom are a married couple. They both work in real estate, Jackie in mortgage financing and Tom in sales. Tom's grandmother died and left each of her five grown grandchildren $50,000. Jackie and Tom were amazed and pleased. As they talked, they agreed to put the money into a money market account until the real estate market settled down, at which time they would make a down payment on their next home. Both Tom and Jackie like the duplex they bought when they married. They can afford the current mortgage because one side of the duplex is rented. They feel no hurry to buy something

(continued)

---

[3] For more on the work of the Jean Baker Miller Institute, go to http://wt.haworthpress.com.

| Case 6.2 | It's Not Yours to Loan! |

larger, although they are quite crowded, especially since the value of their duplex has dropped. In a recent appraisal, they were disappointed at how the duplex had lost value.

Half a year went by. Jackie usually managed the money, paying bills out of a joint checking account to which both contribute. One day Tom was at the bank and as he made a deposit, noticed that the money market account was down by about $20,000. In alarm, he asked the teller to track down the activity on the account. What he found shocked him. Jackie had taken $20,000 out three months before, then had made small deposits back into the account since then. He rushed home and confronted her. After a long, escalating fight in which Jackie was first evasive, then defensive, and Tom was accusing and unbelieving, Jackie confessed what had happened. Her parents had gotten themselves into trouble with credit card debt. Jackie arranged to loan them $20,000 with their promise and assurance that they would quickly pay her back. But Jackie's mother needed an unexpected operation. Her parents had made no payments back to Jackie. Jackie, panicked, tried to replenish the account but knew she could never do it on her salary. Here is part of their first conflict episode:

Tom: I cannot believe you would deceive me and do something so dangerous, dishonest and selfish. What about our plans? You had absolutely no right to touch that money without talking to me.

Jackie: I feel terrible. But my parents had a good plan for paying us back. It's not their fault that Mom had to have surgery. Have a heart, Tom.

Tom: They needed help for their credit card problems and stupid debts. I might have wanted to help, but you didn't ask. Now I can't trust you. You are not the woman I thought you were—you are a sneak and I will never be able to trust you again.

Jackie: Fine!!! I'll put every cent of my salary in the fund and you can tell my parents that you wouldn't help them. I'll tell them how selfish you are. What daughter wouldn't want to help her parents when they had gotten in trouble because of terrible jobs and a sinking economy? We had the money, and they didn't. They'll pay us back. I had no idea you were so heartless.

Tom: And I had no idea you were so gullible and deceitful! There's no earthly way your parents could have paid us back, even without your Mom's operation. You care more about them than our plans.

Jackie: And you apparently care more about money than love and helping out.

Using Welwood and Jordan's ideas from above, let's see what *awareness, flexibility, compassion, and vulnerability* might sound like. A counselor asked each of them to reflect on the storm of emotion they were feeling before they talked with each other about the conflict again. They each wrote in a journal as they reflected.

(continued)

Case 6.2   It's Not Yours to Loan!

Jackie: *I can see from the look on Tom's face and hear in his voice that he is shocked and dismayed. It's extremely painful to me to know that I betrayed his trust. I wish I had talked to him and told him about my parents' need. I was afraid that he would say no, and I believed that with a bonus coming in at Dad's business, they would be able to pay us back. Well, I see that I was not thinking. I just wanted to help and I felt guilty having the money and not helping them. I want to let Tom know that our values are different. In my culture, you help people in your family who are in need, period. But I hated feeling scared all the time and I'm actually glad Tom found out. I don't know what to do.*

Tom: *I feel awful about blowing up at Jackie the way I did. I humiliated her. And yet I felt so shocked and scared that she took my money without telling me. More than that, I realize that I don't like or trust her parents. I am furious that they manipulated her, the way they have done before with kids in the family. Jackie's right, in a way. I do feel ungenerous with them. Her dad's an alcoholic and her mom works way too hard. Her dad expects people to take care of him. I think her mom put all those charges on the credit cards because he feels entitled to whatever he wants. I feel sorry for her mom. I'm still angry at Jackie, but I have seen for years how her parents take advantage of their kids. But I can't talk to Jackie about that—she'd be really hurt. And now we are furious with each other. But under all that, I feel scared and sad. It's not really the money, it's the trust issue. And I can imagine something like this happening in the future.*

Tom and Jackie are on their way to becoming "warriors of the heart." They are telling the truth to themselves, which will enable them to tell the truth to each other, and solve their problems.

Before the counselor asked them to reflect in their journals, and then talk with each other again, Tom and Jackie had begun to tell themselves stories, make predictions, and believe these predictions. If they had listed their "stories," or **automatic thoughts**, they would have been following "hot thoughts" (Greenberger and Padesky 1995, 55).

You might think of "hot thoughts" this way. Perhaps you have had the experience of walking into a room, turning on the lamp switch, and having no light appear. You may have discovered that the wall switch connected to the lamp's plug was turned off so the lamp was not receiving electricity. Activating the wall switch causes electricity to flow in the circuit, allowing the lamp to turn on.

Wires that carry electricity are called "hot wires." Similarly, the automatic thoughts that are most connected to strong feelings are called "hot" thoughts. These thoughts conduct the emotional charge, so these are the thoughts that are important to identify, examine, and sometimes alter to change our feelings (adapted from Greenberg and Padesky 1995).

Case 6.3 — Strong Emotions and Automatic Thoughts

Write down a situation that you are experiencing in the present or immediate past about which you have strong emotions, like Tom and Jackie did. Then write down the automatic thoughts (the hot ones) that lead from your emotional situation. Some questions that might help you discover your automatic stories are these:

- What was going through my mind just before I started to feel this way?
- What am I afraid might happen?
- What is the worst thing that could happen if it is true?
- What does this mean about how the other person(s) feels and thinks about me?
- What images or memories do I have in this situation? (from Greenberger and Padesky 1995, 51).

Here is one example of a situation full of feeling.

Case 6.4 — You Voted for Who?!

You have just discovered that your fiancé has voted the opposite ticket from you in the general election. You have both argued over this; you cannot believe that he/she feels so differently. You fiancé reminds you that you share a lot of values in common, but you are disbelieving and shocked. Automatic thoughts:

If we are so different on something as important as who is president, what will this mean for our future together?

I am ashamed to tell my family how s/he voted.

I never saw myself as being married to someone so different from me.

[handwritten: This could be good] → Is there more about him/her that I don't know? How can I find out?

Is this marriage right for me?

Using awareness to gain clarity, to build in space to reflect, to stop oneself from telling stories, and to remain gentle with oneself and others is a key tool for working with feelings. Feelings are facts, but with attention and care, we can change our feelings and still be honest and be ourselves.

Second Steps: Working with Emotions

The following techniques will help you work with strong emotion.

A) Express Anger Responsibly

Anger can be relationally lethal if you express it with contempt, disgust, exaggeration, shaming, and other mixtures of strong negative feelings. We have explored Gottman's

[handwritten margin note: Anger—but without · contempt · disgust · exaggeration · shaming]

ideas of "The Four Horsemen," which are communication responses steeped in negative emotions. Yet anger can be expressed in a way that is *clear, calm, firm, respectful, honest, and compassionate*. This way of speaking works well as you express any strong emotion.

Mace (1987) suggests the following guidelines for **responsible expression** of anger:

1. Verbally state the anger. Just as one says, "I am hungry," say, "I am angry."
2. Distinguish between venting and acknowledging anger.
3. Agree that you will never attack each other in a state of anger.
4. Work to find the stimulus for the anger. It won't go away just because it is expressed.

Mace summarizes his approach (for use with intimate partners) as follows: "I find myself getting angry with you. But you know I am pledged not to attack you, which would only make you angry too, and alienate us. What I need is your help to get behind my anger to what really is causing it, so that we can do something about it together." The response to this is, "I don't like your being angry with me, but I don't blame you for it. And since I know you won't attack me, I needn't put up my defenses and get angry with you in turn. I appreciate your invitation to help you get through to the underlying cause of your anger, because I care about our relationship, and it should help both of us to find out what is really happening to us" (97). When you practice this approach to communicating anger, you will find it doesn't seem strange. The rewards for this kind of expression will help you keep using the approach.

B Use the X-Y-Z Formula for Clarity

Often, finding the right words to communicate anger is difficult. The **X-Y-Z** formula will help one express any difficult emotion (Gottman et al. 1976). Here are its components:

- When you do X
- In situation Y
- I feel Z

An administrative assistant might say, "When you interrupt me (X) when I am on the phone (Y), I feel rattled and belittled (Z)." Her response, taking responsibility for feeling upset yet letting the other person know what produced her feelings, is more likely to result in a constructive solution than if she had said, "I don't get any respect around here!"

The X-Y-Z skill has the advantage of clarifying the issue of concern for the recipient of strong emotion and urging the sender to take responsibility for his or her emotional reaction. While X-Y-Z does not prescribe the desired change, the complaint is lodged in a specific, descriptive form so that the recipient might reduce defensiveness and respond appropriately.

C Actively Listen to Emotional Communication

As you listen to someone you care about express a negative emotion, you experience a natural tendency to experience your own fear and then to respond defensively, as in, "I only interrupt you when it is important to the company—get off my case." Remember, however, that when someone is upset with you, he or she needs to express that feeling or the feeling will turn into resentment, despair, sadness, or some other emotion. *You can't "argue" or "reason" someone out of any feeling.* When you say, "You <u>shouldn't</u> feel disappointed/angry/sad," this injunction may increase, not decrease, the emotion. The other person may feel <u>frustrated and misunderstood</u> because you are devaluing the other's real feelings. You don't have to agree with feelings to listen respectfully.

Case 6.5	Roommate to Roommate

Here is an <u>example of respectful listening</u> to someone who is upset. Your roommate has just said:

When you leave your clothes on the floor (X) and I have people in after my night class (Y), I feel disgusted (Z).

Recipient: So my clothes on the floor really get you mad?

1. Does it make you mad all the time or just if people are coming over?

2. Is this a big deal that bothers you a lot, or is it a minor irritation, or somewhere in between?

3. Let's both come up with some ideas. I'll bet we'll figure something out

4. It's important to me that we give and take because I like having you as a roommate.

Protect Yourself from Verbal Abuse

When another's expression of anger, rage, or contempt burns out of control, you have a responsibility to *protect yourself.* <u>Listening to belittling; hostile blame; ridicule; demeaning or untrue accusations; sarcastic name-calling; contempt; or actual physical threats is <u>*not*</u> good conflict management.</u> The other person should be told, firmly and consistently, "I won't listen to this kind of talk. I can't hear anything important you're trying to say when you're this out of control." Then you can leave or hang up the phone, <u>giving the other person a chance to cool off</u>. You can say, "<u>Wait!</u>" <u>or "Stop!</u>" in a firm voice. <u>Never try to argue </u>with a person who is engaged in verbal abuse. (It's like arguing with an alcoholic—nothing healing can happen until the person is not drinking.) But just as you would move to stop the abuse of a child, you have the responsibility to <u>stop verbal abuse in a conflict</u>, if you possibly can.

   <u>Verbal abuse leads to escalation or withdrawal</u>, <u>hinders conflict resolution</u>, and <u>lowers the dignity and self-esteem of all parties</u>. Productive reception of someone's anger may not be possible until boundaries are reset and conversation takes a more constructive tone. You can r<u>aise your voice</u> (without shouting) and speak in a firm, <u>no-nonsense</u> tone. Of course, as a student of conflict resolution, you possess skills that will make it unnecessary for you to ever use verbal abuse!

   <u>Conflict is not always polite, but constructive conflict is never abusive or violent.</u> When you know you are o<u>verpowered</u>, or cannot stop the verbal abuse from another, leave. You may need <u>help from friends or professionals</u> to do so. You are never responsible for someone else's verbal abuse, as long as you are using reasonably constructive communication.

Never abusive or violent ||

(E) *Use Fractionation*

The essential conflict reduction tactic known as fractionating is an idea developed by Follett (1940) and later called "fractionation" by Fisher (1971). Fractionation reduces the intensity of emotion in conflicts by focusing attention on the *sizing of disputes*. Conflicts can be broken down from one big mass into several smaller, more manageable conflicts. Fractionating conflict does not make it disappear, of course; it simply makes the components of large conflicts more approachable by parties who are trying to manage their disputes. Conflicts "do not have objective edges established by external events" (158). Rather, conflicts are like a seamless web, with indistinguishable beginnings and endings. Choices are almost always available as to how to size, and therefore manage, conflicts. When you choose to "downsize" a conflict, you probably also downsize the big emotion. This simple idea is one of the most useful conflict management tactics. Almost all conflicts can be made smaller without being trivialized. Smaller conflicts carry less strong emotion.

Can make conflicts smaller (fractionation) without trivializing

(F) *Use Positive Language to Work with Strong Emotion*

As we discussed earlier in this chapter, positive emotions help people broaden their thinking, reflect, and build on integrative ideas. You can adopt the "contribution system" (essentially, each person acknowledges that he or she contributes something to the problem, rather than blaming the other person.) You can use Fisher and Shapiro's ideas from *Beyond Reason: Using Emotions as You Negotiate* (2005) to change your language from negative language to positive language. Study *Difficult Conversations* for excellent language that leads to moderated emotion (Stone, Patton, and Heen 1999). Express appreciation, use "we" language, involve people in decisions that affect them (which reduces defensiveness), and show respect by asking for opinions and advice from others. (For more resources from the Harvard Project on Negotiation, go to www.beyond-reason.net.) We also recommend Marshall Rosenberg's influential book *Speak Peace in a World of Conflict* (2005), another resource full of the language of peaceful communication.

Marshall Rosenberg

❧Personal Responsibility for Emotional Transformation

As we have explored, emotions naturally arising in conflict often "feel bad." Peacemaking is a crucial stress reduction mechanism for people (Aureli and Smucny 2000). In fact, "post-conflict anxiety and reconciliation may function as part of the human homeostatic mechanism, which regulates and stabilizes relationships between former opponents" (Butovskaya, 2008, 1557).

Often try to change the other –

As we think about change, we often try to change the other. This "change the other" attempt usually yields little that is constructive. Sometimes we can *change the situation*. Finally, the only person we can deeply influence, from the inside out, is ourself. Change in your interior communication or thoughts changes the entire system. This is especially true as we work with our own emotions, taking responsibility for how we feel. No longer can we accurately say, "I couldn't help it. He pushed all my buttons." With reflection, we know where our buttons are, how to manage our actions, and how to gain enough space to think while feeling. Boulding (1989) calls this the watershed principle, based on where water flows along the Continental Divide. On one side, it flows toward the Atlantic, yet just a few feet over, it flows toward the Pacific. Very small changes can produce enormous effects. Similarly, in conflict interactions, small personal

Small changes → enormous effects

changes reverberate throughout the entire system and bring results that are much larger than you would ever imagine.

Because self-change in a conflict is difficult, it usually requires prerequisites. If you are going to alter your own emotionally based behavior rather than assert that your feelings and actions are "only natural" or "only in response to what she did," you have to care about the relationship. If the relationship is of no consequence to you, then you feel little impetus to change. The essential point is that you are not waiting for the other to change first—someone has to "step up to the plate."

In conclusion, working with strong emotions by understanding them, reflecting, choosing actions instead of reacting, and learning to express yourself precisely when you are feeling strongly—all this personal growth and responsibility leads to better conflict resolution. Radical self-responsibility means we take seriously our own possibilities for infusing hope and positive change into the world. This is a life-long work in progress.

Radical self-responsibility.

> Out beyond the ideas of right doing and wrong doing,
> There is a field.
> I'll meet you there.

Jelaluddin Rumi

Summary

Emotions are states of feeling that arise naturally during conflict. During conflict a natural tension of opposite occurs—to soften or harden. We noted that emotional intensity varies, our self-protective moves are processed in the right hemisphere of our brain, participants see emotions as good or bad, and relationships are defined by the kind of emotion that is expressed.

Emotions serve a variety of functions, and negative emotions such as anger can serve as a wake-up call. The popular notion that you can get rid of emotions by expressing them (the catharsis view) is not accurate. The anger-fear cycle details what is underneath feelings of anger. Other emotions such as sadness and depression can alert us to trouble in the relationship. We also note that in general, men find it easier to express anger while women find expressing sadness more common. We provide a long list of "feeling words" to help identify some emotional states that occur in conflict.

You have a better chance of productive conflict if you neither deny nor blow up—rather, express whatever feelings you have in the midrange. We note that awareness, flexibility, compassion, and vulnerability are ways to express strong emotions for a positive result. Learning how to catch your automatic thoughts, express anger responsibly, and take personal responsibility for your own emotional transformation yields big payoffs for managing conflict productively.

Key Terms

emotions 194

states of feeling 194

feeling words 194

move toward or against 197

right hemisphere of the brain 198

prosocial 198

left hemisphere of the brain 199

functions of negative emotions 201

anger-fear sequence 203

vulnerability 203

gender differences 205

mid-range 207

warrior of the heart 208

awareness 208

compassion 209

automatic thoughts 211

responsible expression 213

X-Y-Z 213

Review Questions

1. Define emotions.
2. What is the tension of opposites that occurs with emotions and conflict?
3. Describe the main function of emotions in relationship to engagement in conflict resolution activities.
4. List some common misconceptions about emotions.
5. How do these misconceptions hinder effective conflict resolution?
6. How do negative emotions serve us in conflicts?
7. What is the anger-fear sequence?
8. How do sadness, disgust, and shame and guilt influence conflict parties?
9. What are "feeling words"? What makes the study of feeling words useful?
10. Explain the adaptive theory of emotions applied to negative and positive emotions.
11. Why would one want to be in the mid-range of emotional expression? What happens when you are at either end of the bell-curve description of conflict?
12. What is "warrior of the heart"?
13. What are automatic thoughts and how are they connected to emotions?
14. List ways to express anger productively.
15. Why would you want to change yourself rather than others?
16. What are some of the reasons change is difficult?
17. Explain self-responsibility in relation to emotional understanding and regulation.

Chapter 7

Mapping Your Conflicts

Have you ever been in a conflict where you were so perplexed you asked, either silently or out loud, "What is going on here?" For most of us, conflicts are confusing—we can't clearly see the interpersonal dynamics that unfold. And, as we saw in the last chapter, when our emotions are running high, it is even more difficult to understand the conflict dynamics. When you can "map" your conflicts on both (1) macro and (2) micro levels, you will be empowered to make more productive choices in the midst of the chaos.

At the macro level, most people cannot accurately describe the **system dynamics** impacting them. Steve, for example, when asked, "why do your workgroup meetings always end in people shouting?" says, "I just don't know—it seems to be something we do." Steve feels trapped in a system. As with Steve, we are always embedded in a wider system impacting us. In this chapter, we will give you an orientation to system dynamics and some tools for understanding how systems work. When you are in a conflict you will have a better chance to understand the overall dynamics at work.

At the micro level, most of us are notoriously inaccurate in describing our own behavior in a conflict. We develop blind spots about our own behavior, and rigid ways of seeing the other. People repeatedly impose on others that which they later claim was imposed on them. The person who believes the world is a competitive, win/lose place often doesn't see that this view sets competitive processes in motion (Weick 1979). **Self-fulfilling prophecies** are enacted over and over as we provoke the very behavior we accuse the other in the conflict of perpetuating. Then we each make ourselves out to be the other's victim (Warner and Olson 1981). This chapter will help illuminate your conflicts, letting you see gaps in what you know and giving you detailed assessment guides.

Self-fulfilling prophecies

❧Macro-Level Mapping

Systems Theory

Full assessment of a conflict can best be accomplished by (1) assessing the workings of the overall system and how those connect to (2) recurring communication patterns inside the system. One of the most helpful macro-level approaches is general systems theory, which tells us about the workings of entire systems and subsystems in organizations, small groups, and families.

Systems theory helps us answer the question, "How does this work?" Conflicts are seldom managed productively by attention to blame or causality. If you tag someone with the "fault" label, you have not managed the conflict; you have only created an enemy. We call this blame process "putting the black hat on the villain."

Extensive discussions of systems theory applied to various contexts can be found in Gregory Bateson's two major works *Steps to an Ecology of Mind* (1972) and *Mind and Nature* (1980), cornerstones of systems theory writing and research.[1] These approaches give us a new "lens" through which to see what happens—that conflicts are interlocking sequences, like a play production in which everyone plays a part. Key concepts of systems thinking follow:

Conflicts= interlocking Sequences

- **Wholeness.** We must look at the entire system, not just a collection of individual behaviors. Every individual is embedded within a larger system.

- **Organization.** It is true that the unit is made up of individuals, but it nevertheless functions as a unit. Each unit has its own patterns of organization—what is the overall picture?

- **Patterning.** We are interested in what patterns seem connected. What patterns are predictable, and what functions do these patterns serve? Many times people cling to patterns of behavior that seem to make no sense, but from the whole system perspective, they do make sense (Papp, Silverstein, and Carter, 1973).

Selected principles derived from systems theory will help you understand the holistic, or systemic, nature of any conflict. The following suggestions are adapted from a practical and helpful article by Papp, Silverstein, and Carter (1973):

1. **Conflict in Systems Occurs in Chain Reactions. People Cannot Be Identified as Villains, Heroes, Good and Bad People, or Healthy and Unhealthy Members.** Rather than pinpointing one person as the cause of the conflict, look instead for predictable "chain reactions," because what every person does affects every other person. Study the chain reactions—see who picks up what cues and identify the part each plays in the runaway spiral. Satir (1972) uses an image of a family as a mobile in which members respond to changes in each other. If one member responds to a situation, the other members must consciously or unconsciously respond to the movement in the system. The same kind of interdependence exists in organizations and small groups. One cannot *not* affect other members of a system.

   Systems operate with **circular causality,** a concept that suggests that assigning a beginning is less important than looking at the sequence of patterns in the conflict process. Almost always, conflict participants identify the other as the cause while portraying the self as innocent. The boy who runs home screaming "Sasha hit me!" is clearly ignoring his part in the system (he threw dirt at her). All systems are characterized by circular causality—each one affects the other. We might take e-mail messages as an example. When people start sending negative e-mail messages, especially at work, they often feel justified and do not see the negative effect that inflammatory e-mails create. The person who "fires off" a nasty e-mail feels better, but the person who receives it (or hears about it) feels worse, fires off

---

[1]The systems approach to describing normal family processes is discussed thoroughly by Galvin and Brommel (1986) and Walsh (1984). Overviews of systems theory and the change process are provided by Minuchin (1974), Neill and Kniskern (1982), Hoffman (1981), Napier and Whitaker (1978), Weick (1979), Johnson (1977), and Papp, Silverstein, and Carter (1973). These classic approaches provide a fresh perspective for viewing conflict.

another message, and so forth. We suggest that negative information be communicated on the phone or in person, not by e-mail.

Descriptive language is the basic tool for assessing the system from a "no blame" perspective. Note the difference in the following vignettes:

> Wife: He's too needy. I don't know how he expects me to come home from a pressured day at work, wade through the three kids, all of whom want my attention, and ask him calmly, "How was your day?" while kissing him sweetly on the cheek. He should grow up. (Evaluative language.)

The same vignette using descriptive language.

> Wife: Scott wants to be greeted by me when I first get home. What happens, though, is that by the time I hit the front door, all three children clamor for my attention. Scott's usually in the back of the house, so by the time I physically get back to him, I'm involved with one of the children. Then he doesn't get my full attention. And frankly, I don't want to try to split myself in four pieces at that particular time.

In the second scenario, ideas for change already present themselves, whereas in the first scenario, Scott's wife labels Scott as the problem. The couple is not likely to find solutions to the conflict while the wife views Scott as the villain who is causing the problem.

When you are a conflict party it is a stretch to move out of blaming the other, and describing how your behavior and the other's behavior trigger one another. Recently, we worked with David, a VP in a firm. He was in charge of hiring a video producer for their product. When the video production people didn't solve a problem but said, "Maybe you can find a solution," he responded by writing in an e-mail "What is the matter with you people? What don't you understand about 'You are responsible'? Do I have to do all your work for you? Is everyone in your organization a slacker?" Yet, in conversation David was able to say, "Well, I did raise my voice with them in the initial phone call. Maybe that did keep them from taking the initiative."

2. **Each Member Gets Labeled, or Programmed, into a Specific Role in the System.** Labeling serves an explanatory function for the entire group. Most labels keep people from changing; however, the labeling process itself can be changed. For instance, the "watchdog" in an organization may be carrying too much of the quality control. A person labeled as the watchdog may also be excluded, or seen as ready to pounce on any wrongdoing. Conflicts arise because if the watchdog stops performing the function reinforced by the group, others will try to pull her back into the role. The role may, however, limit her and others.

When certain individuals in the system specialize in specific functions, others may not develop those capabilities. For instance, in one sorority house, Jan was known as the "peacemaker" of the group. She could be counted on to help people solve their problems. In one ongoing conflict, however, Theresa and Pat disagreed vehemently with each other over how literally to enforce some house rules. They blew up at each other, knowing they could count on Jan to help patch things up. Theresa and Pat were not forced to make their own peace because Jan always rushed in.

3. **Cooperation Is Necessary among System Members to Keep Conflicts Going.** One person cannot sustain an interaction. Therefore, the cycle can be changed by any one person changing his or her behavior. Healthy systems are characterized by **"morphogenesis,"** or "constructive system-enhancing behaviors that enable the system to grow, innovate and change" (Olson, Sprenkle, and Russell 1979). Conflict can be changed by one person initiating change or by members deciding together to initiate a change in their structure. A system that maintains conflicts by avoiding genuine change is called a "morphostatic" system, one characterized by moves designed to sustain the status quo, or no change.

If you are stuck in a system that does not change, one choice you always have is to change your own behavior, even if you cannot get others to change. In the Shepherd family, for instance, one of the five members usually felt left out. The family expectation was that four people together were enough but five people together were trouble, since each parent wanted to "take care of" one child. The family was able to change and make more room on the merry-go-round when Dad began sharing his time with all three children instead of paying attention to one child at a time.

4. **Triangles Tend to Form in Systems When Relationships Are Close and Intense.** When one person feels a lower level of power, the tendency is to bring in another person to bolster the low-power position. Since the person brought in to build up the position of the low-power person maintains multiple relationships in the system, interlocking triangles begin functioning over and over in predictable ways. If these triangles lead to destructive behavior, they are termed toxic triangles (Satir 1972; Hoffman 1981; Minuchin 1974). Triangles are so important, we will discuss them in more depth in a later section of this chapter.

5. **Systems Develop Rules for Conflict That Are Followed Even if They Work Poorly.** A family might, for example, say "If we are a happy family, we do not have conflict," or "We have polite conflict." At work there may be a rule that "If you have conflict with the boss, you will be fired." Some departments only enact conflict in writing. Others require conflicts to happen only in meetings, whereas some postpone or "table" most potential conflicts.

Such system rules often block collaborative conflict. At one time they may have served the system well. Parents may have decided, for instance, never to fight in front of the children. When the children were infants, the rule protected them from angry faces and loud voices. But with children 12 and 16 years old, the rule doesn't work well because the children can always tell when Mom and Dad are in a conflict.

6. **The Conflict Serves the System in Some Way.** The conflict may be substituting for intimacy and connection, or may serve as a launching pad for problem solving. Never assume that members of a system want the conflict to be resolved. They may fear a vacuum in their interaction if the conflict is no longer serving its particular function.

Although almost everyone in a conflict will say, "Of course we want this over and done with," the fact that people keep conflicts going, sometimes for years at a time, indicates that some system function is served by the conflict. One church congregation carried on a repetitive conflict at board meetings about the propriety of using the church buildings for partisan and special interest group meetings. A third party helped them discover that the debate was a substitute for a subgroup's voicing dissatisfaction with the minister's involvement in social action projects. The board had been reluctant to confront the minister with their disapproval, so they always centered the discussion on "use of the building." The conflict allowed them to express their disapproval in an indirect way. The following section presents techniques for identifying exactly how the conflicts occur inside the system.

Application 7.1	A Brief Systems Analysis

Write a brief paragraph about a group (system) you know inside and out. This may be a family, social group, work group, blended family, or any other group. Based on the principles just discussed, answer the following questions:

- What seems to "set off" conflicts? What are predictable trigger events?

- Does anyone have a label that people joke about? How does the label work for that person and the group?

- Who is the most likely person to change—to not do things the same old way?

- Are there any secret coalitions?

- Are there any expectations that now seem crazy, or nuts, to you, but that people more or less follow?

- What if there were no conflicts? Would anything be lost? What?

You can make use of this system analysis for a larger paper, or for understanding the principles by discussing them with others in your class.

Conflict Patterns

All recurring conflicts follow patterns, predictable actions of communication and response. Even when you can't determine when a pattern "starts," system regularities pervade. Often the structure of the conflict is only expressed indirectly or implicitly so you can't just ask, "What is the structure of your conflict?" Rather, the structure has to be derived from inductive approaches such as (1) identifying specific system patterns, (2) charting conflict triangles, and (3) drawing coalitions.

System-Wide Patterns

Conflicts never occur in a vacuum. If Mary and Marty, just married, are having an ongoing dispute about finances, it is likely that Mary's sister and Marty's buddy, Samuel, are also involved in the conflict. We are all embedded within wider systems, so whether a conflict rages out of control or just simmers on the back burner, there are system-wide forces at work. Everyone affects everyone else.

Just as individuals develop characteristic styles, so do entire systems. Papp, Silverstein, and Carter (1973) note that in systems theory analyses:

- . . . attention is focused on connections and relationships rather than on individual characteristics
- the whole is considered to be greater than the sum of its parts
- each part can only be understood in the context of the whole
- a change in any one part will affect every other part (197).

Each communication system has an identity that is more than the sum of the individual players. If Sally is aggressive, Tom is accommodating, and Linda avoids, simply combining their individual preferences for conflict does not tell us how they will manage conflict as a system. The following comments reflect system-wide observations:

> The research and development department ducks for cover whenever the bottom line is mentioned.
> They fight like cats and dogs, but they always make up.
> That whole group is plastic. They look so sweet, but I wouldn't trust them farther than I could throw them.

Unlike individual styles, system-wide styles have not been widely researched, but many useful system descriptions have emerged from researchers of family interaction. Lederer and Jackson's seminal book on the *Mirages of Marriage* (1968) focused attention on how marital partners act as a unit rather than as individuals. In that book, such phrases as the "gruesome twosome" and the "heavenly twins" were used to describe marriages rather than individuals.

More complete descriptions come from Cuber and Haroff (1955), who described marriages as:

1. *Conflict-habituated* relationships, in which conflict recurs constantly but has little productive effect; the fighters "don't get anywhere."

2. *Devitalized* marriages, in which the relationship is a hollow shell of what originally was vibrant and living.

3. *Passive-congenial* relationships, in which both partners accept a conventional, calm, ordered marriage that maintains little conflict.

4. *Vital* relationships, which involve intense mutual sharing of important life events.

5. *Total* marriages, characterized by the sharing of virtually every aspect of life, fulfilling each other almost completely. (This may be more of an ideal than an observation of real marriages!)

The impact of conflict itself, as well as the way it is enacted, differs depending on the relational type. In a conflict-habituated couple, for example, conflict is so common that it may go almost unnoticed, but it slowly drains the energy that the couple needs for important growth or conflict. Devitalized partners might experience conflict as being so devastating that it tears apart the fragile fabric of their shared life. Conflict, after all, is energy producing and energy draining, and it therefore may destroy a devitalized couple. Likewise, avoidance in a total relationship would be a distress signal, whereas anything but avoidance in a passive-congenial relationship might break its implicit rules.

Another system-level description comes from Rands, Levinger, and Mellinger (1981), who provided an alternate view of conflict resolution types. They found that couples could be seen as belonging to one of four types:

Type I: *Nonintimate-aggressive* relationships foster escalation without any corresponding intimacy. Couples are aggressive toward each other without enjoying the benefit emotional closeness. Conflict for couples who maintain this pattern is usually not satisfying, since more energy is drained than is gained.

Type II: *Nonintimate-nonaggressive* couples lack vitality, intimacy, and escalation. Thus they are more satisfied than Type I people, since they do not have to contend with escalating conflict.

Type III: *Intimate-aggressive* couples combine intimate behavior with aggressive acts. Their conflict usually results in intimacy, even though they use aggressive conflict modes. Their satisfaction depends on whether their conflicts lead to intimacy or someone derails the predictable outcome by aggression that is too vicious or comments that are "below the belt."

Type IV: *Intimate-nonaggressive* partners use small amounts of attacking or blaming behavior, retaining their intimacy in other ways. These couples are satisfied, whether they are "congenial" (i.e., they avoid full discussion of issues) or "expressive" (i.e., they confront important issues).

Application 7.2　　　　My Family Patterns

Describe families, work places or a living situation you are part of, using some of the preceding system pattern descriptions.

- Identify the family itself (family of origin, step-family, current family, former family, extended family).

- Who are the members?

- What patterns best describe each family system?

- What are some advantages of each pattern? Disadvantages?

- Choose two or three constructive changes *you yourself* could put into motion.

- What is the emotional effect on you based on your role in each family system?

In another simpler scheme, David Mace (1987), one of the originators of marital enrichment programs, has looked at conflict patterns in marital systems. He found that couples react to conflict in one of four ways. They may avoid it, tolerate it, attempt to fight fairly, or process it, which involves active listening and telling the emotional as well as factual truth. In your own conflicts, for example, as an overall

[handwritten margin note: Mace – Couples react to conflict in one of 4 ways: ① Avoid it ② Tolerate it ③ Attempt – Fight fairly ④ Process it]

pattern is there avoidance, toleration, fighting, or processing? These become *system styles* when they are repeated.

Whatever your system-wide patterns, they can be classified according to the following **conflict stages** (Guerin et al. 1987):

Stage I: Members experience a minimal amount of conflict, openly communicate, and share power. The level of conflict causes no distress for the system.

Stage II: Members experience significant conflict that they see as causing a problem. Criticism increases, but still there is little power polarization or overt struggle for control. Usually, one person is pursuing and the other is distancing, and as a system, they have some difficulty agreeing on how much separateness they should have.

Stage III: Members are in turbulence, experience high intensity, and are moving toward polarization. They are unable to exchange information accurately, and frequently criticize each other. Their power struggle is now serious and there is a life-or-death quality to much of their communication.

Stage IV: Members have lost the ability to work through their conflicts and have engaged the services of a third party. They see the relationship as adversarial and work to enhance their individual bargaining positions. At this stage, a couple is headed toward disengagement and divorce (Guerin et al. 1987).

Just as with individual approaches to styles, a system-wide view has some limitations. First, conflict can be occurring in the system because the participants disagree about the type of system they want. One partner may want to be enmeshed, involving the other in all decisions, whereas the other may want more disengagement. In such cases, individual behaviors indicate a struggle with the definition of the system as a whole. Rather than being "nonintimate-aggressive," the system may reflect a struggle in process.

When people work toward defining who they will be together, the rules that shape their interaction may be in flux. Some of the typologies discussed in the previous section may have given the impression that conflict patterns are fixed. However, they actually may change rapidly. Sharon and Don, for example, are the parents of three children who are entering their teens. In the past, the family could be described as "nonintimate-nonaggressive." Now that the children are growing up, the parents are rediscovering their intimacy with each other, which results in confusion in the family interactions, since the children are used to being the center of attention. No system description adequately reflects the complexity the family experiences during transition.

Second, just as with individual styles, various system patterns can be functional or not, depending on the needs of the situation. Not all groups are automatically better off with a highly processed, or "intimate-nonaggressive," style all the time. Relationships go through cycles of change on various dimensions. Mutual avoidance of conflict may be appropriate, for instance, if a remarried couple is determined to avoid the tense escalatory behavior of their first marriages. Avoidance may not continue to work for this couple for 10 years, but it may serve their goals well at first.

Conflict Triangles

If you have a conflict with John and you talk to Julia about it, you are in a conflict triangle. All conflicts inherently possess a system-wide structure, and **conflict triangles** occur frequently. Why triangles?[2] When people perceive that they are the low-power person in a conflict, their typical response is to try to form a coalition with another person. That person may indeed bolster their power, but the addition of the third person forms a triangle. "Three's a crowd" is a cultural saying based on sound communication theory. Three people find it difficult to maintain balance in a **conflicted** relationship. Usually they become structured as a "dyad plus one" (Wilmot 1987). Communication triangles are often unstable—the power will flow to two of the people, leaving one person out.

Let's take a typical workplace situation. Terry is the boss, and Marty and Miranda both report to him. Marty and Miranda have a conflict. Marty is very critical of Miranda, and goes to Terry frequently to complain about the "quality of her work." Miranda, on the other hand, is critical about how Marty treats her—interrupting her in meetings and always "second-guessing" her work. She also hears from Tom that Marty "is not pleased with the quality of your work." Everyone is trapped—Terry says, "Why can't they just get along?"; Marty says, "Her quality of work is sub-par," and Miranda says "He doesn't treat me professionally." When Marty and Miranda are together (without Terry) they both say, "He is so hands off he doesn't solve any problems—he just keeps pushing the issue back to us." The following triangle illustrates the recurring conflicts.

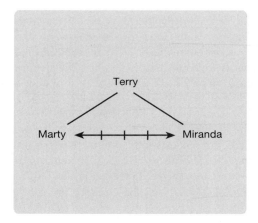

Since there is ongoing conflict, the triangle is inherently unstable—Terry might form up closer to Marty, or spend lunch time with Miranda, thus bringing instability to the system. In any triangle, a shift in any degree of closeness affects the other participant.

Triangles can also be stable. In a relationship with very little conflict, three may be just fine, and even fun. For instance, Helen is a university senior. She is an honors student who enjoys living off campus with her closest friend, Jean. Jean and Helen have

[2]Several researchers and practitioners have noted that the triangle is the basic unit of analysis for conflict communication (Satir 1972; Hoffman 1981; Minuchin 1974; Wilmot 1987).

known each other since high school, and have discovered that their eating habits, how they like to keep up their two-bedroom apartment, their study times and habits, and their sense of fun and frivolity are very similar. Both enjoy solitary time as well as time with each other and friends. Recently Jean began spending a lot of time with her boyfriend, Jeff. For a while, Jeff stayed at Helen and Jean's apartment often, hanging out, studying and just "living." Helen talked to Jean about this, saying that she felt slightly intruded upon and wished for more time alone or just with Jean in the apartment. Since Helen and Jean had already agreed to this basic principle, "the apartment is for us," Jean was not upset. She began to spend more time at Jeff's. Now Helen feels lonely some of the time, but she understands Jean's choices.

Are Jean, Helen, and Jeff in a **toxic triangle?** The word toxic (Satir 1972) was first applied to relationships that are poisonous, dangerous, and potentially devastating to the relationship. Clearly Helen and Jean are *not* in a toxic triangle—they have developed direct, straightforward, communication which is keeping them out of a toxic situation. Helen may be lonely, but she doesn't blame Jean for spending time with Jeff and she knows they are still friends. This is an example of a normal, healthy communication style that does not result in a toxic triangle.

Of course, we aren't always so skilled or fortunate: When conflict erupts, the system tends to cluster into triangles. For example, Tom and Mary are a couple in their second marriages. Tom has a daughter, Susan, age seven, and Mary has a son, Brian, age six. Tom's first wife, Brenda lives in the same town. Mary's first husband, Sam, lives in another state. The current conflict can be described like this:

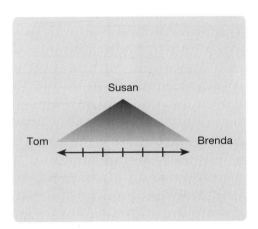

Application 7.3	A Conflict Triangle

Tom and Mary have a close and usually constructive relationship. They learned from their unhappy first marriages to talk problems out and to be direct and honest (as well as respectful, kind, and clear.) But they have some problems. Tom and his former wife, Brenda, do not agree with the parenting plan they agreed to, with a court-appointed

(continued)

Application 7.3   A Conflict Triangle

mediator's help, two years before. Since they remained at an impasse, the mediator sent the parenting plan to a court-appointed "special master," or arbitrator, who recommended a plan to the judge. Tom and Brenda argue via phone and e-mail about exceptions to the "one week with each one" plan. They argue about timing of vacations and holiday visits. Unfortunately, they draw Susan into their conflict, sending messages through her and notes back and forth via Susan. An example would be a note Brenda sent Tom via Susan that said, "Susan will be spending Thanksgiving at my house because she told me that is what she wants to do. Therefore, I will pick her up Wednesday at 4:00." You can draw the toxic triangle of these three people like this:

Conflicting dyads are marked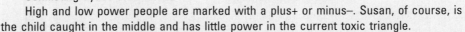

High and low power people are marked with a plus+ or minus–. Susan, of course, is the child caught in the middle and has little power in the current toxic triangle.

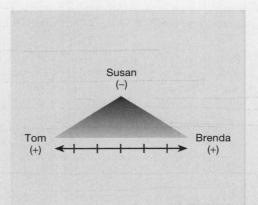

One time Mary, Susan's stepmother, found Susan crying at home. Susan and Mary have a good, warm relationship. Susan said "I hate this. Mom and Dad fight all the time and I can't do anything about it. I just want to do what the judge said because somebody is always mad at me. Whether she was aware of it or not, Susan needed a friend, an ally—Mary.

Allies can be drawn this way:

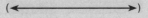

Mary knows she cannot talk directly with Brenda, having tried that communication strategy before. But Mary is tired of being ineffective and watching the ongoing conflict. She has been an **isolate**. A diagram of the conflict so far might look like this. Allies are drawn with parentheses around the arrow connecting their communication bond:

(continued)

Application 7.3   **A Conflict Triangle**

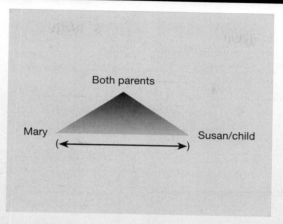

You pick up the conflict from here.   In a small group, draw potential new triangles, involving Mary, Susan, Tom, and Brenda. Remember also that Brian, Mary's son, might have some input here. Propose some conflict resolution strategies, drawing the new triangles. One example might be that Mary decides to talk with Tom about Susan's distress, proposing that Tom talk directly to Brenda, leaving Susan out of any communication. Susan is in the room. How would that triangle look?

The reason to analyze toxic triangles is to discover where the ongoing conflict lies. The goal of triangle analysis is to make toxic triangles into direct, collaborative communication interactions. These new dyads would be drawn like this:

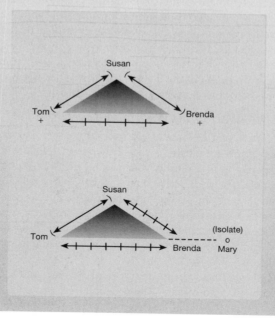

(continued)

Application 7.3   A Conflict Triangle

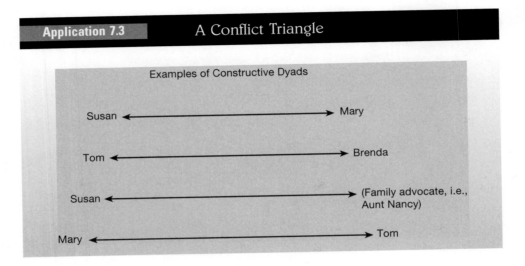

The purpose of diagramming toxic triangles is so you can understand the "stuck places" of the conflict patterns. The goal of triangle analysis is to remove the toxic triangles and make them into direct dyadic communication. This strategy may not resolve all conflicts, but you will take steps toward removing intractable conflicts if you pay attention to toxic triangles.

In organizations, a leader can openly diagram triangles of "failed communication" on a whiteboard at a staff meeting. We have seen managers and team leaders use this technique very effectively. Even without outside intervention, leaders in the organization can say, "We have some failed communication strategies going on. Let's draw them, and brainstorm ways to get ourselves out of the stuck tangle of triangles." When this communication strategy is used without blame, lights go on and people begin to realize why they are in conflict and what they might do about it. Direct communication is usually the constructive strategy of choice. People form triangles when they feel low power. People feel more empowered when communication is direct.

Drawing Coalitions—Who Is In, Who Is Out?

While triangles are part of the system-wide picture, other patterns also emerge. A **coalition** forms when some are closer to each other than they are to others. A private bond emerges. For example, in a family, you may be the "outsider," the last to hear of important family events. At work, there may be two groups, those who like the supervisor and those who do not. In a large organization, some departments join together every time there is a decision; they exclude other departments. When someone is in a coalition, they include select people in the information flow and not others. That communication is often hidden in some way. Figure 7.1 is a simple diagram showing one possible set of coalitions.

When two people are "coalesced," they orient to one another, share more information, and feel closer than to others. When people feel excluded, they call the other people's coalitions "cliques." As you can see from the Williams family diagram, mom

Figure 7.1   Coalitions in the Wlliams Family

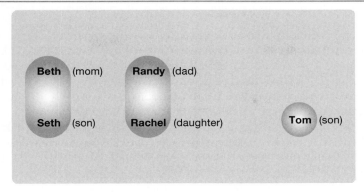

and son Seth are close, as are dad and daughter, Rachel. And son #2, Tom, is the "isolate"—the one who is out of the loop with others.

Coalitions also form in workplaces. Here are two examples to illustrate some of the diverse patterns that develop. In figure 7.2, the executive director has a close relationship with four of her staff, and the other four form a coalition "against" the original group.

Even without knowing any of the people involved, you can sense the system dynamics. In this case, the executive director shared a close bond with one person, and also with about one-half of the staff. The remainder of the professional staff, feeling excluded by the director, formed their own counter-coalition. Whatever one group wanted, the other resisted, and vice versa. Over time, the coalitions became so rigid that outside help was requested.

Drawing coalitions gives us an overall view of the system—who is in, who is out, who is closest to whom, and who has the most power.

In all organizations and families with more than three members, coalitions exist. As the members go about their relating, they tend to "cluster" their communication.

- A parent talks more to one child than to the other.

- One group of elementary school teachers in an elementary school forms into two groups—smokers and nonsmokers.

Figure 7.2   Coalitions With/Against the Boss

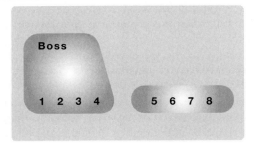

- Half of a group of community college faculty give allegiance to the academic vice president while the other half allies itself with the president.

People form coalitions in order to (1) share topic information, (2) get support and understanding, (3) have a sense of belonging, and (4) gain power. Thus, coalition formation is a natural process in all families and organizations—people tend to cluster together (and apart). In all the workplaces and families where we have worked as change agents, without exception, members are in coalitions.

Recall from chapter 2 the explanation of the "lens" that people use in conflicts. In an ongoing dispute, people disagree with almost everything the other thinks. Yet, surprisingly, when asked to draw coalitions, they reproduce almost the same diagram. Coalitions are so powerful that all the system members know about them and respond to them. We all know at each point in time who's in and who's out.

Once we are in a coalition (or sometimes left out of one), we tend to feel justified in being "in the group" or "not in the group." If we are central we feel important. If we are isolated, we see ourselves as special and different from the others. One administrative assistant in an office of psychologists felt (and was) excluded by the other two assistants. She began to talk to the psychologists in the office about the assistants, saying polite but negative things about them. Soon, she was going to lunch with several of the psychologists. The two other assistants then began to give her more of the tedious billing work, saying, "If she has so much time on her hands, she can help out more."

Once coalitions form, they become self-justifying. In a family, as a parent and child form a close bond talking about the errant parent, for example, the bond becomes self-reinforcing. As we communicate with a coalition partner, we tend to justify the exclusion of others by stressing how similar we are to our coalition partners. We extend the in-group/out-group phenomenon. As the coalition strengthens, the members (1) stress their similarities to one another, (2) highlight their dissimilarities to those not in the coalition, and (3) accelerate these differences throughout time. Each coalition forms its own reward structure, perceptually driving the members farther and farther from the "others."

Similarly, system isolates justify their exclusion. The teenage child or estranged parent isolated from the family and the lonely employee adopt the stance of, "I didn't want to be part of your group anyway." Isolates, after a certain point in time, resist joining and take pleasure in being "different." Whether the isolate is the loner who likes to work the night shift, the estranged teenager, or the only female employee, they provide for their own internal support system and decline offers to merge with the others. They may, of course, feel sad and disillusioned.

Coalitions become toxic when they become so tight that the groups get locked into destructive conflict with one another. In the eyes of coalition participants, they are "friends" whereas the people in the other group are forming cliques. The coalitions, because of their rigidity and heavy boundaries, begin causing problems for the system. The mother-daughter dyad excludes father so that he gives up on having influence in the family and acts out even more isolating behavior. The organization divides into voting blocks and power plays, with each group vying to outdo the other group on policy issues. Each iteration of communication rigidity reinforces the boundaries already existing and produces more and more perceptual distortion—accelerating the negative behavior and inaccurate meta-perceptions of the other group. Rather than talking to others, each group spins off and takes action based on their guesses about the others' intentions—which they usually see as being negative.

Communication patterns both reflect and create the difficulties. People withhold information, make overt power plays, act in competitive ways, or avoid the others altogether. They stop solving problems. Communication exchanges become more toxic and damaging, with each discussion producing more distrust, hostility, and discord. In this sense, coalitions serve to scapegoat other individuals or coalitions. Inclusion and exclusion remain two of the most powerful human forces in social life.

A good way to "get a picture of a conflict" is to draw the coalesced, partly private, pairings. In one romantic situation, Jane has separated from her husband, Tom. She has met a man at work and is flirting with him, considering a relationship with him. Jane and Noah talk about the problems Jane has with Tom. Tom, however, is isolated. He talks with Jane, but much of the truth of her emotional life is hidden from him. As Tom and Jane enter couples counseling, the counselor challenges Jane, in a private session, to stop telling Noah her complaints about Tom, and, instead, to tell Tom. If she does that, she will soften the coalition that further estranges her from Tom. If she does not, she will almost certainly lose her relationship with Tom. Jane still has the choice not to return to Tom; keeping the coalition with Noah assures that she will stay separated. Her closeness with Noah is self-reinforcing; her distance with Tom is self-reinforcing.

You can also see self-reinforcing patterns by looking at **heavy communicators**—those who are central to passing and receiving messages from members. Heavy communicators typically (1) resist being moved out of that central role and (2) at the same time complain about the "overwork," involved in keeping the system happy. For young students in a typical college classroom, about 85 percent of the time mother is a heavy communicator in the family. In an organization, if someone is in a central or mediating role, he or she will complain about others' apathy and lack of involvement—while maintaining their central role at all cost.

Organizational and family isolates also engage in self-reinforcing patterns. If there is an isolate, one member who is "out" compared to the others, the isolate (1) complains about the decisions or personalities of central people yet (2) resists coming closer to the center of communication flow. Both the isolate and the central members cooperate to keep him or her out. In the community college we mentioned above, the academic vice president was accused by half of the faculty of being "weak."

Meanwhile, every time this group disagreed with one of his decisions, they went "over his head" to the president, undercutting him and reinforcing his "weakness." Similarly, in a family, a grandparent might be concerned that a son is not a "good parent" to the grandchildren, yet the grandparent criticizes the son as a parent, and undermines the son's confidence in being a parent.

Softening coalitions lessons their destructive impact. In a women's group formed to read fiction and discuss contemporary books, several members have begun attending erratically. Marcy and Tina talk with each other about how disgusted they are with the overly specialized and obscure fiction some of the natural leaders choose. Ruth and Jane talk with each other, and sometimes with Marcy and Tina, about how the group is becoming just a showcase for the most talkative leaders. By coalescing and isolating themselves, they lose influence in the group, lessening their interdependence on the group, and creating uncertainty in the other members. The solution? For each woman to say to the whole group (and those she usually doesn't talk to!) that her preferences aren't getting much regard, or for each woman to make suggestions about what she'd like to see the group read. One could offer to lead a book discussion. More involvement in the group and less involvement in the coalitions will probably solve the immediate problem.

| Application 7.4 | Draw a System |

For some system you know well (your family, your workplace, your social group), draw the coalitions, isolates, and lines of communication. Label the coalitions with a title, including the initials of each person in the coalition. Remember that some people may be in more than one coalition. Draw lines that indicate whether communication is interrupted or flows easily between the coalitions. Now, show your drawing to someone else, without telling him or her the specific content. See what that person can predict about (1) emotions, (2) tactics used, and (3) predictable communication problems.

Micro-Level Mapping

When you go on a car trip to visit a friend, you need two levels of maps—one showing the two states you are motoring across and another showing the streets in Pittsburgh, where your friend lives. The same kind of information is needed in your conflicts—overall system-wide views and also maps of the smaller details. There are two helpful approaches to mapping your micro-level details of your conflicts: mapping interaction rules and micro-events.

Interaction Rules

You have undoubtedly experienced conflicts in which you wanted to say, "Here we go again. Same song, 14th verse." Sometimes no matter what content is being discussed, the outcome is the same. The same people collude together, the same people are left out, and the same indirect strategies are used (like "forgetting," avoiding the issue, and putting off a decision until something must be done). As we have seen, repetitive, unsatisfactory conflicts often operate on a set of unstated but very powerful rules that limit genuine change.

"Rules" *describe* the *underlying communication structure* of the interaction. Underlying rules are like the structure of a language. Usually, no one person dictates the rules. Instead, the rules guide behavior in more subtle ways. They are "the way things are done" in a family, a business, a department, or a group of friends. A more precise definition of a rule is that it is "a followable prescription that indicates what behavior is obligated, preferred, or prohibited in certain contexts" (Shimanoff 1980, 57).

Usually the rules of communication remain implicit. If you begin to map the rules, however, you bring them to the surface, and then they can be changed. The following are some examples of rules that conform to the above definition. Keep in mind that people can sometimes tell you the rules if you interview them, but the rules are never printed and posted. Those are different kinds of rules.

- Rules are prescriptions for behavior stated in the following form:

  "When in context X, Y must/must not occur."

  "When Father shows sadness or anger, Mother must soothe him."

  "When the program director decides to assign a case to a counselor, the counselor must accept the case or convince the program director to reassign it."

- Rules are stated in prescriptive, not evaluative, language. They focus on communication behavior:

  "When brother and sister fight, Dad must intervene to stop it," not "Dad feels responsible for stopping brother and sister's fights even though they can handle them without interference" (this is interpretive and evaluative).

Rules against knowing the rules abound. People must follow the rules but can't say what they are. For that reason, listing rules for interaction may not be easy. But you can elicit **system rules** from conflict parties by following these steps:

1. List explicit and implicit rules that prescribe your own and others' behavior in conflicts.

2. If you have trouble thinking of rules for your system, think of times when the rule was broken. How did you know the rule was broken? How was the violation communicated? Write about the prescription that became obvious upon breaking the rule.

3. Make sure you generate rules for both behavior that must and behavior that must not be performed.

4. Go back over your list. Make each rule simple and prescriptive. Write rules even for "obvious" communication patterns. They may prove to be important possibilities for change.
   Example:
   When new staff members attend the staff meeting, they must not express opinions unless they have a sponsor who is an older staff member.

5. Code each rule as to the following:

   a. Whose rule is it?
   b. What keeps the rule going?
   c. Who enforces the rule?
   d. Who breaks the rule?
   e. What function does the rule serve?

6. Discuss how the rules help or harm the productive management of conflict. Make decisions for change.
   Example:
   Old rule—When Dad is angry at younger brother, older brother must protect younger brother from Dad's disapproval.

Result—Older brother and Dad engage in conflict often, reducing effect of the protection (a toxic triangle).

New rule—When Dad and younger brother get into a conflict, they must talk about their conflicts without older brother (a new affiliation).

Application 7.5

Discover Your
Rules of Interaction

Choose any of the above steps for your practice. Take 10 minutes or so, and see if you can follow the suggestions. Focus on one particular relationship, and begin to think about, and write some of the rules that define that relationship. Check with others to see if you understand the way rules are written.

Microevents

Microevents are "repetitive loops of observable interpersonal behaviors . . . with a redundant outcome" (Metcoff and Whitaker 1982, 253). Microevents are similar to rules, but microevents are descriptive, not prescriptive, of behavior. They are clusters of behaviors organized into structurally repetitive episodes. In simpler, nontechnical terms, microevents are those small pictures that give a lot of clues about the bigger picture. An outsider could speculate about ongoing relationships based on what she or he sees in a 5- or 10-minute interaction.

Not every short interaction is a microevent; microevents are interactions that give information about other interactions. For instance, your new boyfriend/girlfriend might visit your parents' home with you. After one dinner, the new partner might ask you, "Does your dad always add to whatever you say, and try to kind of improve it? It seems like he's always teaching you. And your mom seems like she's the one who asks questions. Is that the way it usually is?"

Perhaps the clearest keys to the nature of an underlying structure are the "substitutable communication events that reveal the structure" (Metcoff and Whitaker 1982, 258). Metcoff and Whitaker provide the following example of such repeatability:

$$\text{Every time the husband} \left\{ \begin{array}{l} \text{scratched his ear} \\ \text{rubbed his nose} \\ \text{tapped his right foot} \end{array} \right\} \text{during}$$

an argument with his wife, one of the children

$$\text{would} \left\{ \begin{array}{l} \text{ask to go to the bathroom} \\ \text{slap a sibling} \\ \text{begin to cry} \end{array} \right\} \text{so that the}$$

husband-wife dispute was never resolved. (258–259)

The implicit, unstated structure underlying these repetitive conflicts can be summarized as follows: "When the husband and wife initiate a conflict, one of the children makes a move to gain their attention, and the husband-wife conflict is not resolved" (259). Each system will, of course, have a different structure underlying the observable conflict. The microevent serves to define the conflict because it "embodies themes of stability and change within the family system" (263).

Once the underlying structure is decoded, one can begin to predict where, when, or how conflict will erupt. Emily and Gordon are a married couple in their 60s whose children are all grown and living elsewhere. Before each vacation, Gordon decides where they should go, then tries to persuade Emily of the wisdom of his choice. Emily won't agree to go, but neither will she say no. Then, the night before the trip, Gordon stays up most of the night packing, and the next day, Emily reluctantly goes with him. Their repetitive conflicts are structured in the following manner:

1. He always initiates.
2. She is always convinced to go (reluctantly).
3. There is no discussion of their relationship; all issues are handled through content.
4. Neither receives positive results from their respective stances.
5. Neither one can solve or escape the conflict.

Their next conflict, over whether, when, and where to go for Christmas, will be based on a similar structure. One can begin decoding the structure underlying a microevent by focusing on these questions:

Application 7.6	Understanding Your Microevent

1. Who initiates and in what way?
2. Who responds and in what way?
3. Who else is present but is not identified as a party to the conflict?
4. Does anyone "speak for" someone else? If so, does this keep the participants embroiled in the conflict?
5. If there were no conflict, what would be missing?
    a. Who would not be connecting with whom?
    b. How would the parties structure their time?
    c. Would conflicts continue with new parties entering into the fray?
6. Is the conflict serving to fill emotional space so other parties cannot fight?

The communication patterns created in a conflict often cycle back and imprison the players. For example, Beverly went through a divorce two months ago, and her son Randy is having difficulty at school. At least twice a week, Beverly and Randy struggle over his poor work in the fifth grade. He has been labeled a "troublemaker" at school and has been sent home from school three times in the last month. This is embarrassing for

Beverly; she also gets very angry at Randy for his "stupid behavior." The repetitive microevent that Beverly and Randy enact has the following features:

1. Beverly initiates each conflict by being distressed about Randy's school performance or disruptive behavior at school.

2. Randy responds by being sullen, pretending he is deaf and can't hear requests, and withdrawing.

3. The unemployed older brother is present in the house but serves as a bystander.

4. Randy and Beverly are both isolated parties—neither has anyone to come to his or her aid during the conflict.

5. Aside from the conflict, mother and son have few common interests. Beverly can't think of things that might be interesting for the two of them to do together. This recurring conflict both illustrates and crystallizes the family structure.

The following are some ways you can discover and describe microevents:

1. Act as a qualitative researcher who uses observation and interviewing to determine patterns.

2. Obtain a professional third-party (consultant, mediator, or therapist) description of common conflicts.

3. Keep a journal of conflict episodes that seem repetitive—those that have a "here we go again" theme.

4. Ask newcomers to a system, such as new employees, new family members, or new committee members, to describe what they have experienced so far.

~Comprehensive Guides

You can also map your conflicts by using these two comprehensive assessment guides.

Conflict Assessment Guide

The **Conflict Assessment Guide** will help you map all of the central elements of your conflict.

I. **Nature of the Conflict**
    A. What are the "triggering events" that brought this conflict into mutual awareness?
    B. What is the historical context of this conflict in terms of (1) the ongoing relationship between the parties and (2) other, external events within which this conflict is embedded?
    C. Do the parties have assumptions about conflict that are discernable by their choices of conflict metaphors, patterns of behavior, or clear expressions of their attitudes about conflict?
    D. Conflict elements:
        1. How is the struggle being expressed by each party?
        2. What are the perceived incompatible goals?

3. What are the perceived scarce resources?
4. In what ways are the parties interdependent? How are they interfering with one another? How are they cooperating to keep the conflict in motion?

E. Has the conflict vacillated between productive and destructive phases? If so, which elements were transformed during the productive cycles? Which elements might be transformed by creative solutions to the conflict?

II. Orientation to the Conflict

A. What attitudes toward conflict do participants seem to hold?
B. Do they perceive conflict as positive, negative, or neutral? How can you tell?
C. What metaphoric images do conflict participants use? What metaphors might you use to describe the conflict?
D. What is the cultural background of the participants? What is the cultural context in which the conflict takes place?
E. How might gender roles, limitations, and expectations be operating in this conflict?

III. Interests and Goals

A. How do the parties clarify their goals? Do they phrase them in individualistic or systemic terms?
B. What does each party think the other's goals are? Are they similar or dissimilar to the perceptions of self-goals?
C. How have the goals been altered from the beginning of the conflict to the present? In what ways are the prospective, transactive, and retrospective goals similar or dissimilar?
D. What are the topic, relational, identity, and process goals?
E. How do the TRIP goals overlap with one another?
F. Which goals seem to be primary at different stages of the dispute?
G. Are the conflict parties "specializing" in one type or the other?
H. Are the identity and relational issues the "drivers" of this dispute?
I. Are any of the goals emerging in different forms?
J. How do the goals shift during the prospective, transactive, and retrospective phases?

IV. Power

A. What attitudes about their own and the other's power does each party have? Do they talk openly about power, or is it not discussed?
B. What do the parties see as their own and the other's dependencies on one another? As an external observer, can you classify some dependencies that they do not list?
C. What power currencies do the parties see themselves and the other possessing?
D. From an external perspective, what power currencies of which the participants are not aware seem to be operating?
E. In what ways do the parties disagree on the balance of power between them? Do they underestimate their own or the other's influence?

    F. What impact does each party's assessment of power have on subsequent choices in the conflict?

    G. What evidence of destructive "power balancing" occurs?

    H. In what ways do observers of the conflict agree and disagree with the parties' assessments of their power?

    I. What are some unused sources of power that are present?

V. Styles

    A. What individual styles did each party use?

    B. How did the individual styles change during the course of the conflict?

    C. How did the parties perceive the other's style?

    D. In what way did a party's style reinforce the choices the other party made as the conflict progressed?

    E. Were the style choices primarily symmetrical or complementary?

    F. From an external perspective, what were the advantages and disadvantages of each style within this particular conflict?

    G. Can the overall system be characterized as having a predominant style? What do the participants say about the relationship as a whole?

    H. Do the participants appear to strategize about their conflict choices or remain spontaneous?

    I. How does each party view the other's strategizing?

    J. What are the tactical options used by both parties?

    K. Do the tactical options classify primarily into avoidance, competition, or collaboration?

    L. How are the participants' tactics mutually impacting on the others' choices? How are the tactics interlocking to push the conflict through phases of escalation, maintenance, and reduction?

VI. Conflict and emotions

    A. In your situation, what approaches to change have you utilized or are you contemplating? How effective are these approaches?

    B. Choose several emotions that you and the other party have expressed in this conflict. What are the functions of these emotions? How are they mitigated or moderated?

    C. What are you learning about emotions in this particular conflict?

    D. Discuss how you might use positive emotions to help you (and the other party) in this particular conflict.

    E. In this conflict, have you strayed out of the "zone of effectiveness?" How? What have you or might you do about this?

VII. Mapping Interactions and overall patterns

    A. What rules of repetitive patterns characterize this conflict?

    B. What triangles and microevents best characterize the conflict?

    C. How destructive is the tone of this conflict?

    D. Are there coalitions that affect this conflict?

VIII. Attempted Solutions
    A. What options have been explored for managing the conflict?
    B. Have attempted solutions become part of the problem?
    C. Have third parties been brought into the conflict? If so, what roles did they play and what was the impact of their involvement?
    D. Is this conflict a repetitive one, with attempted solutions providing temporary change but with the overall pattern remaining unchanged? If so, what is that overall pattern?
    E. Can you identify categories of solutions that have not been tried?

IX. Negotiation
    A. Are the parties able to negotiate with one another? Why or why not?
    B. What is done to equalize power?
    C. Do the parties use primarily competitive tactics, collaborative tactics, or some combination?
    D. Were the parties able to reach agreements that are durable?

X. Forgiveness & Reconciliation
    A. In your situation, are you working toward forgiveness or reconciliation? Clearly state which in terms of the chapter's information on the difference between the two.
    B. In your situation, what power imbalances should be addressed? How are you doing that?
    C. For you, is forgiveness a decision or a process? Use information in the chapter to discuss your position.
    D. In what way is your situation calling for intrapersonal or interpersonal forgiveness, or both?
    E. Discuss the problems of apology in your situation.
    F. What lessons from other cultures might inform your study of your own conflict?

You can use the *Conflict Assessment Guide* for your own conflicts and also use it when asking others about their conflicts. One other overall approach is the **Difficult Conversations Guide.** This final mapping tool brings forth the narratives (stories) that conflict parties tell themselves and others. It is especially useful for focusing on the emotional component.

Difficult Conversations Guide

Colleagues associated with the Harvard Negotiation Project (Stone, Patton, and Heen 1999) wrote an excellent book, *Difficult Conversations,* that explores what they call "the three conversations." These "conversations" help clarify the structure of a conflict by focusing on the stories people tell themselves and others, the difference between intention and impact, and the way one's identity needs to be restored after an important conflict. The authors of the book make it very clear that you should ask yourself important questions before undertaking a difficult conversation with another person. You prepare for the conversation by assessing the following "stories."

I. What Happened? What Is My Story?
- **A.** What were my intentions?
- **B.** What do I think the other's intentions were?
- **C.** What did I contribute to the problem? (Specifically describe your behavior as well as your feelings and attributions.)

II. What Happened? What Is the Other's Story?
- **A.** What was the impact on me?
- **B.** What impact did I have on the other?
- **C.** What did the other person contribute to the problem?

III. The Feelings Conversation: My Story
- **A.** What feelings underlie my attributions and judgments (e.g., angry, frustrated, disappointed, hurt, guilty, embarrassed, ashamed, grateful, sad)?
- **B.** What do I need or want in order to feel differently in the future?

IV. The Feelings Conversations: The Other's Story
- **A.** What feelings underlie the other's attributions and judgments about me?
- **B.** What information can I get or do I have about this question?
- **C.** What does the other person need to feel differently in the future?

V. The Identity Conversation
- **A.** How has what happened affected my identity?
- **B.** How has what happened affected my sense of influence over the situation?
- **C.** What do I need to do to restore my sense of identity?
- **D.** How has what happened affected the other's identity?
- **E.** How has what happened affected the other's sense of influence over the situation?
- **F.** What does the other need to restore his/her sense of identity?

❧Summary

Conflicts are often perplexing to both participants. Usually, however, an interpersonal conflict is operating as a system of relations, complete with repetitive behavior, rules, and other identifiable dynamics. There are many possible ways to map conflict patterns. Charting triangles and drawing coalitions provides graphic information about system dynamics. One also can focus on system rules, the prescriptions for what one ought to do in a given situation. Microevents are observable, recurring patterns of behavior that can be analyzed for underlying conflict structure. Finally, the *Conflict Assessment Guide* and the *Difficult Conversations* guide are two overall assessment tools to uncover the dynamics of specific conflicts.

❧Key Terms

system dynamics 218	morphogenesis 221	micro-level mapping 234
self-fulfilling prophecies 218	conflict stages 225	system rules 235
macro-level mapping 218	conflict triangles 226	microevent 236
wholeness 219	conflicted 226	Conflict Assessment
organization 219	toxic triangle 227	Guide 238
patterning 219	isolate 228	Difficult Conversations
circular casuality 219	coalitions 230	Guide 241
descriptive language 220	heavy communicator 233	

❧Review Questions

1. Why would you want to map a conflict?
2. Describe systems theory.
3. What are the principles of system theory?
4. What are the advantages of identifying conflict patterns?
5. What are five types of system patterns that occur in marriages?
6. What are the four stages of conflict?
7. Define coalitions, giving an example from your personal life and school.
8. Why do people form coalitions?
9. How can you use a coalition diagram to predict future conflicts?
10. Describe the roles of the heavy communicator and the isolate.
11. What are the characteristics of a healthy system?
12. Define system rules, including personal examples.
13. What are the questions to ask about system rules?
14. Define microevents and give a specific example of one from your life.

Chapter 8

Interpersonal Negotiation

❧Negotiation in Everyday Life

You may not think of yourself as a "negotiator" The word **negotiation** usually brings to mind labor and management representatives negotiating a work contract or representatives of governments meeting with great formality to resolve national disputes. Negotiation simply means to settle by discussion and mutual agreement. Negotiation provides a process of problem solving when the topic, content, or substantive issues rise in importance. The relationship, identity, and process issues remain present and always influence how negotiation proceeds, but the product of negotiation is (a) problem resolution or (b) impasse.

We negotiate for specific agreements. Negotiation occurs every day in both private and public contexts. Even young children negotiate. (Joshi, 2008; Tuval-Mashiach shulman 2006). These situations call on your everyday negotiating skills:

- Your friend wants to have you over for dinner at 8:00 p.m., and you want to come earlier.

- You have a computer problem and want to persuade your professor to give you more time for completion of a paper.

- Your elderly mother, who has lived alone for decades, has fallen and broken her hip, and you and the other siblings need to talk about possible nursing home care. Everyone has a different opinion.

- Your father has agreed to pay for four years of college for you, but you now need one extra semester beyond four years to complete school.

- You and your roommate, who was your best friend, bought many household items together. Recently, because you now are dating her ex-boyfriend, you have had a serious falling out with each other. You agree to stop rooming together but now have to decide who gets what items in the apartment.

- You are in charge of scheduling co-workers, and there is disagreement over who has to take over holiday and late-night shifts.

- You are an hourly employee, and your boss says, "I don't care what hours you guys work just so the store is covered, so the four of you decide what hours you want to work." The co-workers have trouble agreeing.

- You buy carpet from a store and clearly tell the salesperson that you want the old carpet saved so that you can give it to your friend. You come home at the end of the day, and the new carpet looks nice, but the old carpet is gone. A quick phone call reveals that it was taken to the landfill and cannot be retrieved.

- Your daughter, age 15, wants to go on an overnight trip with friends. You want her to be able to go, but she's been slacking off on household agreements. She's in an independent phase. How would you negotiate with her?

In both our personal and work lives, we negotiate to make decisions that are acceptable to everyone concerned. One survey found that human services administrators spend 26 percent of their time negotiating (Files 1981). Further, with the advent of "self-directed work teams," the ability to negotiate both within the team and from the team to the wider organization takes on added importance. Think of negotiation as a back and forth approach to conflict resolution with all the loaded feelings that any approach presents. Negotiation is no more "objective" than any other approach. The TRIP concerns are always present, personal history plays a role, gender matters, power matters, and the history of the friendship, group, marriage or work team matters.

Application 8.1   Negotiation Opportunities

List as many situations as you can think of that involve negotiation possibilities:

- Situations when you could have negotiated, but did not.
- Situations when you did not negotiate well.
- Situations when you were overpowered and could not negotiate at all.
- Situations when you used power as "power over" rather than taking time to negotiate.
- Situations you are involved in that might benefit from negotiating.

Negotiation Is One Path to Conflict Resolution

Negotiation occurs in conflict resolution when the parties recognize their interdependence, are willing to work on both incompatible and overlapping goals (Bartos 1974), have been able to establish enough power balance so people can "come to the table," and they can talk to each other in a problem-solving way. Thus, we think of negotiation as the active phase of conflict resolution when people generate many options, brainstorm ideas, give and take, and attempt to get their mutual goals met. Negotiation can be either competitive ("I want my goals met and I don't care about yours") or collaborative ("We have to reach a mutually satisfying conclusion"). Negotiating involves active engagement, not avoidance.

When people bargain, or negotiate, they "attempt to settle what each shall give and take, or perform and receive" (Rubin and Brown 1975, 2). Negotiation allows conflict parties to state their preferences, discuss their relationship, restrain themselves from certain actions, and increase predictability about each other (Wall 1985). It covers a wide range and falls midway between avoidance and domination, as shown in figure 8.1.

Figure 8.1   The Location of Negotiation in a Conflict Spectrum

Although some writers distinguish between bargaining and negotiation (Keltner 1994), most people treat them as virtually synonymous terms. For the remainder of this chapter, the two terms will be used equally to represent the same activity. Negotiation presumes the following:

- Participants engage in the conflict rather than avoiding.
- Parties resist using domination, or power-over tactics.
- Parties use persuasive communication tactics in a variety of styles.
- Parties have reached an active, problem-solving phase in which specific proposals are traded.

In the active negotiation process, all the parties depend on their assessment of the power and the structure of the situation, regulate their own behavior to maximize their own gains, and search for acceptable proposals so resolution can be achieved. Parties must be able to provide resources and to influence goal achievement, and they must be willing to do so through cooperation (Donohue and Kolt 1992). No purpose is served by negotiating with someone who has nothing to offer you. You need to be induced to struggle together to achieve common and individual goals. Parties in conflict agree tacitly to a framework of ground rules to manage conflict (Putnam and Poole 1987).

⮕Negotiation and Culture

In contemporary Western cultures, we receive contradictory messages about negotiation. On the one hand, you are supposed to "get a good deal," but on the other, you are expected to walk into commercial establishments and pay the listed prices. In intimate relationships, often people don't know how to negotiate with love and respect. We have often thought that marriage vows should contain the phrase, "to love, honor and negotiate!" As we will show, negtotiation can be done in a spirit of close collaboration. Examine the following situations and decide in which ones you would go along with others and in which ones you would negotiate:

Negotiable?

- The price of a new house
- The part(s) of the apartment/house/dorm room you and your roommates will use
- The price of a used car
- The price of an item on sale at a chain store (CD, book, portable radio, etc.)
- The price of pens and paper at the college bookstore

- The salary offered at McDonald's or Burger King for you to "flip burgers"
- The amount of time you work at your job
- The final paper assignment in your class
- The final grade you receive in your conflict class
- The price of a used toaster at a garage sale
- The person(s) who will care for your aging parents
- Where you and your fiancé spend your holidays
- Whether you can move home and work while temporarily dropping out of school
- What will be the guidelines for "house rules" while four friends share a house during college (the roommates have different time, eating and cleaning preferences, but like each other enough to try to make it work.)

As you can see, some items are negotiable and others are not. How do we know? Each culture designates areas that are off limits to negotiation and areas in which negotiation is acceptable. If you have traveled in different cultures, you may have experienced cultural differences relating to negotiating over prices.

The "case of the cheap statue" illustrates a clash of cultures.

Application 8.2 | The Cheap Statue

Wallace, a U.S. citizen, was new to Kathmandu. He had been told by his friend Liz to "be a hard bargainer" when in this culture, where sellers thrive on negotiation. His first day on the streets, many vendors approached him and Liz as they strolled about. One young man, in particular, would not go away. He was selling "good, high-quality statues" for, as he said, a "rock price" (rock-bottom price). When the statue vendor first approached, Wallace stopped and looked intently at the statue. The vendor then stayed close to him for almost an hour, with Wallace saying, "I don't want to buy," but knowing that his looking at the statue made this protest sound rather hollow. The vendor started at 500 rupees (about $10). After the first hour, Wallace gave in and started bargaining. His final offer was 300 rupees, which the vendor would not accept. Wallace and Liz left and returned to the market square some six hours later. The vendor spied them and started tagging along. Wallace bargained for a few minutes, then said, "OK, I now will give you only 250 rupees for the statue." The vendor, after giving a speech about his family starving, and wringing his hands in agony, completed the sale and handed over the statue. Just as Wallace was beginning to feel smug about his fine bargaining ability, the vendor turned to Liz and said, "I'll sell you one for 175 rupees."

Negotiation itself is viewed differently in different cultures. For instance, one would not negotiate over price in Switzerland, but would in Greece and Turkey (but not in restaurants.) Many cultures see North Americans as rude and aggressive in our insistence on trying to get what we want. Others see North Americans as naïve for not bargaining.

What do you know from experience about bargaining in various cultures? What is the approved procedure for bargaining in commercial transactions in various cultures?

We differ considerably from one another in our comfort with negotiating and our willingness to negotiate in different situations. For some of us negotiation in private relationships is fine, whereas for others of us it is off limits or very uncomfortable. Similarly, many people take along a friend to negotiate for them when they buy a large item like a car because they are not comfortable "haggling over price." How do you respond to various negotiation situations?

❧Balancing Power

In negotiations, the most basic task is to actively attempt to structure an **"even playing field,"** a "level table," or balanced power. Since this difficult task of equalizing power is not always possible, sometimes you must decide whether to "leave the table." For example, if you know that you do not have the skills, the support, the power, and the opportunity to negotiate equally, you may decide to disengage, avoid, or get help from someone who can balance the power. That help might come from an attorney, mediator, supervisor, parent, friend, or co-worker. Sometimes, you can't stay at the table and keep your sanity and dignity. Remember that to negotiate effectively, you must be able to give resources that are valued by the other, and to influence the other's goals. You must be "a player." Negotiation depends on at least temporarily balanced power.

If we are in a high-power situation and feel justified in exercising dominance, we may become insensitive to the effects of that dominance on others. After all, we are right and feel justified! When we have the power, we all too often use it to take short-cuts to get what we want. We exercise such control not only to help or protect others, or out of genuine need, but out of "fear, insecurity, vengeance, vanity, habit, self-will, boredom, and laziness" (Kritek 1994, 90). Dominance from one party promotes manipulation and avoidance tactics from those lower in power. The cycle becomes an escalating cycle; seldom do people exercising dominance see that they caused the cycle in the first place. The low-power people feel victimized and begin to act like victims. Some of the most common manipulative tactics are insincere praise, lying and deception, tricks and secret deals, attacks and threats, deliberate stupidity or resistance, flirtatiousness and cuteness, harping on things, withholding something important, and deference (Kritek 1994, 108).

People using dominance often escalate the cycle by not listening to the needs of others, numbing themselves to injustice, focusing only on their own needs and tasks, making light of others' needs, trivializing and minimizing the needs of others, and blaming the victim.

People who use the classic destructive low-power tactics such as deceit and manipulation, and cannot ask for what they want, contribute to an unhealthy dynamic. One way out of these cycles is for both parties to engage in constructive argument.

❧Constructive Argumentation: Test Ideas, Not People

What comes to mind when someone says, "Oh, he is just arguing again"? For many people it implies both disagreeing on content and using a disagreeable tone. The following quotation from a student paper exemplifies this common stance:

> When I get into an argument with a person over something I stand for, then I really like to get involved and have a good battle. If my competitor has a good stand on his issues, then I like to "rip" at him until he breaks or if things go wrong, I break. The excitement of confrontation when I'm battling it out with another person has a tremendous thrill for me if I come out as the victor. I love it when we are at each other's throats.

Clearly this student prefers a competitive stance.

The topic disagreements do not have to contaminate the other TRIP elements. You can disagree on content and be pleasant-maintaining the relationship component. You can offer forcible opinions about an issue, yet protect the face/identity of the other's. Further, you can disagree strongly about content, and still follow the procedural rules. In negotiation situations the following phrases allow participants to disagree on content without being "disagreeable":

- I'm sorry, but I don't agree with your position about the election.
- I'm pretty firm about not agreeing with you, but tell me more.
- We still disagree about the role of government in our private lives, but let's listen to one another one at a time.
- John, that sure isn't my memory about what I agreed to about the deposit.
- We agreed to negotiate on vacation benefits. Our benefits package was circulated without any input from the paralegal staff. As their supervisor, I'm asking you as the human resources director to intervene with the managers and set up a meeting so we can negotiate, as they said they would.

As you can see from these examples, one doesn't have to destroy the relational dimension in order to carry a strong topic argument. In fact, the whole tradition of debate (such as college debates and the presidential debates during campaign years) rests on agreeing on process rules to protect identity, procedural, and relationship dimensions so that the arguments can focus on the topic. Infante says that in "argument" you (1) state what you are claiming, (2) present evidence for your claim, (3) present reasons for your claim, and (4) summarize to show what you have established. All of this is accomplished because you are "testing ideas, not people" (Infante, 1988).

Infante (1988) goes further and specifies exactly what allows an effective "arguer" to make a case, while supporting the other TRIP dimensions. You (1) use the principles of argumentation with compassion, (2) reaffirm your opponent's sense of competence, (3) allow opponents to finish what they are saying, (4) emphasize equality, (5) emphasize shared attitudes, (6) show opponents you are interested in their views, (7) use a somewhat subdued, calm delivery, (8) control the pace of the argument and (9) allow your opponent to save face (Infante, 1988). While this list is lengthy, it does capture the importance of positively supporting the other TRIP dimension while arguing about the topic.

Every day, we see violations of constructive arguing. There are even television shows making money showing people "attack other" and therefore demonstate nonconstructive argumentation. In contrast to this, in professional debate circles, it is considered a logical fallacy to attack the other debater personally. It is called argumentum *ad hominen*, which means "argument against the man." If you are a professional advocate in a courtroom, there are strict rules about not attacking the other side personally, and the rules are interpreted and enforced by the judge—ensuring that argument will occur on the topic level.

The judge won't let you, for example, make the following statement: "The other attorney is just a jerk, and I can't believe the defendant is wasting his money employing him."

Argument is "reason giving" (Benoit 1992; Rowland and Barge 1991; Infante, 1988), trying to convince others of your side of the issue. One makes claims and backs them up (Keough 1992). The arguer tries to get others to "recognize the rightness" of his or her beliefs or actions (Benoit 1983, 550). Interpersonal argumentation, then, has a place in our everyday conflicts and negotiations (Trapp 1981, 1989). One of the positive features of interpersonal arguments (in the sense defined here) is that they are composed of exchanges between two people who feel powerful enough to set forth reasons for their beliefs. If two people are arguing, it is because they are balanced enough in power (or in their desire to re-establish a power balance) to proceed. Lack of argument, in fact, may show that one of the parties feels so powerless that he or she avoids engaging directly with the other (Cloven and Roloff 1991.)

Interpersonal argument, done properly, may in fact be the heart and soul of modern-day interpersonal problem solving and conflict management. We trade positions, set forth evidence, and let the free exchange of ideas reign. But we do not destroy our relationships with others, personally attack them, destroy their face, or violate standards of procedure. When one person says something sarcastic such as, "I wouldn't expect you to understand. You're sitting on a trust fund and couldn't be expected to know the value of money to ordinary people," the relationship and identity levels become the field of argument, with destructive effects. Some recent research about face threat and negotiation shows that threatening face of the other derails the negotiations (White et al. 2004). Furthermore, we respond differently in negotiating (1) a public issue or (2) a personal issue in a relationship. When arguing about public issues, parties tend to enjoy it more and not be so ego-involved as when arguing about their personal relationship (Johnson 2002).

In constructive conflicts, arguments focus on levels of discourse that will move the conflict toward resolution. When argument focuses on relationship or identity issues, the conflict may generate much heat but little light. As in classical debate, the honorable approach is to engage on those issues that are real and will help the dialogue. Anything else blocks progress. In ancient Rome, Quintilian, one of the earliest rhetoricians, wrote of the characteristics of an effective orator: intelligence, character, and goodwill. These attributes describe the effective negotiator as well.

The renewed call to "civility" in public discourse comes from experiences of personal attacks and unproductive negotiation tactics. In civil argumentation and negotiation, cordial, firm, and passionate communication takes place, but attacks on the personhood of the other do not.

| Application 8.3 | Watching an Argument |

Watch a televised argument, live exchange or debate.

- What types of argumentation do they use?
- Do the arguers give evidence for their claims?

(continued)

> ### Application 8.3   Watching an Argument
>
> - Do the arguers show support for relationship, identity, and procedural issues while vigorously disagreeing?
>
> - If there is a moderator, does she or he work to keep the disputants in the "constructive" zone or try to get them to attack one another personally?
>
> - If these two were to actually sit down together and negotiate, what might they do to ensure equal negotiation strength and a productive process?

Approaches to Negotiation

Most views of negotiation present a limited perspective. Since negotiation is such a pervasive conflict management process, it is little wonder that scores of books have been written about it. Unfortunately, some of the popular advice reinforces a **win/lose perspective.** For instance, one book offers "examples to guide you in getting the upper hand every time!" or "33 ways to use the power in you to get your way in any situation" (Ilich 1981). Likewise, much of the research on negotiation focuses exclusively on aggressive maneuvers of negotiators and views negotiation as a debate (Putnam and Jones 1982a). Further, many popular authors see bargaining as a "game of managing impressions and manipulating information. Bargaining is a struggle for advantage, for with the advantage come beneficial outcomes" (Walker 1988, 219). Amateur negotiators often adopt a win/lose view of negotiation (Bazerman and Neale 1983).

Another limited view of negotiation is seeing it as a "*series of compromises*". From this perspective, negotiation is simply a trade-off in which each gives up something to reach a middle ground; the development of creative options is ignored. One final limitation of most literature on negotiation is that it centers on (1) *formal negotiations, between* (2) *negotiating representatives, where* (3) *the beginnings and endings of the negotiations are clearly delineated.* We will discuss some aspects of such negotiations; however, most of us will never be professional negotiators. Therefore, this chapter emphasizes everyday situations.

Competitive Negotiation

Assumptions

Competitive, or "*distributive*," **negotiations** are what most people think of when discussing negotiation. For example, you and your sister both want to use your dad's car for an overnight trip. Competitive negotiators assume that the conflict is win/lose (or "zero-sum" in game theory terms). What you win, she loses, and vice versa. The rewards in such a conflict are seen as a "fixed pie" to be distributed between the parties—thus the name **"distributive" bargaining** (Walton and McKersie 1965). Therefore, if you get to use the car, your sister is out of luck. No one tries joint problem solving, such as dropping your sister off at her destination. In competitive, or distributive, negotiations, each party usually has a "resistance point" or a **"bargaining range"** beyond which he or she will not go (Popple 1984). For example, from a competitive approach, the relevant information for buying a house is this:

Buyer's range: $265,000–$290,000

Seller's range: $275,000–$300,000

Each person's range determines his or her offers and counteroffers. The seller lists the house for $300,000. The buyer makes a first offer of $265,000. After negotiations, through a Realtor the buyer offers $278,000. The seller says that she will not part with the house for less than $290,000. But, in her heart of hearts, she knows that she can buy a new place she wants with $276,500. Buyer and seller slowly move toward their "settlement range" (between $276,500 and $278,000). In this example, the settlement range is already apparent, based on the list price and the first offer, so when the buyer says, "$278,000 is my final offer," the seller takes the offer.

Typically, *the distributive bargainer* is not concerned about a future relationship with the other party and is trying to maximize gain and minimize loss. Unfortunately, some people in ongoing relationships act as if they do not have this relationship, using distributive assumptions. The basic assumptions of distributive, or competitive, negotiation are as follows:

- The negotiating world is controlled by egocentric self-interest.
- The underlying motivation is competitive/antagonistic.
- Limited resources prevail.
- One can make independent choices: tomorrow's decision remains unaffected materially by today's.
- The resource distribution system is distributive in nature (either/or).
- The goal is to win as much as you can—and especially more than the other side. (Murray 1986)

Application 8.4   Mistaken Assumptions

Randy and Jennifer have been married for six years. They have moved back to the city where they met and went to college so Randy could finish his degree in resource management. They now have two children, ages 4 and 2. Jennifer has a job she loves at the university, in her former social work department, where she organizes internships for undergraduate students. She feels fortunate to have this job without an advanced degree; her experience gained her the position. After a miserable time of working for one of his professors doing field research, Randy decided he had no future in the academic research world. His interests lay in working with different constituent groups to manage natural resources. He has a strong communication background to go along with his resource management degree. When a planning and consulting firm offered him a job four hours away, Jennifer and Randy decided he should take it. They have six months to decide whether to move to Denver from Laramie. After several months of four day weeks, then driving back

(continued)

Application 8.4	Mistaken Assumptions

to Laramie for the weekend, Randy told Jennifer he really wanted the family to move to Denver so they could be together. Here's how their first negotiation sounded:

Randy: Jen, I miss you and the kids, and I hate being a weekend dad. It only makes sense for us all to move to Denver. I'm making enough money now that you can go back to school after a year or so. I think we should put the house on the market.

Jennifer: I won't even consider it. I have a wonderful job, the kids have their friends. I know I said I'd consider moving, but I can't bear the idea of leaving this place we love. So, my answer is "no."

Randy: I make enough money now that your continuing in your job and our paying travel costs and for my apartment is just stupid. We need to consolidate our resources in Denver. You'll love it when you get used to it. We can live in a smaller town outside the city.

Jennifer: I'll think about it right when Olivia starts school (two years from this conversation.)

Randy: Maybe I won't care by then. You can just stay in Laramie and we can start working out a parenting plan, since this plan of yours leads to divorce.

Jennifer: I'll never split the kids' time with you. You got yourself into this great job; you can deal with the travel.

(And so on. . .)

Clearly Randy and Jennifer don't know how to negotiate when the relationship is important, ongoing, and there is mutual love and affection. As we discussed in the Emotions chapter, we can assume that Randy and Jennifer's core feelings might be fear, fear of loss and change, and surprise/shock. We will revisit Randy and Jennifer after we present some ideas for collaborative bargaining.

Communication Patterns

Since competitive bargaining assumes that the goals of the parties are in direct conflict and that what you gain, the other loses (Walker 1988), you gain a competitive advantage by starting with a high or extreme offer (Fisher 1985). For instance, if you sue someone, you will ask for large amounts of money—for what the other loses, you gain. Similarly, if you are a competitive negotiator negotiating for a new job and employers ask you, "What salary do you want?" you will say "$65,000," knowing you would be happy with $50,000. Competitive bargainers withhold data from each other and try to throw off each other's ability to predict responses, meanwhile learning as much as possible about each other's position (Putnam and Poole 1987). The competitive bargainer

- Makes high opening demands and concedes slowly.
- Tries to maximize tangible resource gains, within the limits of the current dispute.
- Exaggerates the value of concessions that are offered.

- Uses threats, confrontations, argumentation, and forceful speaking.
- Conceals information.
- Manipulates people and the process by distorting intentions, resources, and goals.
- Tries to resist persuasion on issues.
- Is oriented to quantitative and competitive goals rather than relational goals. (Adapted from Murray 1986; Lax and Sebenius 1986)

The competitive bargainer times concessions (giving in and moving toward the other's position) carefully and moves in a stepwise fashion—giving a little bit at a time until a settlement range can be reached with the other. Since both people are probably in a competitive mode, each is trying to get the other to make concessions. However, you are more likely to receive concessions from someone else when you can convince them you cannot make a concession (Schelling 1960). Thus, each negotiator is trying to convince the other that he or she cannot "give" any more and that the only way the negotiations can reach settlement is if the other gives in (Edwards and White 1977). Former president Jimmy Carter spoke about his role as mediator in the Camp David accords, in which Anwar Sadat of Egypt and Menachem Begin of Israel spent 13 days in isolation negotiating peace in their region. To convince Sadat of his seriousness, Begin had taken a religious oath that he would strike off his right hand if he gave up land in the Sinai desert. Carter came up with the idea that the Israeli parliament, not Begin personally, could enact the moves that would give land back to Egypt. Begin saved face and was able to go ahead with a plan he personally endorsed, after days of negotiating.

Many well-known competitive strategies can be used to advance one's own goals. You only behave cooperatively if it helps you attain a larger share of the pie. You see the "game" of negotiation as one of picking the right maneuvers, much like a military strategy, and you must present a strong defense and try to stay on the offensive. If you show elements of "weakness"—showing your hand or offering concessions too large or too early (Wall 1985)—these weaknesses will work against you. If you are a competitive negotiator you will go to great lengths to convince the opponent that you will not be swayed. When you say, "This is my bottom line!" you are trying to convince the other that you will not make concessions, so the other party had better make some.

If Randy and Jennifer continue to bargain competitively, they might say something like this:

Jennifer: I will consider moving in a year. Olivia will just be starting kindergarten. I can't believe you would uproot us all when we've chosen, you and I together, Laramie as the place we really want to live.

Randy: But you don't want *me* to live there. You don't care about me, just yourself and your friend circle. You supported my taking this job. So now support our family.

Jennifer: I do it my way, you do it yours.

They still don't get it. . .

Disadvantages

As Follett (1940) observed many years ago, working out a position without first consulting others "blocks conflict management." The following list summarizes what Kohn refers to as "the case against competition" (1992).

- Has a strong bias toward confrontation, encouraging the use of coercion and emotional pressure as persuasive means; is hard on relationships, breeding mistrust, feelings of separateness, frustration, and anger, resulting in more frequent breakdowns in negotiations; and distorts communication, producing misinformation and misjudgment.

- Works against responsiveness and openness to opponent, thereby restricting access to joint gains.

- Encourages brinkmanship by creating many opportunities for impasse.

- Increases difficulty in predicting responses of opponent because reliance is on manipulation and confrontation to control process.

- Contributes to an overestimation of the payoffs of competitive actions such as litigation because the focus is not on a relatively objective analysis of substantive merits (Murray 1986, 184).

Competition is seen as a practice that stimulates productivity, but in fact collaboration increases productive ideas.

Competition only builds healthy self-esteem in the winners; losers suffer lack of self-esteem. Winning assumes there are losers.

Women and men view competition differently. Women are as oriented toward achievement, as are men. But as we have seen in previously cited research, women often value self-in-relationship so much that competing with a partner is not worth it. Men tend to orient more toward status, especially with other men. Women and men, therefore, experience different disadvantages when competitive negotiation is the norm (Kohn 1992).

The situations most appropriate for a competitive approach to negotiations are those that are truly win/lose, where one party stands to lose and the other stands to gain. For example, most lawsuits for malpractice can be seen as win/lose. When no ongoing relationship with the conflict partner is predicted, a competitive approach can make sense— take what you can get and leave. Such an approach, obviously, is only acceptable in a culture in which individual gain is valued and relationships are given secondary consideration. If someone is truly Machiavellian, planning each move in life strategically to obtain a payoff, competitiveness is at the center of his or her worldview. Someone with an extreme "dog-eat-dog" worldview may say such things as "I have to treat him well because someday I'll need him." A truly competitive person keeps his or her eyes on the prize at all times! Yet, seldom is competitive negotiation the best choice in an ongoing relationship.

Collaborative Negotiation

Negotiation requires ongoing back-and-forth use of reflective listening and assertion skills by one or both parties. Management of conflict through effective negotiation requires listening to the other party; indicating that you understand his or her concerns; expressing your feelings; stating your points in a firm but friendly manner; linking your points to points expressed by the other party; and working toward a joint resolution that builds on the ideas of both parties and addresses all concerns.

—Umbreit , *Mediating Interpersonal Conflicts*

excellent

Competitive, or distributive, negotiations assume that what one person wins, the other loses. **Integrative, or collaborative, bargaining,** on the other hand, assumes that the parties have both (1) diverse interests and (2) common interests and that the negotiation process can result in both parties' gaining something. Mixed motives, separate needs, and interdependent needs characterize **collaborative negotiation.** Whereas the competitive model assumes that someone loses and someone wins, collaborative negotiation assumes that creativity can transcend the win/lose aspect of competitive negotiations.

One classic example, often repeated in a variety of forms, comes from Mary Parker Follett (1940), who coined the term *integrative*. She illustrates an integrative solution to a conflict that at first appears to be competitive.

In the Harvard Library one day, in one of the smaller rooms, someone wanted the window open, I wanted it shut. We opened the window in the next room, where no one was sitting. This was not a compromise because there was no curtailing of desire; we both got what we really wanted. For I did not want a closed room, I simply did not want the north wind to blow directly on me; likewise the other occupant did not want that particular window open, he merely wanted more air in the room. (32)

Although she doesn't detail her bargaining process, the result was clearly integrative—it integrated the needs of both parties. Integrative, or collaborative, negotiations emphasize maximizing joint benefits for both parties, often in creative ways (Bazerman, Magliozzi, and Neale 1985). Such bargaining places value on the relationship between the conflict parties, requires trust, and relies on full disclosure of relevant information (Walker 1988).

One of the assumptions of collaborative, or integrative, negotiation is that polar opposites are not necessarily in conflict. For example, if two people are negotiating, sometimes they can reach a satisfactory solution precisely because they want different things. Fisher, Ury, and Patton (1991, 74) list some of the polar opposites that can be reconciled in integrative negotiation:

One party cares more about	Other party cares more about
form, appearance	substance
economic considerations	political considerations
internal considerations	external considerations
symbolic considerations	practical considerations
immediate future	more distant future
ad hoc results	the relationship
hardware	ideology
progress	respect for tradition
precedent	this case
prestige, reputation	results
political points	group welfare

Do you recall that in chapter 3, we suggested that conflict parties often specialize in certain kinds of goals? If you are most concerned about "getting things done" (results) and your work associate is more concerned about "looking good" (prestige, reputation), your needs are not necessarily incompatible. For instance, you may want to make sure the work is done for your campus committee and the other may want to make sure there is newspaper coverage of the event you are sponsoring. He can help you get the job done, and you can put him in touch with a reporter you know. Collaborative approaches treat assumed opposites as connected and not incompatible.

Follett (1940) relates yet another story that provides insight into collaborative, or integrative, negotiations. Two sisters were fighting over an orange and, after much acrimony, agreed to split the orange in half—a compromise. One sister used her half of the orange for juice and the other sister used the peel of her half of the orange for a cake. They overlooked the integrative, or collaborative, elements of negotiation. They each could have had a full orange since they wanted different parts! Unlike the sisters, collaborative negotiators engage in joint problem solving, jointly devising solutions that maximize benefits for both parties.

Assumptions

Just as the competitive model of negotiation carries basic assumptions, so does the integrative, or collaborative, model of negotiation. The process presumes the following:

- The negotiating world is controlled by enlightened self-interest.
- Common interests are valued and sought.
- Interdependence is recognized and enhanced.
- Limited resources do exist, but they can usually be expanded through cooperation.
- The resource distribution system is integrative (joint) in nature.
- The goal is a mutually agreeable solution that is fair to all parties and efficient for the community (Murray 1986).

Collaborative bargaining assumes that we can, even in the midst of a conflict, work from "enlightened self-interest." We get what we need from others but do it in a way that also helps them achieve some of their goals. The collaborative bargainer is interested in preserving the relationship with the other. Therefore, driving a hard bargain at the expense of the other is not seen as a victory. Collaborative bargainers must maintain some interest in the other while holding out for their own goals. Unlike a win/lose situation, a collaborative agreement allows both of you to come away from the negotiation with an intact relationship, willing to trust and work with each other in the next bargaining situation.

Communication Patterns

How does one carry out collaborative negotiations? Unless we can specify communicative behaviors that can activate a collaborative negotiation set, the basic principles won't take us very far. All of the collaborative tactics we discussed in chapter 5, can be put to use by the collaborative negotiator. You might want to review that section on collaborative tactics as a basis for collaborative negotiation. Also worthy of note are some specific techniques that lead to collaborative outcomes. If you want more lengthy treatment of these techniques, consult Rubin, Pruitt, and Kim (1994); Lewicki and Litterer (1985), and Smith (2008).

Expanding the pie encourages collaborative outcomes because most conflicts are based on the perception of scarce resources; expanding the resources alters the structure of the conflict. For example, if Jane wants to go to the mountains and Sandy wants to go to the seashore, they might collaborate to find mountainous seashore. Although it won't be the perfect mountain and the shore may have some limitations, they will get to spend their vacation together—they have expanded the pie. Often, children squabble with one another because of the perception that there is not enough parental care and consideration to go around. They fight, say mean things to one another, and struggle over the available love. As the parent, if you refuse to "parcel out" the love and attention, giving each child attention without leaving out the other, you have expanded the pie. Whether the "pie" is actual or metaphoric, its expansion alters the conflict.

Application 8.5   **You've Got to Do It!**

Caitlin, an entry-level employee who had just received her BA, worked for a veterans' program. The program was underfunded, with many demands being placed on the staff members. The program director of the family services division asked Caitlin to design and teach a family communication program to families with preschool children. Caitlin felt unprepared, pushed too far and too fast, and unsupported for this high-visibility program (it would be filmed and put on public-access TV). Although Caitlin was newly hired, she had been given a lot of responsibility and did have legitimate power in the organization. She also wanted to work for the organization so didn't want to resign under the pressure of three times too much work. Two possible scenarios follow:

Competitive Mode

Boss: Caitlin, you've got to do this program, and it has got to be good. Our grant funding for next year depends on delivering this service, which we said we'd provide.

Caitlin: I'd need a master's degree, at least, to be able to design and teach this course. I can't do it and keep track of the after-school program, too. I have too little secretarial support and too many projects that are needing my attention right now. I'm so stressed out I don't know whether I can keep on.

Boss: I hired you to run this entire program. If you didn't think you could do it, you shouldn't have applied. Drop something less important and do this.

(continued)

Application 8.5	You've Got to Do It!

Collaborative Mode

Boss: Caitlin, I really need to get this program on family communication done. Our grant funding for next year depends on delivering this service, which we said we'd provide. Could you take it on?

Caitlin: I don't see how. I have to keep track of the after-school program, and there are a lot of other things that are half-done, too. And I'm stressed out and have almost no secretarial support. Besides, I don't have the training to put this course together. I'd need a master's degree, at least.

Boss: What if I get you some staff help from social work? There's a graduate student over there who said he'd like to do an internship with us. Maybe he could do the program development with you.

Caitlin: That sounds great, but I still need some secretarial help. Could you loan my program someone from your office?

Boss: I can't do that permanently, but you can bring work over and I'll delegate it.

Caitlin: OK, I'll see what I can do. (She continues planning with the boss.)

Nonspecific Compensation

Nonspecific compensation, is a process in which one of the parties is "paid off" with some creative form of compensation, could also help break a competitive spiral and begin a collaborative set. For instance, the boss could have offered extra time off after the project was finished or offered to move up Caitlin's evaluation, which would result in the possibility of an early promotion. If two roommates are bargaining over use of a car, one may say, "OK, you can have my car, but I get to have the apartment for an all-night party after graduation." Another example is looking to purchase a house and discovering that the owner is more interested in moving rapidly than in getting the stated purchase price. Your cousin owns a moving company, so you arrange to have the house owner moved at no cost. Your cousin charges you less than the going rate, and you get the house for less money than was originally asked. If the deal is sealed, you have created a form of nonspecific compensation. (You have found some dimension that is valued by the other and have made an offer to offset your gains in the negotiation.)

Tradeoffs are when one offers to "trade off" issues that are the top priority for the other. The parties have to find multiple issues in the conflict (for example, time is of the essence to you, money to him). Then, you arrange agreements so that each of you gets the top-priority item while giving on the lower-priority item. In one organization the supervisor wanted more hours at work from a particular employee. The employee wanted a fairer (to her) evaluation at the end of the year. With the help of an outsider, they negotiated that (1) the evaluation process would involve discussion before memos were sent and (2) the employee would take on some extra work. Each received acknowledgment of his main concern and gave on the item that was vitally important to the other.

Cost cutting minimizes the other's costs for going along with you. For example, you want to go skiing with your friend. She is overloaded with work, so you offer to ski only half a day and not let her incur the "cost" of missing all her work time. Alternatively, you are negotiating with your romantic partner about going on vacation. He is tied up and feels he can't take off so many days, yet you both want to vacation together. So you offer to drive your car to the resort you wish to visit, giving you the "decompression time" that you value, and suggest he fly to join you two days later. You shorten his total vacation time, yet make it possible for the two of you to vacation together at the resort you want to visit.

Bridging invents new options to meet the other side's needs. You want to rent an apartment, but it is too expensive. You discover that the landlord is concerned about the appearance of the property. So you offer her a rent somewhat below what she wants but agree to do 15 hours of "fix-it work" each month. She receives property improvements, and you receive reduced rent. Everyone gains!

Let's see how Randy and Jennifer might practice collaborative bargaining instead of the "relationship suicide" competitive approach they used first.

Application 8.6   Jennifer and Randy Try Again

After thinking over their angry and unproductive first conversations about whether to move or keep the family where it is, they decided to take a more collaborative approach.

Jennifer: I didn't like the way we talked with each other last weekend about the possibility of our all moving to Denver, or whether we should stay here. I've been thinking. I'm not ready to move yet, and I can't stand the idea of giving up our connection to our friends here. After all, we chose Laramie because of our friend group. I wish we could do both. You know, I do miss you.

Randy: Well, that's a relief. I love my job, but it's not the way I want to live. I've been thinking that I could explore the idea of my working out of Laramie after I have a full year or so with the company.

Jennifer: That's a great idea. I wonder if we could afford some land here so we could build a small vacation place. Then if we do need to move to Denver, we'd have a toehold here.

Randy: I don't think we can afford two places, for sure.

Jennifer: No, I don't either, but I could check out land prices. We could put the money we'd save living in one place toward buying some land. And if you could work more here in the meantime, that would give us some time to look. I need to get used to the idea, and I don't want to sell our house at a fire-sale price.

Randy: OK, I'll talk to my boss, and you can check out some land deals. I can stand it for a few more months as is. It's a relief to me for us to be thinking together again. I've missed that.

What collaborative techniques did Randy and Jennifer use?

In collaborative negotiations, parties brainstorm to invent new and creative options to meet everyone's needs. For example, Sally is negotiating with her work partner. She is frustrated about the job not being done, and Chuck is feeling that the work intrudes too much on his personal time. So, she offers to do more of the work on the spreadsheet if he will bring her coffee and sandwiches. Chuck gains more free time, Sally sees the project moving ahead, and both of them contribute to the task while maintaining their working relationship.

Bargainers who employ collaborative approaches view negotiation as being complex; thus, they find creative ways to "package" agreements and invent new options (Raiffa 1982). The collaborator moves from "fighting" to "conferring" (Follett 1940), assuming that working with the other will bring joint benefits. Information serves as fact-finding material for the bargainers rather than as a wedge that drives between the two parties. Information is not used as a "gotcha now" tactic. With information, one problem solves, explores causes, and generates alternative solutions (Lewicki and Litterer 1985).

Disadvantages

As with competitive tactics, collaborative approaches have some disadvantages. Probably the biggest overall difficulty is that they require "a high order of intelligence, keen perception and discrimination, and, more than all, a brilliant inventiveness" (Follett 1940, 45). If it hasn't been modeled in the home or on the job, collaboration may require specific training. Unless the beginning bargainer (whether an attorney, spouse, friend, or co-worker) has some level of training, the usual approach is to equate "good" bargaining with competitive tactics. Collaborative bargaining requires the same amount of emotional intelligence as all of conflict resolution. One must commit to very high standards. One disadvantage is that this can all seem like a lot of hard work. It is.

According to Murray (1986), collaborative negotiation can be described as follows:

- Is strongly biased toward cooperation, creating internal pressures to compromise and accommodate that may not be in one's best interests.

- Avoids strategies that are confrontational because they carry the risk of impasse, which is viewed as failure.

- Focuses on being sensitive to others' perceived interests; increases vulnerability to deception and manipulation by a competitive opponent; and increases the possibility that the settlement may be more favorable to the other side than fairness would warrant.

- Increases the difficulty of establishing definite aspiration levels and bottom lines because of the reliance on qualitative (value-laden) goals.

- Requires substantial skill and knowledge of the process to do well.

- Requires strong confidence in one's own assessment powers (perception) regarding the interests and needs of the other side and the other's payoff schedule (184).

Collaborative negotiations, then, are not easily used in every conflict. They require considerable skill on the part of the negotiators, who strive to keep the negotiations from disintegrating into a win/lose approach.

❧Seven Elements of Principled Negotiation

In previous editions of this book, we have relied upon Fisher and Ury's *Getting to Yes* (1981) work for their practical approach to collaborative negotiation that has become very popular, for good reason. Fisher and Ury term the process "negotiation on merits" or **"principled negotiation."** Researchers at the Harvard Negotiation Project now present an expansion of that model, which incorporates their widely used previous model (Fisher and Shapiro 2005). The seven elements of principled negotiation are (in a slightly revised form) as follows:

1. Attend to the relationship.

How does each party think and feel about the other? Build a good relationship, working together side by side. Separate the people from the problem. The problem is what the negotiation partners work to resolve. The people are not the problem. Attack and research the problem, not the people involved. This takes self-discipline, of course, since it's so easy to try to tear the other person down. This never works in the long run.

2. Attend to all elements of communication.

Work to build positive, two-way communication, and avoid telling others what to do. Take into account all the discussion of strong emotions we explored in chapter 6. Show you are a person worthy of trust by expressing appreciation, forming affiliations (turn adversaries into colleagues), respecting autonomy (yours and theirs), acknowledging status, and staying within a fulfilling role. In other words, try not to allow the negotiating process to change your positive, chosen role as a good communicator. (Read further on these ideas in *Beyond Reason: Using Emotions as You Negotiate*, Fisher and Shapiro, 2005).

3. Focus on interests, not positions.

Disclose your actual concerns and interests, not "bottom-line positions." **Positions** come from **interests.** When people discuss their actual interests in a transparent way, they are much more likely to be able to come to a mutual agreement. Interestingly, the collaborative bargainer can be just as "tough" as the competitive bargainer. However, you get tough about different aspects. You remain firm about your goals but flexible regarding how to accomplish them—what Pruitt (1983a) calls **firm flexibility.** You work with the other party, but you don't capitulate; your goals are always firm in your mind, but the means you use are flexible and adapted to the other person's needs as well. As Follett (1940) noted, "Mushy people are no more good at this than stubborn people" (40).

Recall that we said earlier that when we are in a dispute, we usually believe we know what the other wants. But this guess is usually inaccurate. When we don't ask the other about his or her interests, we simply project ours onto him or her. In the case of a teenager bargaining with parents over chores and grades, the teenager, when asked what his parent's interests are, is likely to say (with great confidence), "Oh, they are control freaks." The parents might believe that their 15-year-old son wants to do only what he wants and not take family responsibilities. The truth might be that the parents are interested in bargaining (freedom for chores) and the teen is, as well. We don't know what the other wants if we don't ask genuine, open-ended questions, such as "What is your goal here? What are you most interested in? What would make you feel you have ended up with what you most want?" This kind of questioning and listening builds effective conversation about real interests.

Take the case of Joan, who put her house on the market for $325,000. If you are negotiating with her on the price of the house and someone asks you, "why is she asking so much?" you may well answer, "because she wants to make as much as she can." You conclude that based on what your interests would be in her situation. In fact, she asks $325,000 as proof of the value of the improvements she has added to the house during the 10 years she owned it. So, unless the other tells you what he or she wants, you are playing a guessing game.

In disputes, relational and identity interests often remain undiscussed, under the surface of the negotiations. Go back to Joan for a moment. She was raised in a small town; how people treat one another is very important to her. She puts her house on the market for $325,000, as we discussed above. You, as a prospective buyer, try to bargain hard. The Realtor you are sending the offers through tends to be rather tough in negotiations—pushing hard, making "low ball" offers, and using competitive tactics to try and reduce the price. In making your first offer to Joan, the Realtor says, in a nasty tone of voice, "Well, my client will only come up to $218,000 because he feels you have overpriced the house." After many back-and-forth offers and counteroffers, you and Joan agree to $275,000. Then, just before signing the buy-sell agreement, Joan takes the house off the market. A month later, she puts it back on the market and sells it for $250,000 to another buyer going through a realtor who is a friend of Joan's. Joan's relationship and identity issues were more important than the content (the price.)

Application 8.7	Multiple Interests

In small groups of four or five people, take the following *"position"* statements and brainstorm possible *interests* that might underlie them. You should have a minimum of five possible interests for each position, all different from one another.

"I have to take 19 credits next term."

"I want $250 for those skis."

"You have to do the dishes every other night."

"I want the kids to take my name, not their biological father's."

"Quit throwing your clothes on the floor of our apartment."

"Pick me up at 8:00 sharp on Mondays to go to school."

"You have to type the first draft of our project."

4. Generate many options.

When the negotiation begins to look like a win-lose, zero-sum game, explore many options by brainstorming and using creativity. Each possible option should include the genuine interests of the other. A good decision is one that springs from many options generated by concerned conflict parties. A good decision should bring not

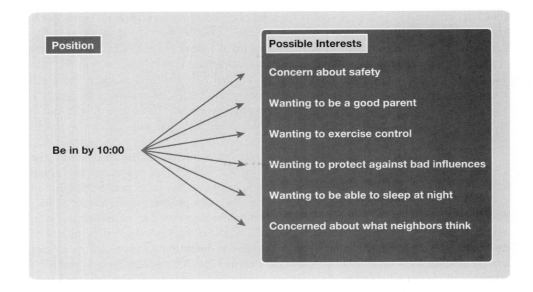

only a sense of relief ("well, we got through that") but also a sense of excitement and hope. "Good for us."

5. Find legitimate criteria

Try to discern whether the outcome is fair, just, reasonable, and respects the interests of each party. When you discover that someone (even yourself!) is only interested in winning or "getting it done," give your attention to how the result will be judged. One can develop objective criteria by using fair procedures (balancing power in the process) and by seeking fair standards. Menzel (1991) suggests six external standards for fairness: (simple success at reaching an agreement, compliance with the agreement, cost of the agreement, efficiency through which the agreement is reached, access to justice presented to disputants, and stability of the agreement over time.) These standards might be important to a court, to a branch of the government such as the department of family services, to family members, or to managers overseeing an agreement in their department. Other fair standards can be based on the following:

market value	moral standards
costs	professional standards
precedent	precedent equal treatment
what a court would decide	efficiency
scientific judgment	reciprocity
	(Fisher and Ury 1981, 89)

6. Analyze the "Best Alternative to a Negotiated Agreement" (BATNA).

Consider your "walk-away" alternative as well as theirs. Recognize that any agreement must be better for everyone involved than simply walking away. Sometimes people say, "I do not need this." If that statement is true, then negotiations will fail. When threats are used, you can say, "we really need to come to agreement. If we don't, the consequences are extremely negative." Then you can review the BATNA to see if it is acceptable.

7. Work with fair and realistic commitments.

Decide whether what you and the other party are asking is reasonable, doable, face-saving, practical, and will enhance the working relationship. If someone is forced into an unrealistic commitment, possibly just to get the problem temporarily solved, the conflict will go underground and have to be revisited. So you gain nothing by "winning" with unrealistic and unfair commitments.

➴The Language of Collaboration

As has been true of other conflict resolution processes throughout this book, no specific set of techniques will assure collaboration. Collaboration is both a mind-set and a set of techniques. If one does not believe that energetic cooperation will provide better solutions than competitive techniques, all the **language of collaboration** that could be memorized will not ultimately produce collaboration. Sometimes, however, you may get stuck looking for the right phrase to help a negotiation move toward collaboration. If so, consider some of the following phrases. Beside each phrase, put the number of the principled negotiation idea that the phrase addresses. There may be several.

| Application 8.8 | Practice the Language and the Principles of Negotiation |

This is a problem you and I haven't had to face before. I'm sure we can work it out. What is it that you are most hoping for?

Let's figure out where we agree, and that will give us a base to work from.

I'd like to postpone making a decision about filing a grievance until our next meeting. Today I want to explore all the options that are available to us in addition to filing a grievance. Is that all right with you?

I can't be satisfied with getting my way if you're disgruntled.

Let's get an example of market value from an objective source.

I know this is difficult, but we can work it out.

I can understand why you want to "split the difference," but let's try for some creative alternatives.

I certainly appreciate your stance. Let's also talk about what I need to be satisfied.

Your threat tells me how important this issue is to you, but it will work better with me not to threaten. Can we back this up and come at it another way?

I don't see any conflict in both of us getting more of what we want, but we have been acting as if what we each get, the other loses.

I really do want a fair and durable settlement for both of us. That requires, of course, more direct information about what we each want. Let's explore that awhile.

(continued)

Application 8.8
Practice the Language and the Principles of Negotiation

I will discuss with you as long as it takes to reach a settlement that will work for both of us.

Yes, I see that you think that is the best solution. Remember, however, that there are two of us here. Let's see if both of us can be satisfied with an outcome.

Most people approach negotiations, at least at the beginning, from a competitive frame of mind—assuming both sides have to lose part of the pie. The competitive or collaborative approaches are more a function of the bargainers than of any other factors. In fact, you can be in a negotiation in which one person takes a cooperative and the other a competitive stance (Walker 1988). If you take a competitive approach, whether you are negotiating about how to spend the evening with a friend or how much to offer on a house, the negotiation process will probably be a competitive, win/lose experience. On the other hand, if you stick firmly to a collaborative approach, you will find creative options that someone with a competitive approach simply would not find. Creative options are often available (Fogg 1985), but unless the negotiators believe them possible and work to jointly produce those options, the negotiations will begin and end on a win/lose footing. Having had experience negotiating and serving as third-party interveners, we are always gratified by how many creative, jointly satisfying options are available and constantly are reminded of how difficult they are for the parties to initially see.

Collaborative language strategies are generally not perceived as genuinely collaborative if the intent is still, as in a competitive system, to promote self-interest at the expense of the other (Kolb and Putnam 1997; Putnam 1996). Kolb and Putnam rightly point out the difference between a relational approach used for personal gain, which is manipulative, and true collaboration. As long as predetermined goals benefiting the self are pursued, the underlying assumptions of both competitive and collaborative modes are

- Self-interest
- Competitiveness
- Rationality
- An individualistic focus
- The exchange model

These underlying assumptions limit the transformative potential of negotiation. Transformation creates something new from what existed before. New ways to cooperate emerge, new feelings arise, and new solutions become possible. The transformative approach to negotiation rests on

- Community concerns
- Cooperativeness
- Subjectivity

Application 8.9   The Rainbow Development Water Problem

A group of summer home owners in the high mountains of Colorado faces an ongoing problem with their water well, which keeps testing as polluted, thus making it necessary for the residents to boil or buy their water. Recently some of the elected officials of the volunteer board authorized a road to be built so heavy equipment could reach the well-head and the well could be dug out and rebuilt. The road was built through wetlands, which raised some federal legal problems, and through a pristine meadow cherished by some of the residents as a quiet, beautiful spot at the end of the property. The road goes through commonly owned property, skirting the edge of privately owned lots. Three factions have formed, and full-scale conflict has erupted, with letters, private conversations, procedural challenges, content arguments, relationship destruction, and face-saving struggles going on at a high level of intensity. Thirty-five or so families are involved. It is a long-standing group of friends and acquaintances who have considerable monetary and emotional investment in the property and dramatically different ecological, political, financial, and community values.

1. The "water first" group: This group consists primarily of engineers, scientists, builders, and practical people who are sick and tired of dealing with a half-solution to the water problem year after year. They want to get a new well, install purification systems if they are needed, and assess the membership for what is required. They rely on scientific studies of the water quality as a database. In their view, the road was simply a means to an important end. They are convinced that their mandate was clear: to provide potable water for the group. They can't understand the outrage of the second group. Many of this group have volunteered countless hours through the years for the practical maintenance of the roads, water system, fences, and governing system. This group is concerned with content goals and face saving. They argue that the content goals are the most important and that they did what they had to do (face saving).

2. The "road has to go" group: This group consists of a few older home owners and their adult children. The view of this group is that environmental concerns are primary. They will not tolerate compromise about the sensitive wetlands along the stream and feel outraged at the destruction of the most beautiful area of common property. They think the board acted without proper authorization by the membership and feel strongly that not only should the road never have been built but that it must be taken out and the area reclaimed. They prefer any solution, including boiling water for drinking, to the degradation of the environment. Many of this group will be second-generation home owners when they inherit the property from their parents. However, these group members have no vote in the association, since only property owners can vote. This group as a whole is concerned about appropriate process and has strongly held content goals.

3. The "we simply have to live with it" group: This group sees itself as the middle group between two extremes. Many of these people feel disappointed or angry about the gravel road and the fact that the water problem still is not solved. They

(continued)

Application 8.9 The Rainbow Development
Water Problem

want to support the elected board but don't like all the conflict and alienation in what used to be a very close and friendly group, which had potlucks, birthday celebrations, and outings together. Now that the road is in, they think it should be accepted and used to solve the water problem. This group is concerned with relationships and face saving for the board. They keep their private opinions, whatever they might be, to themselves. They look to the future.

Now that you have read "The Rainbow Development Water Problem," answer these questions:

- Specify (1) competitive, (2) collaborative, and (3) transformative approaches to defining this problem.
- How can concerns be addressed, relationships be enhanced, and solutions be found?
- What communicative moves from each of the three groups would enhance rather than destroy the ongoing relationships?
- If you were a negotiator for one of the groups, how might you approach the problem?

Competitive and Collaborative Phases

Negotiations are characteristically complex. Early in negotiations, it is common for the participants to have a fixed-sum assumption (Bazerman, Magliozzi, and Neale 1985). Bargainers can, regardless of their initial positions and approaches, move to integrative, or collaborative, outcomes (Tutzauer and Roloff 1988; Gulliver 1979; Lewicki and Litterer 1985). Many negotiations travel between cooperative and competitive phases, often returning to collaborative phases when someone stresses the gains to be had by both sides (Popple 1984; Holmes 1992). Sometimes dyads will reach an impasse, return to earlier phases of negotiations, and seem to regress (Holmes 1992). An example of "impasse dyads" is often found when couples are negotiating details of their divorce. Often, the couple will get stuck on one issue, such as how to work out holiday access to the children, then get so angry they will try to redo all the earlier negotiation, even agreements that had been problem free, such as division of furniture or where each partner would live. Skillful third-party help can often enable the couple to move out of the impasse.

> No matter how far down the wrong road you go, you can always turn back.

The central finding from phase research is that successful negotiations eventually move toward collaborative, or integrative, processes (Holmes 1992; Gulliver 1979). Further, collaborative and competitive processes can be seen as intertwined—as the participants utilize more competitive approaches, a natural tension builds to move toward collaboration (Putnam 1986, 1988). Usually the bargainers begin with a competitive orientation and, through the process of bargaining, move toward a collaborative stance (Jones 1988). The bargainers can be seen as moving from differentiation—stressing their differences with each other, attacking each other's positions, and venting emotions—to integration, or collaboration, in which the negotiators adopt a problem-solving orientation. These processes would look, sequentially, like this:

1. Extreme statements of positions.
2. Clashes about positions.
3. De-emphasis of differences and decreased use of antagonistic tactics (Jones 1988, 472).

An almost identical set of stages also has been specified:

1. Lengthy public orations characterized by a high degree of "spirited" conflict.
2. Tactical maneuvers and arguments for and against proposals.
3. Reducing alternatives to formal agreements (Putnam and Jones 1982a).

Note that these phases have been used in negotiations that resulted in agreements. Also, they are more characteristic of explicit bargaining situations, such as negotiations over contracts. There simply has not been enough research on implicit, informal bargaining processes to specify the phases they involve. Clearly, however, successful negotiations typically arrive at workable agreements by going through collaborative phases.

As noted previously, most inexperienced bargainers automatically assume a competitive stance regarding negotiations since they believe that "toughness" can only be achieved through competitive tactics. Since collaborative tactics generally have to be learned, people often have difficulty understanding them. Yet for negotiations to come to fruition, collaborative tactics have to be called on, or there is a strong possibility of negotiations breaking down and the relationship between the parties being damaged.

One's choice of negotiation strategies sets forces in motion that may be difficult to alter. For example, using pressure tactics increases competitiveness (Tutzauer and Roloff 1988); spirals of competitiveness tend to bring impasse (Putnam 1988b); competitive strategies lessen satisfaction with the process (Putnam and Folger 1988); and a competitive orientation coupled with time pressure secures poorer agreements (Carnevale and Lawler 1986). Basically, cooperative and competitive climates are self-reinforcing—competition encourages more competition and collaboration brings collaboration in return (Folger, Poole & Stutman, 2004, 2008); Carnevale and Lawler 1986; Pace 1988).

How, then, can one move toward collaboration during the negotiation process? Stick to principled negotiation, stay with your chosen role, and maintain optimism that a positive solution can be found. Once you begin succeeding while bargaining collaboratively, your hope and confidence will grow. In negotiation, as in all of conflict resolution, we have to learn to do what comes unnaturally.

❧Summary

Negotiation is one mechanism for solving ongoing conflicts with others and allows us to resolve everyday conflicts peacefully. The negotiation path to conflict management recognizes the stake that all parties have in their joint dispute. Negotiation occurs in everyday life, as well as in structured public arenas such as labor-management bargaining. Each culture, of course, utilizes negotiation in diverse ways.

At the heart of all negotiations are considerations of power. We can equalize power through destructive means or by effective argumentation. The two major types of negotiations are (1) competitive and (2) collaborative. There are assumptions, communication patterns, and downsides associated with each type of negotiation.

Principled negotiation is a collaborative approach that stresses seven principles for successful negotiation. We discuss both the mindset and specific words for being collaborative because often people have difficulty speaking in a collaborative way. We conclude the chapter showing that negotiations often pass between phases—beginning with a competitive tone and concluding with a collaborative tone. Successful negotiators in everyday life eventually collaborate with the other party, manifesting a relational orientation.

Key Terms

Use the text's Online Learning Center at **www.mhhe.com/wilmot8e** to further your understanding of the following terminology.

negotiation   244
even playing field   248
win/lose perspective   251
competitive negotiation   251
distributive bargaining   251
bargaining range   251
integrative or collaborative bargaining   256

collaborative negotiation   256
expanding the pie   258
nonspecific compensation   259
tradeoffs   259
cost cutting   260
bridging   260
principled negotiation   262

positions   262
interests   262
firm flexibility   262
multiple interests   263
BATNA   264
language of collaboration   265

Review Questions

Go to self-quizzes on the Online Learning Center at **www.mhhe.com/wilmot8e** to test your knowledge of the chapter concepts.

1. What is the place of negotiation in everyday life?
2. Explain how negotiation is part of conflict resolution.
3. Define negotiation.
4. How does negotiation fit between avoidance and domination?
5. What impacts do our cultures have on negotiation?
6. List destructive ways to equalize power.
7. How are arguments part of constructive negotiation?
8. List the assumptions and communication elements of competitive negotiation.
9. Describe the assumptions of collaborative negotiation.
10. List some collaborative communication moves.
11. What are the four key elements to principled negotiation?
12. Why are interests so important?
13. What is the difference between positions and interests?
14. List some questions you can use to find interests.
15. What might be some multiple interests you have in a current conflict?
16. Give some examples of collaborative language.
17. How do conflicts move through competitive and collaborative phases?

Chapter 9

Third-Party Intervention

~The Need for Third Parties

Conflicts often are so difficult that we turn to others for help. When you and your romantic partner are not talking, or at the other extreme, yelling at one another, outside help is needed. If your roommate and you have been arguing about rent payments for weeks on end, it may be time for outside help. If you have a family dispute that drags on for years, that is certainly a clear sign of the need for help. If you have a situation at work where you continually fight with your supervisor over your job assignments, it is time to ask for help. When talk is sarcastic, indirect, or defensive, special help may be needed. When you and your partner love each other but keep getting caught in the same destructive spirals, you should consider third-party help. Acquiring competent third-party help can stop destructive spirals and help you and your partner improve your relationship.

When we have conflict trouble, we can turn to friends, advisors, pastors, parents, co-workers, human resource personnel, coaches, counselors, mediators, lawyers—anyone who can help. Third-party help for you or others may be appropriate in situations such as these:

- Your roommate stops paying her share of the rent.
- A friend keeps using your clothes without permission.
- Your sister hangs up on every phone call and refuses to talk, after making bitter comments.
- You and your romantic partner are separating but neither of you wants to.
- You are a teacher and see your elementary students fighting during recess.
- Your workgroup stops meeting and no one cooperates.
- An employee is injured on the job and wants health benefits.
- Violence is beginning to erupt between two young men (Funk et al. 2003).
- Students are being harassed (Newman 2004).
- Two ranchers have a dispute over water rights that involves the entire community.
- A customer tries to return a defective product, but the retailer refuses to accept it.
- Only one worker, a relative of the supervisor, gets a raise. The rest of the employees protest by filing a grievance.
- An employee is fired and seeks redress (Bingham 2004).

These situations call for a variety of third-party interventions, ranging from informal intervention to formal intervention. You might become involved by (1) asking for third-party assistance for yourself or (2) helping a friend or co-worker find appropriate third parties.

Third-party activity is a normal part of everyday life. You may have a friend like Angela, for example, who often helps other friends to "talk it out" when there is a dispute. The third party may be a trained professional. Teachers separate students on the playground, ministers and counselors help families through crises, dormitory resident advisors help students, and mediators help married couples separate and divorce. Lawyers, judges, probation officers, hearings officers, union representatives, professional meeting facilitators, and coaches all help people work through their conflicts.

In this chapter, we will provide an overview of (1) **informal** and (2) **formal** intervention into disputes. For informal interventions (like helping friends, work associates, or family members), we will supply cautions about entering others' disputes and some guidelines for success. For formal interventions (using coaches, mediators, counselors, arbitrators, and the courts, for example), we will acquaint you with the various approaches so you can be an informed consumer of such services.

Advantages of Using Skilled Third Parties

A skilled third party is someone who is trained in intervention and does not have a vested interest in a specific outcome. Whether informal or formal, the goal of all intervention is to transform the conflict elements. The transformation may take many forms. It may

- Change the style of expression in the conflict.
- Alter the degree of interdependence between the parties.
- Change their perceptions or their goals so they are not seen as incompatible.
- Balance the power.
- Modify the actual or perceived **scarcity of resources.**
- Adjust the actual or **perceived interference** by the opposing parties.

Skillful intervention transforms the conflict so that issues can be put to rest and people can move on. After third-party intervention, co-workers may be able to speak to the boss directly instead of forming coalitions, and the boss may agree to give feedback in person instead of in writing. Parents may agree to help their 18-year-old daughter go to college in a different state, or a conflict over scarce parking space may be accurately understood as a relational conflict rather than a content conflict (parking space).

Informal Help

Most everyday conflicts are settled out of court or without the aid of a professional helper but with the assistance of friends, neighbors, and other natural helpers (McGillis 1981). These informal interventions serve "to interrupt a self-maintaining or escalating-malevolent cycle in one way or another and to initiate a de-escalating-benevolent cycle" (Walton 1969).

Informal third parties enter conflicts through diverse routes. A staff person may say, "What would you think about coming to the meeting Tuesday with Julie and Chris? I think we could use your level head." Parties may ask for help indirectly. A friend may call to discuss a potential romantic breakup and you guess he wants you to help out. Children, for instance, sense that parents will step into the role of a third party when they get beaten up on the playground, when "Jill won't give me back my teddy bear," or when big brother picks on them behind their parents' backs. The complaint, accompanied by anger or tears, serves as a request for help. The following are indirect cues indicating that your help may be needed:

Indirectly Asking for Help

1. A person seeks you out, and begins to cry while describing a situation.
2. A person shares private information with you.
3. A person indicates that a crucial decision is impending.
4. A person makes you understand that his or her life is not smooth, that distress is present, or that things seem out of control.
5. A person says "no one knows just how bad my supervisor is."

A teacher may notice that a student, usually happy and in love with life, talks with a very negative tone. A student may say, in a dejected tone, "They won't hire me. They don't think I have any useful experience." She may be indirectly asking for the teacher's help—hoping a phone call or letter of recommendation would help her get hired.

Conditions for Helping

If you want to help people resolve their conflicts, you must choose when to intervene, what your role will be, what your intervention style will be, and what skills you will bring to the conflict. Before you make a commitment to help, answer the following questions:

1. Are they ready for a third party? What evidence do you have to indicate readiness?
2. How do you know that they want *you* to help?
3. What skills prepare you to help them? Can you best help by referring them to someone else?
4. Are you biased, committed to one of the parties, grinding your own ax, or unable to help because of time, position, or other matters?
5. Can you say no? If not, then you are probably too involved in the conflict to be an effective helper. *Interesting*

Once you have answered these questions, take the time to think about the consequences of your intervention. Remember, someone else's problem is not necessarily your problem—you have a choice. If you think you have no choice, you cannot be useful as an informal intervener. For example, many people get involved in conflicts between their parents only to discover the futility of trying to solve marital problems not of their making. If you do not want to get involved but think that you should, your lack of enthusiasm will result in lessened energy, frustration with how hard it is for them to change, and ineffective intervention. If you don't want to help, don't.

If you do choose to enter the conflict, however informal or nonspecific that role may be, take special care to retain your neutrality. Informal third parties often take sides (Van de Vliert 1981, 1985). If one of the parties succeeds in allying with you, the resulting alliance lessens the other side's power in the conflict and creates a new issue in the conflict—that of **unfair bonding.** Consultants to organizations are trained to avoid such biased behavior, but friends and relatives may slip into taking sides only to find that their "help" makes the conflict worse. **Siding** with one party has these effects:

- Siding implies that the outsider adopts the win/lose thinking of the principal parties, which reinforces the destructive effects of such thinking.

- Siding creates a winner (the chosen party) and a loser (the rejected party), causing escalation by the rejected party.

- Siding increases the number of conflict participants.

- By adding additional unbalanced perceptions, siding complicates the conflict issues.

- The siding outsider increases the stake of the parties in the conflict outcome. (Adapted from Van de Vliert 1981, 497–498)

Siding with one conflict party, although not wise for an intervener, does have its place. If, for example, your close friend is breaking off a relationship with her fiancé, you may choose to side with her to give her support. Anything else would be unrealistic. However, you should be aware that siding with one of the conflict parties precludes you from being an effective neutral helper; you will become an additional party to the conflict. There is only one exception to this—when you are formally coaching someone behind the scenes, which we will discuss later.

When you refuse to take sides you can be an effective change agent. A new employee of a hospital was approached by persons on opposite sides of a conflict about nursing shift assignments. One side wanted nursing shifts decided by seniority and the other side by experience. The new nurse found himself being pushed toward the middle—both sides wanted him to persuade the other side of the rightness of their position. He wisely told all parties, "I am too new to have an informed opinion. Besides, I value my relationships with all of you. I prefer not to be involved with this problem." On a university campus, a faculty member's neutrality set the stage for an effective intervention. The faculty member heard from a student who wanted to graduate early and another faculty member refused to consider her petition to waive or substitute a required course. The neutral faculty member offered to intervene by privately asking the resistant faculty member to discuss the issue in a meeting. The intervening professor did not take sides; she provided a forum for handling the matter creatively, and the student was able to graduate at the preferred time.[1]

---

[1] The article "My professor is so unfair," can be found in Harrison, 2007.

If you are going to intervene, clarify any change in your role from your usual role with the conflict parties. If you have been a buddy, boss, romantic partner, co-worker, or casual acquaintance, any change in that role needs to be negotiated. For example, a 14-year-old girl, Toni, lived with a couple in their mid-50s who cared for her as foster parents. The state children's service worker, Anne, had functioned in the past as a person who found placements for Toni, certified potential foster homes for her, and provided her with ongoing counseling. Mr. and Mrs. Black began to quarrel about whether to continue providing care for Toni, since their own children were out of the home and they were beginning to want time without children. Mrs. Black wanted to wait until Toni graduated from high school to request another placement, whereas Mr. Black wanted Toni to move during the summer. Anne was able to act as a third party to their conflict, after making clear that her first loyalty was to Toni's best interests. Since all three people agreed on the interests, they were able, with Anne's help, to find a solution to the conflict. If Anne had not clarified her role, which involved not taking sides with either parent and keeping Toni's interests prominent, both parents would have tried to form a coalition with Anne.

Cautions about Informal Intervention

Several cautions are in order about helping others in conflict:

1. *Be certain the parties want help* in managing their conflict. Did they agree for you to help them, or did you get involved because you felt uncomfortable?

2. *Avoid becoming "the enemy."* The parties might temporarily bond with each other and exclude you. Remember, you are entering an already existing system. Your focus, even if you are taking an informal role, is the relationship. If you become a common enemy by pushing the parties too hard, they will 'gang up' on you.

3. You must constantly *remain aware of coalitions*. Any time a third party enters into an existing relationship, the relationship is changed. Once you coalesce with one person, you lose your helpful role and weaken the relationship between the two parties. Because you cannot predict ahead of time exactly what will happen with your involvement, you must monitor the interactions to watch for shifts in coalitions. If you begin thinking, "No wonder he is struggling with her; she is completely unreasonable," you have formed a coalition and lost your effectiveness.

4. *Once the work is completed, the third party exits from the system*. The goal is to train the parties to manage their own relations. A helper who does not work himself or herself out of a job is not doing the job properly; the parties must become independent of the third party. A helper who improves the parties' relationship and helps them solve the topic issues gives the conflicting parties a real gift.

Application 9.1   My Informal Role

1. List skills you have developed that are useful for helping others. What skills do you lack at this point?

2. Discuss when you have effectively helped others.

(continued)

Application 9.1   My Informal Role

3.   List the times you have tried to help others and your efforts backfired.

   a.   How did the parties ask, directly or indirectly, for help?
   b.   What role did you negotiate ahead of time?
   c.   To whom were you closest? Whom did you know the best?
   d.   What process did they agree to before you intervened?
   e.   How could you tell that your "help" was actually making things worse?

4.   What did you learn from those experiences about being an informal third party?

Formal Intervention

The Intervention Continuum

Formal intervention requires specific training or education. Usually, in Western culture, the formal third party is paid, such as in counseling, mediation, legal interventions, or organizational consultation. However, in some cultures and subcultures of the United States, formal intervention is not paid. Some Native American, Cambodian, Malaysian, and many other cultures use formal intervention to restore peace and justice in the culture. Some religious organizations use a form of unpaid intervention, such as convening a group to decide or advise on an issue. In mainstream Western culture we no longer have access to such traditional councils. Thus, we turn more and more to paid, formal intervention.

Formal intervention modes differ according to the degree to which conflict parties determine the final outcome. In some forms of third-party intervention, the conciliator serves as a facilitator to parties who make their own decisions, whereas other forms impose a resolution to the conflict upon the parties.

Modes of intervention

High ↑

Degree to which
the conflicting
parties determine
the solutions to
their conflicts

Low ↓

- Coaching
- Facilitation
- Mediation
- Counseling and therapy
- Organizational development
- Conciliation
- Quasi-judicial bodies
- Informal tribunals
- Arbitration of all types
- Criminal and civil justice system

In many interventions, combinations of these approaches are used. For instance, both mediation and arbitration can be used by the third party (Buzzard and Eck 1982). Similarly, contracts between labor and management often specify a sequence of steps such as (1) negotiation, (2) mediation, and, if necessary, (3) arbitration. Divorce mediation sometimes uses arbitration as an option (Coogler 1978; Moore 1986).

When the Parties Decide

Coaching

Coaching is a dispute resolution option for those who are unable or unwilling to engage in mediation (Jones and Brinkert 2008). It requires a systems level of thinking and is designed to empower clients to handle conflict. Further, it should be integrated with other approaches. For example, many parties cannot go directly into mediation—they need coaching behind the scenes before entering into mediation or other forms of resolution.

Jones and Brinkert (2008) advance a relational coaching, consistent with the principles we have outlined in this book. They state that the coach helps people with identity, emotion, and power. In our own work as mediator and therapist, we are often asked to coach people through a conflict situation. For example, a good friend, Peter, has two sons who are entering their teen years. Peter's wife died a year ago; one of his wife's sisters, Julianne, explodes at him, blames him for his wife's death (she had cancer from unknown causes), and sends him vitriolic e-mails. Peter asked for coaching on how to respond to Julianne. He is not interested in any joint meetings with her or mediation or counseling—he just wants to know how to deal with her anger in the most productive way. Such is the province of coaching—to help Peter deal with the ongoing dispute in the extended family.

The coach will help parties deal with strong emotions (their own and others'), and assist the person with a more productive response, whether they meet with the other party or not. Take the case of the new CEO, Carl, of a large company. When he gave his "all hands" speech (a presentation to the entire company) at the beginning of his term, people all politely applauded and went on their way. Then, a day later, a long-term and competent employee sent him an email saying, "Ah, what a bunch of B.S.—you will be just like all the other CEO's we have had here." As Carl said, "He acted like there wasn't a human being on the other end of the e-mail." Carl asked for coaching help. After getting all the details, the coach suggested that Carl make sure he was in a good mood, walk to the other building and knock on the employee's door. When the employee saw Carl at his door, he almost had a heart attack—and jumped back. Carl then said, "I could tell from your e-mail that you are concerned about this company. I would like to hear more about what works and doesn't work for you here." The employee talked for almost an hour. Then, five years later, that same employee stood up after another "all hands" presentation by Carl and said, "When Carl first came here I thought he was just like all the rest. I have come to realize that he has a good system in place and really cares about employees—thanks, Carl." Such is the potential power of coaching.

Mike is a recent college graduate, in his first job. He recently found out that his father remarried suddenly, without introducing his new wife to his two grown sons and their wives. Mike came into counseling for one main reason—he wanted to decide how to deal with his father and his new wife. His dad pressured him to visit over Christmas, but Mike felt angry and uncomfortable. Previous conversations with his father, on the phone, ended up with his dad telling him to "deal with it" and stop acting like a child.

The counselor, who knew this would be a short-term coaching relationship, helped Mike decide what to do, for now. Mike decided to write his father a letter and tell him that he was not going to come for Christmas, and that he felt pressured to just go along with a decision that felt disrespectful to him and his brother. Mike continued, in the letter, to say that he agreed that his father had the right to do as he pleased, but that Mike also had the right to wait until he felt more comfortable with his dad's decision, and when he did not feel pressured. He ended by saying that he wanted an ongoing relationship with his father, and might come to like and get to know his wife, but that the timing would need to be something they all decided together. Mike was not interested in devoting more time and money in trying to understand his father or his own reactions. He wanted to deal honestly with the present situation without cutting off future contact. He hoped the letter would be a start in the right direction.

Prerequisite skills for effective coaching are explained in the Comprehensive Coaching Model (Jones and Brinkert 2008). They are the typical skills we have been writing about throughout this book, such as emotional intelligence, listening openly, reframing (like the coach helped Carl do), and supporting the identity of the other.

Unlike when a friend says, "don't take that junk—fight back," a coach looks for opportunities to teach, solve problems, and transform conflicts. Coaching helps people learn to be collaborative. It is a powerful set of techniques for helping parties work with conflict, with or without facing the other party. Coaching is becoming a recognized profession, with certification programs and supervision ensuring quality of coaches.

Counseling

Individuals, couples, and families often seek the services of a professional counselor or therapist to help them resolve disputes. The counselor must have certain, usually licensed, credentials and is paid for her or his services. Counseling might entail (1) meeting with one person individually and/or (2) meeting with two people, or an entire family system. The counselor focuses on all the issues at stake—the emotional and relational issues in addition to the topic dispute, which often simply serves as the "presenting problem." Sometimes, the conflicting parties, such as a committed couple, want to move to forgiveness and reconciliation, but not always.

The counselor might help the parties with personal issues and relational issues. Depending on the counselor and the parties to the conflict, the focus may include psychological issues such as depression, bipolar disorder, anxiety issues, personality disorders, or substance abuse. The counselor might stress the intersection of the personal issues of each party with relationship issues. A professional counselor usually does not control the conversation process in the same way that an arbitrator or mediator might, yet has the task of helping the individuals and the system attain improved functioning, insight, and prevention of future conflict.

When might you seek counseling for a conflict situation? When your own feelings are so highly engaged that you cannot be productive, or use effective communication, you might seek help. When you are very low power in a relationship you may need an advocate. A counselor can help you with self-confidence. When you are suffering emotionally or relationally, and feel isolated, you might benefit from professional counseling. When you want to get counseling help for relationship aspects, remember that you do not have the power to coerce others to enter counseling with you. You can only invite them, and continue to seek help for yourself.

Mediation

The mediator has no power to render a decision or impose a solution. Instead, the mediator helps the parties themselves to work out their differences and to construct a mutually acceptable solution.

—Gray, *Collaborating: Finding Common Ground for Multiparty Problems*

Mediation helps the parties negotiate to reach agreement. Mediation is the "art of changing people's positions with the explicit aim of acceptance of a package put together by both sides, with the mediator as listener, suggestion-giver, the formulator of final agreements to which both sides have contributed" (Alper and Nichols 1981, 31). As Keltner (1983) wrote, "Your job is to facilitate the parties to the dispute to reach an agreement themselves."

The mediator controls the process—not letting the participants interrupt, call names, or engage in other destructive moves. But the mediator does not control the outcome—the solutions to the dispute come from the parties themselves. Sometimes mediators engage in "shuttle diplomacy," keeping the parties separate and bringing messages back and forth. Separation of the parties is common in intense disputes such as war, court-ordered divorce mediation, or other situations in which the parties are unable to be in the same room with each other. However, most mediation is performed with the parties in the same room, with the mediator controlling the communication process for mutual benefit.

The structure of communication in mediation is shown in figure 9.1. The mediator is there to facilitate communication between the parties—not render a judgment. In true mediation, the mediator works to help the parties communicate, and is not a final judge or arbiter. As a result, as figure 9.1 demonstrates, the mediator is present to serve the parties.

Figure 9.1 Mediation (the solid lines indicate flow of communication)

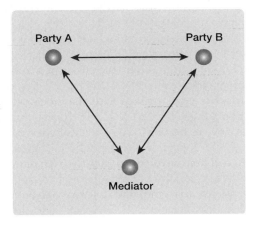

The process of mediation assumes that conflict is inevitable and resolvable. It further assumes that people in a conflict have enough common interest to reach an agreement and that the parties are responsible for settling their own conflict. It assumes that the parties' solutions will be more responsive to their needs than a settlement imposed by a third party (Moore 2003).

Advantages to Mediation   Mediation brings distinct advantages to the management of conflict. First, because it relies on the parties' active negotiation and involvement, it promotes a mutual stake in resolution; therefore, solutions are more likely to be carried out by the parties. The agreement is theirs, not imposed, and as a result there is no "loser" who feels compelled to strike back. The parties created the conflict, and they work for its solution. Their active involvement is a source of mutual empowerment; they take ownership of the conflict and, with the mediator's assistance, impose some limits on the process. In most mediation, the parties "have had some sort of prior relationship that will continue long after the dispute has been resolved" (Alper and Nichols 1981, 13; Kelly 2004).

Second, since mediated agreements represent the work of the parties, the solutions are more likely to be integrative and creative (Billikopf, 2009). The parties know better than any outsider what will work for them, and with the assistance of the mediator, they can craft unique solutions that work for them. An example of this is two businessmen in a mediation. When they first entered, Nick demanded that Paul pay him $60,000 for his part of their business that Paul developed in Hawaii without Nick's input. Had they gone to court or arbitration, they would have "settled" for some amount between $0 and $60,000 (probably $25,000 to $35,000). They would have ruptured their business relationship and friendship. During mediation it was discovered that Nick really wanted (1) to be included and involved and (2) to be valued by his partner for his selling skills. They agreed to have Paul send Nick and Nick's wife twice a year to Hawaii, where Nick would train Paul's salespeople free of charge. This integrative and creative solution never would have happened in adjudication or arbitration.

Third, as this example also illustrates, mediation helps the parties meet their underlying interests rather than fight over positions. Nick's real needs were for involvement and being valued, not money. Fighting over the position of $60,000 would not have kept the business partnership together, and would have obscured the underlying interests. Often, someone wants an apology rather than money.

Fourth, mediation is usually cheaper than adjudication or arbitration. For instance, in one study of 449 cases mediation settled 78 percent of them with an average cost of $2,750, compared to $11,800 for arbitration (Brett, Barsness and Goldberg 1996). The settlement rates for different types of mediation vary but are generally high (Kelly 2004).

Fifth, mediated parties are more satisfied with the process than are participants in adjudication or arbitration. All you have to do is talk to someone who has gone to court and ask, "How was that process for you?" You will hear frustration, blame, and anger. In contrast is a couple whose divorce was successfully mediated some years ago. They remain satisfied as their children have grown and their circumstances changed. They had two young girls and were committed to some form of co-parenting. Since the father planned a move to the West Coast, they had to work out living arrangements, child support, and travel and holiday agreements. Ten years later, the couple came back to the original mediators for help with a problem that developed when the girls went to college. As they called for an appointment, the wife said, "We didn't dare fight. We've told everyone how great this process is, so everybody is looking to us to see how we will do. We *have* to work it out."

The mediation process is becoming more widely available. For example, more than 10,000 schools now have peer mediation programs (Kowalski 1998). Many communities provide nonprofit agencies or groups who train people to be volunteer mediators, or who assist in court-mandated mediation of child living arrangements (Hedeen 2004). Community disputes often are mediated by a neutral party (Alberts et al. 2005a). Neighborhood associations use volunteer mediators to resolve local disputes, centered on such things as zoning violations, rental problems, pet problems, and traffic concerns, as well as more serious issues such as theft and safety.

Limitations to Mediation   Limitations to mediation do exist. First, not all conflict parties can agree to work through their conflict with the "enemy." They may either not want to talk openly about their difficulties with the other or not want to be in the presence of the other person. Many conflicts escalate to the point where conjoint constructive work is not possible. The conflict may be so protracted that the only solution is a win/lose structure in which an outside party decides. In addition, if someone thinks he or she can win by going to court, that person is less likely to want mediation. For example, in one study of couples who either did or did not choose mediation during their divorce, the man's perceived chances of winning in the adversarial system affected his willingness to try mediation (Pearson, Thonnes, and Vanderkooi 1982). Furthermore, attorneys who do not favor mediation will not refer clients to mediation. Attorneys who have not been exposed to non-adversarial methods of conflict resolution are less likely to refer clients to mediation.

Mediation may not be appropriate for certain types of relationships (Cloke, 2001). Mediation involves considerable commitment to working on the conflict. However, many parties are not prepared to reinvest in a relationship that has been problematic for them; they would rather try other routes to settlement or just continue the conflict. For example, Kressel et al. (1980) discovered that enmeshed couples were so intertwined in their dynamics that mediation was not successful for them. Similarly, couples with weak relationship bonds are often not good candidates for mediation. Both too much involvement and too little involvement with the other work against mediation.

Another limitation of mediation is that when one person, usually the woman, has been abused physically or emotionally, she may not be able to speak up with enough authority in mediation to generate options, argue for her perspective, and avoid being manipulated. Even when no overt abuse has occurred, many women are not able to negotiate with the person they once loved (and may still love) even if the relationship is breaking up. Some women try to work on the relationship as it is breaking up, sometimes out of concern for the children, but sometimes because of cultural conditioning. Such power imbalances can also happen in the workplace, where the woman is not able to stand up to supervisors and push for what she wants.

The final limitation of mediation is that involvement in mediation is not worth the effort. Many small disputes may be more efficiently handled by third-party adjudication, such as by small-claims court or a justice of the peace, than by the disputants trying to work with each other. The conflict may not be serious enough to warrant "working through" by the conflict parties.

Mediation Settings   Mediation may be applied to a wide variety of settings and disputes. It has been used successfully in such diverse arenas as

- **Business disputes**
  - partnership concerns
  - contract disagreements
  - management team disputes
  - entire work groups split into coalitions
  - employee grievances
  - sexual harassment
  - employee to employee disputes
- **Domestic disputes**
  - separation and divorce
  - estate distribution after a death
  - parental conflicts
  - parent-child concerns
  - disputes between romantic partners who are splitting up
  - grandparental visitation of children
- **Educational settings**
  - disputes over grades or treatment in class
  - relationships between students and other students
  - student-faculty relationships
  - faculty-to-faculty conflicts
  - faculty-administration disputes
- **Community/neighborhood disputes**
  - barking dogs
  - property line disputes
  - small claims
  - landlord-tenant disputes
- **The criminal justice system**
  - juvenile court situations
  - VOR (victim-offender restitution)
  - treatment in detention facilities
- **Labor-management conflicts**
  - contract disputes

work rules

fringe benefits packages

- **International conflicts**

    border disputes

    rights of citizens traveling

    shared resources such as bodies of water

    land ownership

    wars

Community mediation programs continue to expand across much of the United States, with high rates of settlement success. In Massachusetts, New York, North Carolina, and other states, the success rates for mediating community disputes range from 75 to 95 percent (Umbreit 1995, 59). Community centers typically rely on volunteers who are trained by the local dispute resolution center. Community mediation programs offer excellent training, supervision, and guidance, as well as opportunities to help others resolve disputes. Complaints range from noisy neighbors to "He took my parking space"—almost any issue one can imagine that arises in a neighborhood. You can contact your local mediation center where you might volunteer and receive training.

Schools, ranging from elementary schools to universities, are using considerable amounts of mediation (Association for Conflict Resolution 2004, AC Resolution, 2007). Many grade schools, middle schools, high schools and universities have instituted programs of mediation and standards for programs have been specified (Association for Conflict Resolution, 2007a). When it is a "peer mediation" program, the party's peers will help solve disputes ranging from playground difficulties to teacher-student problems. As an example of peer mediation, here are some tasks for fourth- and fifth-grade mediators when they see a conflict beginning:

1. When you see a conflict brewing during recess or lunch, introduce yourself and ask both parties if they want to solve their problem.

2. If they do, go to the area designated for solving problems. Explain and get agreement to the four basic rules: (a) agree to solve the problem, (b) don't call each other names, (c) do not interrupt, and (d) tell the truth.

3. Decide who will talk first. Ask that person what happened and how he or she feels, using active listening skills to repeat what is said. Do the same with the other person.

4. Ask the first party and then the second party for alternative solutions.

5. Work with the students toward a solution that they both think is good.

6. After the agreement is reached, congratulate the parties and fill out the Conflict Manager Report Form. (Umbreit 1995, 78)

School mediation programs have had considerable success (Kowalski 1998). Of 137 disputes between students in Honolulu, 92 percent resulted in complete agreement, and after the institution of peer mediation in New York schools, suspensions decreased by more than half. Clearly, school mediation is a viable form of third-party intervention for a variety of disputes (Umbreit 1995; Burrell and Cahn 1994). In the university and college setting, campus mediation centers deal with disputes over grades and behavior in classrooms, dorms, and married-student housing. Some of the centers provide family mediation services to students as well.

Family mediation takes many forms, the most common application being separation and divorce. With almost half of all marriages ending in divorce and the pain of going through the court system all too evident, mediation of separation and divorce is becoming increasingly common. It is not a replacement for the legal process but an adjunct to it. By law, the judge retains all the authority to decide the details of a divorce, but a cooperative couple that comes to a judge with a fair agreement will find the process much easier than trying to "prove the other one wrong." The couple, with the mediator's help, fashions (within the constraints of the law) an agreement that will work best for their unique situation. The acrimony, lingering conflict, and repeated trips to court by couples choosing the legal adversarial approach have catalyzed the mediation movement. One study concluded the following after examining mediation in divorces:

Read

> Despite the high levels of stress, anxiety, and fear associated with the breakup of a marriage, the vast majority of the parties in mediation believed that their needs and interests had been considered by the mediator and that the agreements reached in mediation were substantively fair to both parties, and they recommended the mediation process to others. Long-term satisfaction with the agreements was demonstrated by the continued compliance with the original agreements and changes by mutual consent, modifications that were reached through constructive private discussion or by a return to mediation. (Meierding 1993, 169)

In the family context, family business and estate mediation are becoming more popular. When a family owns a small business, for example, and the time comes for Mom or Dad to retire, mediation involves all family members in the decision making so options can be charted that work best for all. Whether it is the family pharmacy, ranch, or Subway® franchise, (1) topic, (2) relationship, (3) identity, and (4) process issues need to be carefully addressed. Mediation provides a framework for discussing important family issues, in addition to the usual issues of taxes, estate planning, and control of decisions. With mediation, all the TRIP issues can be brought to the surface and negotiated, serving the entire family. The following article demonstrates the advantages of using mediation in estate planning.

The Family Estate

Reader: My mother, in her late 70s, is worried about her fairly sizable estate. It includes real estate, stock, and our long-time family cabin in the mountains. She wants to do the "right" thing for her three grown children and their grown families so we won't fight or bicker after she's gone. She vividly remembers a nephew who, after her father's death, broke into the family house and took one of his guns. After 25 years, the family still talks about it! Should Mom think about using mediation?

(continued)

The Family Estate

Mediators: Absolutely. The two biggest mistakes people make about their estates, as well as in other types of mediation, are (1) not preplanning and (2) not dealing with relationship issues.

One cannot, should not, and must not try to pass on a sizable estate without specialized legal help. Estate and tax laws are complex and impose severe consequences for the unprepared (read "$$$"). Issues abound, such as whether to create a trust, if so, what kind, and how to handle the $10,000 annual gift exemption. These "content" issues need careful thought and expert advice. Equally, however, your mother dares not neglect the relational issues in her family—how she and the three children react to the content issues. Before, during, and after consulting with attorneys, she should listen to and address the concerns of each person affected. Current research starkly paints the picture.

If one tries to plan an estate using only legal and financial advisors, the children left out of the discussion will react negatively regardless of the elegance of the plan. Just ask families who've tried to craft even the most thorough estate plan without involving all the impacted players—smoldering resentments and "what ifs" remain. In the safe environment of mediation, both the content and relational issues can be put on the table and examined. Assumptions about people's needs and feelings can be checked out, before they're locked into the text of a will. Creative problem solving can be used to derive solutions that work for the whole family. We have seen cases of people (1) retaining the family business intact in the face of children reluctant to participate and (2) passing on financial assets in ways that work for everyone. Find a competent, experienced mediator to work with the family and with your estate lawyer, and your chances of somebody stealing the guns will diminish.

Reprinted from *The Missoulian*, September 23, 1996 by Bill Wilmot and Roy Andes.

Mediation can be used in conjunction with counseling to resolve adolescent-parent conflicts—those natural calamities that arise in most families. Whereas for some, adolescence is a minor inconvenience, for others it is "a painful exhausting journey that cuts into the bond between parent and child" (Umbreit 1995, 116). A trained mediator can help both the adolescent and the parent(s) develop workable agreements to get them through this often contentious stage of family life. Whatever the need for family mediation, mediators who are members of the Association for Conflict Resolution follow specific standards for practice.

Victim-Offender Restitution (VOR) is a specialized form of mediation designed for cases in which someone is guilty of a crime (Umbreit, Coates, and Vos 2004). Rather than resolving the issue by involving the defendant and the court system, VOR brings the victim into the process. Both the victim and the perpetrator tell their story and review options for compensation of the victim. Such an approach allows the victim participation, brings the reality of the crime home to the offender, and sets the conditions under which the offender can compensate the victim for what was done. It recognizes the victim's rights, allows the offender to take responsibility for what he or she has done, and provides avenues for restoration.[2] A poignant example of a creative use of mediation for a minor crime is presented in the box.

"I Stole Your TV"

An example illustrates the constructive use of mediation to achieve both symbolic and actual restitution. An elderly woman returned to her home one afternoon to find her television set gone. The youth who had stolen it was apprehended and admitted that he had sold the set to a fence. Rather than face a fine or continuance under probation, the defendant, in the presence of the mediation board and of the victim, sat down to work out a nonpunitive resolution to submit to the judge for his approval. The woman broke down in the course of telling the boy, "I watch television all day. This is all I do. I watch 16 hours a day. You have taken the heart of my life away." Confronted with personal implications of his act, the youth agreed to accept a job in order to buy the widow a new set. In addition, he agreed that he would accompany her to the bank to cash her weekly check and escort her to the market to do her shopping. A postscript to the case reports that after inviting the boy to have coffee with her, the woman learned from him that his mother had died and that he lived in an uncongenial relationship with his father and brother. Thereafter these Saturday morning coffee hours became a weekly feature. The closing entry reports that the boy had volunteered to paint the woman's kitchen.

Source: Alper and Nichols 1981, 146–147.

Mediation is used in the business setting as well. When a dispute arises between two co-workers, between a supervisor and an employee, or within a self-directed work team, mediation allows the parties to address the issue in a confidential way. Advantages to using mediation in the workplace include the following:

- Mediation reduces the cost of protracted disputes.
- Mediation increases everyone's satisfaction with the outcomes of the dispute.
- Mediation enhances relationships among people.
- Mediation reduces the recurrence of conflict. (Yarbrough and Wilmot 1995, 3)

Some examples of the use of mediation in business settings are as follows: A wife and husband were co-owners of a business, and he took out loans against the business without consulting her. With the ongoing help of the mediator, they restored their working relationship, got their employees out of the middle of their struggles, and began cooperating fully with each other. In another case, a male supervisor in a large institution was investigated by the personnel office for sexual harassment. After he was found not guilty of harassment, something had to be done to re-establish the working relationship between him and his female administrative aide. The mediator worked with them to (1) set clear boundaries on appropriate behavior on both their parts, (2) stop "end runs"

---

[2]Good reviews of VOR can be found in Umbreit (1995) and in a special issue of *Mediation Quarterly* (vol. 12, no. 3, 1995).

to higher authorities, and (3) establish clear protocols for communication behavior in the office. These are samples of the kinds of disputes that can be successfully handled via mediation. Yarbrough and Wilmot (1995) provide numerous examples of the mediation in diverse organizational disputes ranging from employee-employee disputes to disputes within management teams.

Mediation: Agreement or Transformation? Mediators' views of the mediation process differ on two primary points: (1) what issues are tackled in sessions and (2) what the goals are for the mediation. Some mediators (usually those with technical and/or legal training) will only mediate on the topic or content issues. For example, many legal jurisdictions have a "settlement week" when they convene groups of attorneys to mediate cases that are backlogged on the court calendars. Usually, the process used is **"shuttle diplomacy,"** keeping the parties separate and going back and forth with proposals. This type of mediation is usually quite different from, for example, family mediation that deals with topic, relationship, identity, and process issues where the parties are together a good portion of the time. Both types of mediation have their place, but as a user of the services you should be aware that the mediators' views of mediation result in vastly different processes. A local attorney who was going to mediate between two different factions (an insurance company with an attorney and a tribal elder with a representative) called for advice. In the phone call, it became apparent that his only considerations were topic issues. The parties did settle the topic issues exclusively, primarily because of the natural empathy of the attorney, whom everyone saw as a warm and friendly person.

Disputants with an ongoing relationship do better when mediators expand the issues being considered. The results of research on family mediation are quite clear—when mediators bypass the relational issues and focus only on "facts," they have trouble obtaining agreement from the parties (Donohue 1991; Donohue, Allen, and Burrell 1988; Donohue, Drake, and Roberto 1994). Sustainable agreements take relationship and identity issues into account.

Mediators also differ on whether they search for agreement or transformation (Association for Conflict Resolution 2007b). Bush and Folger (2004) detail goals that range from getting agreement (problem solving) to transformation. Many mediators just want an agreement—to settle the conflict. Others want to see clients undergo transformation—a change in how they see themselves and the other.

Transformation occurs when clients experience empowerment and give recognition to each other. Clients are empowered when they more clearly realize their goals (empowerment of goals), become aware of a wider range of options (empowerment of options), increase their skills (empowerment of skills), gain new awareness of resources (empowerment of resources), and make conscious decisions about what they want to do (empowerment of decision making). As Bush and Folger note, "When these kinds of things occur within relationships, the party experiences a greater sense of self-worth, security, self-determination, and autonomy" (87). In a similar vein, one gives recognition by (1) having the desire to recognize the other, (2) thinking about giving recognition, (3) giving recognition in words, and (4) giving recognition in actions. When these things occur, "The party realizes and enacts his capacity to acknowledge, consider and be concerned about others" (91).

The "just get agreement" problem-solving approach to mediation, Bush and Folger argue, is more aligned with an individualistic world view, in which we see ourselves as separate entities. On the other hand, the transformative view has as its underpinnings a relational view—that we are all interconnected and part of an organic whole. For an overview of these two world views and how they might affect one's mediation, see Bush and Folger (1994) and Wilmot (1995).

Mediation Process and Skills For mediation that includes more than the just the topic dispute, the mediator needs to have an expansive set of skills to control the process of communication, affirm both parties, and move the parties toward creative content and relational solutions, all the while staying within legal and cultural parameters.[3] Yarbrough and Wilmot (1995) specify the primary skills that are necessary at each stage of the mediation process. The mediator needs to have both "reflective" skills and "directive" skills. The parties need to tell their stories, and later move toward solving the joint problems.[4]

The stages of mediation are as follows:

- Entry
- Diagnosis
- Negotiation
- Agreements
- Follow-up

When one follows these steps in mediation, key tasks are accomplished at each step. The mediator wants to do the following things at each stage:

Entry

1. Explain the process.
2. Clarify your role and establish your credibility.
3. Explore consequences of not proceeding.

Diagnosis

1. Gather data with interviews and observations.
2. Look at the conflict elements:
   - Topic
   - Relational
   - Identity/face-saving
   - Procedure
3. Not rush to solutions.

Negotiation

1. Create a safe setting.
2. Establish common ground.

---

[3]For ongoing research and theory on mediation, consult issues of *Conflict Resolution Quarterly*. For example, vol. 22, number 1–2, Fall–Winter 2004 assesses the entire field of conflict resolution.

[4]See Winslade and Monk, 2001 and Kellett (2007) for an in-depth treatments of narrative story telling in mediation.

3. Set an agenda.
4. Balance power/enforce equal talk time.

Agreements

1. Generate different ways to meet interests.
2. Specify who, what, when, where, and how.
3. Agree on the form of the agreement—oral, written, legal.

Follow-up

1. Decide on exact follow-up procedure.
2. Notify other stakeholders of actions.
3. Reach agreement for how to deal with future disputes.
4. Embed the agreement within the system. (Yarbrough and Wilmot 1995)

The key to effective mediation is the level of competence of the mediator and the motivation of the parties (McGuigan and Popp, 2007). It is imperative, if you are to be a mediator or other type of third-party intervener, that you (1) receive extensive training in the necessary skills, (2) have the opportunity to try those skills with co-mediators or mentors, (3) be supervised by experienced mediators, and (4) continue your skill training and exposure to the literature on mediation. One cannot learn mediation skills solely from a book—they have to be practiced and critiqued. You should continually question all of your assumptions about what mediation is and what it can accomplish

Culture In different cultures, the intervention forms will differ from the above. The Hawaiin system of Ho'opopono is so important that it is discussed in depth in the final chapter on forgiveness and reconciliation. In addition, Ury (1990) studied the Kalahari bushmen, who follow a sequence for solving conflicts that taps the **"third force"**—the power of the community. The disputants actually meet in front of others and work the conflict through with the participation of others.

In every serious dispute between two individuals or groups, then, there is a third party at work. The third party is usually not a single individual but a collective of third parties: a third force of concerned relatives, friends, and elders. These third parties are typically "insider third parties" with strong ties to either one or both sides. There can be no private disputes of any seriousness because a dispute affects everyone.

The role of spirit or religion in resolving disputes is also recognized in many societies. In Malay society, for example, the spiritual elements play a prominent role, and the mediator spends informal time with the disputants in all kinds of contexts—attending family gatherings and weddings, for example. Native American cultures that keep their spiritual traditions alive continue to use spiritual force to resolve conflicts. Umbreit (1995) provides a comprehensive overview of some of these approaches and says this about some Native American traditions of dispute resolution:

> A model of mediation that is culturally sensitive to Native Americans and aboriginal people in Canada would be quite different from the dominant Western models. Such a model is likely to include consensus decision making; preference for co-mediation; separate premediation sessions with each person; involvement of elders in the mediation; presence of

chosen family members; circular seating; silence as comfortable; interruptions as inappropriate; nonlinear agenda; and the use of cultural metaphors and symbols. From this culture perspective, mediation occurs within a large cultural context. (37)

Just as we cannot import other cultural forms into mainstream Western culture without modification, neither can we export Western modes directly into other cultural situations. Similarly, within subcultures of Western society, one needs to adapt dispute resolution mechanisms to address their special situations. As Buitrago (1997) says, "with Hispanics the issue of trust is as essential for a positive outcome as for any conflictive party, but can be harder to obtain due to variables like discrimination and powerlessness" (16). Many community mediation centers solicit volunteers who are from unique groups as a way to bridge the gap between traditional mediation techniques and the special needs of subcultures.

Umbreit (1995) provides a step-by-step look at some of the central differences between mediation in modern cultures and mediation in traditional cultures. For example, in a modern culture, mediation might end with a written and signed agreement, whereas in a traditional culture, mediation often ends with participants giving their personal word.

When an Outsider Decides

The structure of communication differs profoundly between a mediation model and adjudication/arbitration. The mediator is there to facilitate communication between the parties. The mediator is the convener, the facilitator, but not the one who makes the decision. Figure 9.2 shows the communication linkages when arbitration or adjudication are used.

Figure 9.2   Lines of communication with professional advocates. (Solid lines indicate heavy communication; broken lines signify that the judge or jury is used as a reference point for the attorneys, often without direct communication; absence of lines signifies no direct communication.)

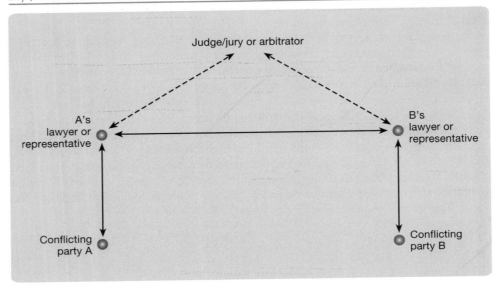

Arbitration: An Expert Decides

Arbitration and adjudication share an identical structure. In both, a third party is empowered to decide the outcome of a conflict. Parties who cannot resolve their conflict go before an arbitrator or judge/jury to solve their conflict. The arbitration might be around a labor contract, or between two business partners. Such contract disputes are a common form of "rights" arbitration; many managers and line workers routinely sign contracts with a clause calling for arbitration in the case of disagreement. (If you buy a car, have to make numerous repairs, and cannot get compensation from the dealer, you can ask for arbitration.) The arbitrator listens to both sides of the dispute, questions you and the car dealer (or your representatives), and renders a judgment. When the parties contractually agree to arbitration, the arbitrated judgment is enforceable in court. This process is called binding arbitration; the judgment is final.

Voluntary, or nonbinding, arbitration is sometimes used when the parties have not contractually agreed to binding arbitration. In nonbinding arbitration, if parties do not accept the judgment they then proceed to more arbitration or court.

Arbitration has some distinct features that make it useful as a form of third-party intervention. First, unlike adjudication, both parties enter into arbitration voluntarily. Second, it keeps one party from using passive-aggressive or impasse tactics on the other—sooner or later the issue will be resolved (Coogler 1978). Third, in many cases the arbitrator has special training in the content area of the dispute, such as in contract arbitration. When the arbitrator has special expertise in the content of the arbitration, he or she can often offer creative content solutions. Fourth, arbitration is readily available for use in situations in which the participants experience a communication breakdown and are no longer able to solve their own problems. Finally, arbitration is a process that can be used for a wide variety of content areas, ranging from contract disputes, medical malpractice, or landlord-tenant conflicts to domestic relations (Alper and Nichols 1981; Tyler 1987; Keltner 1994).

Arbitration does have some limitations. It tends to resolve conflicts solely on a content basis. Arbitration typically does not address the relational or face-saving aspects of the dispute, which is unfortunate because if parties can reach some accord in their relationship, the content issues can often be worked out. Arbitration reinforces the assumption that the parties cannot learn to manage their own difficulties—that only a third party can find a solution. Arbitration reinforces escalation as a legitimate tactic because intransigence will automatically bring in an outsider. Despite these disadvantages, arbitration is still a widely used alternative in conflict management because it binds parties procedurally to seek resolution. The prerequisite that parties agree to arbitrate (either contractually before the dispute begins or voluntarily once they are in conflict) enhances the chances for productive conflict management.

Adjudication: Judge or Jury Decides

Adjudication is a process in which parties present their case before a judge or jury. Adjudication assumes that parties are unable to solve their own conflicts, and a decision must be imported from outside (Wissler 2004). It is similar to arbitration in that a third party decides, but adjudication can be put into motion without mutual consent. In adjudication, you can sue the other party, forcing a decision whether the other wants to participate or not. Additionally, the officials of the criminal justice system can initiate charges, for instance, in cases of bodily assault, robbery, and related offenses. Adjudication assumes that a full argument of each side of a conflict will allow a judge or jury to make a just decision.

Once a suit has been filed with the court (or a petition filed for arbitration), lawyers or other advocates negotiate with each other, often instructing the conflict parties (the litigants) to not talk to each other. In this structure, the litigants set into motion a struggle that the lawyers act out. The original conflict metamorphoses into a conflict between the two lawyers (Irving and Bohm 1978). The attorneys become the prime players, who negotiate with each other, trying to estimate what the judge (or jury) will do with the case. Each lawyer's estimate of the judge's, jury's, or arbitrator's probable response becomes the basis of his or her negotiation strategy. The lawyers then try to persuade each other that their views are correct.

Court processes are fairly well known. One party files charges in court and the other must appear to respond. Between the time of the filing and the court date, the lawyers usually negotiate with each other regarding the case. For example, a landlord charges a tenant with violation of a lease agreement because the tenant signed a one-year lease and moved after four months. The landlord files suit to recover the rent for the eight months the renter was not living there. The two lawyers typically begin negotiations, calling and writing back and forth. If they are not able to reach settlement, the case goes to court; a judge or jury, after hearing testimony and evidence from both sides, may decide that the tenant must pay the eight months' rent, plus attorney fees. If no appeal is filed, the resolution process will end with the enforcement of the action. In a case like this, a justice of the peace may decide the case.

Litigating a dispute is both an alternative to negotiating and at the same time a way to force negotiation. Since most lawsuits are settled before trial (more than 90 percent, according to most studies), it is useful to view litigation not only as a way to "go to court" but also as a highly structured negotiation game, a "refined and constrained version of competitive bargaining" (Goodpaster 1992, 221). Filing a lawsuit forces a nonresponding party to attend to the complaint—avoidance is not possible once a suit is filed.

Advantages of Adjudication *Adjudication as a form of conflict management has a number of positive features.* "Equal protection of the law" allows everyone access to a resolution process and does not require the agreement of the other party. Therefore, adjudication serves as a power-balancing mechanism. For example, individuals can sue large corporations. In the case of abused or neglected children, a state agency can bring the parents before a court to determine their suitability for continued parenting. The children's representative, a guardian ad litem, acts as their agent. As Wehr (1979) notes, "Asymmetrical conflict is best resolved through intervention that empowers the weaker party" (37). A second positive feature of adjudication is that it provides rules for fairness, such as the admission of evidence. In some interpersonal conflicts, one party monopolizes the process, with few restraints. Process restraints are, however, built into the legal system. Each party has equal right to speak. The process rules allow both parties to fully explicate their positions. Third, the use of professionals to speak for the conflict parties is an advantage for parties who need assistance in preparation or presentation of their case. The trained legal expert can develop the best case for the client, ensure fair procedures, and set forth the case with vigor.

Finally, *adjudication serves as a backup for other conflict management procedures.* When arbitration, mediation, conciliation, and negotiation fail to produce agreement, the disputants can go to court. The appeal process allows people to present their case in a higher court if they dislike an earlier judgment. The moral as well as physical power present in our judicial and criminal justice systems provides a last-resort option when necessary.

Limitations of Adjudication   The judicial system also has some limitations in dealing with conflict. First, it has been overused and, as a consequence, is overburdened and misused. Former chief justice Warren Burger, referring to the legal profession, said, "The obligation of our profession is to serve as healers of human conflicts" (Ray 1982), but "suing has become an American parlor game" (Marks 1981). As a result, there is an "unprecedented demand upon the judicial system, leading to considerable frustration and delay . . ." (Sander 1977, 2). Guarantees of speedy justice are difficult to receive; delays of as much as two years between filing and first court appearances are common. Because the judicial system has been used and talked about so much, many individuals automatically think of it as the way to "get even" for some wrong. They often do not realize they have chosen a mode of conflict resolution until "they find themselves caught up in it with apparently no way out" (Coogler 1978, 6). One legal scholar concludes, "It seems clear that it is simply too cumbersome and expensive for most (minor) disputes" (Sander 1977, 24). A continuing round of court battles in order to "win" can deplete almost anyone's finances.

A second disadvantage of using the legal system for conflict resolution is that *conflict parties no longer make their own decisions.* For example, in a dispute involving a community (such as one over an environmental issue), "Litigation takes the decision out of the hands of the communities who must live with its consequences" (Wehr 1979, 123). Similarly, if two people are involved in a protracted domestic dispute such as a contested divorce, the parties stop dealing directly with each other and the attorneys take over the negotiation process. Sometimes the conflict parties, after seeing the communication structure inherent in adjudication, decide to go a different route. For example, Sharon and her ex-husband, Ted, had been divorced for three years and were having difficulties agreeing on child visitation arrangements. They lived in different towns, and each had consulted an attorney about visitation options. One day in April, Sharon flew to Ted's city and called him, only to discover that his attorney had told him, "Don't talk to her, and hold out for all you can get." Sharon told Ted that she had received the same advice from her attorney. They realized that if they both followed their lawyers' advice, they would be in for a long court battle. The two of them wisely decided to empower themselves. They met the next day and worked out an agreement—though the process was difficult for them. They were the original parties to the dispute and were the ones who would have to live with the long-term results of a decision. Therefore, turning over the decision to their representatives wasn't desirable.

A final disadvantage of adjudication is that the *adversarial system operates on a win/lose set of conflict assumptions that encourages escalation tactics* (Menkel-Meadow 1986; Hartje 1984). Often the lawyer is seen as each client's only champion in a hostile world. This belief promotes escalation when, in fact, it might not be necessary. In order to file an action, one has to blow up the magnitude of the conflict to a "You owe us" or "We'll get you" frame of mind; one tries to win at the other's expense. Filing an action is a signal of serious conflict, and unfortunately, filing sets an escalating process in motion. Because attorneys are charged with solely representing the interests of their client, "The client's interest is always perceived as being in opposition to the interests of the other party. The lawyer cannot and does not regard the parties as having a common problem which he or she will help resolve" (Coogler 1978, 7). The gathering of evidence for one side of the conflict disregards the relational and face-saving interests of both parties. While the parties cooperate by following procedural rules, this level of commonality does not open up creative outcomes. The escalating, win/lose atmosphere is often diffi-cult to disengage from once it has been set into motion. Suits and countersuits reflect continual escalation, with each "loser" trying again on some other basis until resources or options are exhausted.

Summary

This chapter gives an overview of resolution for-mats that may be helpful in resolving conflict, ranging from informal to formal modes. The pur-pose of intervening in conflict is to transform the conflict elements, thereby allowing for effective management. You can intervene informally, espe-cially when you are aware of the pitfalls. Formal intervention modes differ according to how much the original conflict parties determine the out-come. In both adjudication and arbitration, an outsider (judge, jury, or arbitrator) decides the out-come of the dispute. Mediation, on the other hand, involves the participants in the management of their own struggle. The mediator facilitates communication and helps the parties reach an agreement that will work for both of them. Vari-ous settings for mediation exist, ranging from fam-ily disputes to business concerns all the way to international conflicts. For instance, school medi-ation programs are useful throughout all levels of schools. Although some mediators want only agreement, others strive for transformation of the conflict parties. There are profound differences in third-party intervention across cultures. In collec-tivist cultures, people often use extended networks of people to help parties reach and keep agree-ments, whereas Western cultures generally do not.

Key Terms

Use the text's Online Learning Center at **www.mhhe.com/wilmot8e** to further your understanding of the following terminology.

informal intervention   272
formal intervention   272
scarcity of resources   272
perceived interference   272
unfair bonding   274
siding   274

coaching   277
counseling   278
mediation   279
Victim-Offender
Restitution   285
shuttle diplomacy   287

third force   289
arbitration (binding and
non-binding)   291
adjudication   291

Review Questions

Go to self-quizzes on the Online Learning Center at **www.mhhe.com/wilmot8e** to test your knowledge of the chapter concepts.

1. Explain the statement, "The goal of all intervention is to transform the conflict elements." Choose an example to illustrate the idea.

2. What are the effects of siding with one of the conflict parties?

3. What are cautions to remember when you are considering being a third-party helper?

4. How do coaches help with conflicts?

5. What is the role of counseling as informal intervention?

6. What are the interpersonal advantages and disadvantages of adjudication?

7. What are the interpersonal advantages and disadvantages of arbitration?

8. Explain how negotiation functions in all the forms of third-party intervention

9. Explain how the mediator controls the process but not the outcome of a conflict.

10. What are the advantages and limitations of mediation?

11. What are the basic tasks of mediation according to "stages of mediation"?

12. What are some differences between Western and traditional cultural expectations and procedures of mediation?

Chapter 10

Forgiveness and Reconciliation
by Gary W. Hawk, M. Div.
University of Montana

He has ruined my past. I'm beginning to toy with the idea of forgiveness so that I don't allow him to destroy my future as well.
—Lynn Shriner (Zehr 2001)

Forgiveness and Reconciliation in the Context of Interpersonal Conflict

In the preceding chapters of this book, we have sought to define conflict and help you understand different attitudes toward and metaphors for conflict. We have explored in depth the patterns of communication that contribute to destructive conflict or reverse the spiral and direct it toward mutual understanding and collaboration. We have offered tools for assessing conflict, feeling and negotiating our way through it, or seeking third-party assistance in processing it. In this chapter we seek to cross the threshold of all our best efforts to understand, process, or resolve conflict. Here we will define forgiveness and reconciliation, recognizing the growing body of literature on this topic. We will note common conceptions and misconceptions about forgiveness. We will explore both the internal process of forgiveness and the way forgiveness can be aided by communication interaction with the other person. We will describe various forms of communication, explicit and implicit, that aid the process. We'll explore the complex role of apology in the movement toward forgiveness, adding necessary words of caution. We also will offer words of hope, calling attention to both some exceptional individuals and key principles that inform and enhance the process of repairing relational wounds. Along the way we'll offer insights from the counselor's office, human history, film, and literature where the story of human conflict and efforts to repair the hurt we cause one another find creative means of expression. Some of these insights, perspectives, and examples flow from the writer's teaching of forgiveness and reconciliation at The Davidson Honors College, University of Montana and a practice in pastoral counseling.

Sometimes our best efforts to prevent conflict or engage in it constructively fail and we are left feeling betrayed, deceived, embittered, or isolated. Despite efforts to learn rather than defend, to tell and hear the truth about a situation, to refrain from retaliation or move empathically toward another person, the bonds of relationship suffer injury or break apart. A marriage once warmed by romance and shared history grows cold or shatters into pieces. An employee's legitimate needs or contributions do not receive the respect they deserve in the workplace. People who live next to each other may become caught up in cycles of increasingly destructive conflict. Rather than reverse the spiral, they begin to avoid one another, accuse one another of failing to honor agreements, or resort to courts of law in an attempt to solve a common problem. Bonds of friendship may weaken from neglect or indifference. A person's addictive behavior can cause emotional distress and financial loss for friends and family members to such an extent that they become lost to one another.

In an effort to find comfort or make sense of things, we sometimes tell ourselves stories about another person. One story can link up with another until a trajectory takes shape that seems impossible to bend in a more positive direction. Sometimes when hurt, afraid, or angry, we do things to other people that seem to violate all that we value and believe. In the process we become incomprehensible to ourselves. Sometimes people do things to us that leave us feeling victimized. An assault or theft, for example, may forever change our view of the world and our place in it. In the aftermath of the things that people do to us, we may wonder about forgiveness.

While forgiveness is not necessarily the last thing we try in a relationship, it often *follows* an effort, more or less determined, to alter the terms of a relationship that has become the source of disappointment, hurt, frustration, or harm (Stone, Patton, and Heen 1999, 140).

❧Some Definitions

What is **forgiveness**? Because of its complexity, forgiveness is defined many ways. These definitions represent *some* of the possibilities. In a conversation with Robert J. Lifton, journalist Bill Moyers quoted William Faulkner as saying that *"Forgiveness is giving up the idea of a better past."* In a volume that reveals how much attention has been given in recent years to the study of forgiveness, Thoresen, Harris, and Luskin say, "Interpersonal forgiveness can be seen as the decision to reduce negative thoughts, affect, and behavior, such as blame and anger, toward an offender or hurtful situation, and to begin to gain better understanding of the offense and the offender" (McCullough, Pargament, and Thoresen 2000). Emphasizing the emotional dimension of forgiveness, Kornfield (2001) says, "Forgiveness is the heart's capacity to release its grasp on the pains of the past and free itself to go on" (236). Sensing how the emotional, cognitive, and behavioral dimensions overlap, Morton Deutsch defines forgiveness as "giving up rage, the desire for vengeance, and a grudge toward those who have inflicted grievous harm on you, your loved ones, or groups with whom you identify. It also implies willingness to accept the other into one's moral community so that he or she is entitled to care and justice" (Deutsch and Coleman 2000, 58).

After studying clinicians who favored forgiveness as a therapeutic strategy, Martin and Denton (1998) concluded that forgiveness is "an inner process, central to psychotherapy, where the injured person without request of the other releases those negative feelings and no longer seeks to hurt, and this process has psychological and emotional benefits" (285).

❧What's to Forgive?

People harm one another not just by what they do to each other but also by what they say and don't say. Relational harm occurs across a wide spectrum from regrettable and hurtful messages to psychological and physical violence. While this array is an entire field of study in itself,[1] a brief review of the elements within it helps us to see very quickly some of the relational transgressions that pose the question of forgiveness.

---

[1]For a more complete treatment of different types of transgressions, see Metts 1994; Roloff and Cloven 1994; and Wilmot 1995.

In a study of "messages that hurt," Vangelisti (1994) describes a variety of "speech acts" that may cause harm. These messages include such things as

- *Accusations:* "You're a liar."
- *Evaluations or judgments:* "I knew you weren't up to the task."
- *Orders or commands:* "Get that done now!"
- *Advice:* "I strongly suggest that you get a job before the Christmas break."
- A *statement of preference or comparison:* "I wish you were more like your brother."
- A *disclosure of information:* "We've decided your job is not needed with the company."
- A *statement disguised as a question or opinion:* "When are you going to quit feeling sorry for yourself?"
- A *threat:* "If I ever see you with her again . . ."
- A *lie:* "I told you I'd quit drinking."

Metts (1994) adds to this list such things as

- *Blunders:* "How's your wife?" (not knowing that the person is divorced)
- *Direct attacks:* "Get out of my face, you mfer."
- *Group reference:* "Well, what did you expect from a white guy?"

These various hurtful and regrettable messages may offend cherished values, pollute the relational climate, make it difficult to maintain closeness, and, in some cases, become grounds for ending the relationship altogether.

Application 10.1   Case: At a Party

At an end-of-the-semester party in a local bar several friends are gathered around a table releasing the tension associated with final exams and demanding projects. A person across the table, someone you've always considered a friend but who does not know that your roommate is lesbian, says something blatantly offensive like, "I'm sick of dykes running that committee in the department." This comment takes you completely by surprise. It completely violates your standards for appropriate speech. You had no idea that this person harbored homophobic feelings. Upset by this remark, you consider your options. What are they? Do you try to break down your dismay privately or do you engage the person directly and try to confront this behavior? If you choose to confront the offense, what approach do you take? Do you get angry, take a moral position, try to educate the person across the table, or try humor? What do you choose and why?

Relationships are strained not just by hurtful messages but by unresolved or poorly resolved conflict. People can remain at odds with each other over money, the use of alcohol and other drugs, time spent with other family members, decisions around health care, family tragedy and loss. These difficulties are particularly common and painful in intimate relationships. Couples argue unproductively and hold each other hostage for years after an affair, or in the aftermath of disagreement about how to manage the multiple requirements of work, recreation, and parenting. For a more thorough treatment of these and other topics over the course of the lifespan of a couple relationship see Harvey (2004) and Waldron and Kelley (2008).

Stewart, Zediker, and Witteborn (2005) describe the damaging effects of deception, betrayal, and aggression. When someone deceives or betrays us, these relational transgressions can erode and jeopardize our sense of identity or well-being, not to mention the relationship. In addition, Cissna and Sieburg (Stewart 2002, 431ff) contend that "that disconfirmation" is a particularly damaging form of interpersonal behavior. A person is being disconfirmed when she feels invisible to another, unrecognized, unacknowledged, or without endorsement. When we are being disconfirmed it seems as though we do not exist in the eyes of someone else. Disconfirmation is a form of psychological abuse with potentially long-term consequences that may actually be more harmful than direct criticism or verbal attack.

Sitting at the far end of the spectrum, but *not* necessarily more damaging than these communicative ways of harming each other, is physical violence that we discussed earlier. It seems important, at the very least, to acknowledge that physical violence includes the neglect, and abuse, of children. In the relationship between adult men and women, we must recognize the prevalence of domestic violence. This expression of the harm we cause one another often follows verbal aggression. While the abuse of men does occur, men are more likely than women to engage in physical violence when faced with noncompliant behavior, challenges to their behavior, or questions about their authority. As the tragedy of domestic violence becomes less concealed, we learn that 40 percent of the women killed each year will be killed by a spouse or lover. For an excellent summary of these and related findings, see Lulofs and Cahn (2000, 324–325).

Whether harm comes to a relationship as the result of something as seemingly minor as a slight or blunder or as major as exclusion on the basis of race, sexual harassment, or an outright assault, all of the ways that people mistreat each other become the backdrop for a discussion of forgiveness. In the classroom and the therapist's office we have learned not to rank these relational transgressions but to recognize their impact.

We have also learned that it is relatively unimportant to distinguish between the effects of a conflict and the effects of an injury. Damage to the person(s) and damage to the relationship occur in both cases making the distinction seem vague. Both the effects of conflict and the effects of injury or violation give rise to questions about forgiveness and the more or less appropriate outcome of reconciliation.

The things that people say and *do* to one another inevitably cause us to ask, "Does this person know who I am?" "Does this person know the harm s/he caused?" "How am I ever going to forgive this person?"

Application 10.2   Case: A Long-Term Intimate Relationship

You have given your heart to a woman in a long-term intimate relationship, though it has not seemed quite right to marry. You have traveled together. You have supported each other as single parents of challenging children. You have both been active participants in

(continued)

Application 10.2   Case: A Long-Term Intimate Relationship

the local arts scene, enjoying film series, museum exhibitions and dancing in downtown clubs. For some time the relationship has not seemed as warm as it once was. Increasingly upset by this loss of honesty and deep sharing, you decide to ask your partner if he or she has sensed a difference in the depth of your relational intimacy. After carefully preparing for this conversation, you make arrangements to have this talk in a safe and private conversation. Your partner listens to your concerns but denies sensing any change in the relationship. Second-guessing yourself, you let the matter go, push your doubts into the background.

A couple of months later you meet your partner at a dance class you both enjoy. In the course of the routines you realize that your partner is unusually intimate with someone else in the class. This time you know what you are seeing. It is painfully clear to you that your partner and this other person are attached to one another in ways that you used to enjoy but have missed of late. You arrange for another private conversation. This time you will not be so quick to give up your concerns. You trust your own eyes. In this second conversation your partner acknowledges this other intimacy. You feel outraged, betrayed, angry, not only about this violation of the terms of your relationship but about the initial denial.

What path do you choose?

- The long path of opening up and sorting out what happened and what this means for the future of the relationship?

- A decision to break off the relationship?

- A long private journey of trying to break down your own hurt and move toward forgiveness?

What factors influence your choice?

Some Misconceptions about Forgiveness

In their formative work at the University of Wisconsin, Enright and others help us to understand what forgiveness is by reminding us of what it is *not* (Enright, Gassin, and Wu 1992, 102; Enright 2001, 23–34):

- *Forgiveness does not dismiss or minimize an event or situation.* It acknowledges the truth about what happened and the consequences that followed. Forgiveness does not excuse or condone the behavior or actions of another. It does not say, "Oh well, he just couldn't help it."

- *Forgiveness is not indifferent about justice.* It might very well hold someone to account, seek restitution or a form of reparation while releasing the resentment that often accompanies a protracted conflict or violation.

In a collection of first-person essays from crime victims, Zehr (2001, 192) recognizes that pursuit of vindication or redress may actually be a relief from the humiliation and shame of having been victimized. Pursuing justice does not necessarily deny the possibility of forgiveness. Drawing a distinction between punitive or retributive justice and "restorative justice," Shriver (1995, 30–32) and others point out that retribution may exacerbate conflict, but "restorative justice" may help people through their victimization and make it possible for the offender to remain in or return to the community. In addition, forgiveness is not the same as a pardon, which refers to a legal transaction that releases someone from a penalty.

Forgiveness is *not* a sign of weakness. Choosing to forgive another person may plunge one into the deepest reflection about (who one is and how that identity is sustained.) It requires us to consider who we are independent of what has been done to us. *Forgiveness requires an act of imagination* because it invites us to consider a future that is not merely a reaction to the past. Forgiveness requires movement, as in a long journey, and cannot possibly be for the faint of heart.

A misuse of forgiveness further obscures the process we hope to clarify. After a crime, a shooting at a school, for example, people other than the victim sometimes presume to offer forgiveness on behalf of the one who was harmed. This gift is often motivated by the best of intentions and may be an attempt to spare an individual, family, or community the suffering it cannot avoid. We take the view, however, that whatever the intentions behind offering forgiveness on behalf of someone else, this form of forgiveness may actually compound the original injury. It violates the moral agency of the person who has been harmed, and it minimizes or may even circumvent the victim's struggle, choice, and freedom. This problem is at the heart of Simon Wiesenthal's book *The Sunflower*. Wiesenthal, a death camp prisoner during World War II, is summoned to the side of a dying S.S. soldier who confesses to heinous crimes against Jews. After listening to the soldier, Wiesenthal leaves him without the reassurance and absolution he craves. Later, Wiesenthal wonders if he has done the right thing by withholding forgiveness on behalf of his Jewish brothers and sisters. The consensus among the renowned people whom Wiesenthal summons to reflect on this problem is that forgiveness, for all its value, cannot be offered by one person on behalf of another (Wiesenthal 1998). Ellis Cose (2004, 49) also reflects on this problem. While he upholds the consensus in *The Sunflower*, he adds that we may choose to offer forgiveness for the harm that the person caused *us*. In other words, we might say something like, "On my child's behalf I cannot forgive you for what you did to her; but I can forgive you for the pain you have caused me." The distinction he makes may seem small; but *we* uphold *the right of people to make a decision about forgiveness on their own behalf.*

One final cautionary note—given the frequency with which women are victimized and that they often fall under pressure to forgive, we want to acknowledge that some authors argue against forgiveness. In an article that stirred up considerable controversy in ecclesiastical circles, Lord (1991) described a situation in which a woman came to him asking if she should forgive the man who shot and killed her sons and nearly killed her as well. Later, and while in prison, the man made an appeal to this woman on the basis of his religious conversion and asked her to forgive him. After a period of study, Lord concluded that the woman was not obligated to forgive in this situation. Other authors reflecting on this kind of problem come to similar conclusions. Placing greater emphasis on righteous anger and remembrance—over forgiveness—may represent a steadfast commitment to the truth, hold people to moral account appropriately, and serve as a necessary protest against things that should not have occurred. McFall

(1991, 156) says that bitterness can serve "as a necessary reminder that something hoped for and greatly valued has been lost."

One last misconception needs clarification. Although the two words are often used together, as in the title of this chapter, or in a course name, forgiveness and reconciliation are *not* the same thing. In the context of interpersonal conflict, *forgiveness* is a process undertaken by one person in relation to another, with or without interaction with that person. On the other hand, *reconciliation* is a process of reestablishing relationship, renewing trust, settling differences so that cooperation and a sense of harmony are restored. Reconciliation brings two parties together in a way that forgiveness may not. For this reason, in speaking of forgiveness and reconciliation, we believe it is essential to emphasize that forgiveness does not necessarily reestablish relationship. Forgiveness neither obligates one to reconciliation nor necessitates it. As countless students have told us, "If I have to reconcile, I won't even consider forgiveness." Forgiveness, then, may benefit the one who violates the terms of a relationship, but first and foremost it is for the benefit of the person who has been harmed. Reconciliation, on the other hand, reflects the mutual interests of two parties and embodies a willingness to reengage in the relationship in the belief that further injury is less likely to occur and that the benefits of a new association outweigh the risks. Because it is difficult to buck the tide of popular usage in which the two words are linked in a casual fashion, we will continue to speak of "forgiveness and reconciliation," but only with the awareness that the two words do not mean the same thing.

When There Is an Imbalance of Power

This distinction between forgiveness and reconciliation is particularly crucial when there is a serious imbalance in power between two parties or between an individual and an institution. Chapter 4 gives attention to power imbalances in conflict situations. Conscience requires that we return briefly to the matter here.

With numerous anecdotes from students in mind, we have learned that children are often confused about the role of power in the forgiveness process. Trying to make sense of a damaging encounter or a long period of exploitation, children can overlook the power differential between themselves and the babysitter, teacher, uncle, stepfather, or any other adult with proportionately greater power. Assuming that power in the situation is equal, children may put themselves under undue pressure to forgive. Dependency needs may make children particularly prone to forgive and reconcile, especially when the person with greater power uses coercion. Possibly for developmental reasons, children are unable to perceive that the person with greater power must assume more responsibility for harm to the person or relationship, not less. Transferring this responsibility to the child, more often than not, creates another layer of harm that the child may carry into adulthood.

Deeply concerned about hierarchical institutions, the church in particular, Keene (1995) tells a story about a woman who was sexually abused as an adolescent by her priest, a man who was clearly in a position of superior power. He describes the pressure to forgive that can be brought to bear on women in this situation. The church's teachings on forgiveness can be used against someone in the form of added pressure, as though a woman resisting forgiveness is guilty of moral failure. This pressure may be compounded when combined with the assertion that forgiveness is good for one's mental health and spiritual well-being.

Keene warns that pressure to forgive, especially when it is applied by those with more power, may serve to protect the hierarchical structures that made the abuse possible in the first place. Sometimes people in positions of greater authority or power expect those with less power to forgive because this release of another in the form of forgiveness *preserves* the **imbalance of power.** Necessary accountability and potential consequences for the actions of those in power can be evaded if the less powerful are pressured to forgive. Furthermore, pressure to forgive a person who retains a position of power may, in effect, ask an injured person to bear the additional suffering of remaining in contact with the abuser. The additional burden, on top of the original injury, may become unbearable. At the very least, it is an affront to justice. In such situations, proximity threatens the person who has already suffered harm. While we continue to hold the view that forgiveness is a choice and not an obligation, situations like those cited above make it extremely clear why forgiveness and reconciliation must not be easily blended. In situations like these, forgiveness, if chosen, should never obligate a person to reconcile. We will say much more about reconciliation later in the chapter.

Thinking specifically of the therapy setting, McKay, Hill, Freedman, and Enright (2007) have warned that encouraging people to forgive before they are ready to take this action may be particularly damaging to women who in many cases already feel responsible for relational repair. A sense of shame and guilt for not being ready to forgive may fall like an additional weight on the shoulders of people who are struggling to rise in the aftermath of a serious offense. Failure to take into account relative differences in power between the client and the perpetrator of harm may further compound the problem. *Requiring* forgiveness or *prescribing* it in a therapeutic situation may at best be untimely and at worst cause additional harm to an injured party. Concerned about such an outcome, these authors contend that "female clients (in particular) should view forgiveness as an informed choice they are making, not a gender-related mandate" (24).

Application 10.3   Taking Advantage of Power

As a junior at a university where you major in Biology you take an elective class in Philosophy. You know this class will be a stretch but you need a break from "hard science" classes. With some anxiety you turn in your first paper on Plato. A week later your professor returns your paper. After looking through his critical comments, you see that he has given you a "D" for the paper. Because your scholarship depends on maintaining a certain grade point, and a "D" would hurt that average, you make arrangements to meet your professor during his office hour.

During your meeting he explains his critical remarks. Suddenly, though, you sense that the conversation has changed directions. He begins to ask more personal questions

(continued)

Application 10.3   Taking Advantage of Power

that leave you feeling uncomfortable. Eventually he seems to hint that he is willing to discuss your grade over a meal or movie together.

- Do you trust your instincts about the shift in the conversation?
- Do you pretend that you haven't heard what you think you heard?
- Do you ask him to clarify his expectations?
- Do you discuss this situation with friends or even the chair of the department?
- Or, are you clear enough about his boundary violation that you confront your professor on the spot and point out the transgression?
- How might you balance the power, temporarily, so you can choose your actions?
- What are your reasons for your decision?

The Matter of Memory

Just as the words forgiveness and reconciliation are often joined, people often say, "Forgive and forget." This is a particularly unfortunate conjunction. The relationship between memory and forgiveness is extremely complex and important. We will give an overview of the problem.

Memory is absolutely essential to the forgiveness process. People say "Forgive and forget" with the best of intentions, hoping to reduce a person's pain. But "Forgive and forget" seems like dangerous counsel to an abused woman who believed she was safe, only to discover upon returning to a relationship that she has again been physically harmed. It is unwise advice to an employee who trusted his employer to communicate expectations in person only to find that the employer consistently exposes the employee in front of a group. To ask a child abused by a priest or other religious figure to forget what happened, for example, creates a **secondary wound** because it asks the child not to trust his own perceptions. If no one remembers what happened, if no one receives a person's story about a transgression, the person who was harmed may come to feel that his or her identity is in jeopardy. While it is true that we are not what happened to us, we almost certainly are what we make of what happened to us. People who have suffered some form of sexual abuse or violence, for example, often feel as though the recovery of memory after a period of suppression or repression seems like the first step in the recovery of self. There can be no deep healing without it. The denial of memory comes to feel like the denial of being and is a genuine threat to personhood. Memory denied or ignored is like an untreated infection. It festers and threatens the whole body. Using exactly this metaphor, Isabel Amaral-Gueterres, truth commissioner for East Timor, says in relation to conflict within his country, "For some people, it may seem better to leave the past untouched. But the past does not go away and, if untreated, may eat away at those people and maybe even destroy them. Remembering is not easy, but forgetting may be impossible" (Cose, 2004, 182).

Archbishop Desmond Tutu makes much the same point throughout his book on South Africa's Truth and Reconciliation Commission (Tutu, 1999). In the case of South

Africa, the commissioners felt so strongly about the value of historical memory that they were willing to trade criminal prosecution of apartheid's torturers and executioners in exchange for the truth about what happened. While it may have seemed a "devil's bargain" to offer partial amnesty in exchange for truth, Tutu asserted that "To be able to *Tutu* forgive one needs to know whom one is forgiving and why. That is why the truth is so central to this whole exercise" (Cose, 2004, 182).

Yet the matter of memory in relation to forgiveness is complex. While forgiveness does not require the denial of memory, the recollection of past injuries can be used as the basis for causing harm to others. The misuse of memory may contribute to what Hannah Arendt calls "the predicament of irreversibility" (Shriver, 34) in which the memory of one violation can be used as the pretext or justification for revenge, perpetuating and deepening the cycles of injury and retribution. Forgiveness does not cast memory out of the equation but cancels the debt that revenge purports to repay. Forgiveness takes the accounting back to zero and offers the possibility of a new starting point. All this becomes especially clear when one looks on the international stage. In the 1990s the battle of Kosovo in 1389 was used by Bosnian Serbs to justify the murder of Muslim Croats. The memory of European favoritism toward Tutsis in Rwanda provided the pretext for their murder by Hutus. The memory of the destruction of the World Trade Towers may have seemed to justify the mistreatment of prisoners at the Abu Ghraib prison in Iraq or at Guantanamo Bay, which became the basis for beheading U.S. citizens and allies by Islamists. As one can see, memories misused can become the basis for inflicting more harm. The challenge, then, is to learn to remember in what one author calls "a living way"—in a way that serves individuals, families, and societies in the future (Anonymous 1993, 24). To get over something in the hope of creating something new in our lives requires that we remember the harm we experienced without letting that memory create momentum that leads to revenge. *Memory is absolutely essential to the forgiveness process* because it is central to the identity of individuals, peoples, and nations and may reduce the susceptibility to repeated injury in the future.

Application 10.4	Bad Memories

Imagine that you are a junior at the university. In the fall of the year, you begin to suffer from insomnia. You lose your appetite. Your interest in sports, basketball in particular, seems to have waned. You begin to withdraw from friends and make excuses when they invite you to participate in social events.

After several weeks of deepening depression, you consult a doctor at the health center. In the course of the interview, you tell the doctor about persistent memories of an incident when you were about eight years old. As you recall, you were at home one day after school. Your mom was still at work. Three teenage boys, living in the neighborhood, came to your house. Initially, they expressed interest in seeing your remote-controlled car. After a while, however, they began to engage in coercive sexual play and forced you to participate. As you give an account of this violation, you realize that, as horrible as the original incident had been, in the present you are even more troubled

(continued)

Application 10.4   Bad Memories

by the way your mother reacted when you tried to tell her the story on the telephone. She expressed skepticism about your account and eventually denied that the incident happened.

You tell the doctor that you feel doubly betrayed, first by your mother's failure to protect you, and second, by her refusal to believe you. You attribute much of your current depression to the lasting trauma of this incident and to your mother's refusal to take your story seriously.

Planning to return home for Thanksgiving, you feel a lot of internal pressure to work through your anger and sense of betrayal. In the two weeks leading up to Thanksgiving, what do you do to try to help yourself?

- What do you do with the anger?
- How do you think you'll approach your mother?
- If you decide to approach your mother, hoping for a conversation, how will you begin?

Now that we have presented a few definitions for forgiveness and have discussed some misconceptions about it, we are ready to look more carefully at how it works.

❧Decision or Process?

Is forgiveness a **decision or a process**? It is not easy to answer this question. An element of decision enters almost every forgiveness process and a process element figures in every decision. In the end, the answer to this question may be "Yes."

In cases involving marital infidelity, but influenced by the forgiveness that takes place by the bedside of dying patients, DiBlasio (2000) argues for a *decision* to let go of resentment and bitterness rather than waiting for a more or less lengthy process to unfold. He contends that "emotional readiness" is not necessarily a factor in the decision to forgive; forgiveness is more "an act of will," temporarily separating reason and feeling. Not wanting to bog clients down in a protracted emotional process, he says, "When clients discover that they need not be victims of their feelings but can decide to move forward despite the hurt, they become empowered" (151). DiBlasio then goes on to describe an intense and ambitious therapeutic session that may last two to three hours. It includes such things as

1. The therapist explains decision-based forgiveness to the client(s).
2. The therapist gives the client(s) an opportunity to establish the wrongful action that needs to be forgiven.
3. The "forgiveness treatment" is explained.
4. The offense(s) is stated.
5. The offender is given an opportunity to provide an explanation.
6. A question and answer period about the infidelity takes place.

7. The offended person responds, expressing feelings and explaining the impact.

8. The offender extends empathy for the hurt he or she caused.

9. The offender develops a plan to stop or prevent similar future behavior, giving the partner an opportunity to check up on commitment to this plan.

10. The offended party recognizes the offender's shame and/or regret.

11. Emphasis is placed on choice and commitment to letting go.

12. The offender makes a formal request for forgiveness.

13. A ceremonial act follows in which both parties recognize that a decision to forgive has taken place.

In a meta-analysis of this question about decision and process, Baskin and Enright (2004) explains that DiBlasio's proposal is one among several that emphasizes the centrality of a **decision to forgive**. In the context of psychotherapy a decision-based model may save time and serve to empower the client(s) trying to move toward forgiveness. Helping people *decide* to forgive gives them something to *do* at a time when they may feel helpless to change their situation. This approach may seem excessively prescriptive, even heavy-handed. For this reason Enright (2001) emphasizes that willingness to forgive is more important than "willfulness."

Interestingly, outside of the therapy setting, people sometimes commit themselves to forgiving another person by a certain date. So, someone in the Christian tradition may decide to forgive someone in the weeks between Ash Wednesday and Easter or before receiving the sacrament of Holy Communion. Or someone in the Jewish tradition may decide to forgive by Yom Kippur. There may be analogous dates in other religious traditions that provide the impetus for a decision to forgive. Stories we hear about people deciding to forgive by a specific date, especially one sanctioned by a religious institution or spiritual tradition, require us to take this approach seriously.

Emphasizing Process over Decision

Molly Layton (1999) describes a **three-step model of forgiveness** that is particularly helpful because it is easy to remember. She uses her own divorce to explain how she entered these three stages on the road to forgiveness:

Injured innocence. In this stage it feels as though everything we believe about life is suddenly in question, especially the idea that if we are good we will never have to suffer. A deep personal injury; an escalating, costly, and dangerous spiral of conflict; or a gross violation of trust threatens what we believe about the world and how to function in it. This is especially true for victims of crime. In the stage of injured innocence, we feel as if the ground on which we stand is unreliable and that we cannot move across its surface. In this stage we are likely to ask, "Am I no longer safe in the world?"

Obsession. In this stage we replay things that were done to us, words that were spoken, all the details of our suffering. It is common in this stage to feel fully victimized. It feels as though our lives are defined by what we have suffered. In this stage we are likely to ask, "Will he/she ever be held accountable? Am I stuck picturing this situation forever?" While "obsession" may have a negative connotation for us, this stage of the process takes seriously the impact of what happened. In this stage one reality is trying to catch up with another—what we believe we deserved and what actually happened. The work of this stage cannot be rushed.

Transcendence. No longer contending with the shock of realizing that the world is not as fair as we first believed, and no longer replaying every scene in the death of a marriage, or some other relationship, we come to believe, despite everything, that life will continue and that it may still be a "prize" worth having. In Layton's case, it was at this stage of her adjustment to the loss of her marriage that she began to give up her hatred, the desire for revenge, and her sense of being at the center of the world's unjust treatment of the innocent. She began to realize that the distinctions we make between perpetrator and victim are often drawn too sharply, that the hardness around each identity can soften in the balm of forgiveness, and that both sides need compassion. She began to realize that through our own suffering we become more deeply acquainted with the suffering of others. In time she learned to transcend what had happened to her and to join the rest of the human family. It was this movement from injured innocence and through the self-absorbed cycles of obsession that helped her get to the point where she could transcend her own pain. In this stage we are likely to wonder, "What will this experience mean to me in the future? How will I be able to integrate it into the whole picture of my life?"

Other researchers in the field delineate many more steps in the process. Robert Enright (2001) and the Human Development Study Group (1991) provide a notable example of this model. They describe 20 separate "guideposts" in four different categories by which people mark their journey. Having tested these guideposts or markers along a path in many different settings, we believe it is worthwhile to list them. In addition, these 20 steps apply whether one is the injured party seeking to forgive, or the one who has caused harm and in need of forgiveness. We list the steps and the kinds of questions one asks at each stage:

Guideposts along the Forgiveness Journey

A: Questions we ask when we are the injured party and consider forgiving others, including ourselves

B: Questions we ask when we have caused harm to another person

The Uncovering Phase

1. Examine psychological defenses

    A: What pain am I feeling and how am I defending myself against it?
    B: What pain have I caused another and am I in denial about it?

2. Face anger so as to release it

    A: Am I able to admit to myself what I am feeling, anger in particular?
    B: Am I able to face the other person's anger and my own sense of guilt or remorse?

3. Admit shame when appropriate

    A: Am I able to face the shame I feel about what happened?
    B: Am I able to face the shame I feel about what I did?

4. Become aware of emotional energy tied up in this (Cathexis)

   A: Am I aware of how much of my own emotional energy is tied up in this memory?

   B: Is my emotional energy tied up in what I did?

5. Become conscious of repetitive thoughts

   A: Am I repeating in my mind or obsessing over what happened?

   B: Am I repeating in my mind or obsessing over what I did?

6. Compare oneself to the other

   A: Am I comparing myself and my life since the transgression to the life of the person who harmed me?

   B: Am I comparing myself and my life since causing harm to the life of the person I harmed?

7. Realize that your life may be adversely changed, sometimes permanently

   A: Am I willing to acknowledge how my life has been changed by what happened?

   B: Am I willing to acknowledge that I have changed another person's life, perhaps forever?

8. Gain insight about how this injury/transgression has changed your world view

   A: Can I face how this event has changed my world view or sense of fairness?

   B: Can I face how what I did changed another person's world view?

Decision Phase

9. Recognize that old strategies may not be working

   A: Am I willing to see that my old ways of dealing with this event may not be working? Can I cope with my pain in a new way?

   B: Can I change the course I'm on in relation to the person I harmed?

10. Consider forgiveness as an option

    A: Am I willing to consider forgiveness as an option?

    B: Am I willing to receive forgiveness, rather than continue to defend myself?

11. Commit to forgiveness

    A: Am I willing to work at forgiving the one who caused harm?

    B: Am I willing to receive the gift of the other person's forgiveness, waiting for it, if necessary?

Work Phase

12. Reframe the picture of the other person

    A: Can I begin to see the other person in context (what life was like for him/her)?

    B: Can I begin to see the person I harmed as vulnerable and needing time to forgive?

13. Empathize

    A: Am I able to feel some empathy for the other person?

    B: Am I able to feel the other person's hurt to which I contributed?

14. Let compassion emerge

    A: Am I able to extend compassion to the person who caused harm?

    B: Am I willing to suffer patiently with the person I harmed?

15. Let the pain in

    A: Am I able let myself accept or absorb the pain I feel?

    B: Can I let the other person be angry, accepting the long path to receiving forgiveness?

Outcome Phase

16. Find meaning in what happened

    A: Can I begin to formulate a new meaning for myself in relation to what I suffered?

    B: Can I find new meaning in the harm I caused and the process of learning to receive forgiveness?

17. Realize that you have needed forgiveness in the past

    A: Have I ever harmed another person as I have been harmed?

    B: Have I ever been in the position of needing to forgive someone else?

18. Realize that you are not alone

    A: Is it possible that I am one of many who has gone through this process?

    B: Where can I find social support while waiting to receive forgiveness?

19. Realize a new purpose

    A: Can I find a new purpose for my life after this injury?

    B: Can I live a new life from this point forward?

20. Release

    A: Can I open myself now to the rest of life, having forgiven, even to the possibility of joy and hope after moving through this process?

    B: Will I let myself experience relief and freedom from guilt and remorse, having learned from this whole process? (Revised by Gary Hawk, 2009)

While such a long list may seem overly detailed, in practice we have found it very helpful to people. It helps them see where they are on this list and what might be needed to proceed further. Some therapists have even rendered this list in a graphic form that resembles a map (Velez 2009).

This section began with the question, "Is forgiveness a decision or a process?" The two models, *decision* and *process*, help us to see that in every case a person is faced with a decision: will I forgive or not? The element of decision is actually present in both of the models. The variation is in the *amount of emotional distress that is explored and experienced before* making the decision. The models also may differ with respect to the amount of time devoted to this exploration. As with any attempt to delineate stages of change, as Kübler-Ross (1970) has done with the grieving process, these models can be misconstrued. People in the process of grieving need to be reassured that there is no right order to the sequence and that it is often necessary to cycle back through earlier stages. In much the same way, before we reach a decision to forgive, we may need to review an offense repeatedly, search a long time for reasons to be empathic toward the offender, or dismantle and reconstruct his view of the world numerous times. We may need to reject the notion that we are anything like the person who did him harm before coming back to the realization that we have things in common with those who hurt us. The struggle to forgive may be arrested at almost any point, be completed only partially, or come so easily that some stages seem unnecessary. Whether we decide to forgive and *then* have to work through the emotions later, or work through the emotions *before* deciding to forgive, forgiveness can be both a decision *and* a process.

Getting Stuck: Eddies in the River

We live in a valley where powerful rivers descend from the mountains and converge on a long journey to the ocean. The landscape affects how we view things. One of our rivers drops through a gorge with major rapids with names like "Fang," "Tumbleweed," and "Cliffside." Wherever the river bends sharply or pushes up against a boulder, the current creates an eddy. People who raft or paddle this river often rest or recover in the **eddies,** areas where it is safe to pull over. This feature of our watershed has given us an image that has proven helpful in explaining forgiveness. If you live in an urban area, you might think instead of traffic jams. Listening to students, clients, and other people, we find that people sometimes get stuck in an *eddy of long-term, low-grade, simmering resentment* (see figure 10.1). In this eddy a person may circle round and round looking for an opportunity to get even. Here we may concentrate on the other person's offense, how that person has fared since doing us harm, and how they are in our debt, a debt they will never be able to pay. The desire and impulse to get even may or may not be contained.

If we do not get caught in this eddy of *resentment and revenge*, we may get caught in an eddy of *depression and withdrawal*. In this eddy the hurt we have suffered seems so great that it seems better to withdraw from life because it poses too many challenges. In this eddy a person attempts to create a small and safe world out of the current. As a collective example of this phenomenon, Enright discovered that nearly half of a group of over 200 seven-year-olds in Northern Ireland were clinically depressed as a result of *Ireland* "the troubles."

Figure 10.1   Eddies in the River

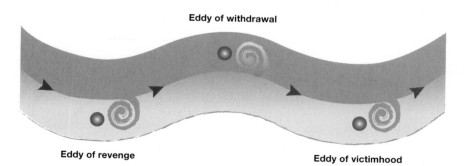

Eddy of withdrawal

Eddy of revenge

Eddy of victimhood

Around the next bend someone may become caught in the eddy of *being a victim*. In this whirlpool a person may ascribe special status to having been victimized. In this eddy people become what happened to them, and may use their story to elicit sympathy from others, demand extra attention, induce guilt in others, or excuse their own passivity (Exline and Baumeister 2000).

When we see a friend or family member in an eddy, we may grow impatient and be tempted to *push* that person back out into the current. Having observed this process carefully in many situations, we believe that it is best to be patient, to see the eddies as resting places, to have a keen sense of timing, and to watch for a person's own motivation to return to the flow of life. This observation may be helpful to you as a friend, family member, or third-party agent. A friend who has expertise in the world of river-running tells us that in certain rapids, it may be necessary to take off one's life-jacket, temporarily at least, so as to descend deeper into the current and be carried back into the river. This image seems particularly helpful when we encounter people who seem to take a very long time to forgive. Even the first step in the process (recognizing one's defenses against the pain of what happened) can seem like an overwhelming task. Sometimes people need to use dissociation, denial, or anger, for example, to protect themselves for a while before reengaging with life after a major violation or betrayal.

The Personal and Interpersonal Dimensions of Forgiveness

Reflecting on the models developed by Enright, applied by Palmer, or distilled by Layton, the reader might conclude that forgiveness is something we work toward by ourselves and without interaction with the person who caused us harm. In some cases, after a violent incident, for example, or because of a person's extreme defensiveness, unwillingness, or inability to accept responsibility, interaction with such a person can seem unsafe, unwise, or undesirable, but this does not foreclose the possibility of forgiveness; it means that forgiveness takes place internally. In a closely argued article from a philosophical point of view, Holmgren (1993) describes the value of this approach. Internal or "intrapersonal" forgiveness is not dependent upon the responsiveness, contrition, attitudes, or apologies of the person who caused the harm. This kind of forgiveness is "unilateral" in that it focuses strictly on the beliefs, feelings, attitudes, decisions, and behavior of the victim (345).

The beauty of these intrapersonal models is that they accurately describe an intricate process that does not depend on the penitence, remorse, or direct actions of the person who caused us harm. We can sometimes wait a very long time for a person to express regret about stealing from us, causing a car accident, or filing for divorce. These models emphasize that we are free to begin the work leading to liberation whether or not the other person acknowledges responsibility, seems aware of the impact of his or her actions, apologizes for harm done, expresses regret, and asks to be forgiven. In effect intrapersonal models for forgiveness say, "You can begin the work of breaking free from a legacy of harm on your own. You don't have to wait for someone else to act before you can begin the process of liberating yourself." In other words we may proceed without waiting on subsequent action, communication, or acknowledgment from the person who caused the injury. We cease to be the prisoner of someone else's actions. We reclaim ourselves as the active center of our own choices.

At the same time we must recognize that all of us belong to networks of relationships from which we are not easily removed. We often encounter, work across from, eat meals, or share children with people who have caused us harm or whom we have harmed. In *some* cases we can go on about our lives after being harmed without needing to interact with the one who hurt us. But in a great many cases we are not so disconnected. The woman who left us is still the mother of our children. For complex reasons having to do with our investment in the relationship, our moral code, the support of friends, and the history of the relationship, we may decide to stay with the husband who betrayed us. The uncle who fondled us shows up at the table at Thanksgiving. We may see the rapist in court. We sit next to the alcoholic father during the Superbowl. We now see more clearly than ever that the process of forgiveness must be intrapersonal—within our own control—to preserve freedom from bondage to the behavior of another human being *but* that the process may be more interpersonal and require more interaction than we previously thought because our lives continue to intersect, overlap, and collide. There are some relationships from which we cannot escape. This means that the interactive and communicative aspects of this process are more important than ever.

After one person has injured another the injured party has a great need to speak about the impact of this event. The injured party has a great need to be heard. At the same time, searching to increase a level of understanding and potentially the capacity for empathy, the injured party may have questions about why this harm took place, how it could have happened, what factors were involved, and if the one who caused the harm understands the impact of his or her actions. These kinds of questions are at the heart of victim offender dialogue programs, for example.

Looking at the situation from the opposite side (and assuming that the transgressor has the courage to accept responsibility), the one who caused the harm may have a great need to tell his or her story, not to justify the actions but to lighten the load of shame or at least explain factors that influenced the harmful choices. In short, forgiveness is likely to be a communicative process, not just a solitary labor hidden from sight. Careful listening, free of judgment, makes possible more complete disclosure that can inform and liberate both the listener and the teller. Courageous truth-telling, a deeply sincere apology, the full acceptance of responsibility, and complete acknowledgment of the impact of an event or action can make possible a more kind and generous response—and possibly the direct or indirect expression of forgiveness. (In other words, where a relationship has not been entirely ruptured and abandoned, full and honest disclosure and grace-filled response dance around each other, approach and then step back, listen to the same music of the relationship, interact together, seek the gift of forgiveness for the perpetrator and liberation from resentment for the one who was harmed.)

And all of this takes time, much more time than we have usually been willing to recognize. An interactive process cannot be completed in one conversation. It may take many conversations and require countless efforts to clarify and understand. In the course of these conversations people often find that each side may have contributed to the injury, rift, or alienation. Therefore, the communicative, interactive nature of forgiveness is one of the growing edges of our thinking.

People renegotiate a relationship after an offense and work toward forgiveness in both implicit and explicit forms of communication (Worthington and Drinkard 2000). Sharing this perspective, Exline and Baumeister (2000) say, "In implicit forgiveness, one's statements or behaviors communicate either that no transgression was committed . . . or that the transgression was so minor as to be of no consequence" (136). In effect a person is able to interact with the person who caused the harm without reference to the injury, transcending it indirectly.

Implicit forgiveness remains communicative, however. It can be communicated by the tone of voice, gentleness in stressful situations, inclination toward humor and lightness of mood. Implicit forgiveness may be expressed through face saving approaches that precede a request rather than through abrasive complaint. A willingness to engage with another person may signal the beginnings of restored trust. These forms of communication are aspects of implicit forgiveness.

Exploring long-term couple relationships, Waldron and Kelley (2005 and 2008) have made major contributions to our understanding of the role of direct communication in the forgiveness process. They delineate various forms of forgiveness-granting communication that involve such things as open discussion, explicit expressions of forgiveness, nonverbal displays, and efforts to minimize the harm to the relationship (735). Interestingly, they have discovered that conditional expressions of forgiveness such as "I told him I would forgive him if the offense never happened again" or "I told her that I would forgive her only if things changed" may help people "reclaim respect, rebuild trust, and assure themselves that the transgression will not be repeated" (739). At the same time, looking at relational outcomes, they discovered that conditional expressions of forgiveness are actually associated with a deterioration of the relationship perhaps because the conditions imply lack of trust and may set in motion various forms of self-protective behavior. This finding makes it very clear that how people communicate about their grievances and how they communicate their forgiveness after grievances take place have enormous implications for the future of relationships and the prospect of reconciliation.

Having both an appreciation for the intrapersonal and interpersonal dimensions of forgiveness, it now appears to us that these two approaches may each have their time and place and may weave around each other in a dynamic fashion. Assuming that interaction is emotionally and physically safe, we sometimes take a direct route to relational repair, engage in discussion, risk self-disclosure, listen as much as speak, work actively within the framework of the relationship in the hope of clarity, understanding, and the freedom that comes with forgiveness. We may then need to drop down into the interior work, more reflective than interactive, where we continue to work our way along the path. At the same time we sometimes take an indirect route, processing the intense feelings, working toward the guideposts on a long journey that Enright and others describe and then assume the risks of interaction, revealing our discoveries, asking for an explanation, issuing an apology, etc. The two approaches serve each other, prepare for and precede each other, each serving the larger purpose of relational repair. See figure 10.2 on next page.

❧Gestures

We are particularly intrigued by communicative **gestures,** not necessarily verbal, that indicate that the process of forgiveness is underway or may have been completed in an implicit way. For example, one person in a romantic relationship may kiss another as a sign that an earlier conflict or disappointment has been transcended. We may visit someone who caused us harm, attend their musical performance, graduation, wedding, or thesis

Figure 10.2   Direct and indirect routes for relational repair

Direct Route:

Possibilities

- Interpersonal communication about situation
- Learn more through interaction
- Receive/offer forgiveness, apology
- Move toward relational repair

Risks

- Exposure to defensiveness and resistance
- Exposure to inadequate apology self-justification

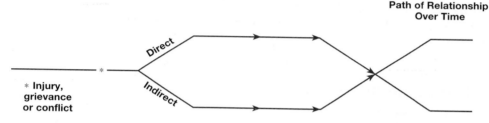

Path of Relationship Over Time

Direct

Indirect

* Injury, grievance or conflict

Indirect Route:

Possibilities

- The intrapersonal process
- Search for meaning of event(s)
- Prepare psychologically for interaction
- Observe others, explore implications for self and other(s)

Risks

- Cut oneself off from helpful information
- Deny oneself benefit of restored relationship

defense. In these instances the willingness to be physically present becomes a sign that a wound is beginning to mend. A willingness to collaborate in a work setting after a time of estrangement may be a sign of forgiveness. Two colleagues may agree to work again on a joint project without first verbally processing an old conflict. One neighbor might bring a meal to another as a sign that a boundary line dispute has been resolved satisfactorily, the offer of food being an ancient gesture that helps to mend a relationship. Very often a touch signals the shift away from resentment, putting a hand on someone's shoulder, for example. Historically speaking, a handshake is such a gesture. It signals that the open hand does not contain a weapon. A small gift is a highly communicative act—presenting a vase of flowers, offering a glass of water, sending a humorous cartoon or sketch, offering a ticket to a concert or sporting event—any of these gestures may communicate at least as effectively as words that something has been released and that the door is open. Also, it may be the case that one gesture begets another, setting in motion a positive, even "generative spiral" that replaces longstanding resentment.

To summarize this section, we believe that forgiveness may come about as a result of an intensely private process or it may come about in interpersonal communication. Forgiveness may be influenced by verbal communication, such as an expression of remorse. Or a wide range of communicative and creative gestures may be the means by which people request or convey forgiveness. In one relationship, the process may start in the solitude of one's memories. In another relationship, the decision to forgive may be facilitated by an apology. Both the private and interactive dimensions of this process influence each other. The internal work of forgiveness may eventually make someone more receptive to an apology if it is offered, accelerating the process of repair. Likewise, the internal process that helps a person forgive may change the conditions in a relationship so that it is more likely that an apology is offered, again accelerating the repair and mending the broken branch.

In this review of the "intrapersonal" and "interpersonal" forms and expressions of forgiveness, we came close to talking about reconciliation, especially when describing gestures. Before exploring reconciliation more completely, however, it seems wise to say more about apology and express some words of caution.

The Value and Limits of Apology

In a comprehensive article that explores the role of communication between aggrieved parties, and that corroborates the research of others, Kelley (1998) points out that people who have been harmed by others are more willing to renegotiate a relationship when they know the following three things: (1) *that there is essential agreement as to the nature of the violation,* (2) *that the other person acknowledges the hurt and pain that the violation caused,* and (3) *that the offending person will make an apology for the hurt and pain that the violation caused.* These three elements sound something like "I am so sorry that I failed to return your car in the condition it was in when you loaned it to me. I did not realize how important this is to you and I see now that my carelessness really upset you. I am willing to do everything necessary to set things right."

Confirming the work of McCullough, Worthington, and Rachal (1997), Kelley also found a correlation between a person's apology and the extension of empathy toward the offending partner. This empathic response to a sincere apology sounds something like, "Now that I understand how badly you feel about hurting me, I am willing to forgive you." When an offender makes a direct explanation of the offense, acknowledges responsibility, requests forgiveness, shows remorse, and apologizes, this form of communication is likely in 76 percent of the cases studied to influence the decision to forgive. The influence of this strategy is so significant that Kelley (1998) concludes that we need "to conceptualize forgiveness as a dynamic interpersonal process" (267). Reflecting on this same process, Exline and Baumeister (2000) say that these actions "may intercept a downward spiral started by the transgression . . ." (136).

However valuable apologies may be in the interactive process of forgiveness, we live in an age when apologies have become commonplace without addressing the question of what makes an apology effective. In France the Catholic Church apologizes for complicity with the Nazis in the extermination of the Jews. In America and Canada, apologies have been offered for the treatment of Native children held in boarding schools. New Zealanders apologize to indigenous populations for introducing diseases.

In Australia whites apologize to the aboriginal peoples on "Sorry Day." In 1980 the United States apologized to Japanese-American citizens forced into prison camps during World War II. Former President Bill Clinton apologized for "the Tuskegee Study of Untreated Syphilis in the Negro Male." Secretary of Defense Donald Rumsfeld seemed to take responsibility for the treatment of Iraqi prisoners at Abu Graib. Former Governor of New York, Eliot Spitzer, seemed to apologize for his liaisons with "call girls."

In the flood of apologies, especially public apologies, we fear that apologies can create the illusion that something significant has happened or will soon be set right. Apologies can be another form of manipulation, put an aggrieved party under extraordinary pressure to respond graciously, or merely serve as a means of self-protection. People may apologize as a kind of shortcut to avoid further engagement with an aggrieved party. Concern about the indiscriminant use of apology leads us to make distinctions between kinds of apologies and even develop a set of criteria that may help us make more effective apologies. There are at least three forms of suspect apologies:

- *Expedient apology.* An expedient apology, often arranged in private, merely benefits the one who offers the apology and provides little or no benefit for the person who was harmed. A person offering an expedient apology says something like, "To avoid more controversy over this, let's issue an apology so we can move on." Clearly, the goal is to avoid rather than engage, to escape the consequences of one's actions rather than learn more about the actual harm caused by one's actions. Recently, physicians in Michigan have been encouraged to apologize for medical mistakes. Insurance companies have discovered that malpractice suits have dropped significantly in situations where physicians offer a sincere apology (Merriam 2004). Reporting on similar stories, a Chicago Public Radio program on apology also indicated that patients and families are extremely astute at discerning whether an apology is genuine or designed merely to placate (Glass 2004).

- *Compelled apology.* A compelled apology may be empty because it is offered without an adequate understanding of the full effect of one's actions. Politicians are often compelled to apologize after an affair becomes public, or after failing to pay taxes, for example. These and other forced apologies, sometimes under the glare of the camera's lights, rarely communicate depth of understanding or a full grasp of the impact of our actions. Efforts to explain our actions can make the situation even worse. On the other hand, we have observed that sometimes children must be *taught* to give apologies. In this situation a parent may say to a child, "Please apologize to your mother for hitting her," or "You need to tell the grocer that you are sorry for stealing this candy." In some cases, especially with children, the process of learning to render an adequate apology begins when someone insists on one. While children may need to be taught to apologize, their feelings about the process should not be suppressed or ignored.

- *Delayed or surrogate apology.* In a delayed apology, someone far removed from the wrongdoing accepts responsibility for the harm and offers an apology on behalf of people no longer present. We issue a delayed apology when we say something like, "I know a lot of water has gone under the bridge and the people who did this harm is long gone, but on their behalf I want to say . . ." Delayed or surrogate apologies may be as comprehensive and necessary as an apology to African Americans for the told and untold harm of slavery or as specific as apologizing for the behavior of a friend in a restaurant. The person receiving the apology should be the one to measure its value, not the one offering the apology.

Our concern about inadequate forms of apology has led us to develop a set of criteria for good apologies. Influenced by a comprehensive study of public and private apology (Lazare, A. 2004), we have developed a set of criteria for good apologies. Apologies require:

1. Acknowledgment of harm without an accompanying justification ("I see that my actions impacted you in these ways . . .).

2. Acceptance rather than deflection of responsibility ("I take full responsibility for the harm I caused").

3. Sincere expression of regret or remorse ("I am deeply sorry that my thoughtless action had this effect on you").

4. Reparation in some form ("I would like to compensate you in some way for the harm I caused").

5. Assurance of safety for the sake of the future of the relationship ("This will not happen again").

6. Reaffirmation or clarification of shared values so that both parties will understand the terms of any future relationship ("In the future you can count on me to uphold my promise that . . .").

7. In rare cases an apology may require an explanation *if* it is requested by the injured party ("What was in your mind when you . . . ?")

In addition to these criteria, even with these criteria in mind, we remain concerned about the way a poor apology may compound an injury or conflict. Therefore, we suggest the following:

When Receiving an Apology, Ask:

1. Who is served by this apology?

2. Can I trust that change in behavior will follow this apology?

3. Does the apology seem sincere, genuine, or authentic? Is it accompanied by acceptance of responsibility for the wrongdoing?

4. Was the apology followed by a justification or excuse for the action that harmed me?

5. What is the purpose of this apology? (repair of the relationship, preparation for another harmful act, an attempt to disarm or equalize power?)

6. Is the apology accompanied by pressure to forgive the person who caused the harm, thus transforming a choice into an obligation?

7. Does the apology precede confrontation or follow it? In other words, how well does the person understand the harm he/she caused?

When Offering an Apology, Ask:

1. Do I really understand what hurt or offended the other person?

2. Am I conscious of what I did?

3. Do I intend to change so that the injury or transgression won't be repeated? Am I prepared to make some kind of restitution if that is requested?

4. Do I mean what I say?

5. Is the apology for me, the other person, or the relationship?

6. Can I apologize without also adding justification for my actions?

It may be that no apology can be completely purified of some kind of self-interest. Perhaps it is too much to expect that every apology be cleansed of any effort to secure a lost advantage. But because apology can be a powerful facilitator of forgiveness, and because sincere apology and forgiveness can twine around each other in a braid, we want to uphold high standards for apologies. Our criteria and the suggested questions may lead us to make better apologies, ones that are worthy of the trust we seek to restore. As Lazare (2004) begins and contends throughout his book:

> One of the most profound human interactions is the offering and accepting of apologies. Apologies have the power to heal humiliations and grudges, remove the desire for vengeance, and generate forgiveness on the part of the offended parties. For the offender, they can diminish the fear of retaliation and relieve the guilt and shame that can grip the mind with a persistence and tenacity that are hard to ignore. The result of the apology process, ideally, is the reconciliation and restoration of broken relationships (1).

Application 10.5

Case: Disappointment at a Wedding

For a year you have been preparing for your wedding day. You, your mother, and friends have been working on every detail of the celebration. During the rehearsal you feel as though all this preparation has paid off. People know their parts; dresses are pressed and ready to wear; the florist and photographer are sure to fulfill their promises; the right rings are in the right pockets. On the day of the wedding the groom and groomsmen arrive in their tuxedos and tease each other in playful and affectionate ways. You and your bridesmaids make ready, talk excitedly, and adjust yourselves in front of the mirror. As the prelude begins, your father, who is supposed to accompany you down the aisle, is nowhere in sight. At the last second, just as the doors are about to open for the processional, he shows up disheveled and intoxicated. You alternate between disbelief and despair. On one hand you want to proceed into the sanctuary as if everything is going according to plan. On the other hand you want to give your father a piece of your mind for ruining your day. Seeing the look on your face, your maid of honor acknowledges your distress, but sensing how much is at stake, whispers, "Take his arm." You swallow your upset and take the first step toward your beloved.

(continued)

Application 10.5 Case: Disappointment at a Wedding

After the wedding and honeymoon, having processed some of your feelings with your husband, you know you have to speak to your father. Life cannot go on without this conversation. By what method will you first contact him: in person, by cell phone, e-mail, text message, or a formal letter? Why do you choose this method? How do you balance your need to be heard and your need to hear his side of the story?

Playing the role of the father, do you explain your behavior, dare to justify it, or simply listen? Is this the time for an apology, and if so, what kind of apology? Do you dare reveal any of your deeper feelings—your fear about this day, the anxiety around seeing your former wife again? What do you say or refrain from saying, knowing that the future of your relationship with your daughter is at stake?

In some cases it is very clear that an injured party wants us to go beyond a mere verbal statement. Sometimes a specific action is required before the relationship can be resumed or trust can be restored. For example, in Ian McEwan's novel *Atonement,* he tells a story about a particularly destructive lie. Briony, the younger of two sisters, sees her older sister, Cecilia, making love with her boyfriend Robbie. Later, when another woman at a party is raped, Briony blames Robbie. Tried, imprisoned, and later forced into the British army during WWII, Robbie is severely injured and nearly dies. Toward the end of the novel, Briony decides to visit her sister, confess her lie, acknowledge its effects, and make amends. Upon arriving she discovers that Robbie, on leave from the army, is present in the apartment. An extremely tense drama unfolds. In the course of the conversation, Robbie and Cecilia refuse to forgive Briony but require of her an exacting set of conditions and amends. This novel presents a gripping account of the cost of a lie, the demands of an interactive repair process, the need for apology, and the way we sometimes need to go far beyond apology to restitution and reparation. For a rich analysis of this problem in national and international affairs, see the final chapters of Cose's *Bone to Pick* (2004).

❧Switching the Point of View: Receiving Forgiveness and Forgiving Oneself

Thus far in this chapter, we have approached the subject of forgiveness from the standpoint of the person who is in a position to forgive someone else. This discussion would be incomplete, however, without looking at the process from another angle: what is it like to **receive forgiveness**? While it can be extremely difficult to offer forgiveness to someone who has hurt us, it also can be very hard to receive it after *we* have done the harm. Accepting forgiveness requires that we shift our attention from the fear of retribution or guilt over something we have done wrong to the possibility of freedom from this fear. Such freedom can seem more terrifying than the repercussions we anticipate. Once we receive someone's offer of forgiveness, we can no longer focus exclusively on the harm we caused. Suddenly the vista is broad. We can look beyond what we did and how our actions affected another person. But such a view can sometimes seem daunting because the basis for defining ourselves suddenly becomes more complex. Instead of seeing ourselves only in relation to something we did in the past, we are confronted now with responsibility for new choices.

Receiving forgiveness can be difficult for another reason. In his formative article where he outlines the relationship between forgiveness, receiving forgiveness, and self-forgiveness, Enright (1996) asserts that a person hoping to receive forgiveness must *wait* for the *gift* of forgiveness to come from the person who has been harmed. It is as if there is an interval between the action that hurt another person and the forgiveness that releases that person from resentment and anger. In this interval, a person's choice about whether or not to forgive must be upheld. As we have said, a person is not obligated to forgive. In this profoundly important interval, the person who caused harm has an opportunity to *reflect rather than deflect* awareness about the actual harm that was caused. Waiting in that interval can be extremely difficult because it requires that a person stay close to awareness of the harm he or she caused. Yet, this interval also may be the birthplace for self-forgiveness.

As with receiving forgiveness, self-forgiveness presents some major challenges. Students sometimes report that they may be willing to receive forgiveness from someone they have harmed but find that they will not grant themselves this same gift. To use another image from the novel *Atonement*, the inability to forgive oneself can seem like being held in a locked and doorless room. Inside this room it seems impossible to live past the shame associated with some wrongdoing. Meanwhile, on the *outside* of the room, people talk, eat, dance, or stroll through a marketplace, wonder at the stars, and wait to be joined by the presence of the one who locked himself inside this doorless room. Some people stay in this room for a very long time, sometimes because it seems safe. In fact the refusal of offered forgiveness may be another eddy in which people get stuck, staying out of the current of life that brings people back together.

Forgiving oneself can be particularly difficult because it first requires that we reconcile *two different images of ourselves:* the person we think we are and the person who caused someone harm. The person we think we are (and would like to be) may resist the truth about the self who told the lie, stole some money, or betrayed a friend. It may seem that as long as we withhold forgiveness from ourselves, then we can't possibly be the person who did this deed. To accept forgiveness, whether from someone else or from oneself, is a form of admission that, yes, we are both these people—the one who finds such actions abhorrent and the one who did them. Self-forgiveness requires that we see these two selves clearly and help them recognize and accept each other, extending compassion to each until the self becomes less divided. Undertaking this work requires us to reckon with the complexity of our identity, seeing the "both/and" quality of who we are.

In this chapter we described the internal process of forgiveness, using Enright's four phases and Layton's movement from injured innocence and obsession to transcendence. It is quite possible for people to apply these same steps to themselves. As in the effort to forgive someone else, we must take steps to *uncover* what happened and face that truth courageously. We must *work* at facing our self-protective defenses and begin to let them down. We must be willing to extend empathy and compassion to ourselves in the same way that we might readily offer it to someone else. We must be willing to move toward a *decision* to release ourselves from self-punishing tendencies, without denying accountability. And finally, we must be willing to move toward an *outcome* phase where the truth has been integrated and the story of our life becomes more rich and complicated than we first thought it would be. The end result can be the same sense of freedom as when we forgive someone else, in this case making what we did to someone else less central to the story we tell about ourselves.

| **Application 10.6** | Looking for an Oasis |

Imagine that you are a young female enlisted soldier serving in Iraq. Two days ago, three soldiers from your unit, two men and a woman, were ambushed on a night patrol as they tried to protect an oil facility against sabotage. All three of them were your good friends. You feel devastated by the loss, aware, too, that you could have been on that same patrol. After the losses, your commanding officer warns all of you in the unit to be extra vigilant in the days leading up to the Muslim holiday of Ramadan.

On patrol yourself a few days after this incident, you see a white van traveling toward an Army checkpoint. Estimating speed and distance, you conclude that the van will not be able to stop at the checkpoint and may even be a danger to the soldiers monitoring all vehicles passing through the area. You fire a warning shot in front of the van. It does not stop. Fearing that the van will ram the checkpoint and may even be loaded with explosives, you fire a rapid volley of shots through the side windows of the van. Moments later the van veers into a roadside ditch and stops. You and several soldiers from the checkpoint run toward the van, weapons ready. Encountering no further threat, you open the van and try to determine what has happened. In the front seat are two adults, a man and a woman, both dead. In the back of the van you find a crying child. She has been wounded not by your bullets but by a land mine explosion. Through a translator who communicates with the child, you learn that her parents were rushing her to the hospital after the explosion. Suddenly you realize that you have killed the child's parents as they tried to help their daughter.

Immediately other soldiers come to your aid. They reassure you that you did exactly what the situation required even if these people were not an actual threat to your unit. Despite their support and time off to recover, you have nightly dreams that haunt you. In one you are in the van being shot at. In another you shoot at the van and, as you approach, see your parents in the front seat.

In the days ahead, the post-traumatic stress associated with this event and the death of your comrades makes it increasingly difficult for you to serve effectively. You ask permission to see the chaplain assigned to your unit. As the time for the first appointment approaches,

- What do you want to tell this person?
- What do you want to hear from this person?
- What would make it easier to begin the process of self-forgiveness?
- What would make the process much harder?
- What do you absolutely *not* want to hear?

~Reconciliation: A Late Stage in the Journey

Trying to be clear about forgiveness, we have kept reconciliation waiting for a long time, almost like a friend in a nearby room. Our friend has been patient while waiting in the room next door, but now she wants to claim her rightful place. If forgiveness is a process or decision involving the whole person that releases feelings such as anger, resentment, and the desire to retaliate, **reconciliation** is *the process of repairing a relationship so that reengagement, trust, and cooperation become possible after a transgression or violation.* The things we say and do to each other create chasms that divide us. When we forgive someone, or when someone else forgives us, the chasm may remain in place. It is not necessarily filled in or spanned by a bridge. For reasons we've explained, it may be good to forgive but not safe to reconcile. When it is safe, reconciliation is about the spanning of the chasms between people. It is about the bridges that people build, one stone at a time, sometimes from one side, occasionally from both.

What are the cables in this bridge? We are already familiar with some of them. A genuine and trustworthy apology may be a central cable in the span. Explicit and implicit actions, as well as gestures, help signal that forgiveness has taken place and open the way for reconciliation. What are some of the other ways we cross over toward each other?

Insights from History, Politics, and Literature

Living in the land of rivers, we remember a time when a winter flood wiped out a key bridge linking a community to a major east-west highway. A resourceful man in the community offered to shoot an arrow across the swollen river. He tied to the arrow a strand of monofilament. This fishing line allowed people on the other side to haul a heavier line across the river, and then a rope, and finally a cable strong enough to allow for passage across the river. The cable prepared the way for rebuilding the bridge.

In his remarkably comprehensive book *An Ethic for Enemies, Forgiveness in Politics,* Donald Shriver (1995, 9) develops the same metaphor to help us understand *four key aspects of reconciliation.* He invites the reader to imagine a cable spanning the chasm of conflict and alienation that divides individuals, groups, and nations. Based on his knowledge of history, politics, and world literature, Shriver asserts that this cable is woven of four strands—*truth, forbearance, empathy,* and *a commitment to remain in a relationship because of our essential interdependence.* Let's examine each of these strands that together form the cable spanning the chasm.

The Strand of Truth

Nothing obstructs the effort to repair a relationship as much as the experience of having your own sense of truth denied. When a friend denies having taken a possession you know he borrowed, when an employer denies having made an agreement that you were counting on, or when a person refuses to hear your point of view, movement toward each other seems impossible. For this reason the ability to acknowledge, honor, and communicate about what happened and its effects is the first bundle of wire woven into the cable. When people trust their memory of what happened, when they feel free and safe as they share their memory, conditions are established that make possible each succeeding step.

The film *Dead Man Walking* provides a particularly powerful example of the role truth plays in the process of reconciliation. In the film, Sister Helen Prejean, portrayed by Susan Sarandon, agrees to serve as the spiritual advisor for Matthew Poncelet, portrayed by Sean Penn. Poncelet sits on death row for his part in the rape and murder of two teenagers. Through the course of the movie, Sister Helen goes from being a naïve person of goodwill who has never seen the inside of a prison to being a mature, brave, and loyal advisor to a criminal in search of his soul. Likewise, Poncelet changes from being a smug, truth-denying shell of a man to a human being who finds his liberation, if not his redemption, in an acknowledgment of the truth and genuine expression of sorrow for his crime. This change takes place because Prejean offers Poncelet a carefully distilled combination of kindness that makes the telling of truth seem possible and tough insistence on truth that rejects every attempt to place blame on others. Without Prejean's steadfast commitment to Poncelet, no truth would emerge. Without her unswerving demand that Poncelet tell the truth and assume moral responsibility for his crime, Poncelet would never move toward the penitence that makes forgiveness seem thinkable. Change in Poncelet's relationship with himself, with his family, with the parents of his victims, and with his God is predicated on the telling of truth.

Application 10.7   Discovering an Affair

For a few weeks, your partner's behavior has seemed suspicious. Several times he has arrived home later than he promised. While on a business trip, he called to say that the meetings had been extended for a couple of days and that his return would be delayed. When you called the hotel where you thought he was staying, you were informed that "No one by that name is in the hotel." You feel shaken by your suspicions. After his return you feel irritation as he works on his e-mail late into the night, protecting the screen when you approach. The next day you do something you swore you'd never do. You enter his e-mail records. Torn between a sense of guilt about compromising his privacy and a desperate need to know, you read the record of his affair. Armed with this information, you set a time to confront him.

In a role-play with others, enact the first part of this conversation. Remember and apply the communication approaches we describe and recommend. Speak your truth with as much strength as you are able without degrading the personhood of your partner. Describe in whatever detail you deem necessary the harmful effects of his actions, the impact on your days and nights, the way this affair calls into question everything you have assumed, and how this affair has changed your life from top to bottom. Also include in this conversation your needs and expectations for the future if the relationship is to continue.

Let the role-play include two radically different outcomes. In the first version the betrayer is defensive, resists taking responsibility, justifies his actions, and may even blame his spouse for his actions. What is the effect of this kind of response on the person who discovers the betrayal? In the second approach, although this may be too much

(continued)

to expect of a first conversation, imagine the betrayer saying the kinds of things that Janice Spring says are *minimally* necessary after an affair (Spring 1996).
There will always be temptations, but I promise:

- *To be the gatekeeper of my life, and take full responsibility for remaining faithful to you;*

- *To keep my word that I have said goodbye to the lover; to prove to you with words and actions that this person is not a threat to us;*

- *To work out my problems in the context of our lives together;*

- *To never cheat on you again; to make it unnecessary for you to play the role of detective any longer; to prove to you that you don't have to be afraid to trust me again (p. 245).*

In the second version of this role play, what is the effect on the person who has been betrayed of this kind of radical acceptance of responsibility and the reaffirmation of values that she assumed they once shared?

The Strand of Forbearance

The second strand in the cable that crosses the canyon of alienation is what Shriver calls *forbearance*. To forbear means to refrain from revenge or punishment after someone has hurt us or transgressed against us. Forbearance is essential to the forgiveness process and to reconciliation because its opposite in revenge sets in motion an uncontrollable chain of consequences that often eliminates the possibility of reconciliation. Revenge, especially in the form of violence, seems to settle the score in the short run, but almost always provides justification for counter-revenge. Revenge has no foresight. It is incapable of looking beyond the action it intends, to consider the wider consequences of meeting one terrible act with another. *Resentment enacted in revenge, then, is self-defeating.* It guarantees that the retribution that seems like justice will double back in some form and strike the ones who imposed it.

As we explained in chapter 6, thoughts of revenge may provide emotional relief or seem to equalize power, but enacted thoughts can create the predicament if irreversibility. As Anne Lamott says in *Traveling Mercies* (1999, 134), it is like taking rat poison and hoping that the rat will die. Putting the matter more elegantly, Sobonfu Some (2003, 37) says, "Resentment is like making a cup of tea with poison in it for the other person. Somewhere along the line you always forget and drink it yourself." Or, as Gandhi reminded us, if everyone were to follow the principle of "an eye for an eye," then the whole world would go blind.

In his short story "Pray Without Ceasing," Wendell Berry (1992) provides a particularly clear example of forbearance. In the story we learn that Thad Coulter has spent his life transforming a west Kentucky hillside into a productive farm. Not long after clawing his way out of the hole of debt, Thad mortgages his hard-won farm in order to help his profligate son, who uses his father's money to buy a business in a larger neighboring town. Predictably, the son squanders his father's money and fails at business. Faced with foreclosure, Thad goes to visit his trusted friend Ben Feltner, hoping for a loan sufficient to save the farm. Ashamed of his own foolishness in trying to float his son's grandiose and ungrounded ideas, Thad gets drunk. When Ben finds it impossible to talk sense with him, he shows Thad the door. Later that same day, incensed by this rejection and ruined by his own sense of shame, Thad shoots and kills Ben, his last best friend. Word of his father's murder eventually reaches Ben's son Mat. After kneeling beside his limp father, Mat rises up, strengthened by the idea of revenge. As Berry says, Mat feels "new created by rage" (34). But as Mat turns from his dead father toward what seems like the sacred duty of revenge, his uncle, Jack Beecham, instantly sees that no good will come from trying to balance one murder with another. At great physical and emotional cost to himself, Jack, an older man, takes hold of Mat. He clamps Mat's arms to his side and holds him through the "concentrated fury" of grief and the desire to get even. The men heave and stagger and kick up the dust. But eventually something flows out of Mat and is replaced by something that flows into him from Jack. In the end, Jack can let Mat go because the younger man has become a new man free of the violence that only *seems* to make things right. Later in the story, a group of men, vigilantes really, come to the house where Mat sits with the body of his father. When they ask Mat's permission to hunt down Thad, Mat turns down their request, having already seen that one bad deed cannot be made right by another. In the end, Mat invites the men into the house to eat, a reconciling gesture in itself.

The beauty of fiction is that it allows us to see in concentrated form something that remains obscure or dilute in life. It distills the problem for us until it becomes clear. In this case, when Mat learns to contain the desire for revenge, Jack can let him go. In this way, Mat spares the community the consequences of his own potential violence and stops the spreading contagion of one killing followed by another. While few of us live in small towns and agrarian settings, we are not unfamiliar with the need for forbearance. Hardly a day goes by that someone does not cut in front of us at the grocery store or bank, make a bad move in heavy traffic, justify one sexual infidelity with another, demean or exclude a person worthy of respect and care. Forbearance is essential because its opposite in revenge sets in motion a tide that cannot be predicted and that guarantees that people will have an even harder time coming back together in a renewed state of trust.

The Strand of Empathy

If forgiveness and its sometimes appropriate aim of reconciliation are predicated on truth, and made possible by forbearance rather than revenge, then developing and expressing empathy for the offending person form the third essential strand in the cable stretching across the chasm. Empathy is rooted in the realization that the one who hurt us remains human and needs our kindness. The expression of empathy communicates that we have some understanding of the other person's motives and needs, however confused they may be. Empathy recognizes that at some point we may have done to someone else the very thing we are now trying to transcend. It helps us see that we have the same capacity for such an action.

Mr. Ives' Christmas, a novel by Oscar Hijuelos (1995), provides a particularly powerful narrative about the effects of a crime and the long, difficult journey toward compassion for the person who committed it. Set in New York City, *Mr. Ives' Christmas* tells the story of an advertising executive whose gentle and gifted son is murdered by a teenage thug. Like a sustained rain, the grief and anger that Ives feels over the loss of his son erode the ground on which he stands. The death of Robert affects Ives' concentration at work, his friendships, his marriage, his interest in sex, the once vital quality of his spiritual life, his social commitments and interests, his sleep, his appetite, and his beliefs about the nature of the world. In short, this loss affects everything. Through the course of the novel, a priest makes concerted efforts to bring Ives and Robert's murderer together. Toward the end of his life, Ives consents to meet Daniel Gomez, the man who killed his son. In the tense moments around this event, two images meet, clash, and influence each other—Ives' mental image of the man who shot his son with a handgun and the man who actually appears before him. Ives meets Gomez in the man's rundown apartment, where the furniture is covered in plastic, photographs are placed in cheap Woolworth's frames, a crucifix and plaster Virgin Mary sit on the table, and a back door leads to a porch where garbage and bicycles are indiscriminately piled. Extremely anxious, Gomez has spent the morning throwing up in anticipation of this meeting. As Gomez comes down the stairs, Ives sees a man who has grown to 300 pounds. His scuffed black shoes have been made over with enamel paint. Ives encounters not a vicious murderer, not a hard-shelled teenage boy with contempt for the world around him, but a fairly pathetic figure lost in regret and fear. Not surprisingly, the actual man, rather than the murderer fixed in the mind of Ives by a newspaper photo, awakens in Ives a compassionate response that finally is communicated by an embrace.

While hugging a murderer as a gesture of reconciliation may not be appropriate, this novel helps us to see that both victim and victimizer can suffer as a result of a crime. In starting across the bridge that spans the chasm of human suffering, we may discover our shared vulnerability and that we are human together. We may come to see how all of us can be exposed on the far limb of fate waiting for a kind word or deed. By means of empathy, we begin to cross over toward each other.

Commitment to the Relationship out of Awareness of Our Interdependence

In some ways this fourth strand in Shriver's cable across the chasm is the hardest to understand, yet it is the most crucial. Perhaps we can best approach this concept indirectly. In his song "Earthtown Square," singer/songwriter Peter Mayer reminds us of our global and economic interdependence. Economic realities in 2009 make the singer's words seem even more relevant. After describing advances in our technological capabilities, he sings,

> . . . *Now it's feeling like a small town*
> *With six billion people downtown.*
> *At a little sidewalk fair*
> *In Earth Town Square.*
> *There are Germans selling Audis*
> *Filled with gasoline from Saudis*
> *To Australians sipping Kenyan coffee in their Chinese shoes*
> *Argentines are meeting Mongols*

Over French fries at McDonald's
And the place looks strangely tiny when you see it from the moon.

Peter Mayer 2002

What is true on the economic level is often true on the psychological or relational level as well. If global economics binds us together, so does our web of relationships, whether in our families or our communities. A sense of how what happens to one person affects others, places responsibility on us to work things out with one another. "Because this place looks strangely tiny from the moon," we are charged to work together in the household to which we all belong. People like Martin Luther King Jr. and Archbishop Desmond Tutu have a particularly firm grasp of this fourth strand. In King's case, he knew that the goal was not just a seat on the bus in Montgomery, Alabama, where his activism began, but the creation of a "beloved community" among all the races and classes (Lampman 2005). Deeply steeped in the African tradition of "Ubuntu," which recognizes that no one person can be a human being without belonging in some sense to another human being, Desmond Tutu (1999) has a clear understanding of the same point. He knows that "we experience fleetingly that we are made for togetherness, for friendship, for community, for family, that we are created to live in a delicate network of interdependence" (265). It is because of this interdependence that we are called upon to use all our interpersonal skills and ability to communicate with one another for the sake of some small version of our place in the "beloved community."

The Tie that Binds: A Multicultural Example from Hawaii

In 2008, I traveled to Maui, Hawaii, to learn more about an ancient Hawaiian practice known as Ho'oponopono. I spent time in a predominantly indigenous community where I quickly realized that forgiveness expresses itself differently in different cultures. While in Hawaii I gathered information, like bits of broken shell scattered on the sand, from many sources—an astonishing private library and conversations with community elders, and clergy. What follows is a brief summary of a mostly hidden way that Native Hawaiians help family members untangle the nets of grievance, hurt, and resentment that threaten the vitality and well-being of their families. This account should *not* be taken as a full explication of the practice.

Ho'oponopono, developed by the first Pacific Islanders to inhabit Hawaii, nearly disappeared in the years after James Cook landed on the islands in 1820 and the Congregational Church sought to suppress the practice. Yet it persists in the memory of elders and some families still practice this ritual in the privacy of their homes. Ho'oponopono occasionally reemerges less formally in drug treatment, recreation, and juvenile justice programs. In light of everything else we have said in this chapter on forgiveness and reconciliation, this introduction to a very complex method will shed light on important aspects of the effort to improve relations between individuals who are members of an extended family network.

As it was originally practiced, and for those who continue to use some version of the process, Ho'oponopono assumes an underlying cosmology, a harmonious triangular relationship among God (Akua), the land (Aina), and the people (Kanaka). Any disturbance to any one part of this triangle affects every aspect of this complex set of relationships. Living on an isolated archipelago, the Hawaiians could not afford disharmony in relationships. Travel between islands, collaborative efforts to catch fish, the planting of taro, construction of shelters and ceremonial sites depended on the cooperation of family members and harmony between them. Ho'oponopono was developed to restore this fragile harmony after it had been lost.

The most precise account of this practice is preserved in a two-volume book called *Nana I Ke Kumu*, or *"look to the source."* In this book the principal author, Mary Pukui (1979), describes an intricate process, led by a trusted elder, whose goal is to gather family members for the purpose of discovering what has gone wrong. It aims to restore relationships between supernatural powers, the land, and its people. Literally, Ho'oponopono means to make right. The process begins with an opening prayer led by the elder (Kahuna or Haku), establishing the spiritual context for social relations and their repair. The elder then initiates an investigation into the problems underlying this disharmony. This part of the practice is like peeling an onion or opening bark around a tree (Mahiki). As the parties to the conflict tell their stories, one by one, the elder keeps a close eye on individual conduct and the expression of feelings. If this uncovering phase becomes too intense or dissolves into blaming or excusing, he or she may call for a time-out (Ho'omalu) in which silence is enforced and deep introspection is required. When participants are able to return to the discussion, sometimes days later, participants continue to open up the hidden layers of the conflict or trouble (Pilikia). During the course of the discussion, the leader expects absolute truthfulness and sincerity, examining all parties to the conflict. Likewise, in a resolution phase of the process, the leader expects honest confession, the deepest acknowledgment of wrong-doing, apology, and expressions of regret. The injured party is expected to offer forgiveness (Kala) and release from obligation without further recrimination. At this point in the process the elder prescribes appropriate forms of restitution so that the wrongdoer is not burdened by a sense of guilt or discomfort in social situations, and so that the injured party has no further claim that might again entangle the interdependent relationships. The leader and participants expect that this cycle of acknowledgment, expression of remorse, and the offer of forgiveness, *completes* the process. It is said to be finished or cut off (Oki), so much so that a person who refuses to accept the resolution of the problem may, in rare cases, be excluded from the community, a most severe punishment in the island context. Finally, the elder leads a concluding prayer that summarizes the discoveries and actions of the parties, asking for a blessing on the participants. Occasionally, a modest cleansing ritual follows Ho'oponopono.

Part of the genius of Ho'oponopono is that it recognizes that grievances are often tied together and that one layer of resentment underlies another. In a well-known story told by Mary Pukui, a woman receives a quilt from her mother. In time she was supposed to pass it on to her daughter. But feeling hurt by what she perceives as her daughter's apparent inattention, the mother sells the quilt rather than pass it down to the next generation. Feeling guilty about her action, the mother becomes ill and begins to dream about her daughter. The illness and the dream precipitate the call for Ho'oponopono. Hawaiians see illness and a particularly vivid dream as evidence of disharmony in the cosmic triangle, a kind of trouble that is best addressed through Ho'oponopono. During the course of Ho'oponopono, the daughter communicates her disappointment and resentment toward the mother who failed to pass on the quilt. But peeling back a deeper layer, the elder discovers that the mother is feeling hurt because the daughter has been ignoring her. Peeling to the core, the uncovering process reveals that the daughter is preoccupied with her new husband and child. The restorative part of the process requires the mother to create another quilt for the daughter (with the help of other women in the community) and the daughter to communicate more frequently with her mother. Through this example, Mary Pukui illustrates how family members become entangled in a net of resentments. The Ho'oponopono leader disentangles the binding cords, freeing all the parties caught in this crow's nest of misery. In discussion about this process, other elders likened Ho'oponopono to removing a fish hook caught in the flesh of each family member. The person with the grievance must let go the far end of the line so that the hook can be removed through acknowledgment, confession, and forgiveness. Linguistically speaking, the language surrounding the practice of Ho'oponopono employs a host of metaphors derived from traditional Hawaiian culture that reinforce the spiritual and psychological process of making right a disturbance in once-harmonious relationships.

From the vantage point of a different culture that has wittingly and unwittingly contributed to the destruction of the Hawaiian culture, Ho'oponopono may seem to us as though it depends too much on the skill of a leader at a time when few are trained to carry out this kind of responsibility. Also, it may overestimate the possibility of achieving closure through a stylized ritual process. Nevertheless, Ho'oponopono, wherever it is still practiced or remembered, has much to commend to anyone studying forgiveness and reconciliation. It recognizes and uncovers the layers of grievance that often keep people apart. It sees through the surface glare of one story to get at another deeper story and recognizes how two stories may be deeply intertwined. It creates a container in which multiple truths can emerge. It discourages the most primitive expressions of emotion that can cause additional injuries and interrupt the restorative process. It demands restitution as a part of restorative justice so that the newly freed are not entangled in the future. It asks participants to cleanse themselves of the residue of resentment through the expectation that they achieve closure in relation to one another. And depending on one's point of view, it recognizes and awakens spiritual resources that help people restore the lost harmony of the world.

In an analysis of ancient Polynesian culture, Miura (1999) says that the process of Ho'oponopono consists of:

1. Gathering the parties to a dispute by a high-status family or community member who knows the parties.
2. Opening prayer to the gods (God).
3. A statement of the problem to be solved or prevented from growing worse.
4. Questioning of involved participants by the leader.
5. Replies to the leader and a discussion channeled through the leader.
6. Periods of silence.
7. Honest confession to the gods (or God) and to each of the parties in the dispute.
8. Immediate restitution or arrangements to make restitution as soon as possible.
9. "Setting to right" of each successive problem that becomes apparent as Ho'oponopono proceeds (repeating the preceding steps if necessary).

10. Mutual forgiveness of the other and releasing him or her from guilt, grudges, and tensions for the wrongdoing.

11. Closing prayer.

12. A meal or snack. (Wall and Callister 1995)

Other cultures have developed their own methods of untangling the strands of conflict and retribution that give rise to injury upon injury. The Truth and Reconciliation Commission in South Africa, for example, is only one of many efforts following civil conflict in Africa to reveal painful stories, and to create a setting in which confessions can be made and forgiveness enacted (McLaughlin 2006). In a very different social and historical context, four young women, Israeli and Palestinian, created an organization called Just Vision that provides examples of nonviolent interaction between parties to this ancient conflict. In 2006 they produced a documentary film, *Encounter Point*, that follows the life stories of a handful of ordinary Palestinian and Israeli civilians. In the course of the film we see how they overcome terrible losses suffered in the course of the conflict, and criticism within their own communities as they form partnerships with their supposed enemies in order to work nonviolently toward a greater understanding of the problem. Courageous people from both sides behave in humane, empathic, and thoughtful ways, deeply aware that the dance of vengeance and revenge is deadly for both sides. This film records the highly interactive quality of conversation between Israelis and Palestinians as they work through the memory of conflict within and between these communities. It graphically illustrates the value of speaking and hearing the truth, the necessity of restraint, the social and moral implications of economic interdependence, and the possibility of developing empathy for people thought to be mortal enemies. For an additional example from Amish country see Paul (2008).

❧Conclusion

In 1973 Marietta Jaeger and her family were camping in Montana near the town of Three Forks. During the night, someone slit the tent in which her seven-year-old daughter Susie was sleeping and removed her. A well-coordinated search was set in motion, but Susie was not found. About a week later, a phone call from a man later identified as David Meinhofer, was the first break in the case. In this call, he revealed a detail about one of Susie's fingernails that linked him to the crime. Initially Marietta was filled with rage about what had happened to her daughter. But in time and with the help of her own particular faith, she was able to transcend this initial impulse to kill the man who had taken her daughter. She knew that she had to overcome her hatred, for her own sake and for Susie's, if her daughter were to be found alive. If she hung on to the hate, she would be enslaved to what had happened. Asking for a change of heart, Marietta found a more compassionate way of being. Exactly a year after Susie's abduction, the kidnapper called again. Marietta reached deep inside herself for the implausible kindness she knew was needed. She asked David, "How can I help you?" Her genuine concern for the man kept him on the phone about an hour until he revealed enough information so that police were able to track him down and arrest him. Marietta later met the man face to face. He confessed to kidnapping, molesting, and killing Susie and three other young people. After returning to his jail cell he hung himself. Despite the doubly tragic outcome, Marietta knew in her own heart that she had forgiven her daughter's murderer.

Realizing that she and Meinhofer's mother had something in common in the loss of their children, Marietta eventually reached out to Meinhofer's mother. Years later, Marietta returned to Montana for the 25th anniversary of Susie's death. In touch with Meinhofer's mother since the murder, Marietta and this woman both visited the graves where their children were buried. Years later Marietta moved from her home state of Michigan to the community where Susie and the family had vacationed. Here, she married a local rancher. Marietta is now a tireless and determined advocate for eliminating the death penalty in Montana. She is firmly convinced that carrying out justice as revenge in the form of the death penalty would not have been an appropriate way to honor the memory of her daughter. Marietta's case, while dramatic, is not unique. In less dramatic ways people question the apparently ironclad logic that seems to dictate that revenge must follow injury and bitter conflict. By means of a sometimes circuitous journey or as a result of a relatively swift decision people find their way to the freedom of forgiveness and, in some cases the restored relationship that characterizes reconciliation.

❧ Summary

In this chapter, informed by remarkable stories and a growing body of research, we define forgiveness, discuss misconceptions about it, and describe how the process of forgiving may take a path with many steps or be the result of a decision. Forgiveness does not require forgetting, must take into account differences in power between parties to a conflict or transgression, and stand by the view that forgiveness is more a choice than an obligation. People may get stuck in the process and may need patience and resting places while on the journey to forgiveness. Forgiveness is both intrapersonal and interpersonal in nature. It may take the indirect route of private reflection and nonverbal gestures toward an offending party or may risk direct communication about the offense, the harm it caused, and the need for restitution and amends. We set a high standard for apology, recognizing that good apologies may foster and speed the process of repairing relational damage. Reconciliation is not always be an appropriate goal or outcome. Relying on Shriver, we see great value in telling and hearing the truth, resisting the appeal of revenge, developing empathy that softens the hardened heart, and working toward the awareness that our ties of mutual dependence invite us to keep working at restoring our connections. Informed by insights and practices in other cultures, we have a growing appreciation of the role played by other members of the community who can help us remember and forgive, grieve and let go, and who can help us untangle the nets of our own complicity in destructive interactions.

Listening carefully to the stories people tell, we have realized that the process leading to forgiveness is not always scripted or methodical; sometimes it is simply mysterious. At the end of the journey people say things like, "I found that the stones I wanted to throw simply slipped out of my fingers." "The gate to a future I could not have imagined simply swung open when I let go of what they did to me." "Resentment no longer holds me hostage." "Like a scarred tree, I've begun to heal." "The journey is not over, but I have started out on the road."

Using examples from the lives of our students, from film, fiction, and international relations, we have illustrated some of the challenges inherent in this process. Forgiveness and reconciliation, its close cousin in the next room, are the byproduct of a complex interaction of several factors. Forgiveness that restores us to ourselves and reconciliation that restores us to one another are the result of time, the human desire to transcend injury, the courage to place a violation, betrayal, deception, or some other wound in the larger context of additional experience, and perhaps the mysterious effect of what some call "grace." When we forgive someone else or ourselves, or when we are forgiven by those we have harmed, we affirm the world is much larger than the injury that dominates our thoughts and feelings. An invisible door opens and we step out onto a stage where it is possible to associate with one another in ways less constricted by old memories. In this light we subjugate the memory of past harm to the hope of a new future. In the face of conflict or injury, we see our mutual vulnerability, our inevitable interdependence, and the need for compassion so all of us may transcend the injuries and bitter conflicts associated with the past and move more freely as creators of a new story.

❧Key Terms

Use the text's Online Learning Center at **www.mhhe.com/wilmot8e** to further your understanding of the following terminology.

forgiveness 297
imbalance of power   303
secondary wound   304
decision or a process   306
decision to forgive   307

three-step model
of forgiveness   307
eddies   311
gestures   314
receive forgiveness   320

reconciliation   323
the strand of truth   323
the strand of forbearance   325
the strand of empathy   326
ho'oponopono   328

❧Review Questions

Go to the self-quizzes on the Online Learning Center at **www.mhhe.com/wilmot8e** to test your knowledge of the chapter concepts.

1. Discuss some definitions of forgiveness. What are key components of forgiveness?

2. What are differences between forgiveness and reconciliation?

3. What is the problem with the phrase "forgive and forget"?

4. Compare and contrast the ideas of "forgiveness as decision" and "forgiveness as process," giving your own opinions based on the ideas presented.

5. Explain the "eddies" in which a person may be caught.

6. In what way is forgiveness both intrapersonal and interpersonal? How might these aspects be woven together?

7. How do gestures function to lay the groundwork for further change?

8. What makes apologies ineffective or inappropriate?

9. What makes self-forgiveness so difficult?

10. Explain Shriver's four strands of reconciliation.

11. What are some of the guidelines for a reconciling conversation?

12. Can you describe other cultural practices of the practice of forgiveness?

References

Abe, J. A. and C. E. Izard. 1999. A longitudinal study of emotion expression and personality relations in early development. *Journal of Personality and Social Psychology* 77, no. 3: 566–577.

Acitelli, L. K., E. Douvan, and J. Veroff. 1993. Perceptions of conflict in the first year of marriage: How important are similarity and understanding? *Journal of Social and Personal Relationships* 10: 5–20.

Ackerman, B. P., J. A. Abe, and C. E. Izard 1998. Differential emotions theory and emotional development: Mindful of modularity. In *What develops in emotional development?* edited by M. F. Mascolo and S. Griffin. New York: Plenum Press: 86–106.

Alberts, J., and G. Driscoll. 1992. Containment versus escalation: The trajectory of couples' conversational complaints. *Western Journal of Communication* 56: 394–412.

Alberts, J. K., B. L. Heisterkamp, and R. M. McPhee, 2005a. Disputant perceptions of and satisfaction with a community mediation program. *The International Journal of Conflict Management* 16, no. 3: 218–244.

Alberts, J. K., P. Lutgen-Sandvik, and S. J. Tracy. 2005b. *Bullying in the workplace: A case of escalated incivility*. To be presented at the International Communication Association Convention, New York, May.

Almeida, D. M. (2005). Resilience and vulnerability to daily stressors assessed via diary methods. *Current Directions in Psychological Science* 14, no. 2: 64–68.

Almeida, D. M. and M. C. Horn. 2004. Is daily life more stressful during middle adulthood? In *How healthy are we? A national study of well-being at midlife*, O. G. Brim, C. D. Ryff, and R. C. Kessler. The John D. and Catherine T. MacArthur foundation series on mental health and development. Studies on successful midlife development. Chicago: University of Chicago Press: 425–451.

Alper, B. S., and L. W. Nichols. 1981. *Beyond the courtroom*. Lexington, MA: Lexington Books.

Amato, P. R., and S. R. Rogers. 1999. Do attitudes toward divorce affect marital quality? *Journal of Family Issues* 20: 69–87.

Anonymous, 1993. Getting over, *The New Yorker* 67 (April 5): 24.

Apfelbaum, E. 1974. On conflicts and bargaining. *Advances in Experimental Social Psychology* 7: 103–156.

Applegate, J. L. 1982. The impact of construct system development on communication and impression formation in persuasive contexts. *Communication Monographs* 49 (December): 277–286.

Argyle, M., and A. Furnham. 1983. Sources of satisfaction and conflict in long-term relationships. *Journal of Marriage and the Family* 45: 481–493.

Aslund, C., B. Starrin, J. Leppert, and K. W. Nilsson. 2009. Social status and shaming experiences related to adolescent overt aggression at school. *Aggressive Behavior* 35: 1–13.

Association for Conflict Resolution. 2004. *Conflict resolution education: Fostering peace building in our schools*. Fall.

Association for Conflict Resolution. 2005. *Spirituality and the heart of conflict resolution*. Special issue: Fall.

Association for Conflict Resolution. 2007a. Recommended standards for school-based peer mediation programs.

Association for Conflict Resolution. 2007b. *Paradigms of practice: A mosaic of approaches*. Washington, DC. Winter issue.

Augsburger, D. W. 1992. *Conflict mediation across cultures: Pathways and patterns*. Louisville, KY: Westminster/John Knox Press.

Aureli, F. and D. Smucny. 2000. The role of emotion in conflict and conflict resolution. In F. Aureli, and Frans B. M. de Waal. Natural conflict resolution, 199–224. Berkeley: University of California Press.

Averill, J. R. 1968. Grief: Its nature and significance. *Psychological Bulletin* 70: 721–748.

Bach, G. R., and H. Goldberg. 1974. *Creative aggression: The art of assertive living*. New York: Avon Books.

Bach, G. R., and P. Wyden. 1968. *The intimate enemy: How to fight fair in love and marriage*. New York: Avon Books.

Baldwin, Jr., D. C., and S. R. Daugherty. 2008. Inter-professional conflict and medical errors: Results of a national multi-specialty survey of hospital residents in the US. *Journal of Interprofessional Care* 2, no. 6: 573–586.

Barnett, R. C., N. L. Marshall, and J. H. Pleck. 1992. Men's multiple roles and their relationship to men's psychological distress. *Journal of Marriage and the Family* 54: 358–368.

Barnlund, D. C. 1989. *Communicative styles of Japanese and Americans: Images and realities*. Belmont, CA: Wadsworth.

Baron, R. A. 1984. Reducing organizational conflict: An incompatible response approach. *Journal of Applied Psychology* 69: 272–279.

Bartos, O. J. 1974. *Process and outcome of negotiations*. New York: Columbia University Press.

Baskin, T. and R. Enright. 2004, Winter. Intervention Studies on Forgiveness: A Meta-Analysis, *Journal of Counseling & Development* 82, 79–90.

Bateson, G. 1972. *Steps to an ecology of mind*. New York: Ballantine Books.

———. 1980. *Mind and nature: A necessary unity*. New York: Bantam Books.

Baumeister, R. F., L. Smart, and J. M. Boden. 1996. Relation of threatened egotism to violence and aggression: The dark side of high self-esteem. *Psychological Review* 103: 5–33.

Baumeister, R. R., A. Stillwell, and S. R. Wotman. 1990. Victim and perpetrator accounts of interpersonal conflict: Autobiographical narratives about anger. *Journal of Personality and Social Psychology* 59: 994–1005.

Baxter, L. A. 1982. Conflict management: An episodic approach. *Small Group Behavior* 13, no. 1: 23–42.

Baxter, Leslie A., D. O. Braithwaite, and J. Nicholson. 1999. Turning points in the development of blended family relationships. *Journal of Social and Personal Relationships* 16: 291–313.

Bazerman, M. H., T. Magliozzi, and M. A. Neale. 1985. Integrative bargaining in a competitive market. *Organizational Behavior and Human Decision Processes* 35: 294–313.

Bazerman, M. H., and M. A. Neale. 1983. Heuristics in negotiation: Limitations to effective dispute resolution procedures. In *Negotiating in organizations*, edited by M. Bazerman and R. Lewicki. Beverly Hills, CA: Sage Publications.

Beck, A. T. 1988. *Love is never enough.* New York: Harper & Row.

Belenky, M., B. Clinchy, N. Goldberger, and J. Tarule. 1986. *Women's ways of knowing: The development of self, voice, and mind.* New York: Basic Books.

Bell, C., & F. Song. 2005. Emotions in the conflict process: An application of the cognitive appraisal model of emotions to conflict management. *The International Journal of Conflict Management* 16, no. 1: 30–54.

Bell, D. C., J. S. Chafetz, and L. H. Horn. 1982. Marital conflict resolution: A study of strategies and outcomes. *Journal of Family Issues* 3: 111–131.

Bell, M. L., and D. Forde. 1999. A factorial survey of interpersonal conflict resolution. *Journal of Social Psychology* 139: 369–378.

Bell, R. A., and J. A. Daly. 1984. The affinity-seeking function of communication. *Communication Monographs* 51: 91–115.

Benoit, P. J. 1983. Characteristics of arguing from a naive social actor's perspective. In *Argument in transition: Proceedings of the third summer conference on argumentation*, edited by D. Zarefsky, M. O. Sillars, and J. Rhodes, 544–559. Annandale, VA: Speech Communication Association.

———. 1992. Introduction, special issue: Interpersonal argumentation. *Argumentation and Advocacy* 29: 39–40.

Berger, C. R. 1980. Power and the family. In *Persuasion: New directions in theory and research*, edited by M. E. Roloff and G. R. Miller. Beverly Hills, CA: Sage Publications.

Bergmann, T. J., and R. J. Volkema. 1994. Issues, behavioral responses and consequences in interpersonal conflicts. *Journal of Organizational Behavior* 15: 467–471.

Bernard, M., and J. Bernard. 1983. Violent intimacy: The family as a model for love relationships. *Family Relations* 32: 283–286.

Berry, W. 1992. Pray without ceasing. In *Fidelity*. New York and London: Pantheon Press.

Billikopf, G. 2009. *Party-directed mediation.* Modesto, CA: University of California Press.

Bingham, L. B. 2004. Employment dispute resolution: The case for mediation. *Conflict Resolution Quarterly* 22, no. 1–2: 145–174.

Bjorkqvist, K., K. Osterman, and M. Hjelt-Back. 1994. Aggression among university employees. *Aggressive Behavior* 20: 173–184.

Bjorkqvist, K., K. Osterman, and K. M. J. Lagerspetz. 1994. Sex differences in covert aggression among adults. *Aggressive Behavior* 20: 27–33.

Blau, P. M. 1964. Exchange and power in social life. New York: John Wiley & Sons.

Blood, R. O., Jr., and D. M. Wolfe. 1960. Husbands and wives: The dynamics of married living. Glencoe, IL: Free Press.

Bochner, A. P. 1976. Conceptual frontiers in the study of communication in families: An introduction to the literature. *Human Communication Research* 2, no. 4: 381–397.

Bodtker, A. M., and J. K. Jameson. 2001. Emotion in conflict formation and its transformation: Application to organizational conflict management. *International Journal of Conflict Management* 12, no. 3: 259–275.

Borisoff, D., and D. A. Victor. 1989. *Conflict management: A communication skills approach.* Englewood Cliffs, NJ: Prentice Hall.

Boulding, K. 1989. *Three faces of power.* Newbury Park, CA: Sage Publications.

Bowers, J. W., and D. J. Ochs. 1971. The rhetoric of agitation and control. Reading, MA: Addison-Wesley Publishing.

Braiker, H. B., and H. H. Kelley. 1979. Conflict in the development of close relationships. In *Social exchange in developing relationships*, edited by R. L. Burgess and T. L. Huston. New York: Academic Press.

Braman, R. 1998. Teaching peace to adults: Using critical thinking to improve conflict resolution. *Adult Learning* (Winter): 30–33.

Breggin, P. B. 1992. *Beyond conflict: From self-help and psychotherapy to peacemaking.* New York: St. Martin's Press.

Brett, J. M., Z. I. Barsness, and S. B. Goldberg. 1996. The effectiveness of mediation: An independent analysis of cases handled by four major service providers. *Negotiation Journal* 12: 259–269.

Brockriede, W. 1972. Arguers as lovers. *Philosophy and Rhetoric* 5 (Winter): 1–11.

Brown, B. R. 1977. Face-saving and face-restoration in negotiation. In *Negotiations,* edited by D. Druckman, 275–299. Beverly Hills, CA: Sage Publications.

Brown, L. M., and C. Gilligan. 1992. *Meeting at the crossroads: Women's psychology and girls' development.* Cambridge, MA: Harvard University Press.

Brown, P., and S. Levinson. 1978. Universals in language use: Politeness phenomena. In *Questions and politeness: Strategies in social interaction,* edited by E. Goody. New York: Cambridge University Press.

Browning, J., and O. Dotton. 1986. Assessment of wife assault with the conflict tactics scale: Using couple data to quantify the differential reporting effect. *Journal of Marriage and the Family* 48: 375–379.

Brutz, J., and C. M. Allen. 1986. Religious commitment, peace activism, and marital violence in Quaker families. *Journal of Marriage and the Family* 48: 491–502.

Brygger, M. P., and M. Edleson. 1984. *Gender differences in reporting of battering incidents.* Paper presented at the Second National Conference for Family Violence Researchers, University of New Hampshire, Durham.

Buitrago, Y. 1997. *Mediation through a Hispanic lens.* Paper presented to the Intercultural Communication Division of Western State Communication Association, San Diego, California.

Bullis, C. 1983. *Conflict behavior: An inductive examination of deductive measures.* Paper presented at the Western Speech Communication Association Convention, Albuquerque, New Mexico, February.

Burgoon, J. K., M. L. Johnson, and P. T. Koch. 1998. The nature and measurement of interpersonal dominance. *Communication Monographs* 65, no. 4: 308–310.

Burman, B. and G. Margolin. 1992. "Analysis of the association between marital relationships and health problems: An interactional perspective." *Psychological Bulletin* 112, no. 39: 25.

Burrell, N. A., and D. D. Cahn. 1994. Mediating peer conflicts in education contexts: The maintenance of school relationships. In *Conflict in personal relationships,* edited by D. D. Cahn, 79–94. Hillsdale, NJ: Lawrence Erlbaum Associates.

Bush, R. A. B., and J. P. Folger. 1994. *The promise of mediation: Responding to conflict through empowerment and recognition.* San Francisco: Jossey-Bass.

———. (2004). *The promise of mediation: The transformative approach to conflict.* San Francisco: Jossey-Bass.

Butovskaya, M. L. (2008). Reconciliation, dominance and cortisol levels in children and adolescents (7–15-year-old boys). *Behaviour* 145, no. 11: 1557–1576.

Buttny, R. 2000. Discursive positioning as accounting and dialogic practice. *Narrative Inquiry* 10, no. 1: 147–151.

Buzzard, L. R., and L. Eck. 1982. *Tell it to the church: Reconciling out of court.* Elgin, IL: David C. Cook Publishing.

Cahill, M. 1982. *Couples' perceptions of power.* Paper for Interpersonal Communication 595: Advanced Conflict Management, University of Montana.

Camara, K. A., and G. Resnick. 1989. Styles of conflict resolution and cooperation between divorced parents: Effects on child behavior and adjustment. *American Journal of Orthopsychiatry* 59, no. 4: 560–575.

Cameron, K. S., and D. A. Whetten. 1995. *Developing management skills.* New York: Harper Collins College Publishers.

Campbell, J. 1988. *The power of myth.* New York: Doubleday.

Canary, D. J., E. M. Cunningham, and M. J. Cody. 1988. Goal types, gender, and locus of control in managing interpersonal conflict. *Communication Research* 15: 426–447.

Canary, D. J., and W. R. Cupach. 1988. Relational and episodic characteristics associated with conflict tactics. *Journal of Social and Personal Relationships* 5: 305–322.

Canary, D. J., W. R. Cupach, and S. J. Messman. 1995. *Relationship conflict.* Thousand Oaks, CA: Sage Publications.

Canary, D. J., and B. H. Spitzberg, 1987. Appropriateness and effectiveness perceptions of conflict strategies. *Human Communication Research* 14: 93–118.

Carey, C. M., and P. A. Mongeau. 1996. Communication and violence in courtship relationships. In *Family violence from a communication perspective,* edited by D. D. Cahn and S. A. Lloyd, 127–150. Hillsdale, NJ: Lawrence Erlbaum Associates.

Carnevale, P. J. D., and E. J. Lawler. 1986. Time pressure and the development of integrative agreements in bilateral negotiations. *Journal of Conflict Resolution* 30: 636–659.

Carstensen, L. L., J. M. Gottman, and R. W. Levenson. 2004. Emotional behavior in long-term marriage. In *Close relationships: Key readings,* edited by H. T. Reis, and C. E. Rusbult. 457–470. Philadelphia: Taylor & Francis.

Cavanaugh, M., C. Larson, A. Goldberg, and J. Bellow. 1981a. Power. *Communication* 10, no. 2: 81–107.

———. 1981b. *Power and communication behavior: A formulative investigation.* Unpublished manuscript. Department of Speech Communication, University of Denver.

Charles, S. T., and L. L. Carstensen. 2008. Unpleasant situations elicit different emotional responses in younger and older adults. *Psychology and Aging* 23, no. 3: 495–504.

Cloke, Kenneth. 2001. *Mediating dangerously: The frontiers of conflict resolution.* San Francisco: Jossey-Bass.

Cloke, K., and Joan Goldsmith. 2000. *Resolving conflicts at work: A complete guide for everyone on the job.* San Francisco: Jossey-Bass.

Cloven, D. H., and M. E. Roloff. 1991. Sense-making activities and interpersonal conflict: Communicative cures for the mulling blues. *Western Journal of Speech Communication* 55: 134–158.

Cohen, D., J. Vandello, S. Puente, and A. Rantilla. 1999. "When you call me that, smile!" How norms for politeness, interaction styles, and aggression work together in Southern culture. *Social Psychology Quarterly*, 62, no. 3: 257–275.

Coleman, D. H., and M. A. Straus. 1986. Marital power, conflict, and violence in a nationally representative sample of American couples. *Violence and Victims* 1: 141–157.

Coleman, M. A., M. A. Fine, L. G. Ganong, K. M. Downs, and N. Pauk. 2001. When you're not the Brady Bunch: Identifying perceived conflicts and resolution strategies in stepfamilies. *Personal Relationships* 8: 57–73.

Combs, D. 2004. The way of conflict: Elemental wisdom for resolving disputes and transcending differences. Novato, CA: New World Library.

Comstock, J. 1994. Parent-adolescent conflict: A developmental approach. *Western Journal of Communication* 58: 263–282.

Comstock, J., and K. Strzyzewski. 1990. Interpersonal interaction on television: Family conflict and jealousy on prime time. *Journal of Broadcasting and Electronic Media* 34: 263–282.

Coogler, O. J. 1978. *Structured mediation in divorce settlement*. Lexington, MA: D. C. Heath & Company.

Cose, E. 2004. *Bone to pick*. New York: Atria Books.

Coser, L. A. 1967. *Continuities in the study of social conflict*. New York: Free Press.

Crohan, S. E. 1992. Marital happiness and spousal consensus on beliefs about marital conflict: A longitudinal investigation. *Journal of Social and Personal Relationships* 9: 89–102.

Cromwell, R. E., and D. H. Olson. 1975. *Power in families*. Beverly Hills, CA: Sage Publications.

Cuber, J. F., and P. B. Haroff. 1955. *The significant Americans: A study of sexual behavior among the affluent*. New York: Appleton-Century.

Cupach, W. R. 1980. *Interpersonal conflict: Relational strategies and intimacy*. Paper presented to the Speech Communication Association Convention, New York.

———. 1982. *Communication satisfaction and interpersonal solidarity as outcomes of conflict message strategy use*. Paper presented at the International Communication Association Convention, May.

Dahl, R. A. 1957. The concept of power. *Behavioral Science* 2: 201–215.

Deal, J. E., and K. S. Wampler. 1986. Dating violence: The primacy of previous experience. *Journal of Social and Personal Relationships* 3: 457–471.

Deci, E. L. 1992. On the nature and functions of motivation theories. *Psychological Science* 3: 167–171.

Delia, J. G., and R. A. Clark. 1977. Cognitive complexity, social perception and the development of listener-adapted communication in six-, eight-, ten-, and twelve-year-old boys. *Communication Monographs* 44, no. 4: 326–345.

DeSilvilya, H. S., & Yagil, D. 2005. The role of emotions in conflict management: The case of work teams. *The International Journal of Conflict Management* 16, no. 1: 55–69.

Deutsch, M. 1949. A theory of competition and cooperation. *Human Relations* 2: 129–151.

———. 1958. Trust and suspicion. *Journal of Conflict Resolution* 2: 265–279.

———. 1973. Conflicts: Productive and destructive. In *Conflict resolution through communication*, edited by F. E. Jandt. New York: Harper & Row.

Deutsch, M., and P. Coleman, eds. 2000. *The handbook of conflict resolution*. San Francisco: Jossey-Bass.

DiBlasio, F. 2000. Decision-based forgiveness treatment in cases of marital infidelity. *Psychotherapy* 37, no. 2: 149–158.

Dien, D. S. F. 1982. A Chinese perspective on Kohlberg's theory of moral development. *Developmental Review* 2: 331–341.

Dobash, R. E., and R. P. Dobash. 1979. *Violence against wives*. New York: Free Press.

Donohue, W. A. 1991. *Communication, marital dispute, and divorce mediation*. Hillsdale, NJ: Lawrence Erlbaum Associates.

Donohue, W. A., M. Allen, and N. Burrell. 1988. Mediator communicative competence. *Communication Monographs* 55: 104–119.

Donohue, W. A., L. Drake, and A. J. Roberto. 1994. Mediator issue intervention strategies: A replication and some conclusions. *Mediation Quarterly* 11: 261–274.

Donohue, W. A., and R. Kolt. 1992. *Managing interpersonal conflict*. Newbury Park, CA: Sage Publications.

Dumlao, R., and R. A. Botta. 2000. Family communication patterns and the conflict styles young adults use with their fathers. *Communication Quarterly* 48, no. 2: 174–190.

Dunn, C. W., and C. M. Tucker. 1993. Black children's adaptive functioning and maladaptive behavior associated with quality of family support. *Journal of Multicultural Counseling and Development* 21: 79–87.

Edelgard, M., and W. Colsman. 2002. Conflict resolution style as an indicator of adolescents' substance use and other problem behaviors. *Addictive Behaviors* 26, no. 4: 633–648.

Edwards, H. T., and J. J. White. 1977. *Problems, readings and materials on the lawyer as a negotiator*. St. Paul, MN: West Publishing.

Einarsen, S. 1999. The nature and causes of bullying at work. *International Journal of Manpower* 20: 16–27.

Einarsen, S., and E. G. Mikkelsen. 2003. Individual effects of exposure to bullying at work. In *Bullying and emotional abuse in* the workplace: International perspectives in research and practice, edited by S. Einarsen, H. Hoel, D. Zapf, and C. L. Cooper, 127–144. London: Taylor & Francis Publishers.

Eleff, L. 2001. Paper for mediation class. Arizona State University.

Ellis, D. G. 2006. *Transforming conflict: Communication and ethnopolitical conflict.* Lanham, MD: Rowan & Littlefield Publishers.

El-Sheikh, M. 1994. Children's emotional and physiological responses to interadult angry behavior: The role of history of interparental hostility. *Journal of Abnormal Child Psychology* 22: 661–679.

Emerson, R. M. 1962. Power-dependence relations. *American Sociological Review* 27: 31–41.

Enright, R. 1996. Counseling within the forgiveness triad: On forgiving, receiving forgiveness, and self-forgiveness. *Counseling and Values* 40, no. 2: 107–127.

Enright, R. 2001. *Forgiveness is a choice.* Washington, DC: American Psychological Association.

Enright, R. D., and the Human Development Study Group. 1991. The moral development of forgiveness. In W. Kurtines and Gewirtz (eds.), *Moral behavior and development* 1: 123–152. Hillsdale, NJ: Erlbaum.

Enright, R., E. Gassin, and C. Wu. 1992. Forgiveness: A developmental view. *Journal of Moral Education* 21: 101.

Evans, P. 1992. *The verbally abusive relationship.* Holbrook, MA: Bob Adams.

Exline, J., and R. Baumeister. 2000. Expressing forgiveness and repentance. *Forgiveness, theory, research, and practice,* edited by M. McCullough, K. Pargament, and C. Thoresen. New York: Guilford Press.

Falbo, T., and L. A. Peplau. 1980. Power strategies in intimate relationships. *Journal of Personality and Social Psychology* 38: 618–628.

Felson, R. B. 1996. Big people hit little people: Sex differences in physical power and interpersonal violence. *Criminology* 34, no. 3: 433–452.

Files, L. A. 1981. The human services management task: A time allocation study. *Public Administration Review* 41: 686–692.

Fisher, R. 1971. "Fractionating conflict," in C. Smith (Ed.) *Conflict resolution: Contributions of the behavioral sciences.* Notre Dame: University of Notre Dame Press, 157–169.

Fisher, R. 1985. Beyond yes. *Negotiation Journal* 1: 67–70.

Fisher, R., and S. Brown. 1988. *Getting together: Building a relationship that gets to yes.* Boston: Houghton Mifflin.

Fisher, R., and D. Shapiro. 2005. *Beyond reason: Using emotions as you negotiate.* New York: Penguin Group.

Fisher, R., and W. Ury. 1981. *Getting to yes: Negotiating agreement without giving in.* Boston: Houghton Mifflin.

Fisher, R., W. Ury, and B. Patton. 1991. *Getting to yes.* 2d ed. New York: Penguin Books.

Fletcher, J. 1999. *Disappearing acts: Gender, power, and relational practice at work.* Cambridge, MA: MIT Press.

Fogg, R. W. 1985. Dealing with conflict: A repertoire of creative, peaceful approaches. *Journal of Conflict Resolution* 29: 330–358.

Folger, J. P., M. S. Poole, and R. K. Stutman. 1993. *Working through conflict: A communication perspective.* Glenview, IL: Scott, Foresman & Company.

Folger, J. P., M. S. Poole, and R. K. Stutman. 2004. *Working through conflict: Strategies for relationships, groups, and organizations.* 5th ed. Glenview, IL: Poole, Allyn and Bacon.

———. 2008. *Working through conflict: Strategies for relationships, groups, and organizations.* 6th ed. Glenview, IL: Poole, Allyn and Bacon.

Follett, M. P. 1940. *Dynamic administration: The collected papers of M. P. Follett.* Edited by H. C. Metcalf and L. Urwick. New York: Harper & Brothers.

Forte, P. S. 1997. The high cost of conflict. *Nursing Economics* 15, no. 3: 119–124.

Foss, S., and C. L. Griffin. 1995. Beyond persuasion: A proposal for an invitational rhetoric. *Communication Monographs* 62 (March): 2–18.

Fredrickson, B. L. 2003. The value of positive emotions: The emerging science of positive psychology is coming to understand why it's good to feel good. *American Scientist* 91: 330–335.

Frentz, T., and J. H. Rushing. 1980. *A communicative perspective on closeness/distance and stability/change in intimate ongoing dyads.* Unpublished manuscript. University of Colorado, Boulder.

Frijda, N. 1986. *The emotions.* Cambridge: Cambridge University Press.

Frijda, N. H., A. S. R. Manstead, and S. Bem. (eds.). 2000. *Studies in emotion and social interaction,* New York: Cambridge University Press.

Funk, J., R. Elliott, H. Bechtoldt, T. Pasold, and A. Tsavoussis. 2003. The attitudes toward violence scale: Child version. *Journal of Interpersonal Violence* 18, no. 2: 186–197.

Galvin, K. M., and B. J. Brommel. 1982. *Family communication: Cohesion and change.* Glenview, IL: Scott, Foresman & Company.

———. 1986. *Family communication: Cohesion and change.* 2d ed. Glenview, IL: Scott, Foresman & Company.

Garber, R. J. 1991. Long-term effects of divorce on the self-esteem of young adults. *Journal of Divorce and Remarriage* 17: 131–137.

Gayle, B. M. 1991. Sex equity in workplace conflict management. *Journal of Applied Communication Research* 19: 152–169.

Gayle-Hackett, B. 1989a. *Do females and males differ in the selection of conflict management strategies? A meta-analytic review.* Paper presented to the Western Speech Communication Association Convention, Spokane, Washington, February 17.

———. 1989b. *Gender differences in conflict management strategy selection: A preliminary organizational investigation.* Paper presented to the Western Speech Communication Association Convention, Spokane, Washington, February 17.

Gelles, R. 1981. The myth of the battered husband. In *Marriage and family,* edited by R. Walsh and O. Poes. New York: Guilford Press.

———. 1987. *The violent home.* Beverly Hills, CA: Sage Publications.

Gelles, R. J., and C. P. Cornell. 1990. *Intimate violence in families.* 2d ed. Newbury Park, CA: Sage Publications.

Gerzon, M. 1992. *A choice of heroes: The changing faces of American manhood.* New York: Houghton Mifflin Company; reprint edition.

Gibb, J. 1961. Defensive communication. *Journal of Communication* 11, no. 3: 141–148.

Gilligan, C. 1982. *In a different voice.* Cambridge, MA: Harvard University Press: 18–63.

Gilmore, S. K., and P. W. Fraleigh. 1992. *Style profile for communication at work.* Eugene, OR: Friendly Press.

Gire, J. T., and D. W. Carment. 1993. Dealing with disputes: The influence of individualism-collectivism. *Journal of Social Psychology* 133, no. 1: 81–96.

Glass, I. 2004. Apology. *This American life.* Chicago Public Radio. November 5.

Goffman, E. 1967. *Interaction ritual: Essays on face to face behavior.* Garden City, NY: Doubleday.

Goldberg, A. A., M. S. Cavanaugh, and C. E. Larson. 1983. The meaning of "power." *Journal of Applied Communication Research* 11, no. 2: 89–108.

Goleman, D. 1995. *Emotional intelligence.* New York: Bantam Books.

———. 1998. *Working with emotional intelligence.* New York: Bantam Books.

Goodpaster, G. 1992. Lawsuits as negotiations. *Negotiation Journal* 8, no. 3: 221–239.

Goodrich, T. J. 1991. Women, power, and family therapy: What's wrong with this picture? In *Women and power: Perspectives for family therapy,* edited by T. J. Goodrich, 3–35. New York: W. W. Norton & Company.

Gottman, J., C. Notarius, J. Gonso, and H. Markman. 1976. *A couple's guide to communication.* Champaign, IL: Research Press.

Gottman, J. M. 1982. Emotional responsiveness in marital conversations. *Journal of Communication* 32, no. 8: 108–120.

———. 1994. *What predicts divorce? The relationship between marital process and marital outcomes.* Hillsdale, NJ: Lawrence Erlbaum Associates.

———. 1999. *The marriage clinic: A scientifically based marital therapy.* New York: W. W. Norton and Co.

Gottman, J. M., and L. J. Krokoff. 1989. Marital interaction and satisfaction: A longitudinal view. *Journal of Consulting and Clinical Psychology* 57: 47–52.

Gray, B. 1989. *Collaborating: Finding common ground for multi-party problems.* San Francisco: Jossey-Bass.

Gray-Little, B. 1982. Marital quality and power processes among black couples. *Journal of Marriage and the Family* 44, no. 3: 633–646.

Greenberger, D., and C. A. Padesky. 1995. *Mind over mood: Change how you feel by changing the way you think.* New York: Guilford Press.

Greene, K., and M. Bogo. 2002. The different faces of intimate violence: Implications for assessment and treatment. *Journal of Marital and Family Therapy* 28, no. 4: 455–467.

Grych, J. H., and F. D. Fincham. 1990. Marital conflict and children's adjustment: A cognitive conceptual framework. *Psychological Bulletin* 108: 267–290.

Gudykunst, W. B., and Y. Yun Kim. 2002. *Communicating with strangers: An approach to intercultural communication.* New York: McGraw-Hill.

Gudykunst, W. and S. Ting-Toomey, *Culture and Interpersonal Communication* (Beverly Hills, CA: Sage, 1988).

Guerin, P. J., Jr., L. F. Fay, S. L. Burden, and J. G. Kautto. 1987. *The evaluation and treatment of marital conflict: A four-stage approach.* New York: Basic Books.

Guerrero, L. K. and Angela G. La Valley. 2006. "Conflict, emotion and communication." In *The Sage handbook of conflict communication,* edited by John G. Oetzel and Stella Ting-Toomey. Thousand Oaks, CA: Sage Publications: 69–96.

Guggenbuhl-Craig, A. 1971. *Power and the helping professions.* Translated by M. Gubitz. Dallas: Spring Publications.

Gulliver, P. H. 1979. *Disputes and negotiations: A cross-cultural perspective.* New York: Academic Press.

Haferkamp, C. J. 1991–1992. Orientations to conflict: Gender, attributions, resolution strategies, and self-monitoring. *Current Psychology: Research and Reviews* 10: 227–240.

Haley, J. 1959. An interactional description of schizophrenia. *Psychiatry* 22: 321–332.

Harris, L. M., K. J. Gergen, and J. W. Lannamann. 1986. Aggression rituals. *Communication Monographs* 53: 252–265.

Harrison, T. R. (2007). "My professor is so unfair: Student attitudes and experiences of conflict with faculty," *Conflict Resolution Quarterly,* 24, Issue 3, 349–368.

Harsanyi, J. C. 1962. Measurement of social power in n-person reciprocal power situations. *Behavioral Science* 7: 81–91.

Hart, R. P., and D. M. Burks. 1972. Rhetorical sensitivity and social interaction. *Speech Monographs* 39, no. 2: 75–91.

Hartje, J. H. 1984. Lawyer's skills in negotiations: Justice in unseen hands. *Missouri Journal of Dispute Resolution:* 119–192.

Harvey, J. (2004). Trauma and recovery strategies across the lifespan of long-term married couples. Phoenix: Arizona State University West Press.

Hatfield, E., M. K. Utne, and J. Traupmann. 1979. Equity theory and intimate relationships. In *Social exchange in developing relationships,* edited by R. L. Burgess and T. L. Huston. New York: Academic Press.

Hathaway, W. 1995. A new way of viewing dispute resolution training. *Mediation Quarterly* 13: 37–45.

Hayakawa, S. I. 1978. *Language in thought and action.* 4th ed. New York: Harcourt Brace Jovanovich.

Hayes, Javette Grace and Sandra Metts. October–December 2008. Managing the expression of emotions. *Western Journal of Communication.* 72, no. 4: 374–396.

Hedeen, T. 2004. The evolution and evaluation of community mediation: Limited research suggests unlimited progress. *Conflict Resolution Quarterly* 22, no. 1–2: 101–133.

Heer, D. M. 1963. The measurement and bases of family power: An overview. *Marriage and Family Living* 25: 133–139.

Heim, P., and S. K. Galant, 1993. *Smashing the glass ceiling: Tactics for women who want to win in business.* New York: Simon and Schuster.

Hein, G., and T. Singer. 2008. I feel how you feel but not always: The empathic brain and its modulation. *Current Opinion in Neurobiology,* 18: 153–158.

Heitler, S. 1990. *From conflict to resolution: Skills and strategies for individual, couple, and family therapy.* New York: W. W. Norton & Company.

Hermone, R. H. 1974. How to negotiate and come out the winner. *Management Review* 1: 19–25.

Heydenberk, Roberta A., Warren R. Heydenberk and Vera Tzenova, 2006. Conflict resolution and bully prevention: Skills for school success. *Conflict Resolution Quarterly* 24, no. 1 (Fall).

Hijuelos, O. 1995. *Mr. Ives' Christmas.* New York: Harper Collins.

Hilgerman, R. H. 1994. *Goal management at work.* New York: McGraw-Hill.

Hoffman, L. 1981. *Foundations of family therapy: A conceptual framework for systems change.* New York: Basic Books.

Hogh, A., M. Engstrom-Henriksson, and H. Burr, 2005. A 5-year follow-up study of aggression at work and psychological health. *International Journal of Behavioral Medicine* 12, no. 4: 256–265.

Holloway, S., and G. Brager. 1985. Implicit negotiations and organizational practice. *Administration in Social Work* 9: 15–24.

Holmes, M. E. 1992. Phase structures in negotiation. In *Communication and negotiation,* edited by L. L. Putnam and M. E. Roloff. Newbury Park, CA: Sage Publications: 83–105.

Holmgren, M. 1993. Forgiveness and the intrinsic value of persons. *American Philosophical Quarterly* 30: 4.

Huang, B., H. R. White, R. Kosterman, R. F. Catalano, and J. D. Hawkins. 2001. Developmental associations between alcohol and interpersonal aggression during adolescence. *Journal of Research in Crime and Delinquency* 38, no. 1: 64.

Ilich, J. 1981. *Power negotiating: Strategies for winning in life and business.* Boston: Addison-Wesley Publishing.

Infante, D. 1988. *Arguing constructively.* Prospect Heights, IL: Waveland Press.

Infante, D. A., K. C. Hartley, M. M. Martin, M. A. Higgins, S. D. Bruning, and G. Hur. 1992. Initiating and reciprocating verbal aggression: Effects on credibility and credited valid arguments. *Communication Studies* 43: 182–190.

Infante, D. A., B. L. Riddle, C. L. Horvath, and S. A. Tumlin. 1992. Verbal aggressiveness: Messages and reasons. *Communication Quarterly* 40: 116–126.

Infante, D. A., and C. J. Wigley III. 1986. Verbal aggressiveness: An interpersonal model and measure. *Communication Monographs* 53: 61–69.

Internet Safety Technical Task Force. 2009. *Final report of the internet safety technical task force to the multi-state working group on social networking of state attorneys general of the United States.*

Irving, H. H., and P. E. Bohm. 1978. A social science approach to family dispute resolution. *Canadian Journal of Family Law* 1, no. 1: 39–56.

Isen, A. (1987). Positive affect, cognitive processes, and social behavior. In *Advances in Experimental Social Psychology,* edited by L. Berkowitz San Diego: Academic Press: 20: 203–253.

Ivy, D. K., and P. Backlund. 2003. *Genderspeak: Personal effectiveness in gender communication.* New York: McGraw-Hill.

Izard, C. E., and B. P. Ackerman. 2000. Motivational, organizational, and regulatory functions of discreet emotions. In *Handbook of emotions.* 2nd ed. Edited by M. Lewis & J. M. Haviland-Jones New York: Guilford Press.

Jamieson, D. W., and K. W. Thomas. 1974. Power and conflict in the student-teacher relationship. *Journal of Applied Behavioral Science* 10: 321–333.

Jandt, F. E., ed. 1973. *Conflict resolution through communication.* New York: Harper & Row.

Jaycox, L. H., and R. L. Repetti. 1993. Conflict in families and the psychological adjustment of preadolescent children. *Journal of Family Psychology* 7: 344–355.

Jennings, A. M., C. J. Salts, and T. A. Smith Jr. 1991. Attitudes toward marriage: Effects of parental conflict, family structure, and gender. *Journal of Divorce and Remarriage* 17: 67–79.

Johnson, A. J. 2002. Beliefs about arguing: A comparison of public issue and personal issue arguments. *Communication Reports* 15, no. 2: 99–112.

Johnson, B. 1977. *Communication: The process of organizing.* Boston: Allyn & Bacon.

Johnson, C., and R. Ford. 1996. Dependence power, legitimacy, and tactical choice. *Social Psychology Quarterly* 59, no. 2: 126–141.

Johnson, D. W., and R. T. Johnson. 1996. Reducing school violence through conflict resolution training. *NAASP Bulletin* 80, no. 579: 11–19.

Johnson, P. 1976. Women and power: Toward a theory of effectiveness. *Journal of Social Issues* 32: 99–110.

Johnson, S. M. 2002. *Emotionally focused couple therapy with trauma survivors: Strengthening attachment bonds.* New York: Guilford Press.

Jones, D. C. 1992. Parental divorce, family conflict and friendship networks. *Journal of Social and Personal Relationships* 9: 219–235.

Jones, T. S. 1988. Phase structures in agreement and no-agreement mediation. *Communication Research* 15: 470–495.

Jones, T. S. 2001. *Evaluating your conflict resolution education program.* Columbus, Ohio: Ohio Department of Education.

———. 2004. Conflict resolution education: The field, the findings, and the future. *Conflict Resolution Quarterly* 22, no. 1–2: 233–267.

Jones, Tricia S. and Ross Brinkert. 2008. *Conflict coaching: Conflict management strategies and skills for the individual.* Thousand Oaks, CA: Sage Publications.

Jones, T. S., and R. O. Compton (eds.). 2003. *Kids working it out: Stories and strategies for making peace in our schools.* San Francisco: Jossey-Bass/John Wiley.

Jones, T. S., and D. Kmitta (eds.). 2000. *Does it work? The case for conflict resolution education in our nation's schools.* Washington, DC: Conflict Resolution Education Network.

Jordan, J. S. 1990. Courage in connection: Conflict, compassion, creativity. In *Work in progress.* Stone Center Working Paper Series. Wellesley, MA: Stone Center, Wellesley College.

Jordan, J. V. 2008. Valuing vulnerability: New definitions of courage. *Women and Therapy,* 31, no. 2: 209–233.

Jordan-Jackson, Felecia F., Yang Lin, Andrew S. Rancer, and Dominic A. Infante. 2008. "Perceptions of males' and females' use of aggressive messages in an interpersonal dispute: You've come a long way baby?" *Western Journal of Communication* 72, no. 3, July–September: 239–258.

Jordan, J., S. Kaplan, J. Miller, I. Stiver, and J. Surrey. 1991. *Women's growth in connection.* New York: Guilford Press.

Joshi, A. 2008. Conflict resolution between friends during middle childhood. *The Journal of Genetic Psychology,* 169, no. 2: 133–148.

Jouriles, E. N., W. J. Bourg, and A. M. Farris. 1991. Marital adjustment and child conduct problems: A comparison of the correlation across subsamples. *Journal of Consulting and Clinical Psychology* 59: 354–357.

Jouriles, E. N., and A. Farris. 1992. Effects of marital conflict on subsequent parent-son interactions. *Behavior Therapy* 23: 355–374.

Kalmuss, D. S., and M. A. Straus. 1982. Wife's marital dependency and wife abuse. *Journal of Marriage and the Family* 44: 277–286.

Kam, C. C.-S., and M. H. Bond. 2008. Role of emotions and behavioural responses in mediating the impact of face loss on relationship deterioration: Are Chinese more face-sensitive than Americans? *Asian Journal of Social Psychology* 11: 175–184.

Kaplan, R. E. 1975. Maintaining interpersonal relationships. *Interpersonal Development* 6: 106.

Kaschak, E. 1992. *Engendered lives: A new psychology of women's experience.* New York: Basic Books.

Keashly, L., and J. H. Neuman (eds.). 2008. *Final report: Workplace behavior (bullying) project survey.* Mankato, MN: Minnesota State University.

Keene, F. 1995. The politics of forgiveness. *On the Issues,* Fall: 107–109.

Kellermann, K., and B. C. Shea. 1996. Threats, suggestions, hints and promises: Gaining compliance efficiently and politely. *Communication Quarterly* 44: 145–165.

Kellett, P. M. 2007. *Conflict dialogue: Working with layers of meaning for productive relationships.* Thousand Oaks, CA: Sage Publications.

Kelley, D. 1998. The communication of forgiveness. *Communication Studies* 49: 255–271.

Kelly, J. 2004. Family mediation research: Is there empirical support for the field? *Conflict Resolution Quarterly* 22, no. 1–2: 3–35.

Keltner, J. (Sam). 1983. *You are the mediator.* Unpublished guide. Department of Speech Communication, Oregon State University.

Keltner, J. W. 1987. *Mediation: Toward a civilized system of dispute resolution.* Annandale, VA: Speech Communication Association.

————. 1994. *The management of struggle: Elements of dispute resolution through negotiation, mediation and arbitration.* Cresskill, NJ: Hampton Press.

Kenkel, W. W. 1957. Influence differentiation in family decision making. *Sociology and Social Research* 43: 18–25.

Keough, C. M. 1992. Bargaining arguments and argumentative bargainers. In *Communication and negotiation*, edited by L. L. Putnam and M. E. Roloff, 109–127. Newbury Park, CA: Sage Publications.

Kiecolt-Glaser, J. K., T. Newton, J. T. Cacioppo, R. G. CacCallum, R. Glaser, and W. B. Malarkey. 1996. "Marital conflict and endocrine function: Are men really more physiologically affected than women?" *Journal of Consulting and Clinical Psychology* 64, no. 2: 324(9).

Kilmann, R., and K. W. Thomas. 1975. Interpersonal conflict-handling behavior as reflections of Jungian personality dimensions. *Psychological Reports* 37: 971–980.

Kim, J., and C. Emery. 2003. Marital power, conflict, norm consensus, and marital violence in a nationally representative sample of Korean couples. *Journal of Interpersonal Violence* 18, no. 2: 197–220.

Kimmel, M. J., D. G. Pruitt, J. M. Magenau, E. Konar-Goldband, and P. J. D. Carnevale. 1980. Effects of trust, aspiration, and gender on negotiation tactics. *Journal of Personality and Social Psychology* 38: 9–22.

King, M. L., Jr. 1989. *Strength to love.* Augsburg Fortress Press.

Kipnis, D. 1976. *The powerholders.* Chicago: University of Chicago Press.

Kipnis, D., S. Schmidt, and I. Wilkerson. 1980. Intraorganizational influence tactics: Explorations in getting one's way. *Journal of Applied Psychology* 65: 440–452.

Kluwer, E. S., J. A. M. Heesink, and E. van de Vliert. 1996. Marital conflict about the division of household labor and paid work. *Journal of Marriage and the Family* 58, no. 4: 958–970.

Knapp, M. L., L. L. Putnam, and L. J. Davis. 1988. Measuring interpersonal conflict in organizations: Where do we go from here? *Management Communication Quarterly* 1: 414–429.

Koerner, A. F., and M. A. Fitzpatrick. 2002. You never leave your family in a fight: The impact of family of origin on conflict-behavior in romantic relationships. *Communication Studies* 53, no. 3: 234–252.

Kohlberg, L. 1976. Moral stages and moralization: The cognitive development approach in Licrona. In *Moral development and behavior: Theory, research and social issues.* New York: Holt Reinhart.

Kohn, A. 1992. *No contest: The case against competition.* New York: Houghton Mifflin.

Kolb, D., and L. Putnam. 1992. The multiple faces of conflict in organizations. *Journal of Organizational Behavior* 13: 311–324.

————. 1997. Through the looking glass: Negotiation theory refracted through the lens of gender. In *Frontiers in dispute resolution in industrial relations and human resources*, edited by S. Gleason, 231–257. East Lansing, MI: Michigan State University Press.

Korabik, K., G. L. Baril, and C. Watson. 1993. Managers' conflict management style and leadership effectiveness: The moderating effects of gender. *Sex Roles* 29, no. 5/6: 405–418.

Kornfield, J. 2001. *After the ecstasy, the laundry.* New York: Bantam Press.

Kotter, J. P. 1985. *Power and influence: Beyond formal authority.* New York: Free Press.

Kowalski, K. M. 1998. Peer mediation success stories: In nearly 10,000 schools nationwide, peer mediation helps teens solve problems without violence. *Current Health* 25, no. 2: 13–16.

Kressel, K., N. Jaffee, B. Tuchman, C. Watson, and M. Deutsch. 1980. A typology of divorcing couples: Implications for mediation and the divorce process. *Family Process* 19, no. 2: 101–116.

Kritek, P. B. 1994. *Negotiating at an uneven table: A practical approach to working with difference and diversity.* San Francisco: Jossey-Bass.

Krokoff, L. J., J. M. Gottman, and A. K. Roy. 1988. Blue-collar and white-collar marital interaction and communication orientation. *Journal of Social and Personal Relationships* 5: 201–221.

Kübler-Ross, E. 1970. *Death and dying.* New York: Macmillan.

Kuhn, T., and M. S. Poole. 2000. Do conflict management styles affect group decision making? Evidence from a longitudinal study. *Human Communication Research* 26, no. 4: 558–591.

Kurdek, L. A. 1994. Areas of conflict for gay, lesbian, and heterosexual couples: What couples argue about influences relationship satisfaction. *Journal of Marriage and the Family* 56: 923–935.

Laing, R. D., H. Phillipson, and A. R. Lee. 1966. *Interpersonal perception.* Baltimore: Perennial Library.

Lakoff, G., and M. Johnson. 1980. *Metaphors we live by.* Chicago: University of Chicago Press.

Lamott, A. 1999. *Traveling mercies.* New York: Anchor Books.

Lampman, J., 2005. The civil rights movement must water its spiritual roots, *The Christian Science Monitor,* Boston, 14. January 4.

Lange, J. I. 1993. The logic of competing information campaigns: Conflict over old growth and the spotted owl. *Communication Monographs* 60: 239–257.

Larson, C., and F. LaFasto. 1989. *Teamwork*. Newbury Park, CA: Sage Publications.

Lax, D., and J. Sebenius. 1986. *The manager as negotiator*. New York: Free Press.

Layton, M. 1999. Apology not accepted. *Utne Reader*, March–April, 45–50.

Lazare, A. 2004. *On apology*. New York: Oxford University Press.

Lederer, W. J., and D. D. Jackson. 1968. *Mirages of marriage*. New York: W. W. Norton & Company.

Lenton, R. L. 1995a. Power versus feminist theories of wife abuse. *Canadian Journal of Criminology* 37: 305–330.

———. 1995b. Feminist versus interpersonal power theories of wife abuse revisited. *Canadian Journal of Criminology* 37, no. 4: 567–574.

Lerner, H. G. 1989. *The dance of intimacy*. New York: Harper & Row.

Lewicki, R. J., and J. A. Litterer. 1985. *Negotiation*. Homewood, IL: Irwin.

Lewis, M., and J. M. Haviland-Jones (eds.). 2000. *Handbook of emotions*. 2nd ed. New York: Guilford Press.

Leymann, H. 1990. Mobbing and psychological terror at workplaces. *Violence and Victims* 5: 119–126.

Lilly, E. R. 1989. The determinants of organizational power styles. *Educational Review* 41: 281–293.

Lim, T., and J. Bowers. 1991. Face-work: Solidarity, approbation, and tact. *Human Communication Research* 17: 415–450.

Lindbergh, A. 1955. *Gift from the sea*. New York: Pantheon.

Lloyd, S. A., and B. C. Emery. 1994. Physically aggressive conflict in romantic relationships. In *Conflict in personal relationships*, edited by D. D. Cahn. Hillsdale, NJ: Lawrence Erlbaum Associates: 27–46.

Lord, R. 1991. Do I have to forgive? *The Christian Century* 108: 902–903.

Lulofs, R. S. 1994. *Conflict: From theory to action*. Scottsdale, AZ: Gorsuch Scarisbuck Publishers.

Lulofs, R., and D. Cahn. 2000. *Conflict: From theory to action*. Boston: Allyn and Bacon: 317–325.

Longaretti, L., and R. English. 2007. *Helping your pupils to communicate effectively and manage conflict*. London: Taylor & Francis.

Lutgen-Sandvik, P., S. Tracy, and J. Alberts. 2005. *Burned by bullying in the American workplace: A first time study of U.S. prevalence and delineation of bullying "degree."* Presented at the Western States Communication Convention, February, San Francisco, California.

MacDonald, G., M. P. Zanna, and J. G. Holmes. 2000. An experimental test of the role of alcohol in relationship conflict. *Journal of Experimental Social Psychology* 36, no. 2: 182–194.

Mace, D. R. 1987. *Close companions: The marriage enrichment handbook*. 1982; reprint. New York: Continuum.

Mack, R. M., and R. C. Snyder. 1973. The analysis of social conflict—toward an overview and synthesis. In *Conflict resolution through communication*, edited by F. E. Jandt. New York: Harper & Row.

Mackey, R. A., and B. A. O'Brien. 1998. Marital conflict management: Gender and ethnic differences. *Social Work* 43, no. 2: 128–132.

Madanes, C. 1981. *Strategic family therapy*. San Francisco: Jossey-Bass.

Maiese, M. 2006. Engaging the emotions in conflict intervention. *Conflict Resolution Quarterly* 24, no. 2: 187–195.

Malis, R. S., and M. E. Roloff. 2006. Demand/withdraw patterns in serial arguments: Implications for well-being. *Human Communication Research*, 32: 198–216.

Marano, H. E. 1996. A saga of spouse abuse. *Psychology Today*, May/June, 56–77.

Marin, M. J., J. C. Sherblom, and T. Shipps. 1994. Contextual influences on nurses' conflict management strategies. *Western Journal of Communication* 58: 201–228.

Marks, M. A. 1981. *The suing of America*. New York: Seaview Books.

Marshall, L. L. 1994. Physical and psychological abuse. In *The dark side of interpersonal communication*, edited by W. R. Cupach and B. H. Spitzberg. Hillsdale, NJ: Lawrence Erlbaum Associates: 281–311.

Martin, M. M., C. M. Anderson, and G. L. Horvath. 1996. Feelings about verbal aggression: Justifications for sending and hurt from receiving verbally aggressive messages. *Communication Research Reports* 13: 19–26.

Martin, M. W., and R. T. Denton. 1998. Defining forgiveness: An empirical exploration of process and role. *American Journal of Family Therapy* 26, no. 4: 281–292.

May, R. 1972. *Power and innocence: A search for the sources of violence*. New York: Dell Publishing.

Mayer, P. 2002. *Earthtown square*. Stillwater, MN: Blue Boat Publishing.

McCall, M. W., Jr. 1979. Power, authority, and influence. In *Organizational behavior*, edited by S. Kerr. Columbus, OH: Grid Publishing.

McCann, R. M., and J. M. Honeycutt. 2006. A cross-cultural analysis of imagined interactions. *Human Communication Research* 32: 274–301.

McClelland, D. C. 1969. The two faces of power. *Journal of International Affairs* 24: 141–154.

McCorkle, S., and J. Mills. 1992. Rowboat in a hurricane: Metaphors of interpersonal conflict management. *Communication Reports* 5, no. 2: 57–66.

McCready, V., J. E. Roberts, D. Bengala, H. Harris, G. Kingsley, and C. Krikorian. 1996. A comparison of conflict tactics in the supervisory process. *Journal of Speech and Hearing Research* 39, no. 1: 191–200.

McCullough, M., K. Pargament, and C. Thoresen. 2000. *Forgiveness, theory, research and practice*. New York, London: Guilford Press.

McCullough, M. E., E. L. Worthington, and K. C. Rachal. 1997. Interpersonal forgiving in close relationships. *Journal of Personality and Social Psychology* 73: 321–336.

McDonald, G. W. 1980. Family power: The assessment of a decade of theory and research. *Journal of Marriage and the Family* 42, no. 4: 841–854.

McEwan, I. 2001. *Atonement*. New York, Anchor Books.

McFall, L. 1991. What's wrong with bitterness? In *Feminist ethics*, edited by C. Card. Lawrence: University Press of Kansas.

McGillis, D. 1981. Conflict resolution outside the courts. *Applied Social Psychology Annual* 2: 243–262.

McGonagle, K. A., R. C. Kessler, & I. H. Gotlib, (1993). The effects of marital disagreement style, frequency, and outcome on marital disruption. *Journal of Social and Personal Relationships*, 10, 385–404.

McGuigan, R., and N. Popp. 2007. The self in conflict: The evolution in mediation. *Conflict Resolution Quarterly* 25, no. 2.

McKay, K., M. Hill, S. Freedman, and R. Enright. 2007. Towards a feminist empowerment model of forgiveness psychotherapy. *Psychotherapy: Theory, Practice, & Training* 44, no. 1: 14–29.

McLaughlin, A. Africa after war: Paths to forgiveness. *Christian Science Monitor*. Retrieved from http://www.csmonitor.com/2006/1023-10-26p01s03-woaf.html.

Meierding, N. R. 1993. Does mediation work? A survey of long-term satisfaction and durability rates for privately mediated agreements. *Mediation Quarterly* 11: 157–170.

Menkel-Meadow, C. 1986. The transformation of disputes by lawyers: What the dispute paradigm does and does not tell us. *Missouri Journal of Dispute Resolution*: 25–44.

Menz, F., and A. Al-Roubaie. 2008. Interruptions, status, and gender in medical interviews: The harder you brake, the longer it takes. *Discourse and Society* 19, no. 5: 645–666.

Menzel, K. E. 1991. Judging the fairness of mediation: A critical framework. *Mediation Quarterly* 9, no. 1: 3–20.

Merriam, G. 2004. Author tells docs: Learn and use the word "sorry." *The Missoulian*.

Merrill, D. M. 1996. Conflict and cooperation among adult siblings during the transition to the role of filial caregiver. *Journal of Social and Personal Relationships* 13: 399–413.

Metcoff, J., and C. A. Whitaker. 1982. Family microevents: Communication patterns for problem solving. In *Normal family processes*, edited by F. Walsh. New York: Guilford Press.

Metts, S. 1994. Relational transgressions. In *The dark side of interpersonal communication*, edited by W. R. Cupach and Brian H. Spitzberg. Hillside, NJ: Lawrence Erlbaum Publishers: 217–239.

Metz, M. E., B. R. S. Rosser, and N. Strapko. 1994. Differences in conflict-resolution styles among heterosexual, gay, and lesbian couples. *Journal of Sex Research* 31: 293–308.

Mikula, G., K. R. Scherer, and U. Athenstaedt. 1998. The role of injustice in the elicitation of differential emotional reactions. *Personality and Social Psychology Bulletin* 24, no. 7: 769–783.

Millar, F. E., and L. E. Rogers. 1987. Relational dimensions of interpersonal dynamics. In *Interpersonal processes: New directions in communication research*, edited by M. E. Roloff and G. R. Miller. Vol. 14 of Sage Annual Reviews of Communication Research. Newbury Park, CA: Sage Publications: 117–139.

———. 1988. Power dynamics in marital relationships. In *Perspectives on marital interaction*, edited by O. Noller and M. A. Fitzpatrick. Clevedon, UK: Multilingual Matters: 78–97.

Miller, G. R., and M. Steinberg. 1975. *Between people: A new analysis of interpersonal communication*. Chicago: Science Research Associates.

Miller, J. B. 1986. What do we mean by relationships? In *Work in progress*. Stone Center Working Paper Series, no. 22. Wellesley, MA: Stone Center, Wellesley College.

———. 1991. Women's and men's scripts for interpersonal conflict. *Psychology of Women Quarterly* 15: 15–29.

Minuchin, S. 1974. *Families and family therapy*. Cambridge, MA: Harvard University Press.

Mishler, E. G. and N. E. Waxler. 1968. *Interaction in Families: An experimental study of family processes and schizophrenia*. New York: John Wiley and Sons.

Miura, S. Y. 1999. The mediation of conflict in the traditional Hawaiian family: A collectivist approach. *Communication Quarterly* 47: 19.

Moffitt, T. E., A. Caspi, R. F. Krueger, L. Magdol, P. A. Silva, R. Sydney, and G Margolin. 1997. Do partners agree about abuse in their relationship? *Psychological Assessment* 9, no. 1: 47–57.

Moore, C. 1986. *The mediation process*. San Francisco, CA: Jossey-Bass.

———. 1996. *The mediation process*. 2d ed. San Francisco, CA: Jossey-Bass.

———. 2003. *The mediation process: Practical strategies for resolving conflict*. San Francisco: Jossey-Bass.

Moran, R. T., J. Allen, R. Wichman, T. Ando, and M. Sasano. 1994. Japan. In *Global perspectives on organizational conflict*, edited by M. A. Rahim and A. A. Blum. Westport, CT: Praeger Publishing: 33–52.

Murphy, C. M., and T. J. O'Farrell. 1994. Factors associated with marital aggression in male alcoholics. *Journal of Family Psychology* 8 no. 3: 321–336.

Murray, J. A. 1986. Understanding competing theories of negotiation. *Negotiation Journal* 2 (April): 179–186.

Murray-Close, D., Crick, N. R., & Galotti, K. M. (2006). Children's moral reasoning regarding physical and relational aggression. *Social Development* 15, no. 3: 345–372.

Napier, A., and C. Whitaker. 1978. *The family crucible*. New York: Harper & Row.

Neale, M., and M. Bazerman. 1985. When will externally set aspiration levels improve negotiator performance? A look at integrative behavior in a competitive market. *Journal of Occupational Behavior* 6: 19–32.

Neff, K., and S. Harter. 2002. The authenticity of conflict resolutions among adult couples: Does women's other-oriented behavior reflect their true selves. *Sex Roles: A Journal of Research*, November, 403–421.

Neill, J. R., and D. P. Kniskern. 1982. *From psyche to system: The evolving therapy of Carl Whitaker*. New York: Guilford Press.

Neimeyer, G. J., and R. A. Neimeyer. 1985. Relational trajectories: A personal construct contribution. *Journal of Social and Personal Relationships* 2: 325–349.

Newman, Richard S. 2004. When elementary school students are harassed by peers: A self-regulative perspective on help seeking. *Elementary School Journal* 103: 339–357.

Nicolotti, L., M. el-Sheikh, and S. M. Whitson. 2003. Children's coping with marital conflict and their adjustment and physical health: Vulnerability and protective functions. *Journal of Family Psychology* 17, no. 3: 315–326.

Noller, P., J. A. Feeney, D. Bonnell, and V. Callan. 1994. A longitudinal study of conflict in early marriage. *Journal of Social and Personal Relationships* 11: 233–252.

Nugier, A., P. M. Niedenthal, M. Brauer, and P. Chekroun. 2007. Moral and angry emotions provoked by informal social control. *Cognition and Emotion* 21, no. 8: 1699–1720.

Oetzel, John G. and Stella Ting-Toomey (eds). *The Sage handbook of conflict communication*. Thousand Oaks, CA: Sage Publications, 2006.

O'Leary, K. D., J. Barling, I. Arias, A. Rosenbaum, J. Malone, and A. Tyree. 1989. Prevalence and stability of physical aggression between spouses: A longitudinal analysis. *Journal of Consulting and Clinical Psychology* 57: 263–268.

Olson, D. H., and C. Rabunsky. 1972. Validity of four measures of family power. *Journal of Marriage and Family* 34, no. 2: 224–233.

Olson, D. H., D. H. Sprenkle, and C. Russell. 1979. Circumplex model of marital and family systems. Part 2. Cohesion and adaptability dimensions, family types and clinical applications. *Family Process* 18: 3–28.

Olweus, D. 1993. Bullying at school: What we know and what we can do. Hoboken, NJ.: Wiley-Blackwell.

Ortony, A. 1975. Why metaphors are necessary and not just nice. *Educational Theory* 25, no. 1: 45–53.

Palfrey, J., D. Sacco, D. Boyd, L. DeBonis, and Internet Safety Technical Task Force. 2009. Enhancing child safety and online technologies. *Final report of the internet safety technical task force to the multi-state working group on social networking of state attorneys general of the United States.*

Palmer, J. 1997. Finding a way to forgive: Reclaiming power and wholeness. *Prism: A Theological Forum for the UCC*, Spring, 89–99.

Papa, M. J., and E. J. Natalle. 1989. Gender, strategy selection and discussion satisfaction in interpersonal conflict. *Western Journal of Speech Communication* 53: 260–272.

Papa, M. J., and E. A. Pood. 1988. Coorientational accuracy and differentiation in the management of conflict. *Communication Research* 15: 400–425.

Papp, L. M., E. M. Cummings, and M. C. Goeke-Morey. 2002. Marital conflicts in the home when children are present versus absent. *Developmental Psychology* 38, no. 5: 774(10).

Papp, P., O. Silverstein, and E. Carter. 1973. Family sculpting in preventive work with "well" families. *Family Process* 12, no. 1: 197–212.

Paterson B., Bradley P., Stark C., Saddler D., Leadbetter D. and Allen D., Deaths Associated with Restraint Use in Health and Social Care in the United Kingdom: The Results of A Preliminary Survey, Journal of Psychiatric and Mental Health Nursing, 10, 3–1, 2002.

Paul, G. 2008. *Forgiveness as a cluturalphenomenon: A case study of Amish and English forgiveness.* Paper presented at the meeting of the National Communication Association Annual Meeting, November 22.

Paul, J., and M. Paul. 1983. *Do I have to give up me to be loved by you?* Minneapolis, MN: CompCare Publications.

———. 1987. *If you really loved me.* Minneapolis, MN: CompCare Publications.

Pearson, J., N. Thonnes, and L. Vanderkooi. 1982. The decision to mediate profiles—individuals who accept and reject the opportunity to mediate contested child custody and visitation issues. *Journal of Divorce* 6 (Winter): 17–35.

Pearson, J. C., L. H. Turner, and W. Todd-Mancillas. 1991. *Gender and communication.* 2d ed. Dubuque, IA: William C. Brown Communications.

Phillips, G. M., and N. Metzger. 1976. *Intimate communication.* Boston: Allyn & Bacon.

Pike, G. R., and A. L. Sillars. 1985. Reciprocity of marital communication. *Journal of Social and Personal Relationships* 2: 303–324.

Planalp, S. 1999. Communicating emotion: Social, moral and cultural processes. Cambridge: Cambridge University Press.

Poole, Marshall Scott and Johny T. Garner. "Perspective on Workgroup Conflict and Communication," In *The Sage handbook of conflict communication*, edited by John G. Oetzel and Stella Ting-Toomey. Thousand Oaks, CA: Sage Publications, 2006: 267–292.

Popple, P. R. 1984. Negotiation: A critical skill for social work administrators. *Administration in Social Work* 8: 1–11.

Portello, J. Y., and C. Long. 1994. Gender role orientation, ethical and interpersonal conflicts, and conflict handling styles of female managers. *Sex Roles* 31: 683–701.

Pruitt, D. G. 1981. *Negotiation behavior*. New York: Academic Press.

———. 1983a. Achieving integrative agreements. In *Negotiating in organizations*, edited by M. H. Bazerman and R. Lewicki. Beverly Hills, CA: Sage Publications.

———. 1983b. Strategic choice in negotiation. *American Behavioral Scientist* 27: 167–194.

Pukui, M. 1979. *Nana i ke kumu: Look to the source*. Honolulu, HI: Queen Liliʻuokalani Children's Center.

Putnam, L. L. 1986. *Negotiation of intergroup conflict in organizations*. Lecture delivered at Baylor University, Waco, Texas, October 21.

———. 1988. *Reframing integrative and distributive bargaining: A process perspective*. Revised manuscript. Lafayette, IN: Purdue University, Spring.

———. 1996. *A gendered view of negotiation*. Address to Communication Studies Department, University of Montana, Missoula, September 26.

Putnam, L. L., and J. P. Folger. 1988. Communication, conflict, and dispute resolution: The study of interaction and the development of conflict theory. *Communication Research* 15: 349–359.

Putnam, L. L., and T. S. Jones. 1982a. Reciprocity in negotiations: An analysis of bargaining interaction. *Communication Monographs* 49: 181–191.

———. 1982b. The role of communication in bargaining. *Human Communication Research* 8: 162–280.

Putnam, L. L., and M. S. Poole. 1987. Conflict and negotiation. In *Handbook of organizational communication: An interdisciplinary perspective*, edited by F. M. Jablin, L. L. Putnam, K. H. Roberts, and L. W. Porter. Newbury Park, CA: Sage Publications.

Putnam, L. L., and C. E. Wilson. 1982. Communicative strategies in organizational conflicts: Reliability and validity of a measurement scale. In *Communication yearbook* 6, edited by M. Burgoon. Beverly Hills, CA: Sage Publications, International Communication Association.

Rahim, M. A. 1983. A measure of styles of handling interpersonal conflict. *Academy of Management Journal* 26: 368–376.

———. 1986. *Managing conflict in organizations*. New York: Praeger.

Rahim, M. A., and N. R. Magner. 1995. Confirmatory factor analysis of the styles of handling interpersonal conflict: First-order factor model and its invariance across groups. *Journal of Applied Psychology* 80: 122–132.

Raiffa, H. 1982. *The art and science of negotiation*. Cambridge, MA: Harvard University Press, Belknap Press.

Rands, M., G. Levinger, and G. D. Mellinger. 1981. Patterns of conflict resolution and marital satisfaction. *Journal of Family Issues* 2, no. 3: 297–321.

Raush, H. C., W. A. Barry, R. Hertel, and M. A. Swain. 1974. *Communication, conflict and marriage*. San Francisco: Jossey-Bass.

Raven, B. H., and J. R. P. French Jr. 1956. A formal theory of social power. *Psychological Review* 63: 181–194.

Raven, B. H., and A. W. Kruglanski. 1970. Conflict and power. In *The structure of conflict*, edited by P. Swingel. New York: Academic Press: 69–109.

Ray, L., ed. 1982. *Alternative dispute resolution: Bane or boon to attorneys?* Washington, DC: Special Committee on Alternative Means of Dispute Resolution of the Public Services Division, American Bar Association.

Renwick, P. 1977. The effects of sex differences on the perception and management of superior-subordinate conflict: An exploratory study. *Organizational Behavior and Human Performance* 19: 403–415.

Richmond, V. P., L. M. Davis, K. Saylor, and J. C. McCroskey. 1984. Power strategies in organizations: Communication techniques and messages. *Human Communication Research* 11: 85–108.

Ridley, C. A., and C. M. Feldman. 2003. Female domestic violence toward male partners: Exploring conflict responses and outcomes. *Journal of Family Violence* 18, no. 3: 157–171.

Rivers, S. E., M. A. Brackett, N. A. Katulak, and P. Salovey. 2006. Regulating anger and sadness: An exploration of discreet emotions in emotion regulation. *Journal of Happiness Studies* 8: 393–427.

Robert, M. 1982. *Managing conflict from the inside out*. Austin, TX: Learning Concepts.

Rogan, R. G., and R. Hammer. 1994. Crisis negotiations: A preliminary investigation of facework in naturalistic conflict discourse. *Journal of Applied Communication Research* 22: 216–231.

Rogers, L. E., A. Castleton, and S. A. Lloyd. 1996. Relational control and physical aggression in satisfying marital relationships. In *Family violence from a communication perspective*, edited by D. D. Cahn and S. A. Lloyd. Hillsdale, NJ: Lawrence Erlbaum Associates: 218–239.

Rogers, L. E. and R. Farace, "Analysis of relational communication in dyads," *Human Communication Research*, 1, no.3 (1975): 222–239.

Rogers, M. F. 1974. Instrumental and infra-resources: The bases of power. *American Journal of Sociology* 79: 1418–1433.

Roloff, M. E. 1976. Communication strategies, relationships, and relational change. In *Explorations in interpersonal communication,* edited by G. R. Miller. Newbury Park, CA: Sage Publications.

Roloff, M. E., and D. H. Cloven. 1994. When partners transgress: Maintaining violated relationships. In *Communication and relational maintenance,* edited by D. J. Canary and L. Stafford. New York: Academic Press: 23–24.

Rosen, K. H. 1996. The ties that bind women to violent premarital relationships: Processes of seduction and entrapment. In *Family violence from a communication perspective,* edited by D. D. Cahn and S. A. Loyd. Hillsdale, NJ: Lawrence Erlbaum Associates.

Rosenberg, Marshall. 2003. *Nonviolent communication: A language of life.* Encinitas, CA: Puddle Dancer Press.

Rosenberg, M. B. 2005. *Speak peace in a world of conflict: What you say next will change your world.* Encinitas, CA: Puddle Dancer Press.

Ross, M., and D. Holmberg. 1992. Are wives' memories for events in relationships more vivid than their husbands' memories? *Journal of Social and Personal Relationships* 9: 585–604.

Rossi, A. M., and W. R. Todd-Mancillas. 1987. Male and female differences in managing conflicts. In *Communication, gender, and sex roles in diverse interaction contexts* edited by L. P. Stewart and S. Ting-Toomey. Norwood, NJ: Ablex.

Rowland, R. C., and J. K. Barge. 1991. On international argument. *Argumentation and Advocacy* 28: 24–34.

Rubin, J. Z. 1996. *Proliferation process in conflict.* Address to faculty and students. University of Montana, Missoula, May.

Rubin, J. Z., and B. R. Brown. 1975. *The social psychology of bargaining and negotiation.* New York: Academic Press.

Rubin, J. Z., D. G. Pruitt, and S. H. Kim. 1994. *Social conflict: Escalation, stalemate and settlement.* 2d ed. New York: McGraw-Hill.

Runde, C. E. and Tim A. Flanagan. 2007. *Becoming a conflict competent leader: How you and your organization can manage conflict effectively.* New York: John Wiley.

Rusbult, C. E., D. J. Johnson, and G. D. Morrow. 1984. Impact of couple patterns of problem solving on distress and nondistress in dating relationships. *Journal of Personality and Social Psychology* 50: 744–753.

Rusbult, C. E., I. Zembrodt, and L. K. Gunn. 1982. Exit, voice, loyalty and neglect: Responses to dissatisfaction in romantic involvements. *Journal of Personality and Social Psychology* 43: 1230–1242.

Rushing, J., and T. Frentz. 1995. *Projecting the shadow: The cyborg hero in American film.* Chicago: University of Chicago Press.

Rushing, J. H. 1983. *Rhetorical criticism as analogic process.* Paper presented at the Speech Communication Association/American Forensic Association Summer Conference on Argumentation, Alta, Utah, July.

Rutter, M., C. E. Izard, and P. B. Read (eds.). 1986. *Depression in young people: Developmental and clinical perspectives.* New York: Guilford Press.

Sabourin, T. C. 1995. The role of negative reciprocity in spousal abuse: A relational control analysis. *Journal of Applied Communication Research* 23: 271–283.

Sabourin, T. C., and G. H. Stamp. 1995. Communication and the experience of dialectical tensions in family life: An examination of abusive and nonabusive families. *Communication Monographs* 62: 213–242.

Sadker, M., and D. Sadker. 1994. *Failing at fairness: How American schools cheat girls.* New York: Macmillan Press.

Safilios-Rothschild, C. 1970. The study of family power structure: A review 1960–1969. *Journal of Marriage and the Family* 32, no. 4: 539–549.

Sander, F. E. A. 1977. *Report on the national conference on minor disputes resolution.* Washington, DC: American Bar Association Press.

Sanford, K. (2007). Hard and soft emotions during conflict: Investigating married couples and other relationships. *Personal Relationships* 14: 65–90.

Satir, V. 1967. *Conjoint family therapy.* Palo Alto, CA: Science and Behavior Books.

———. 1972. *Peoplemaking.* Palo Alto, CA: Science and Behavior Books.

Schelling, T. C. 1960. *The strategy of conflict.* Cambridge, MA: Harvard University Press.

Schmidt, S. M., and T. A. Kochan. 1972. Conflict: Toward conceptual clarity. *Administrative Science Quarterly* 17: 359–370.

Schnake, M. E., and D. S. Cochran. 1985. Effect of two goal-setting dimensions on perceived intraorganizational conflict. *Group and Organization Studies* 10: 168–183.

Schuetz, J. 1978. Communicative competence and the bargaining of Watergate. *Western Journal of Speech Communication* 41: 105–115.

Sheldon, A. 1992. Conflict talk: Sociolinguistic challenges to self-assertion and how young girls meet them. *Merrill-Palmer Quarterly* 38: 95–117.

Sherif, M., and C. W. Sherif. 1956. *An outline of social psychology*. Rev. ed. New York: Harper & Brothers.

Shimanoff, S. B. 1980. *Communication rules: Theory and research*. Beverly Hills, CA: Sage.

Shockley-Zalabak, P. 1981. The effects of sex differences on preference for utilization of conflict styles of managers in a work setting: An exploratory study. *Public Personnel Management Journal* 10: 289–295.

Shriver, D. 1995. *An ethic for enemies, forgiveness in politics*. New York: Oxford University Press.

Siegert, J. R., and G. H. Stamp. 1994. "Our first big fight" as a milestone in the development of close relationships. *Communication Monographs* 61: 345–360.

Sillars, A. L. In press 2009. Interpersonal conflict. In C. Berger, M. Roloff, and D. R. Roskos-Ewoldsen (eds.). *Handbook of communication science*. 2nd ed. Thousand Oaks, CA: Sage.

Sillars, A. L. 1980. Attributions and communication in roommate conflicts. *Communication Monographs* 47: 180–200.

———. 1986. *Procedures for coding interpersonal conflict* (revised). Unpublished manuscript. Department of Interpersonal Communication, University of Montana.

———. 2002. For better or worse: Rethinking the role of communication and "misperception" in family conflict. B. Aubrey Fisher Memorial Lecture, Department of Communication, University of Utah.

Sillars, A. L. (2009). Interpersonal conflict. In C. Berger, M. Roloff, and D. R. Roskos-Ewoldsen (eds.). *Handbook of communication science*. 2nd ed. Thousand Oaks, CA: Sage Publications.

Sillars, A. L., S. F. Coletti, D. Parry, and M. A. Rogers. 1982. Coding verbal conflict tactics: Nonverbal and perceptual correlates of the "avoidance-distributive-integrative" distinction. *Human Communication Research* 9, no. 1: 83–95.

Sillars, A. L., and D. Parry. 1982. Stress, cognition, and communication in interpersonal conflicts. *Communication Research* 9: 201–226.

Sillars, A. L., and J. Weisberg. 1987. Conflict as a social skill. In *Interpersonal processes: New directions in communication research*, edited by M. E. Roloff and G. R. Miller. Newbury Park, CA: Sage Publications, 140–171.

Simmel, G. 1953. *Conflict and the web of the group affiliations*. Translated by K. H. Wolff. New York: Free Press.

Simons, H. 1972. Persuasion in social conflicts: A critique of prevailing conceptions and a framework for future research. *Speech Monographs* 39: 227–247.

Smith, D. M. 2008. *Divide or conquer: How great teams turn conflict into strength*. New York: Penguin Group.

Soloman, L. 1960. The influence of some types of power relationships and game strategies upon the development of interpersonal trust. *Journal of Abnormal and Social Psychology* 61: 223–230.

Some, S. 2003. *Falling out of grace: Meditations on loss, healing and wisdom*. El Sobrante, CA: North Bay Books.

Spring, J. 1996. *After the affair*. New York: Harper.

Stafford, W. (1977) "A ritual to read to each other" in William Stafford, *Stories that could be true: New and collected poems*. New York: Harper and Row.

Stets, J. E., and D. A. Henderson. 1991. Contextual factors surrounding conflict resolution while dating: Results from a national study. *Family Relations* 40: 29–36.

Stevens, A. 1989. *The roots of war: A Jungian perspective*. New York: Paragon House.

Stewart, J. 1978. Foundations of dialogic communication. *Quarterly Journal of Speech* 64: 183–201.

Stewart, J., K. Zediker, and S. Witteborn. 2005. *Together: Communicating interpersonally, a social construction approach*. Los Angeles: Roxbury Publishing Company.

Stewart, J. (ed.). 2002. *Bridges, not walls*. New York: McGraw-Hill.

Stone, D., B. Patton, and S. Heen. 1999. *Difficult conversations: How to discuss what matters most*. New York: Penguin Books.

Straus, M. A., R. J. Gelles, and S. K. Steinmetz. 1980. *Behind closed doors: Violence in the American family*. Garden City, NY: Doubleday.

Straus, M. A., S. L. Hamby, S. Boney-McCoy, and D. B. Sugarman. 1996. The revised conflict tactics scale (CTS2): Development and preliminary psychometric data. *Journal of Family Issues* 17: 283–316.

Stuart, R. B. 1980. *Helping couples change: A social learning approach to marital therapy*. New York: Guilford Press.

Stulberg, J. 1987. *Taking charge/Managing conflict*. New York: D. C. Heath & Company.

Sugarman, A. B., and G. T. Hotaling. 1989. Rating violence: Prevalence, context, and risk markers. In *Violence in dating relationships*, edited by M. A. Pirog-Good and J. E. Stets. New York: Praeger: 3–32.

Sun, I. Y., and B. K. Payne. 2004. Racial differences in resolving conflicts: A comparison between black and white police officers. *Crime and Delinquency* 50, no. 4: 516–541.

Survivors of abuse Web site www.ascasupport.org, 2004.

Tannen, D. 1990. *You just don't understand: Women and men in conversation*. New York: William Morrow.

———. 1994. *Gender and discourse*. New York: Oxford University Press.

Tavris, C. 1989. *Anger: The misunderstood emotion.* 1982. Reprint. New York: Simon & Schuster/Touchstone.

Thomas, K. 1976. Conflict and conflict management. In *Handbook of industrial and organizational psychology,* edited by M. D. Dunnette. Chicago: Rand McNally.

Thomas, K. W., and L. R. Pondy. 1977. Toward an "intent" model of conflict management among principal parties. *Human Relations* 30: 1089–1102.

Timmers, M., A. Fischer, and A. Manstead. 1998. Gender differences in motives for regulating closeness. *Personality and Social Psychology Bulletin* 24: 974–985.

Ting-Toomey, S. and J. G. Oetzel. 2001. *Managing intercultural conflict effectively.* Thousand Oaks, CA: Sage Publications.

Tinsley, C. A. 2001. How negotiators get to yes: Predicting the constellation of strategies used across cultures to negotiate conflict. *Journal of Applied Psychology* 86, no. 4: 583.

Tjosvold, D. 1990. The goal interdependence approach to communication in conflict: An organizational study. In *Theory and research in conflict management,* edited by M. A. Rahim, 15–27. New York: Praeger.

Tomkins, S. S. 1962. *Affect, imagery, and consciousness: 1. The positive affects.* New York: Springer.

Tomkins, S. S. 1963. *Affect, imagery, and consciousness: 2. The negative affects.* New York: Springer.

Tracy, S. J., P. Lutgen-Sandvik, and J. K. Alberts. 2004. *Is it really bad? Exploring the emotional pain of workplace bullying through narratives, drawings and metaphors.* Paper presented at the annual convention of the National Communication Association, Chicago, Illinois (November).

Tracy, S. J., P. Lutgen-Sandvik, and J. K. Alberts. 2006. Nightmares, demons, and slaves: Exploring the painful metaphors of workplace bullying. *Management Communication Quarterly* 20, no. 2: 148–185.

Trapp, R. 1981. Special report on argumentation: Introduction. *Western Journal of Speech Communication* 45: 111–117.

———. 1989. Interpersonal argumentation: Conflict and reason-giving. *Communication Reports* 2: 105–109.

Triandis, H. C. 1980. *Handbook of cross cultural psychology.* Boston: Allyn & Bacon.

Trubisky, P., S. Ting-Toomey, and S-L. Lin. 1991. The influence of individualism-collectivism and self-monitoring on conflict styles. *International Journal of Intercultural Relations* 15: 65–83.

Turk, J. L., and N. W. Bell. 1972. Measuring power in families. *Journal of Marriage and Family* 34, no. 2: 215–222.

Turner, C. M., and P. M. Barrett. 1998. Adolescent adjustment to perceived marital conflict. *Journal of Child and Family Studies* 7, no. 4: 499(1).

Tutu, D. 2004. *No future without forgiveness.* New York: Doubleday.

Tutzauer, F., and M. E. Roloff. 1988. Communication processes leading to integrative agreements: Three paths to joint benefits. *Communication Research* 15: 360–380.

Tuval-Mashiach, R., and S. Shulman. 2006. Resolution of disagreements between romantic partners, among adolescents, and young adults: Qualitative analysis of interaction discourses. *Journal of Research on Adolescence* 16, no. 4: 561–588.

Tyler, T. R. 1987. The psychology of disputant concerns in mediation. *Negotiation Journal* 3: 367–374.

Umbreit, M. S. 1995. *Mediating interpersonal conflicts.* West Concord, MN: CPI Publishing.

Umbreit, M., R. B. Coates, and B. Vos. 2004. Victim-offender mediation: Three decades of practice and research. *Conflict Resolution Quarterly* 22, no. 1–2: 279–303.

Ury, William. 2000. *The third side: Why we fight and how we can stop.* New York: Viking Penguin.

Ury, W., J. Brett, and S. Goldberg. 1988. *Getting disputes resolved.* San Francisco: Jossey-Bass.

Ury, W. L. (1990). Dispute resolution notes from the Kalahari. *Negotiation Journal* 6: 229–238.

Van de Vliert, E. 1981. Siding and other reactions to a conflict. *Journal of conflict resolution* 25, no. 3: 495–520.

———. 1985. Escalative intervention in small-group conflicts. *Journal of Applied Behavioral Science* 21: 19–36.

Vangelisti, A. 1994. Messages that hurt. In *The dark side of interpersonal communication,* edited by W. R. Cupach and B. Spitzberg. Hillsdale, NJ: Lawrence Erlbaum Publisher.

VanLear, C. Arthur (1992). "Marital communication across the generations: Learning and rebellion, continuity and change." *Journal of Social and Personal Relationships,* 9, 103–124.

Velez, J. *The road to forgiveness.* Retrieved January 1, 2009, from http://www.feelingsunlimited.com/TheRoadToForgiveness.html.

Vissing, Y., and W. Baily. 1996. Parent-to-child verbal aggression. In *Family violence from a communication perspective,* edited by D. D. Cahn and S. A. Lloyd. Hillsdale, NJ: Lawrence Erlbaum Associates: 85–107.

Vivian, D., and J. Langhinrichsen-Rohling. 1994. Are bidirectionally violent couples mutually victimized? A gender-sensitive comparison. *Violence and Victims* 9: 107–124.

Waldron, V., and D. Kelley. 2005. Forgiving communication as a response to relational transgressions. *Journal of Social and Personal Relationships* 22, no. 6: 723–742.

Waldron, V. R., and D. L. Kelley. 2008. *Communicating forgiveness.* Thousand Oaks, CA: Sage Publications.

Walker, G. B. 1988. Bacharach and Lawler's theory of argument in bargaining: A critique. *Journal of the American Forensic Association* 24: 218–232.

Wall, J. A., Jr. 1985. *Negotiation: Theory and practice.* Glenview, IL: Scott, Foresman & Company.

Wall, J. A., and R. R. Callister. 1995. Ho'oponopono: Some lessons from Hawaiian mediation. *Negotiation Journal* 11: 45–53.

Wall, V. D., Jr., and G. Galanes. 1986. The SYMLOG dimensions and small group conflict. *Central States Speech Journal* 37: 61–78.

Waller, W. 1938. *The family: A dynamic interpretation.* New York: Gordon.

Walsh, F. 1984. *Normal family processes.* New York: Guilford Press.

Walton, R. E. 1969. *Interpersonal peacemaking: Confrontation and third party consultation.* Reading, MA: Addison-Wesley Publishing.

Walton, R. E., and R. B. McKersie. 1965. *A behavioral theory of labor negotiations: An analysis of a social system.* New York: McGraw-Hill.

Warner, C. T., and T. D. Olson. 1981. Another view of family conflict and family wholeness. *Family Relations* 30, no. 4: 493–504.

Watson, C. 1994. Gender versus power as a predictor of negotiation behavior and outcomes. *Negotiation Journal* 10: 117–127.

Watzlawick, P., J. H. Beavin, and D. D. Jackson. 1967. *Pragmatics of human communication: A study of interaction patterns, pathologies and paradoxes.* New York: W. W. Norton & Company.

Weeks, D. 1992. The eight essential steps to conflict resolution. New York: Jeremy T. Tarcher/Putnam Publishing.

Wehr, P. 1979. *Conflict regulation.* Boulder, CO: Westview Press.

Weick, K. E. 1979. *The social psychology of organizing.* 2d ed. New York: Addison-Wesley Publishing.

Welwood, J. (1990). *Journey of the heart: Intimate relationship and the pathos of love.* New York: HarperCollins.

Wenger, A., and D. Mockli. 2003. *Conflict prevention: The untapped potential of the business sector.* Boulder, CO: Lynne Rienner Publishers.

White, J. B., R. Tynan, A. D. Galinsky, and L. Thompson. 2004. Face threat sensitivity in negotiation: Roadblock to agreement and joint gain. *Organizational Behavior and Human Decision Processes* 94, no. 2: 102–125.

White, J. W., and J. A. Humphrey. 1994. Women's aggression in heterosexual conflicts. *Aggressive Behavior* 20: 195–202.

Wiesenthal, S. 1998. *The sunflower.* New York: Schocken Books.

Wilhelm, R., trans. 1977. *The I Ching.* Princeton, NJ: Princeton University Press.

Wilmot, W. W. 1976. *The influence of personal conflict styles of teachers on student attitudes toward conflict.* Paper presented to Instructional Communication Division, International Communication Association Convention, Portland, Oregon, April 15.

———. 1987. *Dyadic communication.* 3d ed. New York: McGraw-Hill.

———. 1995. *Relational communication.* New York: McGraw-Hill.

Wilmot, W. W., and R. H. Andes. 2004. *Better bargains.* Unpublished manuscript.

———. (1996). "The family estate," *The Missoulian,* September 23.

Wilson, S. R. 1992. Face and facework in negotiation. In *Communication and negotiation,* edited by L. L. Putnam and M. E. Roloff, 176–205. Newbury Park, CA: Sage Publications.

Winslade, John and Gerald Monk. 2001. *Narrative mediation: A new approach to conflict resolution.* San Francisco: Jossey-Bass.

Wissler, R. L. 2004. The effectiveness of court-connected dispute resolution in civil cases. *Conflict Resolution Quarterly* 22, no. 2: 55–88.

Wood, J. T. 1997. *Gendered lives: Communication, gender and culture.* 2d. ed. Belmont, CA: Wadsworth Publishing Co.

Workplace Bullying Institute and Zogby International. 2007. *U.S. workplace bullying survey, 2007.*

Worthington, E. L. and D. Drinkard. 2000. Promoting reconciliation through psychoeducational and therapeutic interventions. *Journal of Marital and Family Therapy* 26: 1.

Yankelovich, D. 1999. *The magic of dialogue: Transforming conflict into cooperation.* New York: Simon and Schuster.

Yarbrough, E. 1977. *Rules of observation.* Unpublished monograph. Department of Communication, University of Colorado.

Yarbrough, E., and W. Wilmot. 1995. *Artful mediation: Constructive conflict at work.* Boulder, CO: Cairns Publishing.

Yelsma, P. 1984. Functional conflict management in effective marital adjustment. *Communication Quarterly* 32, no. 1: 56–61.

———. 1995. Couples' affective orientations and their verbal aggressiveness. *Communication Quarterly* 43: 100–114.

Yexley, M., and I. Borowsky. 2002. Correlation between different experiences of intrafamilial physical violence and violent adolescent behavior. *Journal of Interpersonal Violence* 17, no. 7: 707–721.

Yoshimura, S. 2007. Goals and emotional outcomes of revenge activities in interpersonal relationships. *Journal of Social and Personal Relationships* 24, no. 1: 87–98.

Young-Bruehl, E., and F. Bethelard. 2000. *Cherishment: A psychology of the heart*. New York: The Free Press.

Young-Eisendrath, P. 1997. *You're not what I expected: Love after the romance has ended*. New York: Morrow Press.

———. 2000. Self and transcendence: A postmodern approach to analytical psychology in practice. *Psychoanalyic Dialogues* 10, no. 3: 427–428.

Zehr, H. 2001. *Transcending: Reflections of crime victims*. Intercourse, PA: Good Books.

Zhang, Y. B., J. Harwood, and M. L. Hummert. 2005. Perceptions of conflict management styles in Chinese intergenerational dyads. *Communication Monographs* 72, no. 1: 71–97.

Zietlow, P. H., and A. L. Sillars. 1988. Life-stage differences in communication during marital conflicts. *Journal of Social and Personal Relationships* 5: 223–245.

Name Index

Subject Index